A Guide to the Westminster Confession of Faith and Larger Catechism

With Scripture Proofs

Also including

Chapter Summaries and Topical Index

James E. Bordwine

The Trinity Foundation
Jefferson, Maryland

© 1991 James E. Bordwine and The Trinity Foundation
Post Office Box 700
Jefferson, Maryland 21755

ISBN: 0-940931-30-3

Contents

Preface v
Summary of the Westminster Confession of Faith vii

Chapter I: Of the Holy Scripture 1
Chapter II: Of God, and of the Holy Trinity 9
Chapter III: Of God's Eternal Decree 15
Chapter IV: Of Creation 21
Chapter V: Of Providence 25
Chapter VI: Of the Fall of Man, of Sin, and
             the Punishment thereof 33
Chapter VII: Of God's Covenant with Man 39
Chapter VIII: Of Christ the Mediator 47
Chapter IX: Of Free Will 57
Chapter X: Of Effectual Calling 61
Chapter XI: Of Justification 67
Chapter XII: Of Adoption 73
Chapter XIII: Of Sanctification 75
Chapter XIV: Of Saving Faith 79
Chapter XV: Of Repentance unto Life 83
Chapter XVI: Of Good Works 89
Chapter XVII: Of the Perseverance of the Saints 97
Chapter XVIII: Of Assurance of Grace and Salvation 101
Chapter XIX: Of the Law of God 109
Chapter XX: Of Christian Liberty, and Liberty of Conscience ... 117
Chapter XXI: Of Religious Worship, and the Sabbath Day ... 127
Chapter XXII: Of Lawful Oaths and Vows 139

Chapter XXIII: Of the Civil Magistrate 145
Chapter XXIV: Of Marriage and Divorce 153
Chapter XXV: Of the Church 159
Chapter XXVI: Of the Communion of the Saints 165
Chapter XXVII: Of the Sacraments 169
Chapter XXVIII: Of Baptism 173
Chapter XXIX: Of the Lord's Supper 179
Chapter XXX: Of Church Censures 185
Chapter XXXI: Of Synods and Councils 189
Chapter XXXII: Of the State of Men after Death, and
                   of the Resurrection of the Dead 193
Chapter XXXIII: Of the Last Judgment 197

Index 201
Westminster Larger Catechism 303
The Crisis of Our Time 357
Intellectual Ammunition 364

Preface

This work is the result of my deep love and appreciation for the Westminster Standards. It is my conviction that the Confession and Catechisms represent the single best expression of the doctrine contained in the Scriptures. As the reader is probably aware, the Confession has undergone some revision in American Presbyterianism. This volume is based upon the so-called "American Version," but it also includes the original wording in italicized type (see 20-4, 22-3, 23-3, 24-4, 25-6 and 31-2) as it appears in *Westminster Confession of Faith,* published by Free Presbyterian Publications.

I would like to express my appreciation to my father, now residing in heaven, and my mother who taught me the elementary principles of godliness in my childhood; to my wife, Rebecca, for her constant encouragement and many hours of typing and proof-reading; to Jerry Crick, student at Greenville Presbyterian Theological Seminary (Greenville, SC) for his helpful critique of certain portions of this work; to David Dively, PCA pastor, for his reading of the Index; and to Dr. Raymond Dillard of Westminster Theological Seminary (Philadelphia) for supplying the computerized text of the catechism.

May the Head of the Church, whose doctrine is so well explained in the Westminster Standards, be glorified in this endeavor. May His Spirit revive the Old School.

Some readers will be interested to know that this document was prepared using WordPerfect word processing software. This program has an excellent cataloging function which is reflected in the Index. Computerized versions of this work are available from The Trinity Foundation.

Jim Bordwine
Newland, NC
December 1990

A Chapter-by-Chapter Summary of the Primary Teachings of the Westminster Confession of Faith

Chapter I
Of the Holy Scripture

1. The Holy Scripture, given by the inspiration of God, is necessary because the works of creation and providence are not sufficient to give a saving knowledge of God.

2. God's former methods of revelation have ceased now that the Church possesses the written Scripture.

3. The Scripture's infallible authority depends solely upon the fact that God is its author, and only as the Holy Spirit bears witness by and with the Word in our hearts will we become fully persuaded of this truth.

4. Everything necessary for God's glory, our salvation, faith and life is contained in the Scripture and nothing, at any time or for any reason, is to be added to it.

5. In all controversies of religion, the Church is to make final appeal to the Scripture, which, by God's providence, has been kept pure in all ages.

Chapter II
Of God and the Holy Trinity

1. There is only one true God who is not dependent on any creature, but has all life, glory, goodness and blessedness in and of Himself.

2. God exercises absolute dominion over all things and may do with them whatsoever He pleases and is due whatsoever worship, service or obedience He requires of His creatures.

3. In the Godhead, there are three persons, the same in substance, equal in power and eternity.

Chapter III
Of God's Eternal Decree

1. Although God has unchangeably foreordained whatsoever comes to pass and has predestinated some men and angels unto everlasting life and others to everlasting death, He has done so without becoming the author of sin or doing violence to the will of His creatures.

2. Those of mankind whom God has predestinated unto life have been chosen in Christ and are effectually called by His Spirit, are justified, adopted, sanctified and kept by His power; the rest of mankind, from whom God has withheld His mercy, have been ordained to dishonor and wrath for their sin.

Chapter IV
Of Creation

1. In the space of six days, God created the world of nothing.

2. Man, created in the image of God with the law of God written upon his heart, was left to the liberty of his own will having been commanded not to eat of the tree of the knowledge of good and evil.

Chapter V
Of Providence

1. The providence of God, whereby He governs all creatures and actions, extends to the first fall and all other sins of angels and men so that His own holy ends are accomplished; yet He is neither the author nor approver of sin.

2. God sometimes allows His own children to be subjected to manifold temptations so that they might be chastised, humbled and drawn closer to Him.

3. God blinds and hardens the wicked by withholding His grace, withdrawing the gifts which they have and giving them over to the power of Satan.

Chapter VI
Of the Fall of Man, etc.

1. Our first parents, having sinned in eating the forbidden fruit, fell from their original righteousness and communion with God.

2. Because they were the root of all mankind, the guilt of this sin was imputed to all their posterity, along with the corruption of their nature from which proceeds all the sins which we commit.

3. This corruption of nature, though pardoned and mortified through Christ, remains in the regenerate in this life.

Chapter VII
Of God's Covenant with Man

1. God has condescended to man by way of covenant.

2. The first covenant, a covenant of works, promised life in return for perfect obedience; the second covenant, the covenant of grace, freely offers life and salvation to man by Jesus Christ.

3. This covenant of grace, though differently administered in the Old and New Testament eras, is essentially one.

Chapter VIII
Of Christ the Mediator

1. The Mediator, in which are joined the Godhead and the manhood, was chosen and ordained by God and does, in time, redeem, call, justify, sanctify and glorify the seed given to Him from all eternity.

2. The Son of God, who was God, of one substance and equal with the Father, did take upon Him the nature of man with all of its essential properties and infirmities, yet without sin, being conceived by the power of the Holy Spirit in the womb of the virgin Mary.

3. In His role as Mediator, the Lord Jesus perfectly fulfilled the law, triumphed over death by His resurrection, fully satisfied the justice of His Father and purchased reconciliation and an everlasting inheritance for all those whom the Father has given to Him.

4. All of those for whom redemption was purchased, including the elect who lived before the incarnation, have its benefits applied to them by Christ working through His Word and Spirit.

Chapter IX
Of Free Will

1. Having been created with a will which was determined neither to good or evil, man, in his pre-fallen state, had the power to will and do that which was well pleasing to God.

2. Fallen man is dead in sin, is unable to convert himself and can be freed from his natural bondage only when God translates him into the state of grace.

Chapter X
Of Effectual Calling

1. By His Word and Spirit, and wholly of grace, God effectually calls all those predestinated unto life and translates them from sin and death to grace and salvation.

2. Although others may experience some common operations of the Spirit, only the elect, including infants, truly come to Christ and are saved.

Chapter XI
Of Justification

1. God freely justifies the elect by imputing to them the obedience and satisfaction of Christ.

2. Faith, which is the gift of God, is the alone instrument of justification.

3. Although they may suffer the consequences of their sins in this life, those who are justified can never fall from the state of justification.

Chapter XII
Of Adoption

By the grace of adoption, all those who are justified are made the children of God and fully enjoy all accompanying benefits.

Chapter XIII
Of Sanctification

1. Upon regeneration, sin's dominion is broken and a process begins whereby the lusts of the flesh are gradually overcome.

2. This process is incomplete in this life and remnants of sin remain; nevertheless, the working of the Spirit of Christ enables the regenerate to overcome and experience growth in his pursuit of holiness.

Chapter XIV
Of Saving Faith

1. The Spirit of Christ is responsible for the faith whereby the elect are enabled to believe and be saved.

2. The principal acts of this saving faith are accepting, receiving and resting upon Christ alone for salvation.

Chapter XV
Of Repentance unto Life

1. Repentance, which is an act of God's free grace, occurs when a

sinner turns from his sin to God and, thereafter, determines to live according to His commandments.

2. A general repentance is not satisfactory; we are to repent of particular sins particularly and, if necessary, by a private or public confession, declare our repentance to those that are offended.

Chapter XVI
Of Good Works

1. The Word of God alone determines what constitutes good works.

2. The good works of believers, which are evidences of true faith, are produced by the Spirit of Christ.

3. Good works, though essential, do not merit pardon of sin.

4. Even though the good works produced by the Spirit are defiled by the believer's imperfection, they are, nevertheless, accepted in Christ.

Chapter XVII
Of the Perseverance of the Saints

1. The elect, due to the immutability of God's decree, will persevere to the end and be eternally saved.

2. The elect may, for a time, fall into grievous sins and suffer all the miseries which accompany such behavior.

Chapter XVIII
Of the Assurance of Grace and Salvation

1. Believers in the Lord Jesus can be certainly assured that they are in the state of grace.

2. This assurance rests upon God's promises, the evidences of His grace and the inward testimony of the Spirit.

3. Although the assurance of believers may be shaken, in due time it will be revived.

Chapter XIX
Of the Law of God

1. The law given to Adam, by which he and his posterity were bound to absolute obedience, continued to be a perfect rule of righteousness even after the fall and was delivered by God in the form of the Ten Commandments.

2. In addition to this moral law, God gave the people of Israel ceremonial laws, all of which are abrogated under the New Testament, and judicial laws, which expired with that nation.

3. Although the judicial laws expired, the general equity of these statutes remains applicable.

4. God's law reveals His will and our duty and is, therefore, of great use to believers, as well as to others as a rule of life.

Chapter XX
Of Christian Liberty and Liberty of Conscience

1. Freedom from the guilt and dominion of sin, the wrath of God, the sting of death, etc. have all been purchased for believers by Christ.

2. God alone is Lord of the conscience so that the believer is free from man-made rules and regulations.

3. Christian liberty is no pretense for sin.

Chapter XXI
Of Religious Worship, and the Sabbath Day

1. The only acceptable way of worshiping God is that given in the Scriptures and requires the mediation of Christ.

2. The ordinary parts of worship include prayer, the reading of the Scriptures, the sound preaching and conscionable hearing of the Word, the singing of the psalms and the proper administration of the sacraments (to these may be added oaths, vows, fastings and thanksgivings upon special occasions).

3. According to the commandment of God, which binds all men in all ages, one day in seven is to be kept holy unto Him during which men are to engage in the worship of God and the performance of deeds of necessity and mercy.

Chapter XXII
Of Lawful Oaths and Vows

1. An oath involves calling upon God, whose name ought to be used with all fear and reverence, to witness an assertion or promise.

2. A vow, which is to be made to God alone and which must be in accordance with the Word, may be used to express thankfulness or to obtain what we want.

Chapter XXIII
Of the Civil Magistrate

1. Civil magistrates have been ordained by God for the defence and encouragement of good and the punishment of evil.

2. Although civil magistrates are forbidden to encroach upon the authority of the Church, they are obligated to protect the Church so that she may freely discharge her duties, without giving preference to any particular denomination of Christians.

3. The people are obligated to pray for and obey the magistrates regardless of the magistrates' religious orientation.

Chapter XXIV
Of Marriage and Divorce

1. Marriage, which is to be between one man and one woman, was ordained for the mutual help of husband and wife.

2. It is the duty of the godly to avoid being unequally yoked with the wicked in marriage.

3. The bond of marriage may not be legitimately dissolved except in cases of adultery or wilful desertion.

Chapter XXV
Of the Church

1. The invisible Church is composed of the whole number of the elect; the visible Church is composed of all those who profess the true religion, along with their children.

2. It is the duty of the visible Church to gather and perfect the saints.

3. The purity of particular Churches is determined by the manner in which they handle the Gospel, administer the sacraments and perform public worship.

4. Jesus Christ is the alone head of the Church.

Chapter XXVI
Of the Communion of the Saints

1. The saints share in Christ's graces, sufferings, death, resurrection and glory; likewise, they share in each other's gifts and graces and are obligated to pursue their mutual edification.

2. The saints' communion with Christ does not make them partakers of the substance of the Godhead; nor does their communion with one another set aside the right of the private ownership of goods.

Chapter XXVII
Of the Sacraments

1. Sacraments are signs and seals of the covenant of grace which represent Christ and His benefits to believers.

2. The efficacy of a sacrament depends solely upon the work of the Spirit and the word of institution.

3. Only two sacraments, Baptism and the Lord's Supper, have been ordained by Christ in the Gospel.

Chapter XXVIII
Of Baptism

1. Through the sacrament of baptism, which signifies the ingrafting of the believer into Christ, and which is rightly administered by the pouring or sprinkling of water, the party is admitted into the visible Church.

2. All who profess faith in Christ, and their infant children, are to be baptized.

3. Even though grace and salvation are not inseparably attached to the sacrament of baptism nor to the moment of its administration, that which is signified will be conferred by the Holy Spirit to all to whom it is due at the appointed time.

Chapter XXIX
Of the Lord's Supper

1. The sacrament of the Lord's Supper was instituted by Christ Himself as a sealing ordinance and means of grace and is to be observed in His Church until the end of the age.

2. The sacrament of the Lord's Supper reminds us of Christ's sacrifice of Himself but does not involve any real sacrifice itself.

3. The elements of bread and wine are to be set apart by the declaration of the words of institution and prayer, but are not to be worshiped or adored.

4. The doctrine of transubstantiation is contrary to the teaching of Scripture, common sense and reason.

5. Those who partake of the sacrament of the Lord's Supper in a right manner do receive and feed upon Christ crucified after a spiritual manner.

Chapter XXX
Of Church Censures

1. Jesus Christ has established a government for His Church in the hands of officers who have the power to grant or deny admission to the kingdom.

2. Church censures, consisting of admonition, suspension and excommunication, serve to reclaim erring brethren, deter others from similar offences and maintain the purity of the Gospel and the Church.

Chapter XXXI
Of Synods and Councils

1. Synods and councils ought to be convened occasionally as the good of the Church requires.

2. The determinations of synods and councils, which are ecclesiastical in nature, ought to be received as long as they are in agreement with the Word of God; however, it should be remembered that all such assemblies are subject to error.

Chapter XXXII
Of the State of Men after Death, and of the Resurrection of the Dead

1. At the time of death, the body begins to decay, but the soul, being immortal, returns immediately to God whereupon the righteous are received into heaven and the wicked are cast into hell.

2. At the last day, those who are alive shall be changed and the souls of the dead shall be reunited to their bodies; the unjust to dishonor and the just to honor.

Chapter XXXIII
Of the Last Judgment

1. On an appointed day, God will judge the world, including apostate angels, by Jesus Christ who will require an account of every thought, word and deed.

2. The purpose of this day is for the manifestation of God's mercy, in the salvation of the elect, and of His justice, in the damnation of the reprobate.

3. Although the time of this day of judgment is known to God alone, its certainty serves to deter men from evil and console the godly in their adversity.

Chapter I
Of the Holy Scripture

I. Although the light of nature, and the works of creation and providence do so far manifest the goodness, wisdom, and power of God, as to leave men unexcusable;[1] yet are they not sufficient to give that knowledge of God, and of His will, which is necessary unto salvation.[2] Therefore it pleased the Lord, at sundry times, and in divers manners, to

---

[1] ROM 2:14 For when the Gentiles, which have not the law, do by nature the things contained in the law, these, having not the law, are a law unto themselves: 15 Which shew the work of the law written in their hearts, their conscience also bearing witness, and their thoughts the mean while accusing or else excusing one another; 1:19 Because that which may be known of God is manifest in them; for God hath shewed it unto them. 20 For the invisible things of him from the creation of the world are clearly seen, being understood by the things that are made, even his eternal power and Godhead; so that they are without excuse. PSA 19:1 The heavens declare the glory of God; and the firmament sheweth his handiwork. 2 Day unto day uttereth speech, and night unto night sheweth knowledge. 3 There is no speech nor language, where their voice is not heard. ROM 1:32 Who knowing the judgment of God, that they which commit such things are worthy of death, not only do the same, but have pleasure in them that do them. 2:1 Therefore thou art inexcusable, O man, whosoever thou art that judgest: for wherein thou judgest another, thou condemnest thyself; for thou that judgest doest the same things.

[2] 1CO 1:21 For after that in the wisdom of God the world by wisdom knew not God, it pleased God by the foolishness of preaching to save them that believe. 2:13 Which things also we speak, not in the words which man's wisdom teacheth, but which the Holy Ghost teacheth; comparing spiritual things with spiritual. 14 But the natural man receiveth not the things of the Spirit of God; for they are foolishness unto him: neither can he know them, because they are spiritually discerned.

reveal Himself, and to declare that His will unto His Church;[3] and afterwards for the better preserving and propagating of the truth, and for the more sure establishment and comfort of the Church against the corruption of the flesh, and the malice of Satan and of the world, to commit the same wholly unto writing;[4] which make the Holy Scripture to be most necessary;[5] those former ways of God's revealing His will unto His people being now ceased.[6]

[3] HEB 1:1 God, who at sundry times and in divers manners spake in time past unto the fathers by the prophets.
[4] PRO 22:19 That thy trust may be in the Lord, I have made known to thee this day, even to thee. 20 Have not I written to thee excellent things in counsels and knowledge, 21 That I might make thee know the certainty of the words of truth; that thou mightest answer the words of truth to them that send unto thee? LUK 1:3 It seemed good to me also, having had perfect understanding of all things from the very first, to write unto thee in order, most excellent Theophilus, 4 That thou mightest know the certainty of those things, wherein thou hast been instructed. ROM 15:4 For whatsoever things were written aforetime were written for our learning, that we through patience and comfort of the scriptures might have hope. MAT 4:4 But he answered and said, It is written, Man shall not live by bread alone, but by every word that proceedeth out of the mouth of God. 7 Jesus said unto him, It is written again, Thou shalt not tempt the Lord thy God. 10 Then saith Jesus unto him, Get thee hence, Satan: for it is written, Thou shalt worship the Lord thy God, and him only shalt thou serve. ISA 8:19 And when they shall say unto you, Seek unto them that have familiar spirits, and unto wizards that peep, and that mutter: should not a people seek unto their God? for the living to the dead? 20 To the law and to the testimony: if they speak not according to this word, it is because there is no light in them.
[5] 2TI 3:15 And that from a child thou hast known the holy scriptures, which are able to make thee wise unto salvation through faith which is in Christ Jesus. 2PE 1:19 We have also a more sure word of prophecy; whereunto ye do well that ye take heed, as unto a light that shineth in a dark place, until the day dawn, and the day star arise in your hearts.
[6] HEB 1:1 God, who at sundry times and in divers manners spake in time past unto the fathers by the prophets, 2 Hath in these last days spoken unto us by his Son, whom he hath appointed heir of all things, by whom also he made the worlds.

II. Under the name of Holy Scripture, or the Word of God written, are now contained all the books of the Old and New Testament, which are these:

Of the Old Testament:

Genesis	I Kings	Ecclesiastes	Obadiah
Exodus	II Kings	The Song of Songs	Jonah
Leviticus	I Chronicles	Isaiah	Micah
Numbers	II Chronicles	Jeremiah	Nahum
Deuteronomy	Ezra	Lamentations	Habakkuk
Joshua	Nehemiah	Ezekiel	Zephaniah
Judges	Esther	Daniel	Haggai
Ruth	Job	Hosea	Zechariah
I Samuel	Psalms	Joel	Malachi
II Samuel	Proverbs	Amos	

Of the New Testament:

The Gospels according to
  Matthew
  Mark
  Luke
  John
The Acts of the Apostles
Paul's Epistles to the
  Romans
  Corinthians I
  Corinthians II
  Galatians
  Ephesians
  Philippians
  Colossians
  Thessalonians I
  Thessalonians II
  To Timothy I
  To Timothy II
  To Titus
  To Philemon
The Epistle to the Hebrews
The Epistle of James
The first and second Epistles
  of Peter
The first, second, and third
  Epistles of John
The Epistle of Jude
The Revelation of John

All which are given by inspiration of God to be the rule of faith and life.[7]

---

[7] LUK 16:29 Abraham saith unto him, They have Moses and the prophets; let them hear them. 31 And he said unto him, If they hear not Moses and the

III. The books commonly called Apocrypha, not being of divine inspiration, are no part of the canon of Scripture, and therefore are of no authority in the Church of God, nor to be any otherwise approved, or made use of, than other human writings.[8]

IV. The authority of the Holy Scripture, for which it ought to be believed, and obeyed, depends not upon the testimony of any man, or Church; but wholly upon God (who is truth itself) the author thereof: and therefore it is to be received, because it is the Word of God.[9]

---

prophets, neither will they be persuaded, though one rose from the dead. EPH 2:20 And are built upon the foundation of the apostles and prophets, Jesus Christ himself being the chief corner stone. REV 22:18 For I testify unto every man that heareth the words of the prophecy of this book, If any man shall add unto these things, God shall add unto him the plagues that are written in this book: 19 And if any man shall take away from the words of the book of this prophecy, God shall take away his part out of the book of life, and out of the holy city, and from the things which are written in this book. 2TI 3:16 All scripture is given by inspiration of God, and is profitable for doctrine, for reproof, for correction, for instruction in righteousness.

[8] LUK 24:27 And beginning at Moses and all the prophets, he expounded unto them in all the scriptures the things concerning himself. 44 And he said unto them, These are the words which I spake unto you, while I was yet with you, that all things must be fulfilled, which were written in the law of Moses, and in the prophets, and in the psalms, concerning me. ROM 3:2 Much every way: chiefly, because that unto them were committed the oracles of God. 2PE For the prophecy came not in old time by the will of man: but holy men of God spake as they were moved by the Holy Ghost.

[9] 2PE 1:19 We have also a more sure word of prophecy; whereunto ye do well that ye take heed, as unto a light that shineth in a dark place, until the day dawn, and the day star arise in your hearts. 21 For the prophecy came not in old time by the will of man: but holy men of God spake as they were moved by the Holy Ghost. 2TI 3:16 All scripture is given by inspiration of God, and is profitable for doctrine, for reproof, for correction, for instruction in righteousness. 1JO 5:9 If we receive the witness of men, the witness of God is greater: for this is the witness of God which he hath testified of his Son. 1TH 2:13 For this cause also thank we God without ceasing, because, when ye received the word of God which ye heard of us, ye received it not as the word of men, but as it is in truth, the word of God, which effectually worketh also in you that believe.

V. We may be moved and induced by the testimony of the Church to an high and reverent esteem of the Holy Scripture.[10] And the heavenliness of the matter, the efficacy of the doctrine, the majesty of the style, the consent of all the parts, the scope of the whole (which is, to give all glory to God), the full discovery it makes of the only way of man's salvation, the many other incomparable excellencies, and the entire perfection thereof, are arguments whereby it does abundantly evidence itself to be the Word of God: yet notwithstanding, our full persuasion and assurance of the infallible truth and divine authority thereof, is from the inward work of the Holy Spirit bearing witness by and with the Word in our hearts.[11]

VI. The whole counsel of God concerning all things necessary for His own glory, man's salvation, faith and life, is either expressly set down in Scripture, or by good and necessary consequence may be deduced from Scripture: unto which nothing at any time is to be added, whether by new revelations of the Spirit, or traditions of men.[12] Nevertheless, we

[10] 1TI 3:15 But if I tarry long, that thou mayest know how thou oughtest to behave thyself in the house of God, which is the church of the living God, the pillar and ground of the truth.

[11] 1JO 2:20 But ye have an unction from the Holy One, and ye know all things. 27 But the anointing which ye have received of him abideth in you, and ye need not that any man teach you: but as the same anointing teacheth you of all things, and is truth, and is no lie, and even as it hath taught you, ye shall abide in him. JOH 16:13 Howbeit when he, the Spirit of truth, is come, he will guide you into all truth: for he shall not speak of himself; but whatsoever he shall hear, that shall he speak: and he will shew you things to come. 14 He shall glorify me: for he shall receive of mine, and shall shew it unto you. 1CO 2:10 But God hath revealed them unto us by his Spirit: for the Spirit searcheth all things, yea, the deep things of God. 11 For what man knoweth the things of a man, save the spirit of man which is in him? even so the things of God knoweth no man, but the Spirit of God. 12 Now we have received, not the spirit of the world, but the spirit which is of God; that we might know the things that are freely given to us of God. ISA 59:21 As for me, this is my covenant with them, saith the Lord; My spirit that is upon thee, and my words which I have put in thy mouth, shall not depart out of thy mouth, nor out of the mouth of thy seed, nor out of the mouth of thy seed's seed, saith the Lord, from henceforth and for ever.

[12] 2TI And that from a child thou hast know the holy scriptures, which are

acknowledge the inward illumination of the Spirit of God to be necessary for the saving understanding of such things as are revealed in the Word:[13] and that there are some circumstances concerning the worship of God, and government of the Church, common to human actions and societies, which are to be ordered by the light of nature, and Christian prudence, according to the general rules of the Word, which are always to be observed.[14]

VII. All things in Scripture are not alike plain in themselves, nor alike clear unto all:[15] yet those things which are necessary to be known,

able to make thee wise unto salvation through faith which is in Christ Jesus. 16 All scripture is given by inspiration of God, and is profitable for doctrine, for reproof, for correction, for instruction in righteousness: 17 That the man of God may be perfect, thoroughly furnished unto all good works. GAL 1:8 But though we, or an angel from heaven, preach any other gospel unto you than that which we have preached unto you, let him be accursed. 9 As we said before, so say I now again, if any man preach any other gospel unto you than that ye have received, let him be accursed. 2TH 2:2 That ye be not soon shaken in mind, or be troubled, neither by spirit, nor by word, nor by letter as from us, as that the day of Christ is at hand.

[13] JOH 6:45 It is written in the prophets, And they shall be all taught of God. Every man therefore that hath heard, and hath learned of the Father, cometh unto me. 1CO 2:9 But as it is written, Eye hath not seen, nor ear heard, neither have entered into the heart of man, the things which God hath prepared for them that love him. 10 But God hath revealed them unto us by his Spirit: for the Spirit searcheth all things, yea the deep things of God. 11 For what man knoweth the things of a man, save the spirit of man which is in him? even so the things of God knoweth no man, but the Spirit of God. 12 Now we have received, not the spirit of the world, but the spirit which is of God; that we might know the things that are freely given to us of God.

[14] 1CO 11:13 Judge in yourselves: is it comely that a woman pray unto God uncovered? 14 Doth not even nature itself teach you, that, if a man have long hair, it is a shame unto him? 14:26 How is it then, brethren? when ye come together, every one of you hath a psalm, hath a doctrine, hath a tongue, hath a revelation, hath an interpretation. Let all things be done unto edifying. 40 Let all things be done decently and in order.

[15] 2PE 3:16 As also in all his epistles, speaking in them of these things: in which are some things hard to be understood, which they that are unlearned and

believed, and observed for salvation are so clearly propounded, and opened in some place of Scripture or other, that not only the learned, but the unlearned, in a due use of the ordinary means, may attain unto a sufficient understanding of them.[16]

VIII. The Old Testament in Hebrew (which was the native language of the people of God of old), and the New Testament in Greek (which, at the time of the writing of it, was most generally known to the nations), being immediately inspired by God, and, by His singular care and providence, kept pure in all ages, are therefore authentical;[17] so as, in all controversies of religion, the Church is finally to appeal unto them.[18] But, because these original tongues are not known to all the people of God, who have right unto, and interest in the Scriptures, and are commanded, in the fear of God, to read and search them,[19] therefore they are to be translated into the vulgar language of every nation unto which they come,[20] that, the Word of God dwelling plentifully in all, they may

unstable wrest, as they do also the other scriptures, unto their own destruction.

[16] PSA 119:105 Thy word is a lamp unto my feet, and a light unto my path. 130 The entrance of thy words giveth light; it giveth understanding unto the simple.

[17] MAT 5:18 For verily I say unto you, Till heaven and earth pass, one jot or one tittle shall in no wise pass from the law, till all be fulfilled.

[18] ISA 8:20 To the law and to the testimony: if they speak not according to this word, it is because there is no light in them. ACT 15:15 And to this agree the words of the prophets; as it is written. JOH 5:39 Search the scriptures; for in them ye think ye have eternal life: and they are they which testify of me. 46 For had ye believed Moses, ye would have believed me: for he wrote of me.

[19] JOH 5:39 Search the scriptures; for in them ye think ye have eternal life: and they are they which testify of me.

[20] 1CO 14:6 Now, brethren, if I come unto you speaking with tongues, what shall I profit you, except I shall speak to you either by revelation, or by knowledge, or by prophesying, or by doctrine? So likewise ye, except ye utter by the tongue words easy to be understood, how shall it be known what is spoken? for ye shall speak into the air. 11 Therefore if I know not the meaning of the voice, I shall be unto him that speaketh a barbarian, and he that speaketh shall be a barbarian unto me. 12 Even so ye, forasmuch as ye are zealous of spiritual gifts, seek that ye may excel to the edifying of the church. 24 But if all prophesy, and

worship Him in an acceptable manner;[21] and, through patience and comfort of the Scriptures, may have hope.[22]

IX. The infallible rule of interpretation of Scripture is the Scripture itself: and therefore, when there is a question about the true and full sense of any Scripture (which is not manifold, but one), it must be searched and known by other places that speak more clearly.[23]

X. The supreme judge by which all controversies of religion are to be determined, and all decrees of councils, opinions or ancient writers, doctrines of men, and private spirits, are to be examined, and in whose sentence we are to rest, can be no other but the Holy Spirit speaking in the Scripture.[24]

---

there come in one that believeth not, or one unlearned, he is convinced of all, he is judged of all: 27 If any man speak in an unknown tongue, let it be by two, or at the most three, and that by course; and let one interpret. 28 But if there be no interpreter, let him keep silence in the church; and let him speak to himself, and to God.

[21] COL 3:16 Let the word of Christ dwell in you richly in all wisdom; teaching and admonishing one another in psalms, and hymns, and spiritual songs, singing with grace in your hearts to the Lord.

[22] ROM 15:4 For whatsoever things were written aforetime, were written for our learning; that we, through patience and comfort of the scriptures, might have hope.

[23] 2PE 1:20 Knowing this first, that no prophecy of the scripture is of any private interpretation. 21 For the prophecy came not in old time by the will of man; but holy men of God spake as they were moved by the Holy Ghost. ACT 15:15 And to this agree the words of the prophets; as it is written, 16 After this I will return, and will build again the tabernacle of David, which is fallen down; and I will build again the ruins thereof, and I will set it up.

[24] MAT 22:29 Jesus answered and said unto them, Ye do err, not knowing the scriptures, nor the power of God. 31 But as touching the resurrection of the dead, have ye not read that which was spoken unto you by God, saying. EPH 2:20 And are built upon the foundation of the apostles and prophets, Jesus Christ himself being the chief corner-stone. ACT 28:25 And when they agreed not among themselves, they departed, after that Paul had spoken one word, Well spake the Holy Ghost by Esaias the prophet unto our fathers.

Chapter II
Of God, and of the Holy Trinity

I. There is but one only,[1] living, and true God,[2] who is infinite in being and perfection,[3] a most pure spirit,[4] invisible,[5] without body, parts,[6]

---

[1] DEU 6:4 Hear, O Israel; The Lord our God is one Lord. 1CO 8:4 As concerning therefore the eating of those things that are offered in sacrifice unto idols, we know that an idol is nothing in the world, and that there is none other God but one. 6 But to us there is but one God, the Father, of whom are all things, and we in him; and one Lord Jesus Christ, by whom are all things, and we by him.

[2] 1TH 1:9 For they themselves shew of us what manner of entering in we had unto you, and how ye turned to God from idols, to serve the living and true God. JER 10:10 But the Lord is the true God, he is the living God, and an everlasting King.

[3] JOB 11:7 Canst thou by searching find out God? canst thou find out the Almighty unto perfection? 8 It is as high as heaven; what canst thou do? deeper than hell; what canst thou know? 9 The measure thereof is longer than the earth, and broader than the sea. 26:14 Lo, these are parts of his ways; ubt how little a portion is heard of him? but the thunder of his power who can understand?

[4] JOH 4:24 God is a Spirit: and they that worship him must worship him in spirit and in truth.

[5] 1TI 1:17 Now unto the King eternal, immortal, invisible, the only wise God, be honour and glory for ever and ever. Amen.

[6] DEU 4:15 Take ye therefore good heed unto yourselves; for ye saw no manner of similitude on the day that the Lord spake unto you in Horeb out of the midst of the fire: 16 Lest ye corrupt yourselves, and make you a graven image, the similitude of any figure, the likeness of male or female. JOH 4:24 God is a Spirit:

or passions;[7] immutable,[8] immense,[9] eternal,[10] incomprehensible,[11] almighty,[12] all wise,[13] most holy,[14] most free,[15] most absolute;[16] working

and they that worship him must worship him in spirit and in truth. LUK 24:39 Behold my hands and my feet, that it is I myself: handle me, and see; for a spirit hath not flesh and bones, as ye see me have.

[7] ACT 14:11 And when the people saw what Paul had done, they lifted up their voices, saying in the speech of Lycaonia, The gods are come down to us in the likeness of men. 15 And saying, Sirs, why do ye these things? We also are men of like passions with you, and preach unto you that ye should turn from these vanities unto the living God, which made heaven, and earth, and the sea, and all things that are therein.

[8] JAM 1:17 Every good gift and every perfect gift is from above, and cometh down from the Father of lights, with whom is no variableness, neither shadow of turning. MAL 3:6 For I am the Lord, I change not; therefore ye sons of Jacob are not consumed.

[9] 1KI 8:27 But will God indeed dwell on the earth? behold, the heaven and heaven of heavens cannot contain thee; how much less this house that I have builded? JER 23:23 Am I a God at hand, saith teh Lord, and not a God afar off? 24 Can any hide himself in secret places that I shall not see him? saith the Lord. Do not I fill heaven and earth? saith the Lord.

[10] PSA 90:2 Before the mountains were brought forth, or ever thou hadst formed the earth and the world, even from everlasting to everlasting, thou art God. 1TI a:17 Now unto the King eternal, immortal, invisible, the only wise God, be honour and glory for ever and ever. Amen.

[11] PSA 145:3 Great is the Lord, and greatly to be praised; and his greatness is unsearchable.

[12] GEN 17:1 And when Abram was ninety years old and nine, the Lord appeared to Abram, and said unto him, I am the Almighty God; walk before me, and be thou perfect. REV 4:8 And the four beasts had each of them six wings about him; and they were full of eyes within: and they rest not day and night, saying, Holy, holy, holy, Lord God Almighty, which was, and is, and is to come.

[13] ROM 16:27 To God only wise, be glory through Jesus Christ for ever. Amen.

[14] ISA 6:3 And one cried unto another, and said, Holy, holy, holy, is the Lord of hosts: the whole earth is full of his glory. REV 4:8 And the four beasts had each of them six wings about him; and they were full of eyes within: and they rest not day and night, saying, Holy, holy, holy, Lord God Almighty, which was, and is, and is to come.

all things according to the counsel of His own immutable and most righteous will,[17] for His own glory;[18] most loving,[19] gracious, merciful, long-suffering, abundant in goodness and truth, forgiving iniquity, transgression, and sin;[20] the rewarder of them that diligently seek Him;[21] and withal, most just, and terrible in His judgments,[22] hating all sin,[23] and who will by no means clear the guilty.[24]

[15] PSA 115:3 But our God is in the heavens: he hath done whatsoever he hath pleased.

[16] EXO 3:14 And God said unto Moses, I Am That I Am: and he said, Thus shalt thou say unto the children of Israel, I Am hath sent me unto you.

[17] EPH 1:11 In whom also we have obtained an inheritance, being predestinated according to the purpose of him who worketh all things after the counsel of his own will.

[18] PRO 16:4 The Lord hath made all things for himself: yea, even the wicked for the day of evil. ROM 11:36 For of him, and through him, and to him, are all things: to whom be glory for ever. Amen.

[19] 1JO 4:8 He that loveth not knoweth not God; for God is love. 16 And we have known and believed the love that God hath to us. God is love; and he that dwelleth in love dwelleth in God, and God in him.

[20] EXO 34:6 And the Lord passed by before him, and proclaimed, The Lord, The Lord God, merciful and gracious, longsuffering, and abundant in goodness and truth, 7 Keeping mercy for thousands, forgiving iniquity and transgression and sin, and that will by no means clear the guilty; visiting the iniquity of the fathers upon the children, and upon the children's children, unto the third and to the fourth generation.

[21] HEB 11:6 But without faith it is impossible to please him: for he that cometh to God must believe that he is, and that he is a rewarder of them that diligently seek him.

[22] NEH 9:32 Now therfore, our God, the great, the mighty, and the terrible God, who keepest covenant and mercy, let not all the trouble seem little before thee, that hath come upon us, on our kings, on our princes, and on our priests, and on our prophets, and on our fathers, and on all thy people, since the time of the kings of Assyria unto this day. 33 Howbeit thou art just in all that is brought upon us; for thou hast done right, but we have done wickedly.

[23] PSA 5:5 The foolish shall not stand in thy sight: thou hatest all workers of iniquity. 6 Thou shalt destroy them that speak leasing: the Lord will abhor the bloody and deceitful man.

II. God has all life,[25] glory,[26] goodness,[27] blessedness,[28] in and of himself; and is alone in and unto Himself all-sufficient, not standing in need of any creatures which He has made,[29] nor deriving any glory from them,[30] but only manifesting His own glory in, by, unto, and upon them. He is the alone fountain of all being, of whom, through whom, and to whom are all things;[31] and has most sovereign dominion over them; to do by them, for them, or upon them whatsoever Himself pleases.[32] In His

[24] NAH 1:2 God is jealous, and the Lord revengeth; the Lord revengeth, and is furious; the Lord will take vengeance on his adversaries, and he reserveth wrath for his enemies. 3 The Lord is slow to anger, and great in power, and will not at all acquit the wicked: the Lord hath his way in the whirlwind and in the storm, and the clouds are the dust of his feet. EXO 34:7 Keeping mercy for thousands, forgiving iniquity and transgression and sin, and that will by no means clear the guilty; visiting the iniquity of the fathers upon the children, and upon the children's children, unto the third and to the fourth generation.

[25] JOH 5:26 For as the Father hath life in himself; so hath he given to the Son to have life in himself.

[26] ACT 7:2 And he said, Men, brethren, and fathers, hearken; The God of glory appeared unto our father Abraham, when he was in Mesopotamia, before he dwelt in Charran.

[27] PSA 119:68 Thou art good, and doest good; teach me thy statutes.

[28] 1TI 6:15 Which in his times he shall shew, who is the blessed and only Potentate, the King of kings, and Lord of lords. ROM 9:5 Whose are the fathers, and of whom as concerning the flesh Christ came, who is over all, God blessed for ever. Amen.

[29] ACT 17:24 God that made the world and all things therein, seeing that he is Lord of heaven and earth, dwelleth not in temples made with hands; 25 Neither is worshipped with men's hands, as though he needed any thing, seeing he giveth to all life, and breath, and all things.

[30] JOB 22:2 Can a man be profitable unto God, as he that is wise may be profitable unto himself? 3 Is it any pleasure to the Almighty, that thou art righteous? or is it gain to him that thou makest thy ways perfect?

[31] ROM 11:36 For of him, and through him, and to him, are all things: to whom be glory for ever. Amen.

[32] REV 4:11 Thou art worthy, O Lord, to receive glory and honour and power: for thou hast created all things, and for thy pleasure they are and were created. 1TI 6:15 Which in his times he shall shew, who is the blessed and only

sight all things are open and manifest,[33] His knowledge is infinite, infallible, and independent upon the creature,[34] so as nothing is to Him contingent, or uncertain.[35] He is most holy in all His counsels, in all His works, and in all His commands.[36] To Him is due from angels and men, and every other creature, whatsoever worship, service, or obedience He is pleased to require of them.[37]

III. In the unity of the Godhead there be three persons, of one

Potentate, the King of kings, and Lord of lords. DAN 4:25 That they shall drive thee from men, and thy dwelling shall be with the beasts of the field, and they shall make thee to eat grass as oxen, and they shall wet thee with the dew of heaven, and seven times shall pass over thee, till thou know that the most High ruleth in the kingdom of men, and giveth it to whomsoever he will. 35 And all the inhabitants of the earth are reputed as nothing: and he doeth according to his will in the army of heaven, and among the inhabitants of the earth: and none can stay his hand, or say unto him, What doest thou?

[33] HEB 4:13 Neither is there any creature that is not manifest in his sight: but all things are naked and opened unto the eyes of him with whom we have to do.

[34] ROM 11:33 O the depth of the riches both of the wisdom and knowledge of God! how unsearchable are his judgments, and his ways past finding out! 34 For who hath known the mind of the Lord? or who hath been his counsellor? PSA 147:5 Great is our Lord, and of great power: his understanding is infinite.

[35] ACT 15:18 Known unto God are all his works from the beginning of the world. EZE 11:5 And the Spirit of the Lord fell upon me, and said unto me, Speak; Thus saith the Lord; Thus have ye said, O house of Israel: for I know the things that come into your mind, every one of them.

[36] PSA 145:17 The Lord is righteous in all his ways, and holy in all his works. ROM 7:12 Wherefore the law is holy, and the commandment holy, and just, and good.

[37] REV 5:12 Saying with a loud voice, Worthy is the Lamb that was slain to receive power, and riches, and wisdom, and strength, and honour, and glory, and blessing. 13 And every creature which is in heaven, and on the earth, and under the earth, and such as are in the sea, and all that are in them, heard I saying, Blessing, and hnnour, and glory, and power, be unto him that sitteth upon the throne, and unto the Lamb for ever and ever. 14 And the four beasts said, Amen. And the four and twenty elders fell down and worshipped him that liveth for ever and ever.

substance, power, and eternity: God the Father, God the Son, and God the Holy Ghost:[38] the Father is of none, neither begotten, nor proceeding; the Son is eternally begotten of the Father;[39] the Holy Ghost eternally proceeding from the Father and the Son.[40]

[38] 1JO 5:7 For there are three that bear record in heaven, the Father, the Word, and the Holy Ghost: and these three are one. MAT 3:16 And Jesus, when he was baptized, went up straightway out of the water: and, lo, the heavens were opened unto him, and he saw the Spirit of God descending like a dove, and lighting upon him: 17 And lo a voice from heaven, saying, This is my beloved Son, in whom I am well pleased. 28:19 Go ye therefore, and teach all nations, baptizing them in the name of the Father, and of the Son, and of the Holy Ghost. 2CO 13:14 The grace of the Lord Jesus Christ, and the love of God, and the communion of the Holy Ghost, be with you all. Amen.

[39] JOH 1:14 And the Word was made flesh, and dwelt among us, (and we beheld his glory, the glory as of the only begotten of the Father,) full of grace and truth. 15 John bare witness of him, and cried, saying, This was he of whom I spake, He that cometh after me is preferred before me: for he was before me. 18 No man hath seen God at any time; the only begotten Son, which is in the bosom of the Father, he hath declared him.

[40] JOH 15:26 But when the Comforter is come, whom I will send unto you from the Father, even the Spirit of truth, which proceedeth from the Father, he shall testify of me. GAL 4:6 And because ye are sons, God hath sent forth the Spirit of his Son into your hearts, crying, Abba, Father.

Chapter III
Of God's Eternal Decree

I. God from all eternity, did, by the most wise and holy counsel of His own will, freely, and unchangeably ordain whatsoever comes to pass;[1] yet so, as thereby neither is God the author of sin,[2] nor is violence offered to the will of the creatures; nor is the liberty or contingency of second causes taken away, but rather established.[3]

[1] EPH 1:11 In whom also we have obtained an inheritance, being predestinated according to the purpose of him who worketh all things after the counsel of his own will. ROM 11:33 O the depth of the riches both of the wisdom and knowledge of God! how unsearchable are his judgments, and his ways past finding out! HEB 6:17 Wherein God, willing more abundantly to shew unto the heirs of promise the immutability of his counsel, confirmed it by an oath. ROM 9:15 For he saith to Moses, I will have mercy on whom I will have mercy, and I will have compassion on whom I will have compassion. 18 Therefore hath he mercy on whom he will have mercy, and whom he will he hardeneth.

[2] JAM 1:13 Let no man say when he is tempted, I am tempted of God: for God cannot be tempted with evil, neither tempteth he any man. 17 Every good gift and every perfect gift is from above, and cometh down from the Father of lights, with whom is no variableness, neither shadow of turning. 1JO 1:5 This then is the message which we have heard of him, and declare unto you, that God is light, and in him is no darkness at all.

[3] ACT 2:23 Him, being delivered by the determinate counsel and foreknowledge of God, ye have taken, and by wicked hands have crucified and slain. MAT 17:12 But I say unto you, That Elias is come already, and they knew him not, but have done unto him whatsoever they listed. Likewise shall also the Son of man suffer of them. ACT 4:27 For of a truth against thy holy child Jesus, whom thou hast anointed, both Herod, and Pontius Pilate, with the Gentiles, and

II. Although God knows whatsoever may or can come to pass upon all supposed conditions;[4] yet has He not decreed anything because He foresaw it as future, or as that which would come to pass upon such conditions.[5]

III. By the decree of God, for the manifestation of His glory, some men and angels[6] are predestinated unto everlasting life; and others foreordained to everlasting death.[7]

---

the people of Israel, were gathered together, 28 For to do whatsoever thy hand and thy counsel determined before to be done. JOH 19:11 Jesus answered, Thou couldest have no power at all against me, except it were given thee from above: therefore he that delivered me unto thee hath the greater sin. PRO 16:33 The lot is cast into the lap; but the whole disposing thereof is of the Lord.

[4] ACT 15:18 Known unto God are all his works from the beginning of the world. 1SA 23:11 Will the men of Keilah deliver me up into his hand? will Saul come down, as thy servant hath heard? O Lord God of Israel, I beseech thee, tell thy servant. And the Lord said, He will come down. 12 Then said David, Will the men of Keilah deliver me and my men into the hand of Saul? And the Lord said, They will deliver thee up. MAT 11:21 Woe unto thee, Chorazin! woe unto thee, Bethsaida! for if the mighty works, which were done in you, had been done in Tyre and Sidon, they would have repented long ago in sackcloth and ashes. 23 And thou, Capernaum, which art exalted unto heaven, shalt be brought down to hell: for if the mighty works, which have been done in thee, had been done in Sodom, it would have remained until this day.

[5] ROM 9:11 (For the children being not yet born, neither having done any good or evil, that the purpose of God according to election might stand, not of works, but of him that calleth;) 13 As it is written, Jacob have I loved, but Esau have I hated. 16 So then it is not of him that willeth, nor of him that runneth, but of God that sheweth mercy. 18 Therefore hath he mercy on whom he will have mercy, and whom he will he hardeneth.

[6] 1TI 5:21 I charge thee before God, and the Lord Jesus Christ, and the elect angels, that thou observe these things without preferring one before another, doing nothing by partiality. MAT 25:41 Then shall he say also unto them on the left hand, Depart from me, ye cursed, into everlasting fire, prepared for the devil and his angels.

[7] ROM 9:22 What if God, willing to shew his wrath, and to make his power known, endured with much longsuffering the vessels of wrath fitted to destruction: 23 And that he might make known the riches of his glory on the

IV. These angels and men, thus predestinated, and foreordained, are particularly and unchangeably designed, and their number so certain and definite, that it cannot be either increased or diminished.[8]

V. Those of mankind that are predestinated unto life, God, before the foundation of the world was laid, according to His eternal and immutable purpose, and the secret counsel and good pleasure of His will, has chosen, in Christ, unto everlasting glory,[9] out of His mere free grace and love, without any foresight of faith, or good works, or perseverance in either of them, or any other thing in the creature, as conditions, or causes moving Him thereunto;[10] and all to the praise of His glorious grace.[11]

vessels of mercy, which he had afore prepared unto glory. EPH 1:5 Having predestinated us unto the adoption of children by Jesus Christ to himself, according to the good pleasure of his will, 6 To the praise of the glory of his grace, wherein he hath made us accepted in the beloved. PRO 16:4 The Lord hath made all things for himself: yea, even the wicked for the day of evil.

[8] 2TI 2:19 Nevertheless the foundation of God standeth sure, having this seal, The Lord knoweth them that are his. And, Let every one that nameth the name of Christ depart from iniquity. JOH 13:18 I speak not of you all: I know whom I have chosen: but that the scripture may be fulfilled, He that eateth bread with me hath lifted up his heel against me.

[9] EPH 1:4 According as he hath chosen us in him before the foundation of the world, that we should be holy and without blame before him in love: 9 Having made known unto us the mystery of his will, according to his good pleasure which he hath purposed in himself: 11 In whom also we have obtained an inheritance, being predestinated according to the purpose of him who worketh all things after the counsel of his own will. ROM 8:30 Moreover whom he did predestinate, them he also called: and whom he called, them he also justified: and whom he justified, them he also glorified. 2TI 1:9 Who hath saved us, and called us with an holy calling, not according to our works, but according to his own purpose and grace, which was given us in Christ Jesus before the world began. 1TH 5:9 For God hath not appointed us to wrath, but to obtain salvation by our Lord Jesus Christ.

[10] ROM 9:11 (For the children being not yet born, neither having done any good or evil, that the purpose of God according to election might stand, not of works, but of him that calleth;) 13 As it is written, Jacob have I loved, but Esau have I hated. 16 So then it is not of him that willeth, nor of him that runneth, but of God that sheweth mercy. EPH 1:4 According as he hath chosen us in him before the foundation of the world, that we should be holy and without blame before him

VI. As God has appointed the elect unto glory, so has He, by the eternal and most free purpose of His will, foreordained all the means thereunto. Wherefore, they who are elected, being fallen in Adam, are redeemed by Christ,[12] are effectually called unto faith in Christ by His Spirit working in due season, are justified, adopted, sanctified,[13] and kept by His power, through faith, unto salvation.[14] Neither are any other redeemed by Christ, effectually called, justified, adopted, sanctified, and saved, but the elect only.[15]

in love. 9 Having made known unto us the mystery of his will, according to his good pleasure which he hath purposed in himself.

[11] 1 PE 1:2 Elect according to the foreknowledge of God the Father, through sanctification of the Spirit, unto obedience and sprinkling of the blood of Jesus Christ: Grace unto you, and peace, be multiplied. EPH 1:4 According as he hath chosen us in him before the foundation of the world, that we should be holy and without blame before him in love: 5 Having predestinated us unto the adoption of children by Jesus Christ to himself, according to the good pleasure of his will. 2:10 For we are his workmanship, created in Christ Jesus unto good works, which God hath before ordained that we should walk in them. 2TH 2:13 But we are bound to give thanks alway to God for you, brethren beloved of the Lord, because God hath from the beginning chosen you to salvation through sanctification of the Spirit and belief of the truth.

[12] 1TH 5:9 For God hath not appointed us to wrath, but to obtain salvation by our Lord Jesus Christ, 10 Who died for us, that, whether we wake or sleep, we should live together with him. TIT 2:14 Who gave himself for us, that he might redeem us from all iniquity, and purify unto himself a peculiar people, zealous of good works.

[13] ROM 8:30 Moreover whom he did predestinate, them he also called: and whom he called, them he also justified: and whom he justified, them he also glorified. EPH 1:5 Having predestinated us unto the adoption of children by Jesus Christ to himself, according to the good pleasure of his will. 2TH 2:13 But we are bound to give thanks alway to God for you, brethren beloved of the Lord, because God hath from the beginning chosen you to salvation through sanctification of the Spirit and belief of the truth.

[14] 1 PE 1:5 Who are kept by the power of God through faith unto salvation ready to be revealed in the last time.

[15] JOH 17:9 I pray for them: I pray not for the world, but for them which thou hast given me; for they are thine. ROM 8:28 And we know that all things work

VII. The rest of mankind God was pleased, according to the unsearchable counsel of His own will, whereby He extends or withholds mercy, as He pleases, for the glory of His sovereign power over His creatures, to pass by; and to ordain them to dishonor and wrath for their sin, to the praise of His glorious justice.[16]

VIII. The doctrine of this high mystery of predestination is to be

---

together for good to them that love God, to them who are the called according to his purpose. JOH 6:64 But there are some of you that believe not. For Jesus knew from the beginning who they were that believed not, and who should betray him. 65 And he said, Therefore said I unto you, that no man can come unto me, except it were given unto him of my Father. 10:26 But ye believe not, because ye are not of my sheep, as I said unto you. 8:47 He that is of God heareth God's words: ye therefore hear them not, because ye are not of God. 1JO 2:19 They went out from us, but they were not of us; for if they had been of us, they would no doubt have continued with us: but they went out, that they might be made manifest that they were not all of us.

[16] MAT 11:25 At that time Jesus answered and said, I thank thee, O Father, Lord of heaven and earth, because thou hast hid these things from the wise and prudent, and hast revealed them unto babes. 26 Even so, Father: for so it seemed good in thy sight. ROM 9:17 For the scripture saith unto Pharaoh, Even for this same purpose have I raised thee up, that I might shew my power in thee, and that my name might be declared throughout all the earth. 18 Therefore hath he mercy on whom he will have mercy, and whom he will he hardeneth. 21 Hath not the potter power over the clay, of the same lump to make one vessel unto honour, and another unto dishonour? 22 What if God, willing to shew his wrath, and to make his power known, endured with much longsuffering the vessels of wrath fitted to destruction. 2TI 2:19 Nevertheless the foundation of God standeth sure, having this seal, The Lord knoweth them that are his. And, Let every one that nameth the name of Christ depart from iniquity. 20 But in a great house there are not only vessels of gold and of silver, but also of wood and of earth; and some to honour, and some to dishonour. JUD 4 For there are certain men crept in unawares, who were before of old ordained to this condemnation, ungodly men, turning the grace of our God into lasciviousness, and denying the only Lord God, and our Lord Jesus Christ. 1 PE 2:8 And a stone of stumbling, and a rock of offence, even to them which stumble at the word, being disobedient: whereunto also they were appointed.

handled with special prudence and care,[17] that men, attending the will of God revealed in His Word, and yielding obedience thereunto, may, from the certainty of their effectual vocation, be assured of their eternal election.[18] So shall this doctrine afford matter of praise, reverence, and admiration of God;[19] and of humility, diligence, and abundant consolation to all that sincerely obey the Gospel.[20]

[17] ROM 9:20 Nay but, O man, who art thou that repliest against God? Shall the thing formed say to him that formed it, Why hast thou made me thus? 11:33 O the depth of the riches both of the wisdom and knowledge of God! how unsearchable are his judgments, and his ways past finding out! DEU 29:29 The secret things belong unto the Lord our God: but those things which are revealed belong unto us and to our children for ever, that we may do all the words of this law.

[18] 2 PE 1:10 Wherefore the rather, brethren, give diligence to make your calling and election sure: for if ye do these things, ye shall never fall.

[19] EPH 1:6 To the praise of the glory of his grace, wherein he hath made us accepted in the beloved. ROM 11:33 O the depth of the riches both of the wisdom and knowledge of God! how unsearchable are his judgments, and his ways past finding out!

[20] ROM 11:5 Even so then at this present time also there is a remnant according to the election of grace. 6 And if by grace, then is it no more of works: otherwise grace is no more grace. But if it be of works, then is it no more grace: otherwise work is no more work. 20 For when ye were the servants of sin, ye were free from righteousness. 2 PE 1:10 Wherefore the rather, brethren, give diligence to make your calling and election sure: for if ye do these things, ye shall never fall. ROM 8:33 Who shall lay any thing to the charge of God's elect? It is God that justifieth. LUK 10:20 Notwithstanding in this rejoice not, that the spirits are subject unto you; but rather rejoice, because your names are written in heaven.

Chapter IV
Of Creation

I. It pleased God the Father, Son, and Holy Ghost,[1] for the manifestation of the glory of His eternal power, wisdom, and goodness,[2] in the beginning, to create, or make of nothing, the world, and all things therein whether visible or invisible, in the space of six days; and all very good.[3]

[1] HEB 1:2 Hath in these last days spoken unto us by his Son, whom he hath appointed heir of all things, by whom also he made the worlds. JOH 1:2 The same was in the beginning with God. 3 All things were made by him; and without him was not any thing made that was made. GEN 1:2 And the earth was without form, and void; and darkness was upon the face of the deep. And the Spirit of God moved upon the face of the waters. JOB 26:13 By his spirit he hath garnished the heavens; his hand hath formed the crooked serpent. 33:4 The Spirit of God hath made me, and the breath of the Almighty hath given me life.

[2] ROM 1:20 For the invisible things of him from the creation of the world are clearly seen, being understood by the things that are made, even his eternal power and Godhead; so that they are without excuse. JER 10:12 He hath made the earth by his power, he hath established the world by his wisdom, and hath stretched out the heavens by his discretion. PSA 104:24 O Lord, how manifold are thy works! in wisdom hast thou made them all: the earth is full of thy riches. 33:5 He loveth righteousness and judgment: the earth is full of the goodness of the Lord. 6 By the word of the Lord were the heavens made; and all the host of them by the breath of his mouth.

[3] All of Genesis 1; HEB 11:3 Through faith we understand that the worlds were framed by the word of God, so that things which are seen were not made of things which do appear. COL 1:16 For by him were all things created, that are in heaven, and that are in earth, visible and invisible, whether they be thrones, or

II. After God had made all other creatures, He created man, male and female,[4] with reasonable and immortal souls,[5] endued with knowledge, righteousness, and true holiness, after His own image;[6] having the law of God written in their hearts,[7] and power to fulfil it;[8] and yet under a possibility of transgressing, being left to the liberty of their own will, which was subject unto change.[9] Beside this law written in their hearts,

dominions, or principalities, or powers: all things were created by him, and for him. ACT 17:24 God that made the world and all things therein, seeing that he is Lord of heaven and earth, dwelleth not in temples made with hands.

[4] GEN 1:27 So God created man in his own image, in the image of God created he him; male and female created he them.

[5] GEN 2:7 And the Lord God formed man of the dust of the ground, and breathed into his nostrils the breath of life; and man became a living soul. ECC 12:7 Then shall the dust return to the earth as it was: and the spirit shall return unto God who gave it. LUK 23:43 And Jesus said unto him, Verily I say unto thee, To day shalt thou be with me in paradise. MAT 10:28 And fear not them which kill the body, but are not able to kill the soul: but rather fear him which is able to destroy both soul and body in hell.

[6] GEN 1:26 And God said, Let us make man in our image, after our likeness: and let them have dominion over the fish of the sea, and over the fowl of the air, and over the cattle, and over all the earth, and over every creeping thing that creepeth upon the earth. COL 3:10 And have put on the new man, which is renewed in knowledge after the image of him that created him. EPH 4:24 And that ye put on the new man, which after God is created in righteousness and true holiness.

[7] ROM 2:14 For when the Gentiles, which have not the law, do by nature the things contained in the law, these, having not the law, are a law unto themselves: 15 Which shew the work of the law written in their hearts, their conscience also bearing witness, and their thoughts the mean while accusing or else excusing one another.

[8] ECC 7:29 Lo, this only have I found, that God hath made man upright; but they have sought out many inventions.

[9] GEN 3:6 And when the woman saw that the tree was good for food, and that it was pleasant to the eyes, and a tree to be desired to make one wise, she took of the fruit thereof, and did eat, and gave also unto her husband with her; and he did eat. ECC 7:29 Lo, this only have I found, that God hath made man upright; but they have sought out many inventions.

they received a command, not to eat of the tree of the knowledge of good and evil;[10] which while they kept, they were happy in their communion with God, and had dominion over the creatures.[11]

[10] GEN 2:17 But of the tree of the knowledge of good and evil, thou shalt not eat of it: for in the day that thou eatest thereof thou shalt surely die. 3:8 And they heard the voice of the Lord God walking in the garden in the cool of the day: and Adam and his wife hid themselves from the presence of the Lord God amongst the trees of the garden. 9 And the Lord God called unto Adam, and said unto him, Where art thou? 10 And he said, I heard thy voice in the garden, and I was afraid, because I was naked; and I hid myself. 11 And he said, Who told thee that thou wast naked? Hast thou eaten of the tree, whereof I commanded thee that thou shouldest not eat? 23 Therefore the Lord God sent him forth from the garden of Eden, to till the ground from whence he was taken.

[11] GEN 1:26 And God said, Let us make man in our image, after our likeness: and let them have dominion over the fish of the sea, and over the fowl of the air, and over the cattle, and over all the earth, and over every creeping thing that creepeth upon the earth. 28 And God blessed them, and God said unto them, Be fruitful, and multiply, and replenish the earth, and subdue it: and have dominion over the fish of the sea, and over the fowl of the air, and over every living thing that moveth upon the earth.

Chapter V

Of Providence

I. God the great Creator of all things does uphold,[1] direct, dispose, and govern all creatures, actions, and things,[2] from the greatest even to the least,[3] by His most wise and holy providence,[4] according to His

[1] HEB 1:3 Who being the brightness of his glory, and the express image of his person, and upholding all things by the word of his power, when he had by himself purged our sins, sat down on the right hand of the Majesty on high.
 [2] DAN 4:34 And at the end of the day I Nebuchadnezzar lifted up mine eyes unto heaven, and mine understanding returned unto me, and I blessed the Most High, and I praised and honoured him that liveth for ever, whose dominion is an everlasting dominion, and his kingdom is from generation to generation: 35 And all the inhabitants of the earth are reputed as nothing: and he doeth according to his will in the army of heaven, and among the inhabitants of the earth: and none can stay his hand, or say unto him, What doest thou? PSA 135:6 Whatsoever the Lord pleased, that did he in heaven, and in earth, in the seas, and all deep places. ACT 17:25 Neither is worshipped with men's hands, as though he needed any thing, seeing he giveth to all life, and breath, and all things; 26 And hath made of one blood all nations of men for to dwell on all the face of the earth, and hath determined the times before appointed, and the bounds of their habitation; 27 That they should seek the Lord, if haply they might feel after him, and find him, though he be not far from every one of us: 28 For in him we live, and move, and have our being; as certain also of your own poets have said, For we are also his offspring. JOB 38-41.
 [3] MAT 10:29 Are not two sparrows sold for a farthing? and one of them shall not fall on the ground without your Father. 30 But the very hairs of your head are all numbered. 31 Fear ye not therefore, ye are of more value than many sparrows.
 [4] PRO 15:3 The eyes of the Lord are in every place, beholding the evil and

infallible foreknowledge,⁵ and the free and immutable counsel of His own will,⁶ to the praise of the glory of His wisdom, power, justice, goodness, and mercy.⁷

II. Although, in relation to the foreknowledge and decree of God, the first Cause, all things come to pass immutably, and infallibly;⁸ yet, by the same providence, He orders them to fall out, according to the nature of second causes, either necessarily, freely, or contingently.⁹

the good. PSA 104:24 O Lord, how manifold are thy works! in wisdom hast thou made them all: the earth is full of thy riches. 145:17 The Lord is righteous in all his ways, and holy in all his works.

⁵ ACT 15:18 Known unto God are all his works from the beginning of the world. PSA 94:8 Understand, ye brutish among the people: and ye fools, when will ye be wise? 9 He that planted the ear, shall he not hear? he that formed the eye, shall he not see? 10 He that chastiseth the heathen, shall not he correct? he that teacheth man knowledge, shall not he know? 11 The Lord knoweth the thoughts of man, that they are vanity.

⁶ EPH 1:11 In whom also we have obtained an inheritance, being predestinated according to the purpose of him who worketh all things after the counsel of his own will. PSA 33:10 The Lord bringeth the counsel of the heathen to nought: he maketh the devices of the people of none effect. 11 The counsel of the Lord standeth for ever, the thoughts of his heart to all generations.

⁷ ISA 63:14 As a beast goeth down into the valley, the Spirit of the Lord caused him to rest: so didst thou lead thy people, to make thyself a glorious name. EPH 3:10 To the intent that now unto the principalities and powers in heavenly places might be known by the church the manifold wisdom of God. ROM 9:17 For the scripture saith unto Pharaoh, Even for this same purpose have I raised thee up, that I might shew my power in thee, and that my name might be declared throughout all the earth. GEN 45:7 And God sent me before you to preserve you a posterity in the earth, and to save your lives by a great deliverance. PSA 145:7 They shall abundantly utter the memory of thy great goodness, and shall sing of thy righteousness.

⁸ ACT 2:23 Him, being delivered by the determinate counsel and foreknowledge of God, ye have taken, and by wicked hands have crucified and slain.

⁹ GEN 8:22 While the earth remaineth, seedtime and harvest, and cold and heat, and summer and winter, and day and night shall not cease. JER 31:35 Thus saith the Lord, which giveth the sun for a light by day, and the ordinances of the

III. God, in His ordinary providence, makes use of means,[10] yet is free to work without,[11] above,[12] and against them,[13] at His pleasure.

moon and of the stars for a light by night, which divideth the sea when the waves thereof roar; the Lord of hosts is his name: EXO 21:13 And if a man lie not in wait, but God deliver him into his hand; then I will appoint thee a place whither he shall flee. DEU 19:5 As when a man goeth into the wood with his neighbour to hew wood, and his hand fetcheth a stroke with the axe to cut down the tree, and the head slippeth from the helve, and lighteth upon his neighbour, that he die; he shall flee unto one of those cities, and live: 1KI 22:28 And Micaiah said, If thou return at all in peace, the Lord hath not spoken by me. And he said, Hearken, O people, every one of you. 34 And a certain man drew a bow at a venture, and smote the king of Israel between the joints of the harness: wherefore he said unto the driver of his chariot, Turn thine hand, and carry me out of the host; for I am wounded. ISA 10:6 I will send him against an hypocritical nation, and against the people of my wrath will I give him a charge, to take the spoil, and to take the prey, and to tread them down like the mire of the streets. 7 Howbeit he meaneth not so, neither doeth his heart think so; but it is in his heart to destroy and cut off nations not a few.

[10] ACT 27:31 Paul said to the centurion and to the soldiers, Except these abide in the ship, ye cannot be saved. 44 And the rest, some on boards, and some on broken pieces of the ship. And so it came to pass, that they escaped all safe to land. ISA 55:10 For as the rain cometh down, and the snow from heaven, and returneth not thither, but watereth the earth, and maketh it bring forth and bud, that it may give seed to the sower, and bread to the eater: 11 So shall my word be that goeth forth out of my mouth: it shall not return unto me void, but it shall accomplish that which I please, and it shall prosper in the thing whereto I sent it. HOS 2:21 And it shall come to pass in that day, I will hear, saith the Lord, I will hear the heavens, and they shall hear the earth; 22 And the earth shall hear the corn, and the wine, and the oil; and they shall hear Jezreel.

[11] HOS 1:7 But I will have mercy upon the house of Judah, and will save them by the Lord their God, and will not save them by bow, nor by sword, nor by battle, by horses, nor by horsemen. MAT 4:4 But he answered and said, It is written, Man shall not live by bread alone, but by every word that proceedeth out of the mouth of God. JOB 34:10 Therefore hearken unto me, ye men of understanding: far be it from God, that he should do wickedness; and from the Almighty, that he should commit iniquity.

[12] ROM 4:19 And being not weak in faith, he considered not his own body now dead, when he was about an hundred years old, neither yet the deadness of

IV. The almighty power, unsearchable wisdom, and infinite goodness of God so far manifest themselves in His providence, that it extends itself even to the first fall, and all other sins of angels and men;[14] and that not by a bare permission,[15] but such as has joined with it a most wise and

Sara's womb: 20 He staggered not at the promise of God through unbelief; but was strong in faith, giving glory to God; 21 And being fully persuaded that, what he had promised, he was able also to perform.
   [13] 2KI 6:6 And the man of God said, Where fell it? And he shewed him the place. And he cut down a stick, and cast it in thither; and the iron did swim. DAN 3:27 And the princes, governors, and captains, and the king's counsellors, being gathered together, saw these men, upon whose bodies the fire had no power, nor was an hair of their head singed, neither were their coats changed, nor the smell of fire had passed on them.
   [14] ROM 11:32 For God hath concluded them all in unbelief, that he might have mercy upon all. 33 O the depth of the riches both of the wisdom and knowledge of God! how unsearchable are his judgments, and his ways past finding out! 34 For who hath known the mind of the Lord? or who hath been his counsellor? 2SA 24:1 And again the anger of the Lord was kindled against Israel, and he moved David against them to say, Go, number Israel and Judah. 1CH 21:1 And Satan stood up against Israel, and provoked David to number Israel. 1KI 22:22 And the Lord said unto him, Wherewith? And he said, I will go forth, and I will be a lying spirit in the mouth of all his prophets. And he said, Thou shalt persuade him, and prevail also: go forth, and do so. 23 Now therefore, behold, the Lord hath put a lying spirit in the mouth of all these thy prophets, and the Lord hath spoken evil concerning thee. 1CH 10:4 Then said Saul to his armourbearer, Draw thy sword, and thrust me through therewith; lest these uncircumcised come and abuse me. But his armourbearer would not; for he was sore afraid. So Saul took a sword, and fell upon it. 2SA 16:10 And the king said, What have I to do with you, ye sons of Zeruiah? so let him curse, because the Lord hath said unto him, Curse David. Who shall then say, Wherefore hast thou done so? ACT 2:23 Him, being delivered by the determinate counsel and foreknowledge of God, ye have taken, and by wicked hands have crucified and slain: ACT 4:27 For of a truth against thy holy child Jesus, whom thou hast anointed, both Herod, and Pontius Pilate, with the Gentiles, and the people of Israel, were gathered together, 28 For to do whatsoever thy hand and thy counsel determined before to be done.
   [15] ACT 14:16 Who in times past suffered all nations to walk in their own ways.

powerful bounding,[16] and otherwise ordering, and governing of them, in a manifold dispensation, to His own holy ends;[17] yet so, as the sinfulness thereof proceeds only from the creature, and not from God, who, being most holy and righteous, neither is nor can be the author or approver of sin.[18]

V. The most wise, righteous, and gracious God does oftentimes leave, for a season, His own children to manifold temptations, and the corruption of their own hearts, to chastise them for their former sins, or to discover unto them the hidden strength of corruption and deceitfulness of their hearts, that they may be humbled;[19] and, to raise them to a more

[16] PSA 76:10 Surely the wrath of man shall praise thee: the remainder of wrath shalt thou restrain. 2KI 19:28 Because thy rage against me and thy tumult is come up into mine ears, therefore I will put my hook in thy nose, and my bridle in thy lips, and I will turn thee back by the way by which thou camest.

[17] GEN 50:20 But as for you, ye thought evil against me; but God meant it unto good, to bring to pass, as it is this day, to save much people alive. ISA 10:6 I will send him against an hypocritical nation, and against the people of my wrath will I give him a charge, to take the spoil, and to take the prey, and to tread them down like the mire of the streets. 7 Howbeit he meaneth not so, neither doth his heart think so; but it is in his heart to destroy and cut off nations not a few. 12 Wherefore it shall come to pass, that when the Lord hath performed his whole work upon mount Zion and on Jerusalem, I will punish the fruit of the stout heart of the king of Assyria, and the glory of his high looks.

[18] JAM 1:13 Let no man say when he is tempted, I am tempted of God: for God cannot be tempted with evil, neither tempteth he any man: 14 But every man is tempted, when he is drawn away of his own lust, and enticed. 17 Every good gift and every perfect gift is from above, and cometh down from the Father of lights, with whom is no variableness, neither shadow of turning. 1JO 2:16 For all that is in the world, the lust of the flesh, and the lust of the eyes, and the pride of life, is not of the Father, but is of the world. PSA 50:21 These things hast thou done, and I kept silence; thou thoughtest that I was altogether such an one as thyself: but I will reprove thee, and set them in order before thine eyes.

[19] 2CH 32:25 But Hezekiah rendered not again according to the benefit done unto him; for his heart was lifted up: therefore there was wrath upon him, and upon Judah and Jerusalem. 26 Notwithstanding Hezekiah humbled himself for the pride of his heart, both he and the inhabitants of Jerusalem, so that the wrath of the Lord came not upon them in the days of Hezekiah. 31 Howbeit in the

close and constant dependence for their support upon Himself, and to make them more watchful against all future occasions of sin, and for sundry other just and holy ends.[20]

VI. As for those wicked and ungodly men whom God, as a righteous Judge, for former sins, does blind and harden,[21] from them He not only

---

business of the ambassadors of the princes of Babylon, who sent unto him to inquire of the wonder that was done in the land, God left him, to try him, that he might know all that was in his heart. 2SA 24:1 And again the anger of the Lord was kindled against Israel, and he moved David against them to say, Go, number Israel and Judah.

[20] 2CO 12:7 And lest I should be exalted above measure through the abundance of the revelations, there was given to me a thorn in the flesh, the messenger of Satan to buffet me, lest I should be exalted above measure. 8 For this thing I besought the Lord thrice, that it might depart from me. 9 And he said unto me, My grace is sufficient for thee: for my strength is made perfect in weakness. Most gladly therefore will I rather glory in my infirmities, that the power of Christ may rest upon me. PSA 77:1 I cried unto God with my voice, even unto God with my voice; and he gave ear unto me. 10 And I said, This is my infirmity: but I will remember the years of the right hand of the most High. 12 I will meditate also of all thy work, and talk of thy doings. Cf. MAR 14:66-72 with JOH 21:15 So when they had dined, Jesus saith to Simon Peter, Simon, son of Jonas, lovest thou me more than these? He saith unto him, Yea, Lord; thou knowest that I love thee. He saith unto him, Feed my lambs. 16 He saith to him again the second time, Simon, son of Jonas, lovest thou me? He saith unto him, Yea, Lord; thou knowest that I love thee. He saith unto him, Feed my sheep. 17 He saith unto him the third time, Simon, son of Jonas, lovest thou me? Peter was grieved because he said unto him the third time, Lovest thou me? And he said unto him, Lord, thou knowest all things; thou knowest that I love thee. Jesus saith unto him, Feed my sheep.

[21] ROM 1:24 Wherefore God also gave them up to uncleanness through the lusts of their own hearts, to dishonour their own bodies between themselves. 26 For this cause God gave them up unto vile affections: for even their women did change the natural use into that which is against nature. 28 And even as they did not like to retain God in their knowledge, God gabve them over to a reprobate mind, to do those things which are not convenient. 11:7 What then? Israel hath not obtained that which he seeketh for; but the election hath obtained it, and the rest were blinded 8 (According as it is written, God hath given them the spirit of

withholds His grace whereby they might have been enlightened in their understandings, and wrought upon in their hearts;[22] but sometimes also withdraws the gifts which they had,[23] and exposes them to such objects as their corruption makes occasion of sin;[24] and, withal, gives them over to their own lusts, the temptations of the world, and the power of Satan,[25] whereby it comes to pass that they harden themselves, even under those means which God uses for the softening of others.[26]

slumber, eyes that they should not see, and ears that they should not hear;) unto this day.

[22] DEU 29:4 Yet the Lord hath not given you an heart to perceive, and eyes to see, and ears to hear, unto this day.

[23] MAT 13:12 For whosoever hath, to him shall be given, and he shall have more abundance: but whosoever hath not, from him shall be taken away even that he hath. 25:29 For unto every one that hath shall be given, and he shall have abundance: but from him that hath not shall be taken away even that which he hath.

[24] DEU 2:30 But Sihon king of Heshbon would not let us pass by him: for the Lord thy God hardened his spirit, and made his heart obstinate, that he might deliver him into thy hand, as appeareth this day. 2KI 8:12 And Hazael said, Why weepeth my lord? And he answered, because I know the evil that thou wilt do unto the children of Israel: their strong holds wilt thou set on fire, and their young men wilt thou slay with the sword, and wilt dash their children, and rip up their women with child. 13 And Hazael said, But what, is thy servant a dog, that he should do this great thing? And Elisha answered, The Lord hath shewed me that thou shalt be king over Syria.

[25] PSA 81:11 But my people would not hearken to my voice; and Israel would none of me. 12 So I gave them up unto their own hearts' lust: and they walked in their own counsels. 2TH 2:10 And with all deceivableness of unrighteousness in them that perish; because they received not the love of the truth, that they might be saved. 11 And for this cause God shall send them strong delusion, that they should believe a lie: 12 That they all might be damned who believed not the truth, but had pleasure in unrighteousness.

[26] EXO 7:3 And I will harden Pharaoh's heart, and multiply my signs and my wonders in the land of Egypt. 8:15 But when Pharaoh saw that there was respite, he hardened his heart, and hearkened not unto them; as the Lord had said. 32 And Pharaoh hardened his heart at this time also, neither would he let the people go. 2CO 2:15 For we are unto God a sweet savour of Christ, in them that are saved,

VII. As the providence of God does, in general, reach to all creatures; so, after a most special manner, it takes care of His Church, and disposes all things to the good thereof.[27]

and in them that perish: 16 To the one we are the savour of death unto death; and to the other the savour of life unto life. And who is sufficient for these things? ISA 8:14 and he shall be for a sanctuary; but for a stone of stumbling and for a rock of offence to both the houses of Israel, for a gin and for a snare to the inhabitants of Jerusalem. 1PE 2:7 Unto you therefore which believe he is precious: but unto them which be disobedient, the stone which the builders disallowed, the same is made the head of the corner, 8 And a stone of stumbling, and a rock of offence, even to them which stumble at the word, being disobedient: whereunto also they were appointed. ISA 6:9 And he said, Go, and tell this people, Hear ye indeed, but understand not; and see ye indeed, but perceive not. 10 Make the heart of this people fat, and make their ears heavy, and shut their eyes; lest they see with their eyes, and hear with their ears, and understand with their heart, and convert, and be healed. ACT 28:26 Saying, Go unto this people, and say, hearing ye shall hear, and shall not understand; and seeing ye shall see, and not perceive: 27 For the heart of this people is waxed gross, and their ears are dull of hearing, and their eyes have they closed; lest they should see with their eyes, and hear with their ears, and understand with their heart, and should be converted, and I should heal them.

[27] 1TI 4:10 For therefore we both labour and suffer reproach, because we trust in the living God, who is the Saviour of all men, specially of those that believe. AMO 9:8 Behold, the eyes of the Lord God are upon the sinful kingdom, and I will destroy it from off the face of the earth; saving that I will not utterly destroy the house of Jacob, saith the Lord. 9 For, lo, I will command, and I will sift the house of Israel among all nations, like as corn is sifted in a sieve, yet shall not the least grain fall upon the earth. ROM 8:28 And we know that all things work together for good to them that love God, to them who are the called according to his purpose. ISA 43:3 For I am the Lord thy God, the Holy One of Israel, thy Saviour: I gave Egypt for thy ransom, Ethiopia and Seba for thee. 4 Since thou wast precious in my sight, thou hast been honourable, and I have loved thee: therefore will I give men for thee, and people for thy life. 5 Fear not: for I am with thee: I will bring thy seed from the east, and gather thee from the west. 14 Thus saith the Lord, your redeemer, the Holy One of Israel; For your sake I have sent to Babylon, and have brought down all their nobles, and the Chaldeans, whose cry is in the ships.

Chapter VI
Of the Fall of Man, of Sin, and the Punishment thereof

I. Our first parents, being seduced by the subtilty and temptations of Satan, sinned, in eating the forbidden fruit.[1] This their sin, God was pleased, according to His wise and holy counsel, to permit, having purposed to order it to His own glory.[2]

II. By this sin they fell from their original righteousness and communion, with God,[3] and so became dead in sin,[4] and wholly defiled in all the parts and faculties of soul and body.[5]

[1] GEN 3:13 And the Lord God said unto the woman, What is this that thou hast done? And the woman said, The serpent beguiled me, and I did eat. 2CO 11:3 But I fear, lest by any means, as the serpent beguiled Eve through his subtilty, so your minds should be corrupted from the simplicity that is in Christ.

[2] ROM 11:32 For God hath concluded them all in unbelief, that he might have mercy upon all.

[3] GEN 3:6 And when the woman saw that the tree was good for food, and that it was pleasant to the eyes, and a tree to be desired to make one wise, she took of the fruit thereof, and did eat, and gave also unto her husband with her; and he did eat. 7 And the eyes of them both were opened, and they knew that they were naked; and they sewed fig leaves together, and made themselves aprons. 8 And they heard the voice of the Lord God walking in the garden in the cool of the day: and Adam and his wife hid themselves from the presence of the Lord God amongst the trees of the garden. ECC 7:29 Lo, this only have I found, that God hath made man upright; but they have sought out many inventions. ROM 3:23 For all have sinned, and come short of the glory of God.

[4] GEN 2:17 But of the tree of the knowledge of good and evil, thou shalt not eat of it: for in the day that thou eatest thereof thou shalt surely die. EPH 2:1 And you hath he quickened, who were dead in trespasses and sins.

[5] TIT 1:15 Unto the pure all things are pure: but unto them that are defiled

III. They being the root of all mankind, the guilt of this sin was imputed;[6] and the same death in sin, and corrupted nature, conveyed to all their posterity descending from them by ordinary generation.[7]

and unbelieving is nothing pure; but even their mind and conscience is defiled. GEN 6:5 And God saw that the wickedness of man was great in the earth, and that every imagination of the thoughts of his heart was only evil continually. JER 17:9 The heart is deceitful above all things, and desperately wicked: who can know it? ROM 3:10 As it is written, There is none righteous, no, not one: 11 There is none that understandeth, there is none that seeketh after God. 12 They are all gone out of the way, they are together become unprofitable; there is none that doeth good, no, not one. 13 Their throat is an open sepulchre; with their tongues they have used deceit; the poison of asps is under their lips: 14 Whose mouth is full of cursing and bitterness: 15 Their feet are swift to shed blood: 16 Destruction and misery are in their ways: 17 And the way of peace have they not known: 18 There is no fear of God before their eyes.

[6] GEN 1:27 So God created man in his own image, in the image of God created he him; male and female created he them. 28 And God blessed them, and God said unto them, Be fruitful, and multiply, and replenish the earth, and subdue it: and have dominion over the fish of the sea, and over the fowl of the air, and over every living thing that moveth upon the earth. 2:10 And a river went out of Eden to water the garden; and from thence it was parted, and became into four heads. 17 But of the tree of the knowledge of good and evil, thou shalt not eat of it: for in the day that thou eatest thereof thou shalt surely die. ACT 17:26 And hath made of one blood all nations of men for to dwell on all the face of the earth, and hath determined the times before appointed, and the bounds of their habitation. ROM 5:12 Wherefore, as by one man sin entered into the world, and death by sin; and so death passed upon all men, for that all have sinned. 15 But not as the offence, so also is the free gift. For if through the offence of one many be dead, much more the grace of God, and the gift by grace, which is by one man, Jesus Christ, hath abounded unto many. 16 And not as it was by one that sinned, so is the gift: for the judgment was by one to condemnation, but the free gift is of many offences unto justification. 17 For if by one man's offence death reigned by one; much more they which receive abundance of grace and of the gift of righteousness shall reign in life by one, Jesus Christ. 18 Therefore as by the offence of one judgment came upon all men to condemnation; even so by the righteousness of one the free gift came upon all men unto justification of life. 19 For as by one man's disobedience many were made sinners, so by the

IV. From this original corruption, whereby we are utterly indisposed, disabled, and made opposite to all good,[8] and wholly inclined to all evil,[9] do proceed all actual transgressions.[10]

obedience of one shall many be made righteous. 1CO 15:21 For since by man came death, by man came also the resurrection of the dead. 22 For as in Adam all die, even so in Christ shall all be made alive. 45 And so it is written, The first man Adam was made a living soul; the last Adam was made a quickening spirit. 49 And as we have borne the image of the earthy, we shall also bear the image of the heavenly.

[7] PSA 51:5 Behold, I was shapen in iniquity; and in sin did my mother conceive me. GEN 5:3 And Adam lived an hundred and thirty years, and begat a son in his own likeness, after his image; and called his name Seth. JOB 14:4 Who can bring a clean thing out of an unclean? not one. 15:14 What is man, that he should be clean? and he which is born of a woman, that he should be righteous?

[8] ROM 5:6 For when we were yet without strength, in due time Christ died for the ungodly. ROM 8:7 Because the carnal mind is enmity against God: for it is not subject to the law of God, neither indeed can be. ROM 7:18 For I know that in me (that is, in my flesh,) dwelleth no good thing: for to will is present with me; but how to perform that which is good I find not. COL 1:21 And you, that were sometime alienated and enemies in your mind by wicked works, yet now hath he reconciled.

[9] GEN 6:5 And God saw that the wickedness of man was great in the earth, and that every imagination of the thoughts of his heart was only evil continually. 8:21 And the Lord smelled a sweet savour; and the Lord said in his heart, I will not again curse the ground any more for man's sake; for the imagination of man's heart is evil from his youth; neither will I again smite any more every thing living, as I have done. ROM 3:10 As it is written, There is none righteous, no, not one: 11 There is none that understandeth, there is none that seeketh after God. 12 They are all gone out of the way, they are together become unprofitable; there is none that doeth good, no, not one.

[10] JAM 1:14 But every man is tempted, when he is drawn away of his own lust, and enticed. 15 Then when lust hath conceived, it bringeth forth sin: and sin, when it is finished, bringeth forth death. EPH 2:2 Wherein in time past ye walked according to the course of this world, according to the prince of the power of the air, the spirit that now worketh in the children of disobedience: 3 Among whom also we all had our conversation in times past in the lusts of our flesh, fulfilling the desires of the flesh and of the mind; and were by nature the children of wrath,

V. This corruption of nature, during this life, does remain in those that are regenerated;[11] and although it be, through Christ, pardoned, and mortified; yet both itself, and all the motions thereof, are truly and properly sin.[12]

VI. Every sin, both original and actual, being a transgression of the righteous law of God, and contrary thereunto,[13] does in its own nature, bring guilt upon the sinner,[14] whereby he is bound over to the wrath of

even as others. MAT 15:19 For out of the heart proceed evil thoughts, murders, adulteries, fornications, thefts, false witness, blasphemies.

[11] 1JO 1:8 If we say that we have no sin, we deceive ourselves, and the truth is not in us. 10 If we say that we have not sinned, we make him a liar, and his word is not in us. ROM 7:14 For we know that the law is spiritual: but I am carnal, sold under sin. 17 Now then it is no more I that do it, but sin that dwelleth in me. 18 For I know that in me (that is, in my flesh,) dwelleth no good thing: for to will is present with me; but how to perform that which is good I find not. 23 But I see another law in my members, warring against the law of my mind, and bringing me into captivity to the law of sin which is in my members. JAM 3:2 For in many things we offend all. If any man offend not in word, the same is a perfect man, and able also to bridle the whole body. PRO 20:9 Who can say, I have made my heart clean, I am pure from my sin? ECC 7:20 For there is not a just man upon earth, that doeth good, and sinneth not.

[12] ROM 7:5 For when we were in the flesh, the motions of sins, which were by the law, did work in our members to bring forth fruit unto death. 7 What shall we say then? Is the law sin? God forbid. Nay, I had not known sin, but by the law: for I had not known lust, except the law had said, Thou shalt not covet. 8 But sin, taking occasion by the commandment, wrought in me all manner of concupiscence. For without the law sin was dead. 25 I thank God through Jesus Christ our Lord. So then with the mind I myself serve the law of God; but with the flesh the law of sin. GAL 5:17 For the flesh lusteth against the Spirit, and the Spirit against the flesh: and these are contrary the one to the other: so that ye cannot do the things that ye would.

[13] 1JO 3:4 Whosoever committeth sin transgresseth also the law: for sin is the transgression of the law.

[14] ROM 2:15 Which shew the work of the law written in their hearts, their conscience also bearing witness, and their thoughts the mean while accusing or else excusing one another. ROM 3:9 What then? are we better than they? No, in no wise: for we have before proved both Jews and Gentiles, that they are all under

God,[15] and curse of the law,[16] and so made subject to death,[17] with all miseries spiritual,[18] temporal,[19] and eternal.[20]

sin. 19 Now we know that what things soever the law saith, it saith to them who are under the law: that every mouth may be stopped, and all the world may become guilty before God.

[15] EPH 2:3 Among whom also we all had our conversation in times past in the lusts of our flesh, fulfilling the desires of the flesh and of the mind; and were by nature the children of wrath, even as others.

[16] GAL 3:10 For as many as are of the works of the law are under the curse: for it is written, Cursed is every one that continueth not in all things which are written in the book of the law to do them.

[17] ROM 6:23 For the wages of sin is death; but the gift of God is eternal life through Jesus Christ our Lord.

[18] EPH 4:18 Having the understanding darkened, being alienated from the life of God through the ignorance that is in them, because of the blindness of their heart.

[19] ROM 8:20 For the creature was made subject to vanity, not willingly, but by reason of him who hath subjected the same in hope. LAM 3:39 Wherefore doth a living man complain, a man for the punishment of his sins?

[20] MAT 25:41 Then shall he say also unto them on the left hand, Depart from me, ye cursed, into everlasting fire, prepared for the devil and his angels. 2TH 1:9 Who shall be punished with everlasting destruction from the presence of the Lord, and from the glory of his power.

Chapter VII

Of God's Covenant with Man

I. The distance between God and the creature is so great, that although reasonable creatures do owe obedience unto Him as their Creator, yet they could never have any fruition of Him as their blessedness and reward, but by some voluntary condescension on God's part, which He has been pleased to express by way of covenant.[1]

[1] ISA 40:13 Who hath directed the Spirit of the Lord, or being his counsellor hath taught him? 14 With whom took he counsel, and who instructed him, and taught him in the path of judgment, and taught him knowledge, and shewed to him the way of understanding? 15 Behold, the nations are as a drop of a bucket, and are counted as the small dust of the balance: behold, he taketh up the isles as a very little thing. 16 And Lebanon is not sufficient to burn, nor the beasts thereof sufficient for a burnt offering. 17 All nations before him are as nothing; and they are counted to him less than nothing, and vanity. JOB 9:32 For he is not a man, as I am, that I should answer him, and we should come together in judgment. 33 Neither is there any daysman betwixt us, that might lay his hand upon us both. 1SA 2:25 If one man sin against another, the judge shall judge him: but if a man sin against the Lord, who shall intreat for him? Notwithstanding they hearkened not unto the voice of their father, because the Lord would slay them. PSA 113:5 Who is like unto the Lord our God, who dwelleth on high, 6 Who humbleth himself to behold the things that are in heaven, and in the earth! PSA 100:2 Serve the Lord with gladness: come before his presence with singing. 3 Know ye that the Lord he is God: it is he that hath made us, and not we ourselves; we are his people, and the sheep of his pasture. JOB 22:2 Can a man be profitable unto God, as he that is wise may be profitable unto himself? 3 Is it any pleasure to the Almighty, that thou art righteous? or is it gain to him that thou makest thy ways perfect? JOB 35:7 If thou be righteous, what givest thou him? or what receiveth

II. The first covenant made with man was a covenant of works,[2] wherein life was promised to Adam; and in him to his posterity,[3] upon condition of perfect and personal obedience.[4]

he of thine hand? 8 Thy wickedness may hurt a man as thou art; and thy righteousness may profit the son of man. LUK 17:10 So likewise ye, when ye shall have done all those things which are commanded you, say, We are unprofitable servants: we have done that which was our duty to do. ACT 17:24 God that made the world and all things therein, seeing that he is Lord of heaven and earth, dwelleth not in temples made with hands; 25 Neither is worshipped with men's hands, as though he needed any thing, seeing he giveth to all life, and breath, and all things.

[2] GAL 3:12 And the law is not of faith: but, The man that doeth them shall live in them.

[3] ROM 10:5 For Moses describeth the righteousness which is of the law, That the man which doeth those things shall live by them. ROM 5:12 Wherefore, as by one man sin entered into the world, and death by sin; and so death passed upon all men, for that all have sinned: 13 (For until the law sin was in the world: but sin is not imputed when there is no law. 14 Nevertheless death reigned from Adam to Moses, even over them that had not sinned after the similitude of Adam's transgression, who is the figure of him that was to come. 15 But not as the offence, so also is the free gift. For if through the offence of one many be dead, much more the grace of God, and the gift by grace, which is by one man, Jesus Christ, hath abounded unto many. 16 And not as it was by one that sinned, so is the gift: for the judgment was by one to condemnation, but the free gift is of many offences unto justification. 17 For if by one man's offence death reigned by one; much more they which receive abundance of grace and of the gift of righteousness shall reign in life by one, Jesus Christ.) 18 Therefore as by the offence of one judgment came upon all men to condemnation; even so by the righteousness of one the free gift came upon all men unto justification of life. 19 For as by one man's disobedience many were made sinners, so by the obedience of one shall many be made righteous. 20 Moreover the law entered, that the offence might abound. But where sin abounded, grace did much more abound.

[4] GEN 2:17 But of the tree of the knowledge of good and evil, thou shalt not eat of it: for in the day that thou eatest thereof thou shalt surely die. GAL 3:10 For as many as are of the works of the law are under the curse: for it is written, Cursed is every one that continueth not in all things which are written in the book of the law to do them.

III. Man, by his fall, having made himself incapable of life by that covenant, the Lord was pleased to make a second,[5] commonly called the covenant of grace; wherein He freely offers unto sinners life and salvation by Jesus Christ; requiring of them faith in Him, that they may be saved,[6] and promising to give unto all those that are ordained unto eternal life His Holy Spirit, to make them willing, and able to believe.[7]

---

[5] GAL 3:21 Is the law then against the promises of God? God forbid: for if there had been a law given which could have given life, verily righteousness should have been by the law. ROM 8:3 For what the law could not do, in that it was weak through the flesh, God sending his own Son in the likeness of sinful flesh, and for sin, condemned sin in the flesh. ROM 3:20 Therefore by the deeds of the law there shall no flesh be justified in his sight: for by the law is the knowledge of sin. 21 But now the righteousness of God without the law is manifested, being witnessed by the law and the prophets. GEN 3:15 And I will put enmity between thee and the woman, and between thy seed and her seed; it shall bruise thy head, and thou shalt bruise his heel. ISA 42:6 I the Lord have called thee in righteousness, and will hold thine hand, and will keep thee, and give thee for a covenant of the people, for a light of the Gentiles.

[6] MAR 16:15 And he said unto them, Go ye into all the world, and preach the gospel to every creature. 16 He that believeth and is baptized shall be saved; but he that believeth not shall be damned. JOH 3:16 For God so loved the world, that he gave his only begotten Son, that whosoever believeth in him should not perish, but have everlasting life. ROM 10:6 But the righteousness which is of faith speaketh on this wise, Say not in thine heart, Who shall ascend into heaven? (that is, to bring Christ down from above:) 9 That if thou shalt confess with thy mouth the Lord Jesus, and shalt believe in thine heart that God hath raised him from the dead, thou shalt be saved. GAL 3:11 But that no man is justified by the law in the sight of God, it is evident: for, The just shall live by faith.

[7] EZE 36:26 A new heart also will I give you, and a new spirit will I put within you: and I will take away the stony heart out of your flesh, and I will give you an heart of flesh. 27 And I will put my spirit within you, and cause you to walk in my statutes, and ye shall keep my judgments, and do them. JOH 6:44 No man can come to me, except the Father which hath sent me draw him: and I will raise him up at the last day. 45 It is written in the prophets, And they shall be all taught of God. Every man therefore that hath heard, and hath learned of the Father, cometh unto me.

IV. This covenant of grace is frequently set forth in scripture by the name of a testament, in reference to the death of Jesus Christ the Testator, and to the everlasting inheritance, with all things belonging to it, therein bequeathed.[8]

V. This covenant was differently administered in the time of the law, and in the time of the Gospel:[9] under the law it was administered by promises, prophecies, sacrifices, circumcision, the paschal lamb, and other types and ordinances delivered to the people of the Jews, all foresignifying Christ to come;[10] which were, for that time, sufficient and

---

[8] HEB 9:15 And for this cause he is the mediator of the new testament, that by means of death, for the redemption of the transgressions that were under the first testament, they which are called might receive the promise of eternal inheritance. 16 For where a testament is, there must also of necessity be the death of the testator. 17 For a testament is of force after men are dead: otherwise it is of no strength at all while the testator liveth. HEB 7:22 By so much was Jesus made a surety of a better testament. LUK 22:20 Likewise also the cup after supper, saying, This cup is the new testament in my blood, which is shed for you. 1CO 11:25 After the same manner also he took the cup, when he had supped, saying, This cup is the new testament in my blood: this do ye, as oft as ye drink it, in remembrance of me.

[9] 2CO 3:6 Who also hath made us able ministers of the new testament; not of the letter, but of the spirit: for the letter killeth, but the spirit giveth life. 7 But if the ministration of death, written and engraven in stones, was glorious, so that the children of Israel could not stedfastly behold the face of Moses for the glory of his countenance; which glory was to be done away: 8 How shall not the ministration of the spirit be rather glorious? 9 For if the ministration of condemnation be glory, much more doth the ministration of righteousness exceed in glory.

[10] SEE HEB 8-10, ROM 4:11 And he received the sign of circumcision, a seal of the righteousness of the faith which he had yet being uncircumcised: that he might be the father of all them that believe, though they be not circumcised; that righteousness might be imputed unto them also. COL 2:11 In whom also ye are circumcised with the circumcision made without hands, in putting off the body of the sins of the flesh by the circumcision of Christ: 12 Buried with him in baptism, wherein also ye are risen with him through the faith of the operation of God, who hath raised him from the dead. 1CO 5:7 Purge out therefore the old leaven, that ye may be a new lump, as ye are unleavened. For even Christ our passover is sacrificed for us.

efficacious, through the operation of the Spirit, to instruct and build up the elect in faith in the promised Messiah,[11] by whom they had full remission of sins, and eternal salvation; and is called the Old Testament.[12]

VI. Under the Gospel, when Christ, the substance,[13] was exhibited, the ordinances in which this covenant is dispensed are the preaching of the Word, and the administration of the sacraments of Baptism and the Lord's Supper:[14] which, though fewer in number, and administered with more simplicity, and less outward glory, yet, in them, it is held forth in

---

[11] 1CO 10:1 Moreover, brethren, I would not that ye should be ignorant, how that all our fathers were under the cloud, and all passed through the sea; 2 And were all baptized unto Moses in the cloud and in the sea; 3 And did all eat the same spiritual meat; 4 And did all drink the same spiritual drink: for they drank of that spiritual Rock that followed them: and that Rock was Christ. HEB 11:13 These all died in faith, not having received the promises, but having seen them afar off, and were persuaded of them, and embraced them, and confessed that they were strangers and pilgrims on the earth. JOH 8:56 Your father Abraham rejoiced to see my day: and he saw it, and was glad.

[12] GAL 3:7 Know ye therefore that they which are of faith, the same are the children of Abraham. 8 And the scripture, foreseeing that God would justify the heathen through faith, preached before the gospel unto Abraham, saying, In thee shall all nations be blessed. 9 So then they which be of faith are blessed with faithful Abraham. 14 That the blessing of Abraham might come on the Gentiles through Jesus Christ; that we might receive the promise of the Spirit through faith.

[13] COL 2:17 Which are a shadow of things to come; but the body is of Christ.

[14] MAT 28:19 Go ye therefore, and teach all nations, baptizing them in the name of the Father, and of the Son, and of the Holy Ghost: 20 Teaching them to observe all things whatsoever I have commanded you: and, lo, I am with you alway, even unto the end of the world. Amen. 1CO 11:23 For I have received of the Lord that which also I delivered unto you, That the Lord Jesus the same night in which he was betrayed took bread: 24 And when he had given thanks, he brake it, and said, Take, eat: this is my body, which is broken for you: this do in remembrance of me. 25 After the same manner also he took the cup, when he had supped, saying, This cup is the new testament in my blood: this do ye, as oft as ye drink it, in remembrance of me.

more fullness, evidence, and spiritual efficacy,[15] to all nations, both Jews and Gentiles;[16] and is called the New Testament.[17] There are not therefore two covenants of grace, differing in substance, but one and the same, under various dispensations.[18]

[15] HEB 12:22 But ye are come unto mount Sion, and unto the city of the living God, the heavenly Jerusalem, and to an innumerable company of angels, 23 To the general assembly and church of the firstborn, which are written in heaven, and to God the Judge of all, and to the spirits of just men made perfect, 24 And to Jesus the mediator of the new covenant, and to the blood of sprinkling, that speaketh better things than that of Abel. 25 See that ye refuse not him that speaketh. For if they escaped not who refused him that spake on earth, much more shall not we escape, if we turn away from him that speaketh from heaven: 26 Whose voice then shook the earth: but now he hath promised, saying, Yet once more I shake not the earth only, but also heaven. 27 And this word, Yet once more, signifieth the removing of those things that are shaken, as of things that are made, that those things which cannot be shaken may remain. JER 31:33 But this shall be the covenant that I will make with the house of Israel; After those days, saith the Lord, I will put my law in their inward parts, and write it in their hearts; and will be their God, and they shall be my people. 34 And they shall teach no more every man his neighbour, and every man his brother, saying, Know the Lord: for they shall all know me, from the least of them unto the greatest of them, saith the Lord; for I will forgive their iniquity, and I will remember their sin no more.

[16] MAT 28:19 Go ye therefore, and teach all nations, baptizing them in the name of the Father, and of the Son, and of the Holy Ghost. EPH 2:15 Having abolished in his flesh the enmity, even the law of commandments contained in ordinances; for to make in himself of twain one new man, so making peace; 16 And that he might reconcile both unto God in one body by the cross, having slain the enmity thereby: 17 And came and preached peace to you which were afar off, and to them that were nigh. 18 For through him we both have access by one Spirit unto the Father. 19 Now therefore ye are no more strangers and foreigners, but fellowcitizens with the saints, and of the household of God.

[17] LUK 22:20 Likewise also the cup after supper, saying, This cup is the new testament in my blood, which is shed for you.

[18] GAL 3:14 That the blessing of Abraham might come on the Gentiles through Jesus Christ; that we might receive the promise of the Spirit through faith. 16 Now to Abraham and his seed were the promises made. He saith not, And to seeds, as of many; but as of one, And to thy seed, which is Christ.

ACT 15:11 But we believe that through the grace of the Lord Jesus Christ we shall be saved, even as they. ROM 3:21 But now the righteousness of God without the law is manifested, being witnessed by the law and the prophets; 22 Even the righteousness of God which is by faith of Jesus Christ unto all and upon all them that believe: for there is no difference: 23 For all have sinned, and come short of the glory of God. 30 Seeing it is one God, which shall justify the circumcision by faith, and uncircumcision through faith. PSA 32:1 Blessed is he whose transgression is forgiven, whose sin is covered. ROM 4:3 For what saith the scripture? Abraham believed God, and it was counted unto him for righteousness. 6 Even as David also describeth the blessedness of the man, unto whom God imputeth righteousness without works. 16 Therefore it is of faith, that it might be by grace; to the end the promise might be sure to all the seed; not to that only which is of the law, but to that also which is of the faith of Abraham; who is the father of us all, 17 (As it is written, I have made thee a father of many nations,) before him whom he believed, even God, who quickeneth the dead, and calleth those things which be not as though they were. 23 Now it was not written for his sake alone, that it was imputed to him; 24 But for us also, to whom it shall be imputed, if we believe on him that raised up Jesus our Lord from the dead. HEB 13:8 Jesus Christ the same yesterday, and to day, and for ever.

Chapter VIII
Of Christ the Mediator

I. It pleased God, in His eternal purpose, to choose and ordain the Lord Jesus, His only begotten Son, to be the Mediator between God and man,[1] the Prophet,[2] Priest,[3] and King,[4] the Head and Savior of His Church,[5] the Heir of all things,[6] and Judge of the world:[7] unto whom He

---

[1] ISA 42:1 Behold my servant, whom I uphold; mine elect, in whom my soul delighteth; I have put my spirit upon him: he shall bring forth judgment to the Gentiles. 1PE 1:19 But with the precious blood of Christ, as of a lamb without blemish and without spot: 20 Who verily was foreordained before the foundation of the world, but was manifest in these last times for you. JOH 3:16 For God so loved the world, that he gave his only begotten Son, that whosoever believeth in him should not perish, but have everlasting life. 1TI 2:5 For there is one God, and one mediator between God and men, the man Christ Jesus.

[2] ACT 3:22 For Moses truly said unto the fathers, A prophet shall the Lord your God raise up unto you of your brethren, like unto me; him shall ye hear in all things whatsoever he shall say unto you.

[3] HEB 5:5 So also Christ glorified not himself to be made an high priest; but he that said unto him, Thou art my Son, to day have I begotten thee. 6 As he saith also in another place, Thou art a priest for ever after the order of Melchisedec.

[4] PSA 2:6 Yet have I set my king upon my holy hill of Zion. LUK 1:33 And he shall reign over the house of Jacob for ever; and of his kingdom there shall be no end.

[5] EPH 5:23 For the husband is the head of the wife, even as Christ is the head of the church: and he is the saviour of the body.

[6] HEB 1:2 Hath in these last days spoken unto us by his Son, whom he hath appointed heir of all things, by whom also he made the worlds.

[7] ACT 17:31 Because he hath appointed a day, in the which he will judge the

did from all eternity give a people, to be His seed,[8] and to be by Him in time redeemed, called, justified, sanctified, and glorified.[9]

II. The Son of God, the second person of the Trinity, being very and eternal God, of one substance and equal with the Father, did, when the fullness of time was come, take upon Him man's nature,[10] with all the essential properties, and common infirmities thereof, yet without sin;[11]

world in righteousness by that man whom he hath ordained; whereof he hath given assurance unto all men, in that he hath raised him from the dead.

[8] JOH 17:6 I have manifested thy name unto the men which thou gavest me out of the world: thine they were, and thou gavest them me; and they have kept thy word. PSA 22:30 A seed shall serve him; it shall be accounted to the Lord for a generation. ISA 53:10 Yet it pleased the Lord to bruise him; he hath put him to grief: when thou shalt make his soul an offering for sin, he shall see his seed, he shall prolong his days, and the pleasure of the Lord shall prosper in his hand.

[9] 1TI 2:6 Who gave himself a ransom for all, to be testified in due time. ISA 55:4 Behold, I have given him for a witness to the people, a leader and commander to the people. 5 Behold, thou shalt call a nation that thou knowest not, and nations that knew not thee shall run unto thee because of the Lord thy God, and for the Holy One of Israel; for he hath glorified thee. 1CO 1:30 But of him are ye in Christ Jesus, who of God is made unto us wisdom, and righteousness, and sanctification, and redemption.

[10] JOH 1:1 In the beginning was the Word, and the Word was with God, and the Word was God. 14 And the Word was made flesh, and dwelt among us, (and we beheld his glory, the glory as of the only begotten of the Father,) full of grace and truth. 1JO 5:20 And we know that the Son of God is come, and hath given us an understanding, that we may know him that is true, and we are in him that is true, even in his Son Jesus Christ. This is the true God, and eternal life. PHI 2:6 Who, being in the form of God, thought it not robbery to be equal with God. GAL 4:4 But when the fulness of the time was come, God sent forth his Son, made of a woman, made under the law.

[11] HEB 2:14 Forasmuch then as the children are partakers of flesh and blood, he also himself likewise took part of the same; that through death he might destroy him that had the power of death, that is, the devil. 16 For verily he took not on him the nature of angels; but he took on him the seed of Abraham. 17 Wherefore in all things it behooved him to be made like unto his brethren, that he might be a merciful and faithful high priest in things pertaining to God, to make reconciliation for the sins of the people. 4:15 For we have not an high priest

being conceived by the power of the Holy Ghost, in the womb of the virgin Mary, of her substance.[12] So that two whole, perfect, and distinct natures, the Godhead and the manhood, were inseparably joined together in one person, without conversion, composition, or confusion.[13] Which person is very God, and very man, yet one Christ, the only Mediator between God and man.[14]

    III. The Lord Jesus, in His human nature thus united to the divine, was sanctified, and anointed with the Holy Spirit, above measure,[15]

which cannot be touched with the feeling of our infirmities; but was in all points tempted like as we are, yet without sin.

    [12] LUK 1:27 To a virgin espoused to a man whose name was Joseph, of the house of David; and the virgin's name was Mary. 31 And, behold, thou shalt conceive in thy womb, and bring forth a son, and shalt call his name Jesus. 35 And the angel answered and said unto her, The Holy Ghost shall come upon thee, and the power of the Highest shall overshadow thee: therefore also that holy thing which shall be born of thee shall be called the Son of God. GAL 4:4 But when the fulness of the time was come, God sent forth his Son, made of a woman, made under the law.

    [13] LUK 1:35 And the angel answered and said unto her, The Holy Ghost shall come upon thee, and the power of the Highest shall overshadow thee: therefore also that holy thing which shall be born of thee shall be called the Son of God. COL 2:9 For in him dwelleth all the fulness of the Godhead bodily. ROM 9:5 Whose are the fathers, and of whom as concerning the flesh Christ came, who is over all, God blessed for ever. Amen. 1PE 3:18 For Christ also hath once suffered for sins, the just for the unjust, that he might bring us to God, being put to death in the flesh, but quickened by the Spirit. 1TI 3:16 And without controversy great is the mystery of godliness: God was manifest in the flesh, justified in the Spirit, seen of angels, preached unto the Gentiles, believed on in the world, received up into glory.

    [14] ROM 1:3 Concerning his Son Jesus Christ our Lord, which was made of the seed of David according to the flesh. 4 And declared to be the Son of God with power, according to the spirit of holiness, by the resurrection from the dead. 1TI 2:5 For there is one God, and one mediator between God and men, the man Christ Jesus.

    [15] PSA 45:7 Thou lovest righteousness, and hatest wickedness: therefore God, thy God, hath anointed thee with the oil of gladness above thy fellows.

having in Him all the treasures of wisdom and knowledge;[16] in whom it pleased the Father that all fullness should dwell;[17] to the end that, being holy, harmless, undefiled, and full of grace and truth,[18] He might be thoroughly furnished to execute the office of a Mediator and Surety.[19] Which office He took not unto Himself, but was thereunto called by His Father,[20] who put all power and judgment into His hand, and gave Him commandment to execute the same.[21]

IV. This office the Lord Jesus did most willingly undertake;[22] which

JOH 3:34 For he whom God hath sent speaketh the words of God: for God giveth not the Spirit by measure unto him.

[16] COL 2:3 In whom are hid all the treasures of wisdom and knowledge.

[17] COL 1:19 For it pleased the Father that in him should all fulness dwell.

[18] HEB 7:26 For such an high priest became us, who is holy, harmless, undefiled, separate from sinners, and made higher than the heavens. JOH 1:14 And the Word was made flesh, and dwelt among us, (and we beheld his glory, the glory as of the only begotten of the Father,) full of grace and truth.

[19] ACT 10:38 How God anointed Jesus of Nazareth with the Holy Ghost and with power: who went about doing good, and healing all that were oppressed of the devil; for God was with him. HEB 12:24 And to Jesus the mediator of the new covenant, and to the blood of sprinkling, that speaketh better things than that of Abel. HEB 7:22 By so much was Jesus made a surety of a better testament.

[20] HEB 5:4 And no man taketh this honour unto himself, but he that is called of God, as was Aaron. 5 So also Christ glorified not himself to be made an high priest; but he that said unto him, Thou art my Son, to day have I begotten thee.

[21] JOH 5:22 For the Father judgeth no man, but hath committed all judgment unto the Son. 27 And hath given him authority to execute judgment also, because he is the Son of man. MAT 28:18 And Jesus came and spake unto them, saying, All power is given unto me in heaven and in earth. ACT 2:36 Therefore let all the house of Israel know assuredly, that God hath made that same Jesus, whom ye have crucified, both Lord and Christ.

[22] PSA 40:7 Then said I, Lo, I come: in the volume of the book it is written of me, 8 I delight to do thy will, O my God: yea, thy law is within my heart. HEB 10:5 Wherefore when he cometh into the world, he saith, Sacrifice and offering thou wouldest not, but a body hast thou prepared me: 6 In burnt offerings and sacrifices for sin thou hast had no pleasure. 7 Then said I, Lo, I come (in the volume of the book it is written of me,) to do thy will, O God. 8 Above when he

that He might discharge, He was made under the law,[23] and did perfectly fulfil it;[24] endured most grievous torments immediately in His soul,[25] and most painful sufferings in His body;[26] was crucified, and died,[27] was buried, and remained under the power of death, yet saw no corruption.[28]

said, Sacrifice and offering and burnt offerings and offering for sin thou wouldest not, neither hadst pleasure therein; which are offered by the law; 9 Then said he, Lo, I come to do thy will, O God. He taketh away the first, that he may establish the second. 10 By the which will we are sanctified through the offering of the body of Jesus Christ once for all. JOH 10:18 No man taketh it from me, but I lay it down of myself. I have power to lay it down, and I have power to take it again. This commandment have I received of my Father. PHI 2:8 And being found in fashion as a man, he humbled himself, and became obedient unto death, even the death of the cross.

[23] GAL 4:4 But when the fulness of the time was come, God sent forth his Son, made of a woman, made under the law.

[24] MAT 3:15 And Jesus answering said unto him, Suffer it to be so now: for thus it becometh us to fulfil all righteousness. Then he suffered him. 5:17 Think not that I am come to destroy the law, or the prophets: I am not come to destroy, but to fulfil.

[25] MAT 26:37 And he took with him Peter and the two sons of Zebedee, and began to be sorrowful and very heavy. 38 Then saith he unto them, My soul is exceeding sorrowful, even unto death: tarry ye here, and watch with me. LUK 22:44 And being in an agony he prayed more earnestly: and his sweat was as it were great drops of blood falling down to the ground. MAT 27:46 And about the ninth hour Jesus cried with a loud voice, saying, Eli, Eli, lama sabachthani? that is to say, My God, my God, why hast thou forsaken me?

[26] SEE MAT 26-27

[27] PHI 2:8 And being found in fashion as a man, he humbled himself, and became obedient unto death, even the death of the cross.

[28] ACT 2:23 Him, being delivered by the determinate counsel and foreknowledge of God, ye have taken, and by wicked hands have crucified and slain: 24 Whom God hath raised up, having loosed the pains of death: because it was not possible that he should be holden of it. 27 Because thou wilt not leave my soul in hell, neither wilt thou suffer thine Holy One to see corruption. 13:37 But he, whom God raised again, saw no corruption. ROM 6:9 Knowing that Christ being raised from the dead dieth no more; death hath no more dominion over him.

On the third day He arose from the dead,[29] with the same body in which He suffered,[30] with which also He ascended into heaven, and there sits at the right hand of His Father,[31] making intercession,[32] and shall return, to judge men and angels, at the end of the world.[33]

[29] 1CO 15:3 For I delivered unto you first of all that which I also received, how that Christ died for our sins according to the scriptures; 4 And that he was buried, and that he rose again the third day according to the scriptures: 5 And that he was seen of Cephas, then of the twelve.

[30] JOH 20:25 The other disciples therefore said unto him, We have seen the Lord. But he said unto them, Except I shall see in his hands the print of the nails, and put my finger into the print of the nails, and thrust my hand into his side, I will not believe. 27 Then saith he to Thomas, reach hither thy finger, and behold my hands; and reach hither thy hand, and thrust it into my side: and be not faithless, but believing.

[31] MAR 16:19 So then after the Lord had spoken unto them, he was received up into heaven, and sat on the right hand of God.

[32] ROM 8:34 Who is he that condemneth? It is Christ that died, yea rather, that is risen again, who is even at the right hand of God, who also maketh intercession for us. HEB 9:24 For Christ is not entered into the holy places made with hands, which are the figures of the true; but into heaven itself, now to appear in the presence of God for us. 25 Wherefore he is able also to save them to the uttermost that come unto God by him, seeing he ever liveth to make intercession for them.

[33] ROM 14:9 For to this end Christ both died, and rose, and revived, that he might be Lord both of the dead and living. 10 But why dost thou judge thy brother? or why dost thou set at nought thy brother? for we shall all stand before the judgment seat of Christ. ACT 1:11 Which also said, Ye men of Galilee, why stand ye gazing up into heaven? this same Jesus, which is taken up from you into heaven, shall so come in like manner as ye have seen him go into heaven. 10:42 And he commanded us to preach unto the people, and to testify that it is he which was ordained of God to be the Judge of quick and dead. MAT 13:40 As therefore the tares are gathered and burned in the fire; so shall it be in the end of this world. 41 The Son of man shall send forth his angels, and they shall gather out of his kingdom all things that offend, and them which do iniquity; 42 And shall cast them into a furnace of fire: there shall be wailing and gnashing of teeth. JUD 6 And the angels which kept not their first estate, but left their own habitation, he hath reserved in everlasting chains under darkness unto the judgment of the great day.

V. The Lord Jesus, by His perfect obedience, and sacrifice of Himself, which He through the eternal Spirit, once offered up unto God, has fully satisfied the justice of His Father;[34] and purchased, not only reconciliation, but an everlasting inheritance in the kingdom of heaven, for those whom the Father has given unto Him.[35]

2PE 2:4 For if God spared not the angels that sinned, but cast them down to hell, and delivered them into chains of darkness, to be reserved unto judgment.

[34] ROM 5:19 For as by one man's disobedience many were made sinners, so by the obedience of one shall many be made righteous. HEB 9:14 How much more shall the blood of Christ, who through the eternal Spirit offered himself without spot to God, purge your conscience from dead works to serve the living God? 16 For where a testament is, there must also of necessity be the death of the testator. 10:14 For by one offering he hath perfected for ever them that are sanctified. EPH 5:2 And walk in love, as Christ also hath loved us, and hath given himself for us an offering and a sacrifice to God for a sweetsmelling savour. ROM 3:25 Whom God hath set forth to be a propitiation through faith in his blood, to declare his righteousness for the remission of sins that are past, through the forbearance of God; 26 To declare, I say, at this time his righteousness: that he might be just, and the justifier of him which believeth in Jesus.

[35] DAN 9:24 Seventy weeks are determined upon thy people and upon thy holy city, to finish the transgression, and to make an end of sins, and to make reconciliation for iniquity, and to bring in everlasting righteousness, and to seal up the vision and prophecy, and to anoint the Most Holy. 26 And after threescore and two weeks shall Messiah be cut off, but not for himself: and the people of the prince that shall come shall destroy the city and the sanctuary; and the end thereof shall be with a flood, and unto the end of the war desolations are determined. COL 1:19 For it pleased the Father that in him should all fulness dwell; 20 And, having made peace through the blood of his cross, by him to reconcile all things unto himself; by him, I say, whether they be things in earth, or things in heaven. EPH 1:11 In whom also we have obtained an inheritance, being predestinated according to the purpose of him who worketh all things after the counsel of his own will. 14 Which is the earnest of our inheritance until the redemption of the purchased possession, unto the praise of his glory. JOH 17:2 As thou hast given him power over all flesh, that he should give eternal life to as many as thou hast given him. HEB 9:12 Neither by the blood of goats and calves, but by his own blood he entered in once into the holy place, having obtained eternal redemption for us. 15 And for this cause he is the mediator of the new

VI. Although the work of redemption was not actually wrought by Christ till after His incarnation, yet the virtue, efficacy, and benefits thereof were communicated unto the elect, in all ages successively from the beginning of the world, in and by those promises, types, and sacrifices, wherein He was revealed, and signified to be the seed of the woman which should bruise the serpent's head; and the Lamb slain from the beginning of the world; being yesterday and today the same, and forever.[36]

VII. Christ, in the work of mediation, acts according to both natures, by each nature doing that which is proper to itself;[37] yet, by reason of the unity of the person, that which is proper to one nature is sometimes in Scripture attributed to the person denominated by the other nature.[38]

VIII. To all those for whom Christ has purchased redemption, He does certainly and effectually apply and communicate the same;[39]

testament, that by means of death, for the redemption of the transgressions that were under the first testament, they which are called might receive the promise of eternal inheritance.

[36] GAL 4:4 But when the fulness of the time was come, God sent forth his Son, made of a woman, made under the law, 5 To redeem them that were under the law, that we might receive the adoption of sons. GEN 3:15 And I will put enmity between thee and the woman, and between thy seed and her seed; it shall bruise thy head, and thou shalt bruise his heel. REV 13:8 And all that dwell upon the earth shall worship him, whose names are not written in the book of life of the Lamb slain from the foundation of the world. HEB 13:8 Jesus Christ the same yesterday, and to day, and for ever.

[37] HEB 9:14 How much more shall the blood of Christ, who through the eternal Spirit offered himself without spot to God, purge your conscience from dead works to serve the living God? 1PE 3:18 For Christ also hath once suffered for sins, the just for the unjust, that he might bring us to God, being put to death in the flesh, but quickened by the Spirit.

[38] ACT 20:28 Take heed therefore unto yourselves, and to all the flock, over the which the Holy Ghost hath made you overseers, to feed the church of God, which he hath purchased with his own blood. JOH 3:13 And no man hath ascended up to heaven, but he that came down from heaven, even the Son of man which is in heaven. 1JO 3:16 Hereby perceive we the love of God, because he laid down his life for us: and we ought to lay down our lives for the brethren.

[39] JOH 6:37 All that the Father giveth me shall come to me; and him that

making intercession for them,[40] and revealing unto them, in and by the Word, the mysteries of salvation;[41] effectually persuading them by His Spirit to believe and obey, and governing their hearts by His Word and Spirit;[42] overcoming all their enemies by His almighty power and wisdom, in such manner, and ways, as are most consonant to His wonderful and unsearchable dispensation.[43]

cometh to me I will in no wise cast out. 39 And this is the Father's will which hath sent me, that of all which he hath given me I should lose nothing, but should raise it up again at the last day. 10:15 As the Father knoweth me, even so know I the Father: and I lay down my life for the sheep. 16 And other sheep I have, which are not of this fold: them also I must bring, and they shall hear my voice; and there shall be one fold, and one shepherd.

[40] 1JO 2:1 My little children, these things write I unto you, that ye sin not. And if any man sin, we have an advocate with the Father, Jesus Christ the righteous: 2 And he is the propitiation for our sins: and not for ours only, but also for the sins of the whole world. ROM 8:34 Who is he that condemneth? It is Christ that died, yea rather, that is risen again, who is even at the right hand of God, who also maketh intercession for us.

[41] JOH 15:13 Greater love hath no man than this, that a man lay down his life for his friends. 15 Henceforth I call you not servants; for the servant knoweth not what his lord doeth: but I have called you friends; for all things that I have heard of my Father I have made known unto you. EPH 1:7 In whom we have redemption through his blood, the forgiveness of sins, according to the riches of his grace; 8 Wherein he hath abounded toward us in all wisdom and prudence; 9 Having made known unto us the mystery of his will, according to his good pleasure which he hath purposed in himself. JOH 17:6 I have manifested thy name unto the men which thou gavest me out of the world: thine they were, and thou gavest them me; and they have kept thy word.

[42] JOH 14:16 And I will pray the Father, and he shall give you another Comforter, that he may abide with you for ever. HEB 12:2 Looking unto Jesus the author and finisher of our faith; who for the joy that was set before him endured the cross, despising the shame, and is set down at the right hand of the throne of God. 2CO 4:13 We having the same spirit of faith, according as it is written, I believed, and therefore have I spoken; we also believe, and therefore speak. ROM 8:9 But ye are not in the flesh, but in the Spirit, if so be that the Spirit of God dwell in you. Now if any man have not the Spirit of Christ, he is none of his. 14 For as many as are led by the Spirit of God, they are the sons of God. 15:18 For I will

not dare to speak of any of those things which Christ hath not wrought by me, to make the Gentiles obedient, by word and deed, 19 Through mighty signs and wonders, by the power of the Spirit of God; so that from Jerusalem, and round about unto Illyricum, I have fully preached the gospel of Christ. JOH 17:17 Sanctify them through thy truth: thy word is truth.

[43] PSA 110:1 The Lord said unto my Lord, Sit thou at my right hand, until I make thine enemies thy footstool. 1CO 15:25 For he must reign, till he hath put all enemies under his feet. 26 The last enemy that shall be destroyed is death. MAL 4:2 But unto you that fear my name shall the Sun of righteousness arise with healing in his wings; and ye shall go forth, and grow up as calves of the stall. 3 And ye shall tread down the wicked; for they shall be ashes under the soles of your feet in the day that I shall do this, saith the Lord of hosts. COL 2:15 And having spoiled principalities and powers, he made a shew of them openly, triumphing over them in it.

Chapter IX
Of Free Will

I. God has endued the will of man with that natural liberty, that is neither forced, nor, by any absolute necessity of nature, determined, to good or evil.[1]

II. Man, in his state of innocency, had freedom, and power to will and to do that which was good and well pleasing to God;[2] but yet, mutably, so that he might fall from it.[3]

III. Man, by his fall into a state of sin, has wholly lost all ability of will

---

[1] MAT 17:12 But I say unto you, That Elias is come already, and they knew him not, but have done unto him whatsoever they listed. Likewise shall also the Son of man suffer of them. JAM 1:14 But every man is tempted, when he is drawn away of his own lust, and enticed. DEU 30:19 But your wives, and your little ones, and your cattle, (for I know that ye have much cattle,) shall abide in your cities which I have given you.

[2] ECC 7:29 Lo, this only have I found, that God hath made man upright; but they have sought out many inventions. GEN 1:26 And God said, Let us make man in our image, after our likeness: and let them have dominion over the fish of the sea, and over the fowl of the air, and over the cattle, and over all the earth, and over every creeping thing that creepeth upon the earth.

[3] GEN 2:16 And the Lord God commanded the man, saying, Of every tree of the garden thou mayest freely eat: 17 But of the tree of the knowledge of good and evil, thou shalt not eat of it: for in the day that thou eatest thereof thou shalt surely die. 3:6 And when the woman saw that the tree was good for food, and that it was pleasant to the eyes, and a tree to be desired to make one wise, she took of the fruit thereof, and did eat, and gave also unto her husband with her; and he did eat.

to any spiritual good accompanying salvation:[4] so as, a natural man, being altogether averse from that good,[5] and dead in sin,[6] is not able, by his own strength, to convert himself, or to prepare himself thereunto.[7]

IV. When God converts a sinner, and translates him into the state of grace, He frees him from his natural bondage under sin;[8] and, by His

---

[4] ROM 5:6 For when we were yet without strength, in due time Christ died for the ungodly. 8:7 Because the carnal mind is enmity against God: for it is not subject to the law of God, neither indeed can be. JOH 15:5 I am the vine, ye are the branches: He that abideth in me, and I in him, the same bringeth forth much fruit: for without me ye can do nothing.

[5] ROM 3:10 As it is written, There is none righteous, no, not one. 12 They are all gone out of the way, they are together become unprofitable; there is none that doeth good, no, not one.

[6] EPH 2:1 And you hath he quickened, who were dead in trespasses and sins. 5 Even when we were dead in sins, hath quickened us together with Christ, (by grace ye are saved). COL 2:13 And you, being dead in your sins and the uncircumcision of your flesh, hath he quickened together with him, having forgiven you all trespasses.

[7] JOH 6:44 No man can come to me, except the Father which hath sent me draw him: and I will raise him up at the last day. 65 And he said, Therefore said I unto you, that no man can come unto me, except it were given unto him of my Father. EPH 2:2 Wherein in time past ye walked according to the course of this world, according to the prince of the power of the air, the spirit that now worketh in the children of disobedience: 3 Among whom also we all had our conversation in times past in the lusts of our flesh, fulfilling the desires of the flesh and of the mind; and were by nature the children of wrath, even as others. 4 But God, who is rich in mercy, for his great love wherewith he loved us, 5 Even when we were dead in sins, hath quickened us together with Christ, (by grace ye are saved;). 1CO 2:14 But the natural man receiveth not the things of the Spirit of God: for they are foolishness unto him: neither can he know them, because they are spiritually discerned. TIT 3:3 For we ourselves also were sometimes foolish, disobedient, deceived, serving divers lusts and pleasures, living in malice and envy, hateful, and hating one another. 4 But after that the kindness and love of God our Saviour toward man appeared, 5 Not by works of righteousness which we have done, but according to his mercy he saved us, by the washing of regeneration, and renewing of the Holy Ghost.

[8] COL 1:13 Who hath delivered us from the power of darkness, and hath

grace alone, enables him freely to will and to do that which is spiritually good;[9] yet so, as that by reason of his remaining corruption, he does not perfectly, or only, will that which is good, but does also will that which is evil.[10]

V. The will of man is made perfectly and immutably free to do good alone in the state of glory only.[11]

translated us into the kingdom of his dear Son. JOH 8:34 Jesus answered them, Verily, verily, I say unto you, Whosoever committeth sin is the servant of sin. 36 If the Son therefore shall make you free, ye shall be free indeed.

[9] PHI 2:13 For it is God which worketh in you both to will and to do of his good pleasure. ROM 6:18 Being then made free from sin, ye became the servants of righteousness. 22 But now being made free from sin, and become servants to God, ye have your fruit unto holiness, and the end everlasting life.

[10] GAL 5:17 For the flesh lusteth against the Spirit, and the Spirit against the flesh: and these are contrary the one to the other: so that ye cannot do the things that ye would. ROM 7:15 For that which I do I allow not: for what I would, that do I not; but what I hate, that do I. 18 For I know that in me (that is, in my flesh,) dwelleth no good thing: for to will is present with me; but how to perform that which is good I find not. 19 For the good that I would I do not: but the evil which I would not, that I do. 21 I find then a law, that, when I would do good, evil is present with me. 23 But I see another law in my members, warring against the law of my mind, and bringing me into captivity to the law of sin which is in my members.

[11] EPH 4:13 Till we all come in the unity of the faith, and of the knowledge of the Son of God, unto a perfect man, unto the measure of the stature of the fulness of Christ. HEB 12:23 To the general assembly and church of the firstborn, which are written in heaven, and to God the Judge of all, and to the spirits of just men made perfect. 1JO 3:2 Beloved, now are we the sons of God, and it doth not yet appear what we shall be: but we know that, when he shall appear, we shall be like him; for we shall see him as he is. JUD 24 Now unto him that is able to keep you from falling, and to present you faultless before the presence of his glory with exceeding joy.

Chapter X
Of Effectual Calling

I. All those whom God hath predestinated unto life, and those only, He is pleased, in His appointed time, effectually to call,[1] by His Word and Spirit,[2] out of that state of sin and death, in which they are by nature to grace and salvation, by Jesus Christ;[3] enlightening their minds spiritually

---

[1] ROM 8:30 Moreover whom he did predestinate, them he also called: and whom he called, them he also justified: and whom he justified, them he also glorified. 11:7 What then? Israel hath not obtained that which he seeketh for; but the election hath obtained it, and the rest were blinded. EPH 1:10 That in the dispensation of the fulness of times he might gather together in one all things in Christ, both which are in heaven, and which are on earth; even in him: 11 In whom also we have obtained an inheritance, being predestinated according to the purpose of him who worketh all things after the counsel of his own will.

[2] 2TH 2:13 But we are bound to give thanks alway to God for you, brethren beloved of the Lord, because God hath from the beginning chosen you to salvation through sanctification of the Spirit and belief of the truth: 14 Whereunto he called you by our gospel, to the obtaining of the glory of our Lord Jesus Christ. 2CO 3:3 Forasmuch as ye are manifestly declared to be the epistle of Christ ministered by us, written not with ink, but with the Spirit of the living God; not in tables of stone, but in fleshy tables of the heart. 6 Who also hath made us able ministers of the new testament; not of the letter, but of the spirit: for the letter killeth, but the spirit giveth life.

[3] ROM 8:2 For the law of the Spirit of life in Christ Jesus hath made me free from the law of sin and death. EPH 2:1 And you hath he quickened, who were dead in trespasses and sins; 2 Wherein in time past ye walked according to the course of this world, according to the prince of the power of the air, the spirit that now worketh in the children of disobedience: 3 Among whom also we all had our

and savingly to understand the things of God,⁴ taking away their heart of stone, and giving unto them an heart of flesh;⁵ renewing their wills, and, by His almighty power, determining them to that which is good,⁶ and effectually drawing them to Jesus Christ:⁷ yet so, as they come most

conversation in times past in the lusts of our flesh, fulfilling the desires of the flesh and of the mind; and were by nature the children of wrath, even as others. 4 But God, who is rich in mercy, for his great love wherewith he loved us, 5 Even when we were dead in sins, hath quickened us together with Christ, (by grace ye are saved). 2TI 1:9 Who hath saved us, and called us with an holy calling, not according to our works, but according to his own purpose and grace, which was given us in Christ Jesus before the world began, 10 But is now made manifest by the appearing of our Saviour Jesus Christ, who hath abolished death, and hath brought life and immortality to light through the gospel.

⁴ ACT 26:18 To open their eyes, and to turn them from darkness to light, and from the power of Satan unto God, that they may receive forgiveness of sins, and inheritance among them which are sanctified by faith that is in me. 1CO 2:10 But God hath revealed them unto us by his Spirit: for the Spirit searcheth all things, yea, the deep things of God. 12 Now we have received, not the spirit of the world, but the spirit which is of God; that we might know the things that are freely given to us of God. EPH 1:17 That the God of our Lord Jesus Christ, the Father of glory, may give unto you the spirit of wisdom and revelation in the knowledge of him: 18 The eyes of your understanding being enlightened; that ye may know what is the hope of his calling, and what the riches of the glory of his inheritance in the saints.

⁵ EZE 36:26 A new heart also will I give you, and a new spirit will I put within you: and I will take away the stony heart out of your flesh, and I will give you an heart of flesh.

⁶ EZE 11:19 And I will give them one heart, and I will put a new spirit within you; and I will take the stony heart out of their flesh, and will give them an heart of flesh. PHI 2:13 For it is God which worketh in you both to will and to do of his good pleasure. DEU 30:6 And the Lord thy God will circumcise thine heart, and the heart of thy seed, to love the Lord thy God with all thine heart, and with all thy soul, that thou mayest live. EZE 36:27 And I will put my spirit within you, and cause you to walk in my statutes, and ye shall keep my judgments, and do them.

⁷ EPH 1:19 And what is the exceeding greatness of his power to usward who believe, according to the working of his mighty power. JOH 6:44 No man can come to me, except the Father which hath sent me draw him: and I will raise him

freely, being made willing by His grace.⁸

II. This effectual call is of God's free and special grace alone, not from anything at all foreseen in man,⁹ who is altogether passive therein, until, being quickened and renewed by the Holy Spirit,¹⁰ he is thereby enabled to answer this call, and to embrace the grace offered and conveyed in it.¹¹

---

up at the last day. 45 It is written in the prophets, And they shall be all taught of God. Every man therefore that hath heard, and hath learned of the Father, cometh unto me.

⁸ SON 1:4 Draw me, we will run after thee. PSA 110:3 Thy people shall be willing in the day of thy power, in the beauties of holiness from the womb of the morning: thou hast the dew of thy youth. JOH 6:37 All that the Father giveth me shall come to me; and him that cometh to me I will in no wise cast out. ROM 6:16 Know ye not, that to whom ye yield yourselves servants to obey, his servants ye are to whom ye obey; whether of sin unto death, or of obedience unto righteousness? 17 But God be thanked, that ye were the servants of sin, but ye have obeyed from the heart that form of doctrine which was delivered you. 18 Being then made free from sin, ye became the servants of righteousness.

⁹ 2TI 1:9 Who hath saved us, and called us with an holy calling, not according to our works, but according to his own purpose and grace, which was given us in Christ Jesus before the world began. TIT 3:4 But after that the kindness and love of God our Saviour toward man appeared, 5 Not by works of righteousness which we have done, but according to his mercy he saved us, by the washing of regeneration, and renewing of the Holy Ghost. EPH 2:4 But God, who is rich in mercy, for his great love wherewith he loved us, 5 Even when we were dead in sins, hath quickened us together with Christ, (by grace ye are saved). 8 For by grace are ye saved through faith; and that not of yourselves: it is the gift of God: 9 Not of works, lest any man should boast. ROM 9:11 For the children being not yet born, neither having done any good or evil, that the purpose of God according to election might stand, not of works, but of him that calleth.

¹⁰ 1CO 2:14 But the natural man receiveth not the things of the Spirit of God: for they are foolishness unto him: neither can he know them, because they are spiritually discerned. ROM 8:7 Because the carnal mind is enmity against God: for it is not subject to the law of God, neither indeed can be. EPH 2:5 Even when we were dead in sins, hath quickened us together with Christ, (by grace ye are saved).

¹¹ JOH 6:37 All that the Father giveth me shall come to me; and him that

III. Elect infants, dying in infancy, are regenerated, and saved by Christ, through the Spirit,[12] who works when, and where, and how He pleases:[13] so also are all other elect persons who are incapable of being outwardly called by the ministry of the Word.[14]

IV. Others, not elected, although they may be called by the ministry of the Word,[15] and may have some common operations of the Spirit,[16] yet

cometh to me I will in no wise cast out. EZE 36:37 Thus saith the Lord God; I will yet for this be inquired of by the house of Israel, to do it for them; I will increase them with men like a flock. JOH 5:25 Verily, verily, I say unto you, The hour is coming, and now is, when the dead shall hear the voice of the Son of God: and they that hear shall live.

[12] LUK 18:15 And they brought unto him also infants, that he would touch them: but when his disciples saw it, they rebuked them. 16 But Jesus called them unto him, and said, Suffer little children to come unto me, and forbid them not: for of such is the kingdom of God. ACT 2:38 Then Peter said unto them, Repent, and be baptized every one of you in the name of Jesus Christ for the remission of sins, and ye shall receive the gift of the Holy Ghost. 39 For the promise is unto you, and to your children, and to all that are afar off, even as many as the Lord our God shall call. JOH 3:3 Jesus answered and said unto him, Verily, verily, I say unto thee, Except a man be born again, he cannot see the kingdom of God. 5 Jesus answered, Verily, verily, I say unto thee, Except a man be born of water and of the Spirit, he cannot enter into the kingdom of God. 1JO 5:12 He that hath the Son hath life; and he that hath not the Son of God hath not life. ROM 8:9 But ye are not in the flesh, but in the Spirit, if so be that the Spirit of God dwell in you. Now if any man have not the Spirit of Christ, he is none of his.

[13] JOH 3:8 The wind bloweth where it listeth, and thou hearest the sound thereof, but canst not tell whence it cometh, and whither it goeth: so is every one that is born of the Spirit.

[14] 1JO 5:12 He that hath the Son hath life; and he that hath not the Son of God hath not life. ACT 4:12 Neither is there salvation in any other: for there is none other name under heaven given among men, whereby we must be saved.

[15] MAT 22:14 For many are called, but few are chosen.

[16] MAT 7:22 Many will say to me in that day, Lord, Lord, have we not prophesied in thy name? and in thy name have cast out devils? and in thy name done many wonderful works? 13:20 But he that received the seed into stony places, the same is he that heareth the word, and anon with joy receiveth it; 21 Yet hath he not root in himself, but dureth for a while: for when tribulation or

they never truly come unto Christ, and therefore cannot be saved:[17] much less can men, not professing the Christian religion, be saved in any other way whatsoever, be they never so diligent to frame their lives according to the light of nature, and the laws of that religion they do profess.[18] And to assert and maintain that they may, is very pernicious, and to be detested.[19]

persecution ariseth because of the word, by and by he is offended. HEB 6:4 For it is impossible for those who were once enlightened, and have tasted of the heavenly gift, and were made partakers of the Holy Ghost, 5 And have tasted the good word of God, and the powers of the world to come.

[17] JOH 6:64 But there are some of you that believe not. For Jesus knew from the beginning who they were that believed not, and who should betray him. 65 And he said, Therefore said I unto you, that no man can come unto me, except it were given unto him of my Father. 66 From that time many of his disciples went back, and walked no more with him. 8:24 I said therefore unto you, that ye shall die in your sins: for if ye believe not that I am he, ye shall die in your sins.

[18] ACT 4:12 Neither is there salvation in any other: for there is none other name under heaven given among men, whereby we must be saved. JOH 14:6 Jesus saith unto him, I am the way, the truth, and the life: no man cometh unto the Father, but by me. EPH 2:12 That at that time ye were without Christ, being aliens from the commonwealth of Israel, and strangers from the covenants of promise, having no hope, and without God in the world. JOH 4:22 Ye worship ye know not what: we know what we worship: for salvation is of the Jews. 17:3 And this is life eternal, that they might know thee the only true God, and Jesus Christ, whom thou hast sent.

[19] 2JO 1:9 Whosoever transgresseth, and abideth not in the doctrine of Christ, hath not God. He that abideth in the doctrine of Christ, he hath both the Father and the Son. 10 If there come any unto you, and bring not this doctrine, receive him not into your house, neither bid him God speed: 11 For he that biddeth him God speed is partaker of his evil deeds. 1CO 16:22 If any man love not the Lord Jesus Christ, let him be Anathema Maranatha. GAL 1:6 I marvel that ye are so soon removed from him that called you into the grace of Christ unto another gospel: 7 Which is not another; but there be some that trouble you, and would pervert the gospel of Christ. 8 But though we, or an angel from heaven, preach any other gospel unto you than that which we have preached unto you, let him be accursed.

Chapter XI
Of Justification

I. Those whom God effectually calls, He also freely justifies;[1] not by infusing righteousness into them, but by pardoning their sins, and by accounting and accepting their persons as righteous; not for any thing wrought in them, or done by them, but for Christ's sake alone; nor by imputing faith itself, the act of believing, or any other evangelical obedience to them, as their righteousness; but by imputing the obedience and satisfaction of Christ unto them,[2] they receiving and resting on Him

---

[1] ROM 8:30 Moreover whom he did predestinate, them he also called: and whom he called, them he also justified: and whom he justified, them he also glorified. ROM 3:24 Being justified freely by his grace through the redemption that is in Christ Jesus.

[2] ROM 4:5 But to him that worketh not, but believeth on him that justifieth the ungodly, his faith is counted for righteousness. 6 Even as David also describeth the blessedness of the man, unto whom God imputeth righteousness without works, 7 Saying, Blessed are they whose iniquities are forgiven, and whose sins are covered. 8 Blessed is the man to whom the Lord will not impute sin. 2CO 5:19 To wit, that God was in Christ, reconciling the world unto himself, not imputing their trespasses unto them; and hath committed unto us the word of reconciliation. 21 For he hath made him to be sin for us, who knew no sin; that we might be made the righteousness of God in him. ROM 3:22 Even the righteousness of God which is by faith of Jesus Christ unto all and upon all them that believe: for there is no difference. 24 Being justified freely by his grace through the redemption that is in Christ Jesus. 25 Whom God hath set forth to be a propitiation through faith in his blood, to declare his righteousness for the remission of sins that are past, through the forbearance of God. 27 Where is

and His righteousness by faith; which faith they have not of themselves, it is the gift of God.³

II. Faith, thus receiving and resting on Christ and His righteousness, is the alone instrument of justification:⁴ yet is it not alone in the person

---

boasting then? It is excluded. By what law? of works? Nay: but by the law of faith. 28 Therefore we conclude that a man is justified by faith without the deeds of the law. TIT 3:5 Not by works of righteousness which we have done, but according to his mercy he saved us, by the washing of regeneration, and renewing of the Holy Ghost. 7 That being justified by his grace, we should be made heirs according to the hope of eternal life. EPH 1:7 In whom we have redemption through his blood, the forgiveness of sins, according to the riches of his grace. JER 23:6 In his days Judah shall be saved, and Israel shall dwell safely: and this is his name whereby he shall be called, The Lord Our Righteousness. 1CO 1:30 But of him are ye in Christ Jesus, who of God is made unto us wisdom, and righteousness, and sanctification, and redemption: 31 That, according as it is written, He that glorieth, let him glory in the Lord. ROM 5:17 For if by one man's offence death reigned by one; much more they which receive abundance of grace and of the gift of righteousness shall reign in life by one, Jesus Christ. 18 Therefore as by the offence of one judgment came upon all men to condemnation; even so by the righteousness of one the free gift came upon all men unto justification of life. 19 For as by one man's disobedience many were made sinners, so by the obedience of one shall many be made righteous.

³ ACT 10:44 While Peter yet spake these words, the Holy Ghost fell on all them which heard the word. GAL 2:16 Knowing that a man is not justified by the works of the law, but by the faith of Jesus Christ, even we have believed in Jesus Christ, that we might be justified by the faith of Christ, and not by the works of the law: for by the works of the law shall no flesh be justified. PHI 3:9 And be found in him, not having mine own righteousness, which is of the law, but that which is through the faith of Christ, the righteousness which is of God by faith: ACT 13:38 Be it known unto you therefore, men and brethren, that through this man is preached unto you the forgiveness of sins: 39 And by him all that believe are justified from all things, from which ye could not be justified by the law of Moses. EPH 2:7 That in the ages to come he might shew the exceeding riches of his grace in his kindness toward us through Christ Jesus. 8 For by grace are ye saved through faith; and that not of yourselves: it is the gift of God.

⁴ JOH 1:12 But as many as received him, to them gave he power to become the sons of God, even to them that believe on his name: ROM 3:28 Therefore we conclude that a man is justified by faith without the deeds of the law. 5:1 Therefore

justified, but is ever accompanied with all other saving graces, and is no dead faith, but works by love.[5]

III. Christ, by His obedience and death, did fully discharge the debt of all those that are thus justified, and did make a proper, real and full satisfaction to His Father's justice in their behalf.[6] Yet, in as much as He being justified by faith, we have peace with God through our Lord Jesus Christ.

[5] JAM 2:17 Even so faith, if it hath not works, is dead, being alone. 22 Seest thou how faith wrought with his works, and by works was faith made perfect? 26 For as the body without the spirit is dead, so faith without works is dead also. GAL 5:6 For in Jesus Christ neither circumcision availeth anything, nor uncircumcision; but faith which worketh by love.

[6] ROM 5:8 But God commendeth his love toward us, in that, while we were yet sinners, Christ died for us. 9 Much more then, being now justified by his blood, we shall be saved from wrath through him. 10 For if, when we were enemies, we were reconciled to God by the death of his Son, much more, being reconciled, we shall be saved by his life. 19 For as by one man's disobedience many were made sinners, so by the obedience of one shall many be made righteous. 1TI 2:5 For there is one God, and one mediator between God and men, the man Christ Jesus; 6 Who gave himself a ransom for all, to be testified in due time. HEB 10:10 By the which will we are sanctified through the offering of the body of Jesus Christ once for all. 14 For by one offering he hath perfected for ever them that are sanctified. DAN 9:24 Seventy weeks are determined upon thy people and upon thy holy city, to finish the transgression, and to make an end of sins, and to make reconciliation for iniquity, and to bring in everlasting righteousness, and to seal up the vision and prophecy, and to anoint the Most Holy. 26 And after threescore and two weeks shall Messiah be cut off, but not for himself: and the people of the prince that shall come shall destroy the city and the sanctuary; and the end thereof shall be with a flood, and unto the end of the war desolations are determined. ISA 53:4 Surely he hath borne our griefs, and carried our sorrows: yet we did esteem him stricken, smitten of God, and afflicted. 5 But he was wounded for our transgressions, he was bruised for our iniquities: the chastisement of our peace was upon him; and with his stripes we are healed. 6 All we like sheep have gone astray; we have turned every one to his own way; and the Lord hath laid on him the iniquity of us all. 10 Yet it pleased the Lord to bruise him; he hath put him to grief: when thou shalt make his soul an offering for sin, he shall see his seed, he shall prolong his days, and the pleasure of the Lord shall prosper in his hand. 11 He shall see of the travail of his soul, and shall be satisfied: by his knowledge shall my righteous

was given by the Father for them;[7] and His obedience and satisfaction accepted in their stead;[8] and both, freely, not for any thing in them; their justification is only of free grace;[9] that both the exact justice, and rich grace of God might be glorified in the justification of sinners.[10]

IV. God did, from all eternity, decree to justify all the elect,[11] and Christ did, in the fullness of time, die for their sins, and rise again for their justification:[12] nevertheless, they are not justified, until the Holy Spirit

servant justify many; for he shall bear their iniquities. 12 Therefore will I divide him a portion with the great, and he shall divide the spoil with the strong; because he hath poured out his soul unto death: and he was numbered with the transgressors; and he bare the sin of many, and made intercession for the transgressors.

[7] ROM 8:32 He that spared not his own Son, but delivered him up for us all, how shall he not with him also freely give us all things?

[8] 2CO 5:21 For he hath made him to be sin for us, who knew no sin; that we might be made the righteousness of God in him. MAT 3:17 And lo a voice from heaven, saying, This is my beloved Son, in whom I am well pleased. EPH 5:2 And walk in love, as Christ also hath loved us, and hath given himself for us an offering and a sacrifice to God for a sweetsmelling savour.

[9] ROM 3:24 Being justified freely by his grace through the redemption that is in Christ Jesus: EPH 1:7 In whom we have redemption through his blood, the forgiveness of sins, according to the riches of his grace.

[10] ROM 3:26 To declare, I say, at this time his righteousness: that he might be just, and the justifier of him which believeth in Jesus. EPH 2:7 That in the ages to come he might shew the exceeding riches of his grace in his kindness toward us through Christ Jesus.

[11] GAL 3:8 And the scripture, foreseeing that God would justify the heathen through faith, preached before the gospel unto Abraham, saying, In thee shall all nations be blessed. 1PE 1:2 Elect according to the foreknowledge of God the Father, through sanctification of the Spirit, unto obedience and sprinkling of the blood of Jesus Christ: Grace unto you, and peace, be multiplied. 19 But with the precious blood of Christ, as of a lamb without blemish and without spot: 20 Who verily was foreordained before the foundation of the world, but was manifest in these last times for you, ROM 8:30 Moreover whom he did predestinate, them he also called: and whom he called, them he also justified: and whom he justified, them he also glorified.

[12] GAL 4:4 But when the fulness of the time was come, God sent forth his

does, in due time, actually apply Christ unto them.[13]

V. God does continue to forgive the sins of those that are justified;[14] and although they can never fall from the state of justification,[15] yet they may, by their sins, fall under God's fatherly displeasure, and not have the light of His countenance restored unto them, until they humble themselves, confess their sins, beg pardon, and renew their faith and repentance.[16]

Son, made of a woman, made under the law. 1TI 2:6 Who gave himself a ransom for all, to be testified in due time. ROM 4:25 Who was delivered for our offences, and was raised again for our justification.

[13] COL 1:21 And you, that were sometime alienated and enemies in your mind by wicked works, yet now hath he reconciled 22 In the body of his flesh through death, to present you holy and unblameable and unreproveable in his sight. GAL 2:16 Knowing that a man is not justified by the works of the law, but by the faith of Jesus Christ, even we have believed in Jesus Christ, that we might be justified by the faith of Christ, and not by the works of the law: for by the works of the law shall no flesh be justified. TIT 3:4 But after that the kindness and love of God our Saviour toward man appeared, 5 Not by works of righteousness which we have done, but according to his mercy he saved us, by the washing of regeneration, and renewing of the Holy Ghost; 6 Which he shed on us abundantly through Jesus Christ our Saviour; 7 That being justified by his grace, we should be made heirs according to the hope of eternal life.

[14] MAT 6:12 And forgive us our debts, as we forgive our debtors. 1JO 1:7 But if we walk in the light, as he is in the light, we have fellowship one with another, and the blood of Jesus Christ his Son cleanseth us from all sin. 9 If we confess our sins, he is faithful and just to forgive us our sins, and to cleanse us from all unrighteousness. 1JO 2:1 My little children, these things write I unto you, that ye sin not. And if any man sin, we have an advocate with the Father, Jesus Christ the righteous: 2 And he is the propitiation for our sins: and not for ours only, but also for the sins of the whole world.

[15] LUK 22:32 But I have prayed for thee, that thy faith fail not: and when thou art converted, strengthen thy brethren. JOH 10:28 And I give unto them eternal life; and they shall never perish, neither shall any man pluck them out of my hand. HEB 10:14 For by one offering he hath perfected for ever them that are sanctified.

[16] PSA 89:31 If they break my statutes, and keep not my commandments; 32 Then will I visit their transgression with the rod, and their iniquity with stripes.

VI. The justification of believers under the old testament was, in all these respects, one and the same with the justification of believers under the New Testament.[17]

33 Nevertheless my lovingkindness will I not utterly take from him, nor suffer my faithfulness to fail. PSA 51:7 Purge me with hyssop, and I shall be clean: wash me, and I shall be whiter than snow. 8 Make me to hear joy and gladness; that the bones which thou hast broken may rejoice. 9 Hide thy face from my sins, and blot out all mine iniquities. 10 Create in me a clean heart, O God; and renew a right spirit within me. 11 Cast me not away from thy presence; and take not thy holy spirit from me. 12 Restore unto me the joy of thy salvation; and uphold me with thy free spirit. PSA 32:5 I acknowledged my sin unto thee, and mine iniquity have I not hid. I said, I will confess my transgressions unto the Lord; and thou forgavest the iniquity of my sin. MAT 26:75 And Peter remembered the word of Jesus, which said unto him, Before the cock crow, thou shalt deny me thrice. And he went out, and wept bitterly. 1CO 11:30 For this cause many are weak and sickly among you, and many sleep. 32 But when we are judged, we are chastened of the Lord, that we should not be condemned with the world. LUK 1:20 And, behold, thou shalt be dumb, and not able to speak, until the day that these things shall be performed, because thou believest not my words, which shall be fulfilled in their season.

[17] GAL 3:9 So then they which be of faith are blessed with faithful Abraham. 13 Christ hath redeemed us from the curse of the law, being made a curse for us: for it is written, Cursed is every one that hangeth on a tree: 14 That the blessing of Abraham might come on the Gentiles through Jesus Christ; that we might receive the promise of the Spirit through faith. ROM 4:22 And therefore it was imputed to him for righteousness. 23 Now it was not written for his sake alone, that it was imputed to him; 24 But for us also, to whom it shall be imputed, if we believe on him that raised up Jesus our Lord from the dead. HEB 13:8 Jesus Christ the same yesterday, and to day, and for ever.

Chapter XII
Of Adoption

All those that are justified, God vouchsafes, in and for His only Son Jesus Christ, to make partakers of the grace of adoption,¹ by which they are taken into the number, and enjoy the liberties and privileges of the children of God,² have His name put upon them,³ receive the spirit of adoption,⁴ have access to the throne of grace with boldness,⁵ are enabled

---

¹ EPH 1:5 Having predestinated us unto the adoption of children by Jesus Christ to himself, according to the good pleasure of his will. GAL 4:4 But when the fulness of the time was come, God sent forth his Son, made of a woman, made under the law, 5 To redeem them that were under the law, that we might receive the adoption of sons.
² ROM 8:17 And if children, then heirs; heirs of God, and joint-heirs with Christ; if so be that we suffer with him, that we may be also glorified together. JOH 1:12 But as many as received him, to them gave he power to become the sons of God, even to them that believe on his name.
³ JER 14:9 Why shouldest thou be as a man astonied, as a mighty man that cannot save? yet thou, O Lord, art in the midst of us, and we are called by thy name; leave us not. 2CO 6:18 And will be a Father unto you, and ye shall be my sons and daughters, saith the Lord Almighty. REV 3:12 Him that overcometh will I make a pillar in the temple of my God, and he shall go no more out: and I will write upon him the name of my God, and the name of the city of my God, which is new Jerusalem, which cometh down out of heaven from my God: and I will write upon him my new name.
⁴ ROM 8:15 For ye have not received the spirit of bondage again to fear; but ye have received the Spirit of adoption, whereby we cry, Abba, Father.
⁵ EPH 3:12 In whom we have boldness and access with confidence by the faith of him. ROM 5:2 By whom also we have access by faith into this grace

to cry, Abba, Father,[6] are pitied,[7] protected,[8] provided for,[9] and chastened by Him as by a Father:[10] yet never cast off,[11] but sealed to the day of redemption;[12] and inherit the promises,[13] as heirs of everlasting salvation.[14]

wherein we stand, and rejoice in hope of the glory of God.

[6] GAL 4:6 And because ye are sons, God hath sent forth the Spirit of his Son into your hearts, crying, Abba, Father.

[7] PSA 103:13 Like as a father pitieth his children, so the Lord pitieth them that fear him.

[8] PRO 14:26 In the fear of the Lord is strong confidence: and his children shall have a place of refuge.

[9] MAT 6:30 Wherefore, if God so clothe the grass of the field, which to-day is, and to-morrow is cast into the oven, shall he not much more clothe you, O ye of little faith? 32 For after all these things do the Gentiles seek: for your heavenly Father knoweth that ye have need of all these things. 1PE 5:7 Casting all your care upon him; for he careth for you.

[10] HEB 12:6 For whom the Lord loveth he chasteneth, and scourgeth every son whom he receiveth.

[11] LAM 3:31 For the Lord will not cast off for ever.

[12] EPH 4:30 And grieve not the holy Spirit of God, whereby ye are sealed unto the day of redemption.

[13] HEB 6:12 That ye be not slothful, but followers of them who through faith and patience inherit the promises.

[14] 1PE 1:3 Blessed be the God and Father of our Lord Jesus Christ, which according to his abundant mercy hath begotten us again unto a lively hope by the resurrection of Jesus Christ from the dead, 4 To an inheritance incorruptible, and undefiled, and that fadeth not away, reserved in heaven for you. HEB 1:14 Are they not all ministering spirits, sent forth to minister for them who shall be heirs of salvation?

Chapter XIII
Of Sanctification

I. They, who are once effectually called, and regenerated, having a new heart, and a new spirit created in them, are further sanctified, really and personally, through the virtue of Christ's death and resurrection,[1] by His Word and Spirit dwelling in them:[2] the dominion of the whole body of sin is destroyed,[3] and the several lusts thereof are more and more weakened and mortified;[4] and they more and more quickened and

---

[1] 1CO 6:11 And such were some of you: but ye are washed, but ye are sanctified, but ye are justified in the name of the Lord Jesus, and by the Spirit of our God. ACT 20:32 And now, brethren, I commend you to God, and to the word of his grace, which is able to build you up, and to give you an inheritance among all them which are sanctified. PHI 3:10 That I may know him, and the power of his resurrection, and the fellowship of his sufferings, being made conformable unto his death; ROM 6:5 For if we have been planted together in the likeness of his death, we shall be also in the likeness of his resurrection: 6 Knowing this, that our old man is crucified with him, that the body of sin might be destroyed, that henceforth we should not serve sin.

[2] JOH 17:17 Sanctify them through thy truth: thy word is truth. EPH 5:26 That he might sanctify and cleanse it with the washing of water by the word. 2TH 2:13 But we are bound to give thanks alway to God for you, brethren beloved of the Lord, because God hath from the beginning chosen you to salvation through sanctification of the Spirit and belief of the truth.

[3] ROM 6:6 Knowing this, that our old man is crucified with him, that the body of sin might be destroyed, that henceforth we should not serve sin. 14 For sin shall not have dominion over you: for ye are not under the law, but under grace.

[4] GAL 5:24 And they that are Christ's have crucified the flesh with the affections and lusts. ROM 8:13 For if ye live after the flesh, ye shall die: but if ye

strengthened in all saving graces,[5] to the practice of true holiness, without which no man shall see the Lord.[6]

II. This sanctification is throughout, in the whole man;[7] yet imperfect in this life, there abiding still some remnants of corruption in every part;[8] whence arises a continual and irreconcilable war, the flesh lusting against the Spirit, and the Spirit against the flesh.[9]

III. In which war, although the remaining corruption, for a time, may much prevail;[10] yet, through the continual supply of strength from the

---

through the Spirit do mortify the deeds of the body, ye shall live.

[5] COL 1:11 Strengthened with all might, according to his glorious power, unto all patience and longsuffering with joyfulness. EPH 3:16 That he would grant you, according to the riches of his glory, to be strengthened with might by his Spirit in the inner man; 17 That Christ may dwell in your hearts by faith; that ye, being rooted and grounded in love, 18 May be able to comprehend with all saints what is the breadth, and length, and depth, and height; 19 And to know the love of Christ, which passeth knowledge, that ye might be filled with all the fulness of God.

[6] 2CO 7:1 Having therefore these promises, dearly beloved, let us cleanse ourselves from all filthiness of the flesh and spirit, perfecting holiness in the fear of God. HEB 12:14 Follow peace with all men, and holiness, without which no man shall see the Lord.

[7] 1TH 5:23 And the very God of peace sanctify you wholly; and I pray God your whole spirit and soul and body be preserved blameless unto the coming of our Lord Jesus Christ.

[8] 1JO 1:10 If we say that we have not sinned, we make him a liar, and his word is not in us. ROM 7:18 For I know that in me (that is, in my flesh) dwelleth no good thing: for to will is present with me; but how to perform that which is good I find not. 23 But I see another law in my members, warring against the law of my mind, and bringing me into captivity to the law of sin which is in my members. PHI 3:12 Not as though I had already attained, either were already perfect: but I follow after, if that I may apprehend that for which also I am apprehended of Christ Jesus.

[9] GAL 5:17 For the flesh lusteth against the Spirit, and the Spirit against the flesh: and these are contrary the one to the other: so that ye cannot do the things that ye would. 1PE 2:11 Dearly beloved, I beseech you as strangers and pilgrims, abstain from fleshly lusts, which war against the soul.

[10] ROM 7:23 But I see another law in my members, warring against the law

sanctifying Spirit of Christ, the regenerate part does overcome;[11] and so, the saints grow in grace,[12] perfecting holiness in the fear of God.[13]

of my mind, and bringing me into captivity to the law of sin which is in my members.

[11] ROM 6:14 For sin shall not have dominion over you: for ye are not under the law, but under grace. 1JO 5:4 For whatsoever is born of God overcometh the world: and this is the victory that overcometh the world, even our faith. EPH 4:15 But speaking the truth in love, may grow up into him in all things, which is the head, even Christ: 16 From whom the whole body fitly joined together and compacted by that which every joint supplieth, according to the effectual working in the measure of every part, maketh increase of the body unto the edifying of itself in love.

[12] 2PE 3:18 But grow in grace, and in the knowledge of our Lord and Saviour Jesus Christ. To him be glory both now and for ever. Amen. 2CO 3:18 But we all, with open face beholding as in a glass the glory of the Lord, are changed into the same image from glory to glory, even as by the Spirit of the Lord.

[13] 2CO 7:1 Having therefore these promises, dearly beloved, let us cleanse ourselves from all filthiness of the flesh and spirit, perfecting holiness in the fear of God.

Chapter XIV
Of Saving Faith

I. The grace of faith, whereby the elect are enabled to believe to the saving of their souls,[1] is the work of the Spirit of Christ in their hearts,[2] and is ordinarily wrought by the ministry of the Word,[3] by which also, and by the administration of the sacraments, and prayer, it is increased and strengthened.[4]

[1] HEB 10:39 But we are not of them who draw back unto perdition; but of them that believe to the saving of the soul.

[2] 2CO 4:13 We having the same spirit of faith, according as it is written, I believed, and therefore have I spoken; we also believe, and therefore speak. EPH 1:17 That the God of our Lord Jesus Christ, the Father of glory, may give unto you the spirit of wisdom and revelation in the knowledge of him: 18 The eyes of your understanding being enlightened; that ye may know what is the hope of his calling, and what the riches of the glory of his inheritance in the saints, 19 And what is the exceeding greatness of his power to usward who believe, according to the working of his mighty power. 2:8 For by grace are ye saved through faith; and that not of yourselves: it is the gift of God.

[3] ROM 10:14 How then shall they call on him in whom they have not believed? and how shall they believe in him of whom they have not heard? and how shall they hear without a preacher? 17 So then faith cometh by hearing, and hearing by the word of God.

[4] 1PE 2:2 As newborn babes, desire the sincere milk of the word, that ye may grow thereby. ACT 20:32 And now, brethren, I commend you to God, and to the word of his grace, which is able to build you up, and to give you an inheritance among all them which are sanctified. ROM 4:11 And he received the sign of circumcision, a seal of the righteousness of the faith which he had yet being uncircumcised: that he might be the father of all them that believe, though they be

II. By this faith, a Christian believes to be true whatsoever is revealed in the Word, for the authority of God Himself speaking therein;[5] and acts differently upon that which each particular passage thereof contains; yielding obedience to the commands,[6] trembling at the threatenings,[7] and embracing the promises of God for this life, and that which is to come.[8] But the principal acts of saving faith are accepting, receiving, and resting upon Christ alone for justification, sanctification, and eternal life, by virtue of the covenant of grace.[9]

not circumcised; that righteousness might be imputed unto them also. LUK 17:5 And the apostles said unto the Lord, Increase our faith. ROM 1:16 For I am not ashamed of the gospel of Christ: for it is the power of God unto salvation to every one that believeth; to the Jew first, and also to the Greek. 17 For therein is the righteousness of God revealed from faith to faith: as it is written, The just shall live by faith.

[5] JOH 4:42 And said unto the woman, Now we believe, not because of thy saying: for we have heard him ourselves, and know that this is indeed the Christ, the Saviour of the world. 1TH 2:13 For this cause also thank we God without ceasing, because, when ye received the word of God which ye heard of us, ye received it not as the word of men, but as it is in truth, the word of God, which effectually worketh also in you that believe. 1JO 5:10 He that believeth on the Son of God hath the witness in himself: he that believeth not God hath made him a liar; because he believeth not the record that God gave of his Son. ACT 24:14 But this I confess unto thee, that after the way which they call heresy, so worship I the God of my fathers, believing all things which are written in the law and in the prophets.

[6] ROM 16:26 But now is made manifest, and by the scriptures of the prophets, according to the commandment of the everlasting God, made known to all nations for the obedience of faith.

[7] ISA 66:2 For all those things hath mine hand made, and those things have been, saith the Lord: but to this man will I look, even to him that is poor and of a contrite spirit, and trembleth at my word.

[8] HEB 11:13 These all died in faith, not having received the promises, but having seen them afar off, and were persuaded of them, and embraced them, and confessed that they were strangers and pilgrims on the earth. 1TI 4:8 For bodily exercise profiteth little: but godliness is profitable unto all things, having promise of the life that now is, and of that which is to come.

[9] JOH 1:12 But as many as received him, to them gave he power to become

III. This faith is different in degrees, weak or strong;[10] may be often and many ways assailed, and weakened, but gets the victory:[11] growing up in many to the attainment of a full assurance, through Christ,[12] who is both the author and finisher of our faith.[13]

the sons of God, even to them that believe on his name. ACT 16:31 And they said, Believe on the Lord Jesus Christ, and thou shalt be saved, and thy house. GAL 2:20 I am crucified with Christ: nevertheless I live; yet not I, but Christ liveth in me: and the life which I now live in the flesh I live by the faith of the Son of God, who loved me, and gave himself for me. ACT 15:11 But we believe that through the grace of the Lord Jesus Christ we shall be saved, even as they.

[10] HEB 5:13 For every one that useth milk is unskilful in the word of righteousness: for he is a babe. 14 But strong meat belongeth to them that are of full age, even those who by reason of use have their senses exercised to discern both good and evil. ROM 4:19 And being not weak in faith, he considered not his own body now dead, when he was about an hundred years old, neither yet the deadness of Sara's womb: 20 He staggered not at the promise of God through unbelief; but was strong in faith, giving glory to God. MAT 6:30 Wherefore, if God so clothe the grass of the field, which to-day is, and to-morrow is cast into the oven, shall he not much more clothe you, O ye of little faith? 8:10 When Jesus heard it, he marvelled, and said to them that followed, Verily I say unto you, I have not found so great faith, no, not in Israel.

[11] LUK 22:31 And the Lord said, Simon, Simon, behold, Satan hath desired to have you, that he may sift you as wheat: 32 But I have prayed for thee, that thy faith fail not: and when thou art converted, strengthen thy brethren. EPH 6:16 Above all, taking the shield of faith, wherewith ye shall be able to quench all the fiery darts of the wicked. 1JO 5:4 For whatsoever is born of God overcometh the world: and this is the victory that overcometh the world, even our faith. 5 Who is he that overcometh the world, but he that believeth that Jesus is the Son of God?

[12] HEB 6:11 And we desire that every one of you do shew the same diligence to the full assurance of hope unto the end: 12 That ye be not slothful, but followers of them who through faith and patience inherit the promises. HEB 10:22 Let us draw near with a true heart in full assurance of faith, having our hearts sprinkled from an evil conscience, and our bodies washed with pure water. COL 2:2 That their hearts might be comforted, being knit together in love, and unto all riches of the full assurance of understanding, to the acknowledgement of the mystery of God, and of the Father, and of Christ.

[13] HEB 12:2 Looking unto Jesus the author and finisher of our faith; who for the joy that was set before him endured the cross, despising the shame, and is set down at the right hand of the throne of God.

Chapter XV
Of Repentance unto Life

I. Repentance unto life is an evangelical grace,[1] the doctrine whereof is to be preached by every minister of the Gospel, as well as that of faith in Christ.[2]

II. By it, a sinner, out of the sight and sense not only of the danger, but also of the filthiness and odiousness of his sins, as contrary to the holy nature, and righteous law of God; and upon the apprehension of His mercy in Christ to such as are penitent, so grieves for, and hates his sins, as to turn from them all unto God,[3] purposing and endeavouring to walk

---

[1] ZEC 12:10 And I will pour upon the house of David, and upon the inhabitants of Jerusalem, the spirit of grace and of supplications: and they shall look upon me whom they have pierced, and they shall mourn for him, as one mourneth for his only son, and shall be in bitterness for him, as one that is in bitterness for his firstborn. ACT 11:18 When they heard these things, they held their peace, and glorified God, saying, Then hath God also to the Gentiles granted repentance unto life.

[2] LUK 24:47 And that repentance and remission of sins should be preached in his name among all nations, beginning at Jerusalem. MAR 1:15 And saying, The time is fulfilled, and the kingdom of God is at hand: repent ye, and believe the gospel. ACT 20:21 Testifying both to the Jews, and also to the Greeks, repentance toward God, and faith toward our Lord Jesus Christ.

[3] EZE 18:30 Therefore I will judge you, O house of Israel, every one according to his ways, saith the Lord God. Repent, and turn yourselves from all your transgressions; so iniquity shall not be your ruin. 31 Cast away from you all your transgressions, whereby ye have transgressed; and make you a new heart and a new spirit: for why will ye die, O house of Israel? 36:31 Then shall ye remember your own evil ways, and your doings that were not good, and shall

with Him in all the ways of His commandments.[4]

III. Although repentance is not to be rested in, as any satisfaction for sin, or any cause of the pardon thereof,[5] which is the act of God's free

---

loathe yourselves in your own sight for your iniquities and for your abominations. ISA 30:22 Ye shall defile also the covering of thy graven images of silver, and the ornament of thy molten images of gold: thou shalt cast them away as a menstruous cloth; thou shalt say unto it, Get thee hence. PSA 51:4 Against thee, thee only, have I sinned, and done this evil in thy sight: that thou mightest be justified when thou speakest, and be clear when thou judgest. JER 31:18 I have surely heard Ephraim bemoaning himself thus; Thou hast chastised me, and I was chastised, as a bullock unaccustomed to the yoke: turn thou me, and I shall be turned; for thou art the Lord my God. 19 Surely after that I was turned, I repented; and after that I was instructed, I smote upon my thigh: I was ashamed, yea, even confounded, because I did bear the reproach of my youth. JOE 2:12 Therefore also now, saith the Lord, turn ye even to me with all your heart, and with fasting, and with weeping, and with mourning: 13 And rend your heart, and not your garments, and turn unto the Lord your God: for he is gracious and merciful, slow to anger, and of great kindness, and repenteth him of the evil. AMO 5:15 Hate the evil, and love the good, and establish judgment in the gate: it may be that the Lord God of hosts will be gracious unto the remnant of Joseph. PSA 119:128 Therefore I esteem all thy precepts concerning all things to be right; and I hate every false way. 2CO 7:11 For behold this selfsame thing, that ye sorrowed after a godly sort, what carefulness it wrought in you, yea, what clearing of yourselves, yea, what indignation, yea, what fear, yea, what vehement desire, yea, what zeal, yea, what revenge! In all things ye have approved yourselves to be clear in this matter.

[4] PSA 119:6 Then shall I not be ashamed, when I have respect unto all thy commandments. 59 I thought on my ways, and turned my feet unto thy testimonies. 106 I have sworn, and I will perform it, that I will keep thy righteous judgments. LUK 1:6 And they were both righteous before God, walking in all the commandments and ordinances of the Lord blameless. 2KI 23:25 And like unto him was there no king before him, that turned to the Lord with all his heart, and with all his soul, and with all his might, according to all the law of Moses; neither after him arose there any like him.

[5] EZE 36:31 Then shall ye remember your own evil ways, and your doings that were not good, and shall loathe yourselves in your own sight for your iniquities and for your abominations. 32 Not for your sakes do I this, saith the Lord God, be it known unto you: be ashamed and confounded for your own ways, O house of Israel. EZE 16:61 Then thou shalt remember thy ways, and be

grace in Christ,[6] yet it is of such necessity to all sinners, that none may expect pardon without it.[7]

IV. As there is no sin so small, but it deserves damnation;[8] so there is no sin so great, that it can bring damnation upon those who truly repent.[9]

---

ashamed, when thou shalt receive thy sisters, thine elder and thy younger: and I will give them unto thee for daughters, but not by thy covenant. 62 And I will establish my covenant with thee; and thou shalt know that I am the Lord: 63 That thou mayest remember, and be confounded, and never open thy mouth any more because of thy shame, when I am pacified toward thee for all that thou hast done, saith the Lord God.

[6] HOS 14:2 Take with you words, and turn to the Lord: say unto him, Take away all iniquity, and receive us graciously: so will we render the calves of our lips. 4 I will heal their backsliding, I will love them freely: for mine anger is turned away from him. ROM 3:24 Being justified freely by his grace through the redemption that is in Christ Jesus. EPH 1:7 In whom we have redemption through his blood, the forgiveness of sins, according to the riches of his grace.

[7] LUK 13:3 I tell you, Nay: but, except ye repent, ye shall all likewise perish. ACT 17:30 And the times of this ignorance God winked at; but now commandeth all men every where to repent: 31 Because he hath appointed a day, in the which he will judge the world in righteousness by that man whom he hath ordained; whereof he hath given assurance unto all men, in that he hath raised him from the dead.

[8] ROM 6:23 For the wages of sin is death; but the gift of God is eternal life through Jesus Christ our Lord. ROM 5:12 Wherefore, as by one man sin entered into the world, and death by sin; and so death passed upon all men, for that all have sinned. MAT 12:36 But I say unto you, That every idle word that men shall speak, they shall give account thereof in the day of judgment.

[9] ISA 55:7 Let the wicked forsake his way, and the unrighteous man his thoughts: and let him return unto the Lord, and he will have mercy upon him; and to our God, for he will abundantly pardon. ROM 8:1 There is therefore now no condemnation to them which are in Christ Jesus, who walk not after the flesh, but after the Spirit. ISA 1:16 Wash you, make you clean; put away the evil of your doings from before mine eyes; cease to do evil. 18 Come now, and let us reason together, saith the Lord: though your sins be as scarlet, they shall be as white as snow; though they be red like crimson, they shall be as wool.

V. Man ought not to content themselves with a general repentance, but it is every man's duty to endeavour to repent of his particular sins, particularly.[10]

VI. As every man is bound to make private confession of his sins to God, praying for the pardon thereof;[11] upon which, and the forsaking of them, he shall find mercy;[12] so, he that scandalizes his brother, or the Church of Christ, ought to be willing, by a private or public confession, and sorrow for his sin, to declare his repentance to those that are offended,[13] who are thereupon to be reconciled to him, and in love to receive him.[14]

---

[10] PSA 19:13 Keep back thy servant also from presumptuous sins; let them not have dominion over me: then shall I be upright, and I shall be innocent from the great transgression. LUK 19:8 And Zacchaeus stood, and said unto the Lord; Behold, Lord, the half of my goods I give to the poor; and if I have taken any thing from any man by false accusation, I restore him fourfold. 1TI 1:13 Who was before a blasphemer, and a persecutor, and injurious: but I obtained mercy, because I did it ignorantly in unbelief. 15 This is a faithful saying, and worthy of all acceptation, that Christ Jesus came into the world to save sinners; of whom I am chief.

[11] PSA 51:4 Against thee, thee only, have I sinned, and done this evil in thy sight: that thou mightest be justified when thou speakest, and be clear when thou judgest. 5 Behold, I was shapen in iniquity; and in sin did my mother conceive me. 7 Purge me with hyssop, and I shall be clean: wash me, and I shall be whiter than snow. 9 Hide thy face from my sins, and blot out all mine iniquities. 14 Deliver me from bloodguiltiness, O God, thou God of my salvation: and my tongue shall sing aloud of thy righteousness. PSA 32:5 I acknowledged my sin unto thee, and mine iniquity have I not hid. I said, I will confess my transgressions unto the Lord; and thou forgavest the iniquity of my sin. 6 For this shall every one that is godly pray unto thee in a time when thou mayest be found: surely in the floods of great waters they shall not come nigh unto him.

[12] PRO 28:13 He that covereth his sins shall not prosper: but whoso confesseth and forsaketh them shall have mercy. 1JO 1:9 If we confess our sins, he is faithful and just to forgive us our sins, and to cleanse us from all unrighteousness.

[13] JAM 5:16 Confess your faults one to another, and pray one for another, that ye may be healed. The effectual fervent prayer of a righteous man availeth much. LUK 17:3 Take heed to yourselves: If thy brother trespass against thee,

rebuke him; and if he repent, forgive him. 4 And if he trespass against thee seven times in a day, and seven times in a day turn again to thee, saying, I repent; thou shalt forgive him. JOS 7:19 And Joshua said unto Achan, My son, give, I pray thee, glory to the Lord God of Israel, and make confession unto him; and tell me now what thou hast done; hide it not from me. (PSA 51 throughout)

[14] 2CO 2:8 Wherefore I beseech you that ye would confirm your love toward him.

Chapter XVI
Of Good Works

I. Good works are only such as God has commanded in His holy Word,[1] and not such as, without the warrant thereof, are devised by men, out of blind zeal, or upon any pretence of good intention.[2]

II. These good works, done in obedience to God's commandments,

---

[1] MIC 6:8 He hath shewed thee, O man, what is good; and what doth the Lord require of thee, but to do justly, and to love mercy, and to walk humbly with thy God? ROM 12:2 And be not conformed to this world: but be ye transformed by the renewing of your mind, that ye may prove what is that good, and acceptable, and perfect, will of God. HEB 13:21 Make you perfect in every good work to do his will, working in you that which is well-pleasing in his sight, through Jesus Christ; to whom be glory for ever and ever. Amen.

[2] MAT 15:9 But in vain they do worship me, teaching for doctrines the commandments of men. ISA 29:13 Wherefore the Lord said, Forasmuch as this people draw near me with their mouth, and with their lips do honour me, but have removed their heart far from me, and their fear toward me is taught by the precept of men. 1PE 1:18 Forasmuch as ye know that ye were not redeemed with corruptible things, as silver and gold, from your vain conversation received by tradition from your fathers. ROM 10:2 For I bear them record that they have a zeal of God, but not according to knowledge. JOH 16:2 They shall put you out of the synagogues: yea, the time cometh, that whosoever killeth you will think that he doeth God service. 1SA 15:21 But the people took of the spoil, sheep and oxen, the chief of the things which should have been utterly destroyed, to sacrifice unto the Lord thy God in Gilgal. 22 And Samuel said, Hath the Lord as great delight in burnt offerings and sacrifices, as in obeying the voice of the Lord? Behold, to obey is better than sacrifice, and to hearken than the fat of rams. 23 For rebellion is as the sin of witchcraft, and stubbornness is as iniquity and idolatry. Because thou hast rejected the word of the Lord, he hath also rejected thee from being king.

are the fruits and evidences of a true and lively faith:³ and by them believers manifest their thankfulness,⁴ strengthen their assurance,⁵ edify their brethren,⁶ adorn the profession of the Gospel,⁷ stop the mouths of the adversaries,⁸ and glorify God,⁹ whose workmanship they are, created in

    ³ JAM 2:18 Yea, a man may say, Thou hast faith, and I have works: shew me thy faith without thy works, and I will shew thee my faith by my works. 22 Seest thou how faith wrought with his works, and by works was faith made perfect?
    ⁴ PSA 116:12 What shall I render unto the Lord for all his benefits toward me? 13 I will take the cup of salvation, and call upon the name of the Lord. 1PE 2:9 But ye are a chosen generation, a royal priesthood, an holy nation, a peculiar people; that ye should shew forth the praises of him who hath called you out of darkness into his marvellous light.
    ⁵ 1JO 2:3 And hereby we do know that we know him, if we keep his commandments. 5 But whoso keepeth his word, in him verily is the love of God perfected: hereby know we that we are in him. 2PE 1:5 And beside this, giving all diligence, add to your faith virtue; and to virtue knowledge; 6 And to knowledge temperance; and to temperance patience; and to patience godliness; 7 And to godliness brotherly kindness; and to brotherly kindness charity. 8 For if these things be in you, and abound, they make you that ye shall neither be barren nor unfruitful in the knowledge of our Lord Jesus Christ. 9 But he that lacketh these things is blind, and cannot see afar off, and hath forgotten that he was purged from his old sins. 10 Wherefore the rather, brethren, give diligence to make your calling and election sure: for if ye do these things, ye shall never fall.
    ⁶ 2CO 9:2 For I know the forwardness of your mind, for which I boast of you to them of Macedonia, that Achaia was ready a year ago; and your zeal hath provoked very many. MAT 5:16 Let your light so shine before men, that they may see your good works, and glorify your Father which is in heaven.
    ⁷ TIT 2:5 To be discreet, chaste, keepers at home, good, obedient to their own husbands, that the word of God be not blasphemed. 9 Exhort servants to be obedient unto their own masters, and to please them well in all things; not answering again; 10 Not purloining, but shewing all good fidelity; that they may adorn the doctrine of God our Saviour in all things. 11 For the grace of God that bringeth salvation hath appeared to all men, 12 Teaching us that, denying ungodliness and worldly lusts, we should live soberly, righteously, and godly, in this present world. 1TI 6:1 Let as many servants as are under the yoke count their own masters worthy of all honour, that the name of God and his doctrine be not blasphemed.
    ⁸ 1PE 2:15 For so is the will of God, that with well doing ye may put to

Christ Jesus thereunto,[10] that, having their fruit unto holiness, they may have the end, eternal life.[11]

III. Their ability to do good works is not at all of themselves, but wholly from the Spirit of Christ.[12] And that they may be enabled thereunto, beside the graces they have already received, there is required an actual influence of the same Holy Spirit, to work in them to will, and to do, of His good pleasure:[13] yet are they not hereupon to grow negligent, as if they were not bound to perform any duty unless upon a special motion of the Spirit; but they ought to be diligent in stirring up the grace of God that is in them.[14]

silence the ignorance of foolish men.

[9] 1PE 2:12 Having your conversation honest among the Gentiles: that, whereas they speak against you as evildoers, they may by your good works, which they shall behold, glorify God in the day of visitation. PHI 1:11 Being filled with the fruits of righteousness, which are by Jesus Christ, unto the glory and praise of God. JOH 15:8 Herein is my Father glorified, that ye bear much fruit; so shall ye be my disciples.

[10] EPH 2:10 For we are his workmanship, created in Christ Jesus unto good works, which God hath before ordained that we should walk in them.

[11] ROM 6:22 But now being made free from sin, and become servants to God, ye have your fruit unto holiness, and the end everlasting life.

[12] JOH 15:4 Abide in me, and I in you. As the branch cannot bear fruit of itself, except it abide in the vine; no more can ye, except ye abide in me. 5 I am the vine, ye are the branches: He that abideth in me, and I in him, the same bringeth forth much fruit: for without me ye can do nothing. 6 If a man abide not in me, he is cast forth as a branch, and is withered; and men gather them, and cast them into the fire, and they are burned. EZE 36:26 A new heart also will I give you, and a new spirit will I put within you: and I will take away the stony heart out of your flesh, and I will give you an heart of flesh. 27 And I will put my spirit within you, and cause you to walk in my statutes, and ye shall keep my judgments, and do them.

[13] PHI 2:13 For it is God which worketh in you both to will and to do of his good pleasure. 4:13 I can do all things through Christ which strengtheneth me. 2CO 3:5 Not that we are sufficient of ourselves to think any thing as of ourselves; but our sufficiency is of God.

[14] PHI 2:12 Wherefore, my beloved, as ye have always obeyed, not as in my presence only, but now much more in my absence, work out your own salvation

IV. They who, in their obedience, attain to the greatest height which is possible in this life, are so far from being able to supererogate, and to do more than God requires, as that they fall short of much which in duty they are bound to do.[15]

V. We cannot by our best works merit pardon of sin, or eternal life at the hand of God, by reason of the great disproportion that is between them and the glory to come; and the infinite distance that is between us

with fear and trembling. HEB 6:11 And we desire that every one of you do shew the same diligence to the full assurance of hope unto the end: 12 That ye be not slothful, but followers of them who through faith and patience inherit the promises. 2PE 1:3 According as his divine power hath given unto us all things that pertain unto life and godliness, through the knowledge of him that hath called us to glory and virtue. 5 And beside this, giving all diligence, add to your faith virtue; and to virtue knowledge. 10 Wherefore the rather, brethren, give diligence to make your calling and election sure: for if ye do these things, ye shall never fall: 11 For so an entrance shall be ministered unto you abundantly into the everlasting kingdom of our Lord and Saviour Jesus Christ. ISA 64:7 And there is none that calleth upon thy name, that stirreth up himself to take hold of thee: for thou hast hid thy face from us, and hast consumed us, because of our iniquities. 2TI 1:6 Wherefore I put thee in remembrance that thou stir up the gift of God, which is in thee by the putting on of my hands. ACT 26:6 And now I stand and am judged for the hope of the promise made of God unto our fathers: 7 Unto which promise our twelve tribes, instantly serving God day and night, hope to come. For which hope's sake, king Agrippa, I am accused of the Jews. JUD 20 But ye, beloved, building up yourselves on your most holy faith, praying in the Holy Ghost, 21 Keep yourselves in the love of God, looking for the mercy of our Lord Jesus Christ unto eternal life.

[15] LUK 17:10 So likewise ye, when ye shall have done all those things which are commanded you, say, We are unprofitable servants: we have done that which was our duty to do. NEH 13:22 And I commanded the Levites that they should cleanse themselves, and that they should come and keep the gates, to sanctify the sabbath day. Remember me, O my God, concerning this also, and spare me according to the greatness of thy mercy. JOB 9:2 I know it is so of a truth: but how should man be just with God? 3 If he will contend with him, he cannot answer him one of a thousand. GAL 5:17 For the flesh lusteth against the Spirit, and the Spirit against the flesh: and these are contrary the one to the other: so that ye cannot do the things that ye would.

and God, whom, by them, we can neither profit, nor satisfy for the debt of our former sins,[16] but when we have done all we can, we have done but our duty, and are unprofitable servants:[17] and because, as they are good, they proceed from His Spirit,[18] and as they are wrought by us, they are defiled, and mixed with so much weakness and imperfection, that they cannot endure the severity of God's judgment.[19]

[16] ROM 3:20 Therefore by the deeds of the law there shall no flesh be justified in his sight: for by the law is the knowledge of sin. 4:2 For if Abraham were justified by works, he hath whereof to glory; but not before God. 4 Now to him that worketh is the reward not reckoned of grace, but of debt. 6 Even as David also describeth the blessedness of the man, unto whom God imputeth righteousness without works. EPH 2:8 For by grace are ye saved through faith; and that not of yourselves: it is the gift of God: 9 Not of works, lest any man should boast. TIT 3:5 Not by works of righteousness which we have done, but according to his mercy he saved us, by the washing of regeneration, and renewing of the Holy Ghost; 6 Which he shed on us abundantly through Jesus Christ our Saviour; 7 That being justified by his grace, we should be made heirs according to the hope of eternal life. ROM 8:18 For I reckon that the sufferings of this present time are not worthy to be compared with the glory which shall be revealed in us. PSA 16:2 O my soul, thou hast said unto the Lord, Thou art my Lord: my goodness extendeth not to thee. JOB 22:2 Can a man be profitable unto God, as he that is wise may be profitable unto himself? 3 Is it any pleasure to the Almighty, that thou art righteous? or is it gain to him that thou makest thy ways perfect? 35:7 If thou be righteous, what givest thou him? or what receiveth he of thine hand? 8 Thy wickedness may hurt a man as thou art; and thy righteousness may profit the son of man.

[17] LUK 17:10 So likewise ye, when ye shall have done all those things which are commanded you, say, We are unprofitable servants: we have done that which was our duty to do.

[18] GAL 5:22 But the fruit of the Spirit is love, joy, peace, longsuffering, gentleness, goodness, faith, 23 meekness, temperance: against such there is no law.

[19] ISA 64:6 But we are all as an unclean thing, and all our righteousnesses are as filthy rags; and we all do fade as a leaf; and our iniquities, like the wind, have taken us away. GAL 5:17 For the flesh lusteth against the Spirit, and the Spirit against the flesh: and these are contrary the one to the other: so that ye cannot do the things that ye would. ROM 7:15 For that which I do I allow not: for what I

VI. Notwithstanding, the persons of believers being accepted through Christ, their good works also are accepted in Him;[20] not as though they were in this life wholly unblamable and unreproveable in God's sight;[21] but that He, looking upon them in His Son, is pleased to accept and reward that which is sincere, although accompanied with many weaknesses and imperfections.[22]

would, that do I not; but what I hate, that do I. 18 For I know that in me (that is, in my flesh,) dwelleth no good thing: for to will is present with me; but how to perform that which is good I find not. PSA 143:2 And enter not into judgment with thy servant: for in thy sight shall no man living be justified. PSA 130:3 If thou, Lord, shouldest mark iniquities, O Lord, who shall stand?

[20] EPH 1:6 To the praise of the glory of his grace, wherein he hath made us accepted in the beloved. 1PE 2:5 Ye also, as lively stones, are built up a spiritual house, an holy priesthood, to offer up spiritual sacrifices, acceptable to God by Jesus Christ. EXO 28:38 And it shall be upon Aaron's forehead, that Aaron may bear the iniquity of the holy things, which the children of Israel shall hallow in all their holy gifts; and it shall be always upon his forehead, that they may be accepted before the Lord. GEN 4:4 And Abel, he also brought of the firstlings of his flock and of the fat thereof. And the Lord had respect unto Abel and to his offering. HEB 11:4 By faith Abel offered unto God a more excellent sacrifice than Cain, by which he obtained witness that he was righteous, God testifying of his gifts: and by it he being dead yet speaketh.

[21] JOB 9:20 If I justify myself, mine own mouth shall condemn me: if I say, I am perfect, it shall also prove me perverse. PSA 143:2 And enter not into judgment with thy servant: for in thy sight shall no man living be justified.

[22] HEB 13:20 Now the God of peace, that brought again from the dead our Lord Jesus, that great shepherd of the sheep, through the blood of the everlasting covenant, 21 Make you perfect in every good work to do his will, working in you that which is well-pleasing in his sight, through Jesus Christ; to whom be glory for ever and ever. Amen. 2CO 8:12 For if there be first a willing mind, it is accepted according to that a man hath, and not according to that he hath not. HEB 6:10 For God is not unrighteous to forget your work and labour of love, which ye have shewed toward his name, in that ye have ministered to the saints, and do minister. MAT 25:21 His lord said unto him, Well done, thou good and faithful servant: thou hast been faithful over a few things, I will make thee ruler over many things: enter thou into the joy of thy lord. 23 His lord said unto him, Well done, good and

VII. Works done by unregenerate men, although for the matter of them they may be things which God commands; and of good use both to themselves and others:[23] yet, because they proceed not from an heart purified by faith;[24] nor are done in a right manner, according to the Word;[25] nor to a right end, the glory of God,[26] they are therefore sinful

faithful servant; thou hast been faithful over a few things, I will make thee ruler over many things: enter thou into the joy of thy lord.

[23] 2KI 10:30 And the Lord said unto Jehu, Because thou hast done well in executing that which is right in mine eyes, and hast done unto the house of Ahab according to all that was in mine heart, thy children of the fourth generation shall sit on the throne of Israel. 31 But Jehu took no heed to walk in the law of the Lord God of Israel with all his heart: for he departed not from the sins of Jeroboam, which made Israel to sin. 1KI 21:27 And it came to pass, when Ahab heard those words, that he rent his clothes, and put sackcloth upon his flesh, and fasted, and lay in sackcloth, and went softly. 29 Seest thou how Ahab humbleth himself before me? because he humbleth himself before me, I will not bring the evil in his days: but in his son's days will I bring the evil upon his house. PHI 1:15 Some indeed preach Christ even of envy and strife; and some also of good will: 16 The one preach Christ of contention, not sincerely, supposing to add affliction to my bonds. 18 What then? notwithstanding, every way, whether in pretence, or in truth, Christ is preached; and I therein do rejoice, yea, and will rejoice.

[24] GEN 4:5 But unto Cain and to his offering he had not respect. And Cain was very wroth, and his countenance fell. HEB 11:4 By faith Abel offered unto God a more excellent sacrifice than Cain, by which he obtained witness that he was righteous, God testifying of his gifts: and by it he being dead yet speaketh. 6 But without faith it is impossible to please him: for he that cometh to God must believe that he is, and that he is a rewarder of them that diligently seek him.

[25] 1CO 13:3 And though I bestow all my goods to feed the poor, and though I give my body to be burned, and have not charity, it profiteth me nothing. ISA 1:12 When ye come to appear before me, who hath required this at your hand, to tread my courts?

[26] MAT 6:2 Therefore when thou doest thine alms, do not sound a trumpet before thee, as the hypocrites do in the synagogues and in the streets, that they may have glory of men. Verily I say unto you, They have their reward. 5 And when thou prayest, thou shalt not be as the hypocrites are: for they love to pray standing in the synagogues and in the corners of the streets, that they may be seen of men. Verily I say unto you, They have their reward. 16 Moreover when ye fast,

and cannot please God, or make a man meet to receive grace from God:[27] and yet, their neglect of them is more sinful and displeasing unto God.[28]

be not, as the hypocrites, of a sad countenance: for they disfigure their faces, that they may appear unto men to fast. Verily I say unto you, They have their reward.

[27] HAG 2:14 Then answered Haggai, and said, So is this people, and so is this nation before me, saith the Lord; and so is every work of their hands; and that which they offer there is unclean. TIT 1:15 Unto the pure all things are pure: but unto them that are defiled and unbelieving is nothing pure; but even their mind and conscience is defiled. AMO 5:21 I hate, I despise your feast days, and I will not smell in your solemn assemblies. 22 Though ye offer me burnt offerings and your meat offerings, I will not accept them: neither will I regard the peace offerings of your fat beasts. HOS 1:4 And the Lord said unto him, Call his name Jezreel; for yet a little while, and I will avenge the blood of Jezreel upon the house of Jehu, and will cause to cease the kingdom of the house of Israel. ROM 9:16 So then it is not of him that willeth, nor of him that runneth, but of God that sheweth mercy. TIT 3:15 All that are with me salute thee. Greet them that love us in the faith. Grace be with you all. Amen.

[28] PSA 14:4 Have all the workers of iniquity no knowledge? who eat up my people as they eat bread, and call not upon the Lord. 36:3 The words of his mouth are iniquity and deceit: he hath left off to be wise, and to do good. JOB 21:14 Therefore they say unto God, Depart from us; for we desire not the knowledge of thy ways. 15 What is the Almighty, that we should serve him? and what profit should we have, if we pray unto him? MAT 25:41 Then shall he say also unto them on the left hand, Depart from me, ye cursed, into everlasting fire, prepared for the devil and his angels: 42 For I was an hungered, and ye gave me no meat: I was thirsty, and ye gave me no drink: 43 I was a stranger, and ye took me not in: naked, and ye clothed me not: sick, and in prison, and ye visited me not. 45 Then shall he answer them, saying, Verily I say unto you, Inasmuch as ye did it not to one of the least of these, ye did it not to me. MAT 23:23 Woe unto you, scribes and Pharisees, hypocrites! for ye pay tithe of mint and anise and cummin, and have omitted the weightier matters of the law, judgment, mercy, and faith: these ought ye to have done, and not to leave the other undone.

Chapter XVII
Of the Perseverance of the Saints

I. They, whom God has accepted in His Beloved, effectually called, and sanctified by His Spirit, can neither totally nor finally fall away from the state of grace, but shall certainly persevere therein to the end, and be eternally saved.[1]

II. This perseverance of the saints depends not upon their own free will, but upon the immutability of the decree of election, flowing from the free and unchangeable love of God the Father;[2] upon the efficacy of the merit and intercession of Jesus Christ,[3] the abiding of the Spirit, and of

---

[1] PHI 1:6 Being confident of this very thing, that he which hath begun a good work in you will perform it until the day of Jesus Christ. 2PE 1:10 Wherefore the rather, brethren, give diligence to make your calling and election sure: for if ye do these things, ye shall never fall. JOH 10:28 And I give unto them eternal life; and they shall never perish, neither shall any man pluck them out of my hand. 29 My Father, which gave them me, is greater than all; and no man is able to pluck them out of my Father's hand. 1JO 3:9 Whosoever is born of God doth not commit sin; for his seed remaineth in him: and he cannot sin, because he is born of God. 1PE 1:5 Who are kept by the power of God through faith unto salvation ready to be revealed in the last time. 9 Receiving the end of your faith, even the salvation of your souls.

[2] 2TI 2:18 Who concerning the truth have erred, saying that the resurrection is past already; and overthrow the faith of some. 19 Nevertheless the foundation of God standeth sure, having this seal, The Lord knoweth them that are his. And, Let every one that nameth the name of Christ depart from iniquity. JER 31:3 The Lord hath appeared of old unto me, saying, Yea, I have loved thee with an everlasting love: therefore with lovingkindness have I drawn thee.

[3] HEB 10:10 By the which will we are sanctified through the offering of the

the seed of God within them,⁴ and the nature of the covenant of grace:⁵

---

body of Jesus Christ once for all. 14 For by one offering he hath perfected for ever them that are sanctified. HEB 13:20 Now the God of peace, that brought again from the dead our Lord Jesus, that great shepherd of the sheep, through the blood of the everlasting covenant, 21 Make you perfect in every good work to do his will, working in you that which is well-pleasing in his sight, through Jesus Christ; to whom be glory for ever and ever. Amen. HEB 9:12 Neither by the blood of goats and calves, but by his own blood he entered in once into the holy place, having obtained eternal redemption for us. 13 For if the blood of bulls and of goats, and the ashes of an heifer sprinkling the unclean, sanctifieth to the purifying of the flesh: 14 How much more shall the blood of Christ, who through the eternal Spirit offered himself without spot to God, purge your conscience from dead works to serve the living God? 15 And for this cause he is the mediator of the new testament, that by means of death, for the redemption of the transgressions that were under the first testament, they which are called might receive the promise of eternal inheritance. ROM 8:33 Who shall lay any thing to the charge of God's elect? It is God that justifieth. 34 Who is he that condemneth? It is Christ that died, yea rather, that is risen again, who is even at the right hand of God, who also maketh intercession for us. 35 Who shall separate us from the love of Christ? shall tribulation, or distress, or persecution, or famine, or nakedness, or peril, or sword? 36 As it is written, For thy sake we are killed all the day long; we are accounted as sheep for the slaughter. 37 Nay, in all these things we are more than conquerors through him that loved us. 38 For I am persuaded, that neither death, nor life, nor angels, nor principalities, nor powers, nor things present, nor things to come, 39 Nor height, nor depth, nor any other creature, shall be able to separate us from the love of God, which is in Christ Jesus our Lord. JOH 17:11 And now I am no more in the world, but these are in the world, and I come to thee. Holy Father, keep through thine own name those whom thou hast given me, that they may be one, as we are. 24 Father, I will that they also, whom thou hast given me, be with me where I am; that they may behold my glory, which thou hast given me: for thou lovedst me before the foundation of the world. LUK 22:32 But I have prayed for thee, that thy faith fail not: and when thou art converted, strengthen thy brethren. HEB 7:25 Wherefore he is able also to save them to the uttermost that come unto God by him, seeing he ever liveth to make intercession for them.

⁴ JOH 14:16 And I will pray the Father, and he shall give you another Comforter, that he may abide with you for ever; 17 Even the Spirit of truth; whom the world cannot receive, because it seeth him not, neither knoweth him: but ye

from all which arises also the certainty and infallibility thereof.⁶

III. Nevertheless, they may, through the temptations of Satan and of the world, the prevalency of corruption remaining in them, and the neglect of the means of their preservation, fall into grievous sins;⁷ and, for a time, continue therein:⁸ whereby they incur God's displeasure,⁹ and

know him; for he dwelleth with you, and shall be in you. 1JO 2:27 But the anointing which ye have received of him abideth in you, and ye need not that any man teach you: but as the same anointing teacheth you of all things, and is truth, and is no lie, and even as it hath taught you, ye shall abide in him. 3:9 Whosoever is born of God doth not commit sin; for his seed remaineth in him: and he cannot sin, because he is born of God.

⁵ JER 32:40 And I will make an everlasting covenant with them, that I will not turn away from them, to do them good; but I will put my fear in their hearts, that they shall not depart from me.

⁶ JOH 10:28 And I give unto them eternal life; and they shall never perish, neither shall any man pluck them out of my hand. 2TH 3:3 But the Lord is faithful, who shall stablish you, and keep you from evil. 1JO 2:19 They went out from us, but they were not of us; for if they had been of us, they would no doubt have continued with us: but they went out, that they might be made manifest that they were not all of us.

⁷ MAT 26:70 But he denied before them all, saying, I know not what thou sayest. 72 And again he denied with an oath, I do not know the man. 74 Then began he to curse and to swear, saying, I know not the man. And immediately the cock crew.

⁸ PSA 51 (the title) To the chief musician, A psalm of David, when Nathan the prophet came unto him, after he had gone in to Bathsheba. 51:14 Deliver me from bloodguiltiness, O God, thou God of my salvation: and my tongue shall sing aloud of thy righteousness.

⁹ ISA 64:5 Thou meetest him that rejoiceth and worketh righteousness, those that remember thee in thy ways: behold, thou art wroth; for we have sinned: in those is continuance, and we shall be saved. 7 And there is none that calleth upon thy name, that stirreth up himself to take hold of thee: for thou hast hid thy face from us, and hast consumed us, because of our iniquities. 9 Be not wroth very sore, O Lord, neither remember iniquity for ever: behold, see, we beseech thee, we are all thy people. 2SA 11:27 And when the mourning was past, David sent and fetched her to his house, and she became his wife, and bare him a son. But the thing that David had done displeased the Lord.

grieve His Holy Spirit,[10] come to be deprived of some measure of their graces and comforts,[11] have their hearts hardened,[12] and their consciences wounded;[13] hurt and scandalize others,[14] and bring temporal judgments upon themselves.[15]

[10] EPH 4:30 And grieve not the holy Spirit of God, whereby ye are sealed unto the day of redemption.

[11] PSA 51:8 Make me to hear joy and gladness; that the bones which thou hast broken may rejoice. 10 Create in me a clean heart, O God; and renew a right spirit within me. 12 Restore unto me the joy of thy salvation; and uphold me with thy free spirit. REV 2:4 Nevertheless I have somewhat against thee, because thou hast left thy first love. SON 5:2 I sleep, but my heart waketh: it is the voice of my beloved that knocketh, saying, Open to me, my sister, my love, my dove, my undefiled: for my head is filled with dew, and my locks with the drops of the night. 3 I have put off my coat; how shall I put it on? I have washed my feet; how shall I defile them? 4 My beloved put in his hand by the hole of the door, and my bowels were moved for him. 6 I opened to my beloved; but my beloved had withdrawn himself, and was gone: my soul failed when he spake: I sought him, but I could not find him; I called him, but he gave me no answer.

[12] ISA 63:17 O Lord, why hast thou made us to err from thy ways, and hardened our heart from thy fear? Return for thy servants' sake, the tribes of thine inheritance. MAR 6:52 For they considered not the miracle of the loaves: for their heart was hardened. 16:14 Afterward he appeared unto the eleven as they sat at meat, and upbraided them with their unbelief and hardness of heart, because they believed not them which had seen him after he was risen.

[13] PSA 32:3 When I kept silence, my bones waxed old through my roaring all the day long. 4 For day and night thy hand was heavy upon me: my moisture is turned into the drought of summer. Selah. 51:8 Make me to hear joy and gladness; that the bones which thou hast broken may rejoice.

[14] 2SA 12:14 Howbeit, because by this deed thou hast given great occasion to the enemies of the Lord to blaspheme, the child also that is born unto thee shall surely die.

[15] PSA 89:31 If they break my statutes, and keep not my commandments; 32 Then will I visit their transgression with the rod, and their iniquity with stripes. 1CO 11:32 But when we are judged, we are chastened of the Lord, that we should not be condemned with the world.

Chapter XVIII
Of Assurance of Grace and Salvation

I. Although hypocrites and other unregenerate men may vainly deceive themselves with false hopes and carnal presumptions of being in the favor of God, and estate of salvation[1] (which hope of theirs shall perish):[2] yet such as truly believe in the Lord Jesus, and love Him in sincerity, endeavouring to walk in all good conscience before Him, may, in this life, be certainly assured that they are in the state of grace,[3] and

---

[1] JOB 8:13 So are the paths of all that forget God; and the hypocrite's hope shall perish: 14 Whose hope shall be cut off, and whose trust shall be a spider's web. MIC 3:11 The heads thereof judge for reward, and the priests thereof teach for hire, and the prophets thereof divine for money: yet will they lean upon the Lord, and say, Is not the Lord among us? none evil can come upon us. DEU 29:19 And it come to pass, when he heareth the words of this curse, that he bless himself in his heart, saying, I shall have peace, though I walk in the imagination of mine heart, to add drunkenness to thirst. JOH 8:41 Ye do the deeds of your father. Then said they to him, We be not born of fornication; we have one Father, even God.

[2] MAT 7:22 Many will say to me in that day, Lord, Lord, have we not prophesied in thy name? and in thy name have cast out devils? and in thy name done many wonderful works? 23 And then will I profess unto them, I never knew you: depart from me, ye that work iniquity.

[3] 1JO 2:3 And hereby we do know that we know him, if we keep his commandments. 3:14 We know that we have passed from death unto life, because we love the brethren. He that loveth not his brother abideth in death. 18 My little children, let us not love in word, neither in tongue; but in deed and in truth. 19 And hereby we know that we are of the truth, and shall assure our hearts before him. 21 Beloved, if our heart condemn us not, then have we confidence

may rejoice in the hope of the glory of God, which hope shall never make them ashamed.⁴

II. This certainty is not a bare conjectural and probable persuasion grounded upon a fallible hope;⁵ but an infallible assurance of faith founded upon the divine truth of the promises of salvation,⁶ the inward evidence of those graces unto which these promises are made,⁷ the testimony of the Spirit of adoption witnessing with our spirits that we are

toward God. 24 And he that keepeth his commandments dwelleth in him, and he in him. And hereby we know that he abideth in us, by the Spirit which he hath given us. 1JO 5:13 These things have I written unto you that believe on the name of the Son of God; that ye may know that ye have eternal life, and that ye may believe on the name of the Son of God.

⁴ ROM 5:2 By whom also we have access by faith into this grace wherein we stand, and rejoice in hope of the glory of God. 5 And hope maketh not ashamed; because the love of God is shed abroad in our hearts by the Holy Ghost which is given unto us.

⁵ HEB 6:11 And we desire that every one of you do shew the same diligence to the full assurance of hope unto the end. 19 Which hope we have as an anchor of the soul, both sure and stedfast, and which entereth into that within the veil.

⁶ HEB 6:17 Wherein God, willing more abundantly to shew unto the heirs of promise the immutability of his counsel, confirmed it by an oath: 18 That by two immutable things, in which it was impossible for God to lie, we might have a strong consolation, who have fled for refuge to lay hold upon the hope set before us.

⁷ 2PE 1:4 Whereby are given unto us exceeding great and precious promises: that by these ye might be partakers of the divine nature, having escaped the corruption that is in the world through lust. 5 And beside this, giving all diligence, add to your faith virtue; and to virtue knowledge. 10 Wherefore the rather, brethren, give diligence to make your calling and election sure: for if ye do these things, ye shall never fall: 11 For so an entrance shall be ministered unto you abundantly into the everlasting kingdom of our Lord and Saviour Jesus Christ. 1JO 2:3 And hereby we do know that we know him, if we keep his commandments. 3:14 We know that we have passed from death unto life, because we love the brethren. He that loveth not his brother abideth in death. 2CO 1:12 For our rejoicing is this, the testimony of our conscience, that in simplicity and godly sincerity, not with fleshly wisdom, but by the grace of God, we have had our conversation in the world, and more abundantly to you-ward.

the children of God,[8] which Spirit is the earnest of our inheritance, whereby we are sealed to the day of redemption.[9]

III. This infallible assurance does not so belong to the essence of faith, but that a true believer may wait long, and conflict with many difficulties, before he be partaker of it:[10] yet, being enabled by the Spirit to know the things which are freely given him of God, he may, without extraordinary revelation in the right use of ordinary means, attain thereunto.[11] And therefore it is the duty of every one to give all diligence

---

[8] ROM 8:15 For ye have not received the spirit of bondage again to fear; but ye have received the Spirit of adoption, whereby we cry, Abba, Father. 16 The Spirit itself beareth witness with our spirit, that we are the children of God.

[9] EPH 1:13 In whom ye also trusted, after that ye heard the word of truth, the gospel of your salvation: in whom also after that ye believed, ye were sealed with that Holy Spirit of promise, 14 Which is the earnest of our inheritance until the redemption of the purchased possession, unto the praise of his glory. 4:30 And grieve not the Holy Spirit of God, whereby ye are sealed unto the day of redemption. 2CO 1:21 Now he which stablisheth us with you in Christ, and hath anointed us, is God; 22 Who hath also sealed us, and given the earnest of the Spirit in our hearts.

[10] 1JO 5:13 These things have I written unto you that believe on the name of the Son of God; that ye may know that ye have eternal life, and that ye may believe on the name of the Son of God. ISA 1:10 Hear the word of the Lord, ye rulers of Sodom; give ear unto the law of our God, ye people of Gomorrah. MAR 9:24 And straightway the father of the child cried out, and said with tears, Lord, I believe; help thou mine unbelief. (see PSA 88; PSA 77)

[11] 1CO 2:12 Now we have received, not the spirit of the world, but the spirit which is of God; that we might know the things that are freely given to us of God. 1JO 4:13 Hereby know we that we dwell in him, and he in us, because he hath given us of his Spirit. HEB 6:11 And we desire that every one of you do shew the same diligence to the full assurance of hope unto the end: 12 That ye be not slothful, but followers of them who through faith and patience inherit the promises. EPH 3:17 That Christ may dwell in your hearts by faith; that ye, being rooted and grounded in love, 18 May be able to comprehend with all saints what is the breadth, and length, and depth, and height; 19 And to know the love of Christ, which passeth knowledge, that ye might be filled with all the fulness of God.

to make his calling and election sure,[12] that thereby his heart may be enlarged in peace and joy in the Holy Ghost, in love and thankfulness to God, and in strength and cheerfulness in the duties of obedience,[13] the proper fruits of this assurance; so far is it from inclining men to looseness.[14]

[12] 2PE 1:10 Wherefore the rather, brethren, give diligence to make your calling and election sure: for if ye do these things, ye shall never fall.

[13] ROM 5:1 Therefore being justified by faith, we have peace with God through our Lord Jesus Christ: 2 By whom also we have access by faith into this grace wherein we stand, and rejoice in hope of the glory of God. 5 And hope maketh not ashamed; because the love of God is shed abroad in our hearts by the Holy Ghost which is given unto us. 14:17 For the kingdom of God is not meat and drink; but righteousness, and peace, and joy in the Holy Ghost. 15:13 Now the God of hope fill you with all joy and peace in believing, that ye may abound in hope, through the power of the Holy Ghost. EPH 1:3 Blessed be the God and Father of our Lord Jesus Christ, who hath blessed us with all spiritual blessings in heavenly places in Christ: 4 According as he hath chosen us in him before the foundation of the world, that we should be holy and without blame before him in love. PSA 4:6 There be many that say, Who will shew us any good? Lord, lift thou up the light of thy countenance upon us. 7 Thou hast put gladness in my heart, more than in the time that their corn and their wine increased. 119:32 I will run the way of thy commandments, when thou shalt enlarge my heart.

[14] 1JO 2:1 My little children, these things write I unto you, that ye sin not. And if any man sin, we have an advocate with the Father, Jesus Christ the righteous: 2 And he is the propitiation for our sins: and not for ours only, but also for the sins of the whole world. ROM 6:1 What shall we say then? Shall we continue in sin, that grace may abound? 2 God forbid. How shall we, that are dead to sin, live any longer therein? TIT 2:11 For the grace of God that bringeth salvation hath appeared to all men. 12 Teaching us, that, denying ungodliness and worldly lusts, we should live soberly, righteously and godly, in this present world. 14 Who gave himself for us, that he might redeem us from all iniquity, and purify unto himself a peculiar people, zealous of good works. 2CO 7:1 Having therefore these promises, dearly beloved, let us cleanse ourselves from all filthiness of the flesh and spirit, perfecting holiness in the fear of God. ROM 8:1 There is therefore now no condemnation to them which are in Christ Jesus, who walk not after the flesh, but after the Spirit. 12 Therefore, brethren, we are debtors, not to the flesh, to live after the flesh. 1JO 3:2 Beloved, now are we the sons of God, and it doth not yet appear what we shall be: but we know that, when

IV. True believers may have the assurance of their salvation divers ways shaken, diminished, and intermitted; as, by negligence in preserving of it, by falling into some special sin which wounds the conscience and grieves the Spirit; by some sudden or vehement temptation, by God's withdrawing the light of His countenance, and suffering even such as fear Him to walk in darkness and to have no light:[15] yet are they never so

he shall appear, we shall be like him; for we shall see him as he is. 3 And every man that hath this hope in him purifieth himself, even as he is pure. PSA 130:4 But there is forgiveness with thee, that thou mayest be feared. 1JO 1:6 If we say that we have fellowship with him, and walk in darkness, we lie, and do not the truth: 7 But if we walk in the light, as he is in the light, we have fellowship one with another, and the blood of Jesus Christ his Son cleanseth us from all sin.

[15] SON 5:2 I sleep, but my heart waketh: it is the voice of my beloved that knocketh, saying, Open to me, my sister, my love, my dove, my undefiled: for my head is filled with dew, and my locks with the drops of the night. 3 I have put off my coat; how shall I put it on? I have washed my feet; how shall I defile them? 6 I opened to my beloved; but my beloved had withdrawn himself, and was gone: my soul failed when he spake: I sought him, but I could not find him; I called him, but he gave me no answer. PSA 51:8 Make me to hear joy and gladness; that the bones which thou hast broken may rejoice. 12 Restore unto me the joy of thy salvation; and uphold me with thy free spirit. 14 Deliver me from bloodguiltiness, O God, thou God of my salvation: and my tongue shall sing aloud of thy righteousness. EPH 4:30 And grieve not the holy Spirit of God, whereby ye are sealed unto the day of redemption. 31 Let all bitterness, and wrath, and anger, and clamour, and evil speaking, be put away from you, with all malice. PSA 77:1 I cried unto God with my voice, even unto God with my voice; and he gave ear unto me. 2 In the day of my trouble I sought the Lord: my sore ran in the night, and ceased not: my soul refused to be comforted. 3 I remembered God, and was troubled: I complained, and my spirit was overwhelmed. Selah. 4 Thou holdest mine eyes waking: I am so troubled that I cannot speak. 5 I have considered the days of old, the years of ancient times. 6 I call to remembrance my song in the night: I commune with mine own heart: and my spirit made diligent search. 7 Will the Lord cast off for ever? and will he be favourable no more? 8 Is his mercy clean gone for ever? doth his promise fail for evermore? 9 Hath God forgotten to be gracious? hath he in anger shut up his tender mercies? Selah. 10 And I said, This is my infirmity: but I will remember the years of the right hand of the most High. MAT 26:69 Now Peter sat without in the palace: and a damsel came unto him,

utterly destitute of that seed of God, and life of faith, that love of Christ and the brethren, that sincerity of heart, and conscience of duty, out of which, by the operation of the Spirit, this assurance may, in due time, be revived;[16] and by the which, in the mean time, they are supported from utter despair.[17]

saying, Thou also wast with Jesus of Galilee. 70 But he denied before them all, saying, I know not what thou sayest. 71 And when he was gone out into the porch, another maid saw him, and said unto them that were there, This fellow was also with Jesus of Nazareth. 72 And again he denied with an oath, I do not know the man. PSA 31:22 For I said in my haste, I am cut off from before thine eyes: nevertheless thou heardest the voice of my supplications when I cried unto thee. (PSA 88 throughout) ISA 50:10 Who is among you that feareth the Lord, that obeyeth the voice of his servant, that walketh in darkness, and hath no light? let him trust in the name of the Lord, and stay upon his God.

[16] 1JO 3:9 Whosoever is born of God doth not commit sin; for his seed remaineth in him: and he cannot sin, because he is born of God. LUK 22:32 But I have prayed for thee, that thy faith fail not: and when thou art converted, strengthen thy brethren. JOB 13:15 Though he slay me, yet will I trust in him: but I will maintain mine own ways before him. PSA 73:15 If I say, I will speak thus; behold, I should offend against the generation of thy children. PSA 51:8 Make me to hear joy and gladness; that the bones which thou hast broken may rejoice. 12 Restore unto me the joy of thy salvation; and uphold me with thy free spirit. ISA 50:10 Who is among you that feareth the Lord, that obeyeth the voice of his servant, that walketh in darkness, and hath no light? let him trust in the name of the Lord, and stay upon his God.

[17] MIC 7:7 Therefore I will look unto the Lord; I will wait for the God of my salvation: my God will hear me. 8 Rejoice not against me, O mine enemy: when I fall, I shall arise; when I sit in darkness, the Lord shall be a light unto me. 9 I will bear the indignation of the Lord, because I have sinned against him, until he plead my cause, and execute judgment for me: he will bring me forth to the light, and I shall behold his righteousness. JER 32:40 And I will make an everlasting covenant with them, that I will not turn away from them, to do them good; but I will put my fear in their hearts, that they shall not depart from me. ISA 54:7 For a small moment have I forsaken thee; but with great mercies will I gather thee. 8 In a little wrath I hid my face from thee for a moment; but with everlasting kindness will I have mercy on thee, saith the Lord thy Redeemer. 9 For this is as the waters of Noah unto me: for as I have sworn that the waters of Noah should no more go

over the earth; so have I sworn that I would not be wroth with thee, nor rebuke thee. 10 For the mountains shall depart, and the hills be removed; but my kindness shall not depart from thee, neither shall the covenant of my peace be removed, saith the Lord that hath mercy on thee. PSA 22:1 My God, my God, why hast thou forsaken me? why art thou so far from helping me, and from the words of my roaring? (PSA 88 throughout)

Chapter XIX
Of the Law of God

I. God gave to Adam a law, as a covenant of works, by which He bound him and all his posterity, to personal, entire, exact, and perpetual obedience, promised life upon the fulfilling, and threatened death upon the breach of it, and endued him with power and ability to keep it.[1]

[1] GEN 1:26 And God said, Let us make man in our image, after our likeness: and let them have dominion over the fish of the sea, and over the fowl of the air, and over the cattle, and over all the earth, and over every creeping thing that creepeth upon the earth. 27 So God created man in his own image, in the image of God created he him; male and female created he them. 2:17 But of the tree of the knowledge of good and evil, thou shalt not eat of it: for in the day that thou eatest thereof thou shalt surely die. ROM 2:14 For when the Gentiles, which have not the law, do by nature the things contained in the law, these, having not the law, are a law unto themselves: 15 Which shew the work of the law written in their hearts, their conscience also bearing witness, and their thoughts the mean while accusing or else excusing one another. 10:5 For Moses describeth the righteousness which is of the law, That the man which doeth those things shall live by them. ROM 5:12 Wherefore, as by one man sin entered into the world, and death by sin; and so death passed upon all men, for that all have sinned: 19 For as by one man's disobedience many were made sinners, so by the obedience of one shall many be made righteous. GAL 3:10 For as many as are of the works of the law are under the curse: for it is written, Cursed is every one that continueth not in all things which are written in the book of the law to do them. 12 And the law is not of faith: but, The man that doeth them shall live in them. ECC 7:29 Lo, this only have I found, that God hath made man upright; but they have sought out many inventions. JOB 28:28 And unto man he said, Behold, the fear of the Lord, that is wisdom; and to depart from evil is understanding.

II. This law, after his fall, continued to be a perfect rule of righteousness; and, as such, was delivered by God upon Mount Sinai, in ten commandments, and written in two tables:[2] the first four commandments containing our duty towards God; and the other six, our duty to man.[3]

III. Besides this law, commonly called moral, God was pleased to give to the people of Israel, as a church under age, ceremonial laws, containing several typical ordinances, partly of worship, prefiguring Christ, His graces, actions, sufferings, and benefits;[4] and partly, holding

---

[2] JAM 1:25 But whoso looketh into the perfect law of liberty, and continueth therein, he being not a forgetful hearer, but a doer of the work, this man shall be blessed in his deed. 2:8 If ye fulfil the royal law according to the scripture, Thou shalt love thy neighbour as thyself, ye do well: 10 For whosoever shall keep the whole law, and yet offend in one point, he is guilty of all. 11 For he that said, Do not commit adultery, said also, Do not kill. Now if thou commit no adultery, yet if thou kill, thou art become a transgressor of the law. 12 So speak ye, and so do, as they that shall be judged by the law of liberty. ROM 13:8 Owe no man any thing; but to love one another: for he that loveth another hath fulfilled the law. 9 For this, Thou shalt not commit adultery, Thou shalt not kill, Thou shalt not steal, Thou shalt not bear false witness, Thou shalt not covet; and if there be any other commandment, it is briefly comprehended in this saying, namely, Thou shalt love thy neighbour as thyself. DEU 5:32 Ye shall observe to do therefore as the Lord your God hath commanded you: ye shall not turn aside to the right hand or to the left. 10:4 And he wrote on the tables, according to the first writing, the ten commandments, which the Lord spake unto you in the mount out of the midst of the fire in the day of the assembly: and the Lord gave them unto me. EXO 24:1 And he said unto Moses, Come up unto the Lord, thou, and Aaron, Nadab, and Abihu, and seventy of the elders of Israel; and worship ye afar off.

[3] MAT 22:37 Jesus said unto him, Thou shalt love the Lord thy God with all thy heart, and with all thy soul, and with all thy mind. 38 This is the first and great commandment. 39 And the second is like unto it, Thou shalt love thy neighbour as thyself. 40 On these two commandments hang all the law and the prophets.

[4] (HEB 9) HEB 10:1 For the law having a shadow of good things to come, and not the very image of the things, can never with those sacrifices which they offered year by year continually make the comers thereunto perfect. GAL 4:1 Now I say, That the heir, as long as he is a child, differeth nothing from a servant, though he be lord of all; 2 But is under tutors and governors until the time appointed of the

forth divers instructions of moral duties.⁵ All which ceremonial laws are now abrogated, under the New Testament.⁶

IV. To them also, as a body politic, He gave sundry judicial laws, which expired together with the state of that people; not obliging any other now, further than the general equity thereof may require.⁷

father. 3 Even so we, when we were children, were in bondage under the elements of the world. COL 2:17 Which are a shadow of things to come; but the body is of Christ.

⁵ 1CO 5:7 Purge out therefore the old leaven, that ye may be a new lump, as ye are unleavened. For even Christ our passover is sacrificed for us. 2CO 6:17 Wherefore come out from among them, and be ye separate, saith the Lord, and touch not the unclean thing; and I will receive you. JUD 23 And others save with fear, pulling them out of the fire; hating even the garment spotted by the flesh.

⁶ COL 2:14 Blotting out the handwriting of ordinances that was against us, which was contrary to us, and took it out of the way, nailing it to his cross. 16 Let no man therefore judge you in meat, or in drink, or in respect of an holyday, or of the new moon, or of the sabbath days: 17 Which are a shadow of things to come; but the body is of Christ. DAN 9:27 And he shall confirm the covenant with many for one week: and in the midst of the week he shall cause the sacrifice and the oblation to cease, and for the overspreading of abominations he shall make it desolate, even until the consummation, and that determined shall be poured upon the desolate. EPH 2:15 Having abolished in his flesh the enmity, even the law of commandments contained in ordinances; for to make in himself of twain one new man, so making peace; 16 And that he might reconcile both unto God in one body by the cross, having slain the enmity thereby.

⁷ (EXO 21-22) GEN 49:10 The sceptre shall not depart from Judah, nor a lawgiver from between his feet, until Shiloh come; and unto him shall the gathering of the people be. 1PE 2:13 Submit yourselves to every ordinance of man for the Lord's sake: whether it be to the king, as supreme; 14 Or unto governors, as unto them that are sent by him for the punishment of evildoers, and for the praise of them that do well. MAT 5:17 Think not that I am come to destroy the law, or the prophets: I am not come to destroy, but to fulfil. 38 Ye have heard that it hath been said, An eye for an eye, and a tooth for a tooth: 39 But I say unto you, That ye resist not evil: but whosoever shall smite thee on thy right cheek, turn to him the other also. 1CO 9:8 Say I these things as a man? or saith not the law the same also? 9 For it is written in the law of Moses, Thou shalt not muzzle the mouth of the ox that treadeth out the corn. Doth God take care for oxen? 10 Or

V. The moral law does forever bind all, as well justified persons as others, to the obedience thereof;[8] and that, not only in regard of the matter contained in it, but also in respect of the authority of God the Creator, who gave it.[9] Neither does Christ, in the Gospel, any way dissolve, but much strengthen this obligation.[10]

VI. Although true believers be not under the law, as a covenant of

---

saith he it altogether for our sakes? For our sakes, no doubt, this is written: that he that ploweth should plow in hope; and that he that thresheth in hope should be partaker of his hope.

[8] ROM 13:8 Owe no man any thing, but to love one another: for he that loveth another hath fulfilled the law. 9 For this, Thou shalt not commit adultery, Thou shalt not kill, Thou shalt not steal, Thou shalt not bear false witness, Thou shalt not covet; and if there be any other commandment, it is briefly comprehended in this saying, namely, Thou shalt love thy neighbour as thyself. 10 Love worketh no ill to his neighbour: therefore love is the fulfilling of the law. EPH 6:2 Honour thy father and mother; (which is the first commandment with promise.) 1JO 2:3 And hereby we do know that we know him, if we keep his commandments. 4 He that saith, I know him, and keepeth not his commandments, is a liar, and the truth is not in him. 7 Brethren, I write no new commandment unto you, but an old commandment which ye had from the beginning. The old commandment is the word which ye have heard from the beginning. 8 Again, a new commandment I write unto you, which thing is true in him and in you: because the darkness is past, and the true light now shineth.

[9] JAM 2:10 For whosoever shall keep the whole law, and yet offend in one point, he is guilty of all. 11 For he that said, Do not commit adultery, said also, Do not kill. Now if thou commit no adultery, yet if thou kill, thou art become a transgressor of the law.

[10] MAT 5:17 Think not that I am come to destroy the law, or the prophets: I am not come to destroy, but to fulfil. 18 For verily I say unto you, Till heaven and earth pass, one jot or one tittle shall in no wise pass from the law, till all be fulfilled. 19 Whosoever therefore shall break one of these least commandments, and shall teach men so, he shall be called the least in the kingdom of heaven: but whosoever shall do and teach them, the same shall be called great in the kingdom of heaven. JAM 2:8 If ye fulfil the royal law according to the scripture, Thou shalt love thy neighbour as thyself, ye do well. ROM 3:31 Do we then make void the law through faith? God forbid: yea, we establish the law.

works, to be thereby justified, or condemned;[11] yet is it of great use to them, as well as to others; in that, as a rule of life informing them of the will of God, and their duty, it directs and binds them to walk accordingly;[12] discovering also the sinful pollutions of their nature, hearts and lives;[13] so as, examining themselves thereby, they may come to

---

[11] ROM 6:14 For sin shall not have dominion over you: for ye are not under the law, but under grace. GAL 2:16 Knowing that a man is not justified by the works of the law, but by the faith of Jesus Christ, even we have believed in Jesus Christ, that we might be justified by the faith of Christ, and not by the works of the law: for by the works of the law shall no flesh be justified. 3:13 Christ hath redeemed us from the curse of the law, being made a curse for us: for it is written, Cursed is every one that hangeth on a tree. 4:4 But when the fulness of the time was come, God sent forth his Son, made of a woman, made under the law, 5 To redeem them that were under the law, that we might receive the adoption of sons. ACT 13:39 And by him all that believe are justified from all things, from which ye could not be justified by the law of Moses. ROM 8:1 There is therefore now no condemnation to them which are in Christ Jesus, who walk not after the flesh, but after the Spirit.

[12] ROM 7:12 Wherefore the law is holy, and the commandment holy, and just, and good. 22 For I delight in the law of God after the inward man. 25 I thank God through Jesus Christ our Lord. So then with the mind I myself serve the law of God; but with the flesh the law of sin. PSA 119:4 Thou hast commanded us to keep thy precepts diligently. 5 O that my ways were directed to keep thy statutes! 6 Then shall I not be ashamed, when I have respect unto all thy commandments. 1CO 7:19 Circumcision is nothing, and uncircumcision is nothing, but the keeping of the commandments of God. GAL 5:14 For all the law is fulfilled in one word, even in this; Thou shalt love thy neighbour as thyself. 16 This I say then, Walk in the Spirit, and ye shall not fulfil the lust of the flesh. 18 But if ye be led of the Spirit, ye are not under the law. 19 Now the works of the flesh are manifest, which are these; Adultery, fornication, uncleanness, lasciviousness, 20 Idolatry, witchcraft, hatred, variance, emulations, wrath, strife, seditions, heresies, 21 Envyings, murders, drunkenness, revellings, and such like: of the which I tell you before, as I have also told you in time past, that they which do such things shall not inherit the kingdom of God. 22 But the fruit of the Spirit is love, joy, peace, longsuffering, gentleness, goodness, faith, 23 Meekness, temperance: against such there is no law.

[13] ROM 7:7 What shall we say then? Is the law sin? God forbid. Nay, I had

further conviction of, humiliation for, and hatred against sin,[14] together with a clearer sight of the need they have of Christ, and the perfection of His obedience.[15] It is likewise of use to the regenerate, to restrain their corruptions, in that it forbids sin:[16] and the threatenings of it serve to show what even their sins deserve; and what afflictions, in this life, they may expect for them, although freed from the curse thereof threatened in the law.[17] The promises of it, in like manner, show them God's

not known sin, but by the law: for I had not known lust, except the law had said, Thou shalt not covet. ROM 3:20 Therefore by the deeds of the law there shall no flesh be justified in his sight: for by the law is the knowledge of sin.

[14] JAM 1:23 For if any be a hearer of the word, and not a doer, he is like unto a man beholding his natural face in a glass: 24 For he beholdeth himself, and goeth his way, and straightway forgetteth what manner of man he was. 25 But whoso looketh into the perfect law of liberty, and continueth therein, he being not a forgetful hearer, but a doer of the work, this man shall be blessed in his deed. ROM 7:9 For I was alive without the law once: but when the commandment came, sin revived, and I died. 14 For we know that the law is spiritual: but I am carnal, sold under sin. 24 O wretched man that I am! who shall deliver me from the body of this death?

[15] GAL 3:24 Wherefore the law was our schoolmaster to bring us unto Christ, that we might be justified by faith. ROM 7:24 O wretched man that I am! who shall deliver me from the body of this death? 25 I thank God through Jesus Christ our Lord. So then with the mind I myself serve the law of God; but with the flesh the law of sin. 8:3 For what the law could not do, in that it was weak through the flesh, God sending his own Son in the likeness of sinful flesh, and for sin, condemned sin in the flesh: 4 That the righteousness of the law might be fulfilled in us, who walk not after the flesh, but after the Spirit.

[16] JAM 2:11 For he that said, Do not commit adultery, said also, Do not kill. Now if thou commit no adultery, yet if thou kill, thou art become a transgressor of the law. PSA 119:101 I have refrained my feet from every evil way, that I might keep thy word. 104 Through thy precepts I get understanding: therefore I hate every false way. 128 Therefore I esteem all thy precepts concerning all things to be right; and I hate every false way.

[17] EZR 9:13 And after all that is come upon us for our evil deeds, and for our great trespass, seeing that thou our God hast punished us less than our iniquities deserve, and hast given us such deliverance as this; 14 Should we again break thy commandments, and join in affinity with the people of these abominations?

approbation of obedience, and what blessings they may expect upon the performance thereof:[18] although not as due to them by the law as a covenant of works.[19] So as, a man's doing good, and refraining from evil, because the law encourages to the one and deters from the other, is no evidence of his being under the law: and not under grace.[20]

wouldest not thou be angry with us till thou hadst consumed us, so that there should be no remnant nor escaping? PSA 89:30 If his children forsake my law, and walk not in my judgments; 31 If they break my statutes, and keep not my commandments; 32 Then will I visit their transgression with the rod, and their iniquity with stripes. 33 Nevertheless my lovingkindness will I not utterly take from him, nor suffer my faithfulness to fail. 34 My covenant will I not break, nor alter the thing that is gone out of my lips.

[18] (LEV 26) 2CO 6:16 And what agreement hath the temple of God with idols? for ye are the temple of the living God; as God hath said, I will dwell in them, and walk in them; and I will be their God, and they shall be my people. EPH 6:2 Honour thy father and mother; (which is the first commandment with promise;) 3 That it may be well with thee, and thou mayest live long on the earth. PSA 37:11 But the meek shall inherit the earth; and shall delight themselves in the abundance of peace. MAT 5:5 Blessed are the meek: for they shall inherit the earth. PSA 19:11 Moreover by them is thy servant warned: and in keeping of them there is great reward.

[19] GAL 2:16 Knowing that a man is not justified by the works of the law, but by the faith of Jesus Christ, even we have believed in Jesus Christ, that we might be justified by the faith of Christ, and not by the works of the law: for by the works of the law shall no flesh be justified. LUK 17:10 So likewise ye, when ye shall have done all those things which are commanded you, say, We are unprofitable servants: we have done that which was our duty to do.

[20] ROM 6:12 Let not sin therefore reign in your mortal body, that ye should obey it in the lusts thereof. 14 For sin shall not have dominion over you: for ye are not under the law, but under grace. 1PE 3:8 Finally, be ye all of one mind, having compassion one of another, love as brethren, be pitiful, be courteous: 9 Not rendering evil for evil, or railing for railing: but contrariwise blessing; knowing that ye are thereunto called, that ye should inherit a blessing. 10 For he that ill love life, and see good days, let him refrain his tongue from evil, and his lips that they speak no guile: 11 Let him eschew evil, and do good; let him seek peace, and ensue it. 12 For the eyes of the Lord are over the righteous, and his ears are open unto their prayers: but the face of the Lord is against them that do evil. PSA 34:12

VII. Neither are the forementioned uses of the law contrary to the grace of the Gospel, but do sweetly comply with it;[21] the Spirit of Christ subduing and enabling the will of man to do that freely, and cheerfully, which the will of God, revealed in the law, requires to be done.[22]

What man is he that desireth life, and loveth many days, that he may see good? 13 Keep thy tongue from evil, and thy lips from speaking guile. 14 Depart from evil, and do good; seek peace, and pursue it. 15 The eyes of the Lord are upon the righteous, and his ears are open unto their cry. 16 The face of the Lord is against them that do evil, to cut off the remembrance of them from the earth. HEB 12:28 Wherefore we receiving a kingdom which cannot be moved, let us have grace, whereby we may serve God acceptably with reverence and godly fear. 29 For our God is a consuming fire.

[21] GAL 3:21 Is the law then against the promises of God? God forbid: for if there had been a law given which could have given life, verily righteousness should have been by the law.

[22] EZE 36:27 And I will put my spirit within you, and cause you to walk in my statutes, and ye shall keep my judgments, and do them. HEB 8:10 For this is the covenant that I will make with the house of Israel after those days, saith the Lord; I will put my laws into their mind, and write them in their hearts: and I will be to them a God, and they shall be to me a people. JER 31:33 But this shall be the covenant that I will make with the house of Israel; After those days, saith the Lord, I will put my law in their inward parts, and write it in their hearts; and will be their God, and they shall be my people.

Chapter XX
Of Christian Liberty, and Liberty of Conscience

I. The liberty which Christ has purchased for believers under the Gospel consists in their freedom from the guilt of sin, and condemning wrath of God, the curse of the moral law;[1] and, in their being delivered from this present evil world, bondage to Satan, and dominion of sin;[2] from the evil of afflictions, the sting of death, the victory of the grave, and everlasting damnation;[3] as also, in their free access to God,[4] and their

---

[1] TIT 2:14 Who gave himself for us, that he might redeem us from all iniquity, and purify unto himself a peculiar people, zealous of good works. 1TH 1:10 And to wait for his Son from heaven, whom he raised from the dead, even Jesus, which delivered us from the wrath to come. GAL 3:13 Christ hath redeemed us from the curse of the law, being made a curse for us: for it is written, Cursed is every one that hangeth on a tree.

[2] GAL 1:4 Who gave himself for our sins, that he might deliver us from this present evil world, according to the will of God and our Father. COL 1:13 Who hath delivered us from the power of darkness, and hath translated us into the kingdom of his dear Son. ACT 26:18 To open their eyes, and to turn them from darkness to light, and from the power of Satan unto God, that they may receive forgiveness of sins, and inheritance among them which are sanctified by faith that is in me. ROM 6:14 For sin shall not have dominion over you: for ye are not under the law, but under grace.

[3] ROM 8:28 And we know that all things work together for good to them that love God, to them who are the called according to his purpose. PSA 119:71 It is good for me that I have been afflicted; that I might learn thy statutes. 1CO 15:54 So when this corruptible shall have put on incorruption, and this mortal shall have put on immortality, then shall be brought to pass the saying that is written, Death is swallowed up in victory. 55 O death, where is thy sting? O

yielding obedience unto Him, not out of slavish fear, but a child-like love and willing mind.⁵ All which were common also to believers under the law.⁶ But, under the New Testament, the liberty of Christians is further enlarged, in their freedom from the yoke of the ceremonial law, to which the Jewish Church was subjected;⁷ and in greater boldness of access to the throne of grace,⁸ and in fuller communications of the free Spirit of

grave, where is thy victory? 56 The sting of death is sin; and the strength of sin is the law. 57 But thanks be to God, which giveth us the victory through our Lord Jesus Christ. ROM 8:1 There is therefore now no condemnation to them which are in Christ Jesus, who walk not after the flesh, but after the Spirit.

⁴ ROM 5:1 Therefore being justified by faith, we have peace with God through our Lord Jesus Christ: 2 By whom also we have access by faith into this grace wherein we stand, and rejoice in hope of the glory of God.

⁵ ROM 8:14 For as many as are led by the Spirit of God, they are the sons of God. 15 For ye have not received the spirit of bondage again to fear; but ye have received the Spirit of adoption, whereby we cry, Abba, Father. 1JO 4:18 There is no fear in love; but perfect love casteth out fear: because fear hath torment. He that feareth is not made perfect in love.

⁶ GAL 3:9 So then they which be of faith are blessed with faithful Abraham. 14 That the blessing of Abraham might come on the Gentiles through Jesus Christ; that we might receive the promise of the Spirit through faith.

⁷ GAL 4:1 Now I say, That the heir, as long as he is a child, differeth nothing from a servant, though he be lord of all; 2 But is under tutors and governors until the time appointed of the father. 3 Even so we, when we were children, were in bondage under the elements of the world. 6 And because ye are sons, God hath sent forth the Spirit of his Son into your hearts, crying, Abba, Father. 7 Wherefore thou art no more a servant, but a son; and if a son, then an heir of God through Christ. 5:1 Stand fast therefore in the liberty wherewith Christ hath made us free, and be not entangled again with the yoke of bondage. ACT 15:10 Now therefore why tempt ye God, to put a yoke upon the neck of the disciples, which neither our fathers nor we were able to bear? 11 But we believe that through the grace of the Lord Jesus Christ we shall be saved, even as they.

⁸ HEB 4:14 Seeing then that we have a great high priest, that is passed into the heavens, Jesus the Son of God, let us hold fast our profession. 16 Let us therefore come boldly unto the throne of grace, that we may obtain mercy, and find grace to help in time of need. 10:19 Having therefore, brethren, boldness to enter into the holiest by the blood of Jesus, 20 By a new and living way, which he

God, than believers under the law did ordinarily partake of.⁹

II. God alone is Lord of the conscience,¹⁰ and has left it free from the doctrines and commandments of men, which are, in any thing, contrary to His Word; or beside it, if matters of faith, or worship.¹¹ So that, to believe such doctrines, or to obey such commands, out of conscience, is to betray true liberty of conscience:¹² and the requiring of an implicit

hath consecrated for us, through the veil, that is to say, his flesh; 21 And having an high priest over the house of God; 22 Let us draw near with a true heart in full assurance of faith, having our hearts sprinkled from an evil conscience, and our bodies washed with pure water.

⁹ JOH 7:38 He that believeth on me, as the scripture hath said, out of his belly shall flow rivers of living water. 39 (But this spake he of the Spirit, which they that believe on him should receive: for the Holy Ghost was not yet given; because that Jesus was not yet glorified.) 2CO 3:13 And not as Moses, which put a vail over his face, that the children of Israel could not stedfastly look to the end of that which is abolished. 17 Now the Lord is that Spirit: and where the Spirit of the Lord is, there is liberty. 18 But we all, with open face beholding as in a glass the glory of the Lord, are changed into the same image from glory to glory, even as by the Spirit of the Lord.

¹⁰ JAM 4:12 There is one lawgiver, who is able to save and to destroy: who art thou that judgest another? ROM 14:4 Who art thou that judgest another man's servant? to his own master he standeth or falleth. Yea, he shall be holden up: for God is able to make him stand.

¹¹ ACT 4:19 But Peter and John answered and said unto them, Whether it be right in the sight of God to hearken unto you more than unto God, judge ye. 5:29 Then Peter and the other apostles answered and said, We ought to obey God rather than men. 1CO 7:23 Ye are bought with a price; be not ye the servants of men. MAT 23:8 But be not ye called Rabbi: for one is your Master, even Christ; and all ye are brethren. 9 And call no man your father upon the earth: for one is your Father, which is in heaven. 10 Neither be ye called masters: for one is your Master, even Christ. 2CO 1:24 Not for that we have dominion over your faith, but are helpers of your joy: for by faith ye stand. MAT 15:9 But in vain they do worship me, teaching for doctrines the commandments of men.

¹² COL 2:20 Wherefore if ye be dead with Christ from the rudiments of the world, why, as though living in the world, are ye subject to ordinances, 22 Which all are to perish with the using;) after the commandments and doctrines of men? 23 Which things have indeed a shew of wisdom in will worship, and humility, and

faith, and an absolute and blind obedience, is to destroy liberty of conscience, and reason also.[13]

III. They who, upon pretence of Christian liberty, do practice any sin, or cherish any lust, do thereby destroy the end of Christian liberty, which is, that being delivered out of the hands of our enemies, we might serve the Lord without fear, in holiness and righteousness before Him, all the days of our life.[14]

neglecting of the body; not in any honour to the satisfying of the flesh. GAL 1:10 For do I now persuade men, or God? or do I seek to please men? for if I yet pleased men, I should not be the servant of Christ. 2:4 And that because of false brethren unawares brought in, who came in privily to spy out our liberty which we have in Christ Jesus, that they might bring us into bondage: 5 To whom we gave place by subjection, no, not for an hour; that the truth of the gospel might continue with you. 5:1 Stand fast therefore in the liberty wherewith Christ hath made us free, and be not entangled again with the yoke of bondage.

[13] ROM 10:17 So then faith cometh by hearing, and hearing by the word of God. 14:23 And he that doubteth is damned if he eat, because he eateth not of faith: for whatsoever is not of faith is sin. ISA 8:20 To the law and to the testimony: if they speak not according to this word, it is because there is no light in them. ACT 17:11 These were more noble than those in Thessalonica, in that they received the word with all readiness of mind, and searched the scriptures daily, whether those things were so. JOH 4:22 Ye worship ye know not what: we know what we worship: for salvation is of the Jews. HOS 5:11 Ephraim is oppressed and broken in judgment, because he willingly walked after the commandment. REV 13:12 And he exerciseth all the power of the first beast before him, and causeth the earth and them which dwell therein to worship the first beast, whose deadly wound was healed. 16 And he causeth all, both small and great, rich and poor, free and bond, to receive a mark in their right hand, or in their foreheads: 17 And that no man might buy or sell, save he that had the mark, or the name of the beast, or the number of his name. JER 8:9 The wise men are ashamed, they are dismayed and taken: lo, they have rejected the word of the Lord; and what wisdom is in them?

[14] GAL 5:13 For, brethren, ye have been called unto liberty; only use not liberty for an occasion to the flesh, but by love serve one another. 1PE 2:16 As free, and not using your liberty for a cloke of maliciousness, but as the servants of God. 2PE 2:19 While they promise them liberty, they themselves are the servants of corruption: for of whom a man is overcome, of the same is he brought in

IV. And because the powers which God has ordained, and the liberty which Christ has purchased are not intended by God to destroy, but mutually to uphold and preserve one another, they who, upon pretence of Christian liberty, shall oppose any lawful power, or the lawful exercise of it, whether it be civil or ecclesiastical, resist the ordinance of God.[15] And, for their publishing of such opinions, or maintaining of such practices, as are contrary to the light of nature, or to the known principles of Christianity (whether concerning faith, worship, or conversation), or to

bondage. JOH 8:34 Jesus answered them, Verily, verily, I say unto you, Whosoever committeth sin is the servant of sin. LUK 1:74 That he would grant unto us, that we being delivered out of the hand of our enemies might serve him without fear, 75 In holiness and righteousness before him, all the days of our life.

[15] MAT 12:25 And Jesus knew their thoughts, and said unto them, Every kingdom divided against itself is brought to desolation; and every city or house divided against itself shall not stand. 1PE 2:13 Submit yourselves to every ordinance of man for the Lord's sake: whether it be to the king, as supreme; 14 Or unto governors, as unto them that are sent by him for the punishment of evildoers, and for the praise of them that do well. 16 As free, and not using your liberty for a cloke of maliciousness, but as the servants of God. ROM 13:1 Let every soul be subject unto the higher powers. For there is no power but of God: the powers that be are ordained of God. 2 Whosoever therefore resisteth the power, resisteth the ordinance of God: and they that resist shall receive to themselves damnation. 3 For rulers are not a terror to good works, but to the evil. Wilt thou then not be afraid of the power? do that which is good, and thou shalt have praise of the same: 4 For he is the minister of God to thee for good. But if thou do that which is evil, be afraid; for he beareth not the sword in vain: for he is the minister of God, a revenger to execute wrath upon him that doeth evil. 5 Wherefore ye must needs be subject, not only for wrath, but also for conscience sake. 6 For for this cause pay ye tribute also: for they are God's ministers, attending continually upon this very thing. 7 Render therefore to all their dues: tribute to whom tribute is due; custom to whom custom; fear to whom fear; honour to whom honour. 8 Owe no man any thing, but to love one another: for he that loveth another hath fulfilled the law. HEB 13:17 Obey them that have the rule over you, and submit yourselves: for they watch for your souls, as they that must give account, that they may do it with joy, and not with grief: for that is unprofitable for you.

the power of godliness; or, such erroneous opinions or practices, as either in their own nature, or in the manner of publishing or maintaining them, are destructive to the external peace and order which Christ has established in the Church, they may lawfully be called to account,[16] and

[16] ROM 1:32 Who knowing the judgment of God, that they which commit such things are worthy of death, not only do the same, but have pleasure in them that do them. 1CO 5:1 It is reported commonly that there is fornication among you, and such fornication as is not so much as named among the Gentiles, that one should have his father's wife. 5 To deliver such an one unto Satan for the destruction of the flesh, that the spirit may be saved in the day of the Lord Jesus. 11 But now I have written unto you not to keep company, if any man that is called a brother be a fornicator, or covetous, or an idolater, or a railer, or a drunkard, or an extortioner; with such an one no not to eat. 13 But them that are without God judgeth. Therefore put away from among yourselves that wicked person. 2JO 1:10 If there come any unto you, and bring not this doctrine, receive him not into your house, neither bid him God speed: 11 For he that biddeth him God speed is partaker of his evil deeds. 2TH 3:14 And if any man obey not our word by this epistle, note that man, and have no company with him, that he may be ashamed. 1TI 6:3 If any man teach otherwise, and consent not to wholesome words, even the words of our Lord Jesus Christ, and to the doctrine which is according to godliness; 4 He is proud, knowing nothing, but doting about questions and strifes of words, whereof cometh envy, strife, railings, evil surmisings, 5 Perverse disputings of men of corrupt minds, and destitute of the truth, supposing that gain is godliness: from such withdraw thyself. TIT 1:10 For there are many unruly and vain talkers and deceivers, specially they of the circumcision: 11 Whose mouths must be stopped, who subvert whole houses, teaching things which they ought not, for filthy lucre's sake. 13 This witness is true. Wherefore rebuke them sharply, that they may be sound in the faith. TIT 3:10 A man that is an heretic after the first and second admonition reject. MAT 18:15 Moreover if thy brother shall trespass against thee, go and tell him his fault between thee and him alone: if he shall hear thee, thou hast gained thy brother. 16 But if he will not hear thee, then take with thee one or two more, that in the mouth of two or three witnesses every word may be established. 17 And if he shall neglect to hear them, tell it unto the church: but if he neglect to hear the church, let him be unto thee as an heathen man and a publican. 1TI 1:19 Holding faith, and a good conscience; which some having put away concerning faith have made shipwreck: 20 Of whom is Hymenaeus and Alexander; whom I have

proceeded against, by the censures of the Church. *[and by the power of the civil magistrate.]* ¹⁷

delivered unto Satan, that they may learn not to blaspheme. REV 2:2 I know thy works, and thy labour, and thy patience, and how thou canst not bear them which are evil: and thou hast tried them which say they are apostles, and are not, and hast found them liars. 14 But I have a few things against thee, because thou hast there them that hold the doctrine of Balaam, who taught Balac to cast a stumblingblock before the children of Israel, to eat things sacrificed unto idols, and to commit fornication. 15 So hast thou also them that hold the doctrine of the Nicolaitans, which thing I hate. 20 Notwithstanding I have a few things against thee, because thou sufferest that woman Jezebel, which calleth herself a prophetess, to teach and to seduce my servants to commit fornication, and to eat things sacrificed unto idols. 3:9 Behold, I will make them of the synagogue of Satan, which say they are Jews, and are not, but do lie; behold, I will make them to come and worship before thy feet, and to know that I have loved thee.

¹⁷ DEU 13:6 If thy brother, the son of thy mother, or thy son, or thy daughter, or the wife of thy bosom, or thy friend, which is as thine own soul, entice thee secretly, saying, Let us go and serve other gods, which thou hast not known, thou, nor thy fathers; 7 Namely, of the gods of the people which are round about you, nigh unto thee, or far off from thee, from the one end of the earth even unto the other end of the earth; 8 Thou shalt not consent unto him, nor hearken unto him; neither shall thine eye pity him, neither shalt thou spare, neither shalt thou conceal him: 9 But thou shalt surely kill him; thine hand shall be first upon him to put him to death, and afterwards the hand of all the people. 10 And thou shalt stone him with stones, that he die; because he hath sought to thrust thee away from the Lord thy God, which brought thee out of the land of Egypt, from the house of bondage. 11 And all Israel shall hear, and fear, and shall do no more any such wickedness as this is among you. ROM 13:3 For rulers are not a terror to good works, but to the evil. Wilt thou then not be afraid of the power? do that which is good, and thou shalt have praise of the same: 4 For he is the minister of God to thee for good. But if thou do that which is evil, be afraid; for he beareth not the sword in vain: for he is the minister of God, a revenger to execute wrath upon him that doeth evil. 2JO 1:10 If there come any unto you, and bring not this doctrine, receive him not into your house, neither bid him God speed: 11 For he that biddeth him God speed is partaker of his evil deeds. EZR 7:23 Whatsoever is commanded by the God of heaven, let it be diligently done for the house of the God of heaven: for why should there be wrath against the realm of the king and

his sons? 25 And thou, Ezra, after the wisdom of thy God, that is in thine hand, set magistrates and judges, which may judge all the people that are beyond the river, all such as know the laws of thy God; and teach ye them that know them not. 26 And whosoever will not do the law of thy God, and the law of the king, let judgment be executed speedily upon him, whether it be unto death, or to banishment, or to confiscation of goods, or to imprisonment. 27 Blessed be the Lord God of our fathers, which hath put such a thing as this in the king's heart, to beautify the house of the Lord which is in Jerusalem: 28 And hath extended mercy unto me before the king, and his counsellers, and before all the king's mighty princes. And I was strengthened as the hand of the Lord my God was upon me, and I gathered together out of Israel chief men to go up with me. REV 17:12 And the ten horns which thou sawest are ten kings, which have received no kingdom as yet; but receive power as kings one hour with the beast. 16 And the ten horns which thou sawest upon the beast, these shall hate the whore, and shall make her desolate and naked, and shall eat her flesh, and burn her with fire. 17 For God hath put in their hearts to fulfil his will, and to agree, and give their kingdom unto the beast, until the words of God shall be fulfilled. NEH 13:15 In those days saw I in Judah some treading wine presses on the sabbath, and bringing in sheaves, and lading asses; as also wine, grapes, and figs, and all manner of burdens, which they brought into Jerusalem on the sabbath day: and I testified against them in the day wherein they sold victuals. 17 Then I contended with the nobles of Judah, and said unto them, What evil thing is this that ye do, and profane the sabbath day? 21 Then I testified against them, and said unto them, Why lodge ye about the wall? if ye do so again, I will lay hands on you. From that time forth came they no more on the sabbath. 22 And I commanded the Levites that they should cleanse themselves, and that they should come and keep the gates, to sanctify the sabbath day. Remember me, O my God, concerning this also, and spare me according to the greatness of thy mercy. 25 And I contended with them, and cursed them, and smote certain of them, and plucked off their hair, and made them swear by God, saying, Ye shall not give your daughters unto their sons, nor take their daughters unto your sons, or for yourselves. 30 Thus cleansed I them from all strangers, and appointed the wards of the priests and the Levites, every one in his business. 2KI 23:5 And he put down the idolatrous priests, whom the kings of Judah had ordained to burn incense in the high places in the cities of Judah, and in the places round about Jerusalem; them also that burned incense unto Baal, to the sun, and to the moon, and to the planets, and to all the host of heaven. 6 And he brought out the grove from the house of the Lord, without Jerusalem, unto the brook Kidron, and burned it at the brook Kidron, and stamped it small to powder, and cast the powder thereof upon the graves of the children of the people. 9 Nevertheless the priests of the high places came not up to the altar of the Lord in Jerusalem, but they did eat of the unleavened bread among their brethren. 20 And he slew all the

Chapter XXI

Of Religious Worship, and the Sabbath Day

I. The light of nature shows that there is a God, who has lordship and sovereignty over all, is good, and does good unto all, and is therefore to be feared, loved, praised, called upon, trusted in, and served, with all the heart, and with all the soul, and with all the might.[1] But the acceptable way of worshipping the true God is instituted by Himself, and so limited by His own revealed will, that He may not be worshipped according to the imaginations and devices of men, or the suggestions of Satan, under

---

[1] ROM 1:20 For the invisible things of him from the creation of the world are clearly seen, being understood by the things that are made, even his eternal power and Godhead; so that they are without excuse. ACT 17:24 God that made the world and all things therein, seeing that he is Lord of heaven and earth, dwelleth not in temples made with hands. PSA 119:68 Thou art good, and doest good; teach me thy statutes. JER 10:7 Who would not fear thee, O King of nations? for to thee doth it appertain: forasmuch as among all the wise men of the nations, and in all their kingdoms, there is none like unto thee. PSA 31:23 O love the Lord, all ye his saints: for the Lord preserveth the faithful, and plentifully rewardeth the proud doer. PSA 18:3 I will call upon the Lord, who is worthy to be praised: so shall I be saved from mine enemies. ROM 10:12 For there is no difference between the Jew and the Greek: for the same Lord over all is rich unto all that call upon him. PSA 62:8 Trust in him at all times; ye people, pour out your heart before him: God is a refuge for us. Selah. JOS 24:14 Now therefore fear the Lord, and serve him in sincerity and in truth: and put away the gods which your fathers served on the other side of the flood, and in Egypt; and serve ye the Lord. MAR 12:33 And to love him with all the heart, and with all the understanding, and with all the soul, and with all the strength, and to love his neighbour as himself, is more than all whole burnt offerings and sacrifices.

any visible representation, or any other way not prescribed in the holy Scripture.[2]

II. Religious worship is to be given to God, the Father, Son, and Holy Ghost; and to Him alone;[3] not to angels, saints, or any other creature:[4] and, since the fall, not without a Mediator; nor in the mediation of any other but of Christ alone.[5]

[2] DEU 12:32 What thing soever I command you, observe to do it: thou shalt not add thereto, nor diminish from it. MAT 15:9 But in vain they do worship me, teaching for doctrines the commandments of men. ACT 17:25 Neither is worshipped with men's hands, as though he needed any thing, seeing he giveth to all life, and breath, and all things. MAT 4:9 And saith unto him, All these things will I give thee, if thou wilt fall down and worship me. 10 Then saith Jesus unto him, Get thee hence, Satan: for it is written, Thou shalt worship the Lord thy God, and him only shalt thou serve. (see also DEU 15:1-19) EXO 20:4 Thou shalt not make unto thee any graven image, or any likeness of any thing that is in heaven above, or that is in the earth beneath, or that is in the water under the earth: 5 Thou shalt not bow down thyself to them, nor serve them: for I the Lord thy God am a jealous God, visiting the iniquity of the fathers upon the children unto the third and fourth generation of them that hate me; 6 And shewing mercy unto thousands of them that love me, and keep my commandments.

[3] MAT 4:10 Then saith Jesus unto him, Get thee hence, Satan: for it is written, Thou shalt worship the Lord thy God, and him only shalt thou serve. JOH 5:23 That all men should honour the Son, even as they honour the Father. He that honoureth not the Son honoureth not the Father which hath sent him. 2CO 13:14 The grace of the Lord Jesus Christ, and the love of God, and the communion of the Holy Ghost, be with you all. Amen.

[4] COL 2:18 Let no man beguile you of your reward in a voluntary humility and worshipping of angels, intruding into those things which he hath not seen, vainly puffed up by his fleshly mind. REV 19:10 And I fell at his feet to worship him. And he said unto me, See thou do it not: I am thy fellowservant, and of thy brethren that have the testimony of Jesus: worship God: for the testimony of Jesus is the spirit of prophecy. ROM 1:25 Who changed the truth of God into a lie, and worshipped and served the creature more than the Creator, who is blessed for ever. Amen.

[5] JOH 14:6 Jesus saith unto him, I am the way, the truth, and the life: no man cometh unto the Father, but by me. 1TI 2:5 For there is one God, and one mediator between God and men, the man Christ Jesus. EPH 2:18 For through him we both have access by one Spirit unto the Father. COL 3:17 And

III. Prayer, with thanksgiving, being one special part of religious worship,[6] is by God required of all men:[7] and, that it may be accepted, it is to be made in the name of the Son,[8] by the help of His Spirit,[9] according to His will,[10] with understanding, reverence, humility, fervency, faith, love and perseverance;[11] and, if vocal, in a known tongue.[12]

whatsoever ye do in word or deed, do all in the name of the Lord Jesus, giving thanks to God and the Father by him.

[6] PHI 4:6 Be careful for nothing; but in every thing by prayer and supplication with thanksgiving let your requests be made known unto God.

[7] PSA 65:6 Which by his strength setteth fast the mountains; being girded with power.

[8] JOH 14:13 And whatsoever ye shall ask in my name, that will I do, that the Father may be glorified in the Son. 14 If ye shall ask any thing in my name, I will do it. 1PE 2:5 Ye also, as lively stones, are built up a spiritual house, an holy priesthood, to offer up spiritual sacrifices, acceptable to God by Jesus Christ.

[9] ROM 8:26 Likewise the Spirit also helpeth our infirmities: for we know not what we should pray for as we ought: but the Spirit itself maketh intercession for us with groanings which cannot be uttered.

[10] 1JO 5:14 And this is the confidence that we have in him, that, if we ask any thing according to his will, he heareth us.

[11] PSA 47:7 For God is the King of all the earth: sing ye praises with understanding. ECC 5:1 Keep thy foot when thou goest to the house of God, and be more ready to hear, than to give the sacrifice of fools: for they consider not that they do evil. 2 Be not rash with thy mouth, and let not thine heart be hasty to utter any thing before God: for God is in heaven, and thou upon earth: therefore let thy words be few. HEB 12:28 Wherefore we receiving a kingdom which cannot be moved, let us have grace, whereby we may serve God acceptably with reverence and godly fear. GEN 17:27 And all the men of his house, born in the house, and bought with money of the stranger, were circumcised with him. JAM 5:16 Confess your faults one to another, and pray one for another, that ye may be healed. The effectual fervent prayer of a righteous man availeth much. JAM 1:6 But let him ask in faith, nothing wavering. For he that wavereth is like a wave of the sea driven with the wind and tossed. 7 For let not that man think that he shall receive any thing of the Lord. MAR 11:24 Therefore I say unto you, What things soever ye desire, when ye pray, believe that ye receive them, and ye shall have them. MAT 6:12 And forgive us our debts, as we forgive our debtors. 14 For if ye forgive men their trespasses, your heavenly Father will also forgive you: 15 But if ye forgive not men their trespasses, neither will your Father forgive your

IV. Prayer is to be made for things lawful;[13] and for all sorts of men living, or that shall live hereafter:[14] but not for the dead,[15] nor for those of whom it may be known that they have sinned the sin unto death.[16]

trespasses. COL 4:2 Continue in prayer, and watch in the same with thanksgiving. EPH 6:18 Praying always with all prayer and supplication in the Spirit, and watching thereunto with all perseverance and supplication for all saints.

[12] 1CO 14:14 For if I pray in an unknown tongue, my spirit prayeth, but my understanding is unfruitful.

[13] 1JO 5:14 And this is the confidence that we have in him, that, if we ask any thing according to his will, he heareth us.

[14] 1TI 2:1 I exhort therefore, that, first of all, supplications, prayers, intercessions, and giving of thanks, be made for all men; 2 For kings, and for all that are in authority; that we may lead a quiet and peaceable life in all godliness and honesty. JOH 17:20 Neither pray I for these alone, but for them also which shall believe on me through their word. 2SA 7:29 Therefore now let it please thee to bless the house of thy servant, that it may continue for ever before thee: for thou, O Lord God, hast spoken it: and with thy blessing let the house of thy servant be blessed for ever. RUT 4:12 And let thy house be like the house of Pharez, whom Tamar bare unto Judah, of the seed which the Lord shall give thee of this young woman.

[15] 2SA 12:21 Then said his servants unto him, What thing is this that thou hast done? thou didst fast and weep for the child, while it was alive; but when the child was dead, thou didst rise and eat bread. 22 And he said, While the child was yet alive, I fasted and wept: for I said, Who can tell whether God will be gracious to me, that the child may live? 23 But now he is dead, wherefore should I fast? can I bring him back again? I shall go to him, but he shall not return to me. LUK 16:25 But Abraham said, Son, remember that thou in thy lifetime receivedst thy good things, and likewise Lazarus evil things: but now he is comforted, and thou art tormented. 26 And beside all this, between us and you there is a great gulf fixed: so that they which would pass from hence to you cannot; neither can they pass to us, that would come from thence. REV 14:13 And I heard a voice from heaven saying unto me, Write, Blessed are the dead which die in the Lord from henceforth: Yea, saith the Spirit, that they may rest from their labours; and their works do follow them.

[16] 1JO 5:16 If any man see his brother sin a sin which is not unto death, he shall ask, and he shall give him life for them that sin not unto death. There is a sin unto death: I do not say that he shall pray for it.

V. The reading of the Scriptures with godly fear,[17] the sound preaching[18] and conscionable hearing of the Word, in obedience unto God, with understanding, faith and reverence,[19] singing of psalms with grace in the heart;[20] as also, the due administration and worthy receiving of the sacraments instituted by Christ, are all parts of the ordinary religious worship of God:[21] beside religious oaths,[22] vows,[23] solemn

[17] ACT 15:21 For Moses of old time hath in every city them that preach him, being read in the synagogues every sabbath day. REV 1:3 Blessed is he that readeth, and they that hear the words of this prophecy, and keep those things which are written therein: for the time is at hand.

[18] 2TI 4:2 Preach the word; be instant in season, out of season; reprove, rebuke, exhort with all longsuffering and doctrine.

[19] JAM 1:22 But be ye doers of the word, and not hearers only, deceiving your own selves. ACT 10:33 Immediately therefore I sent to thee; and thou hast well done that thou art come. Now therefore are we all here present before God, to hear all things that are commanded thee of God. MAT 13:19 When any one heareth the word of the kingdom, and understandeth it not, then cometh the wicked one, and catcheth away that which was sown in his heart. This is he which received seed by the way side. HEB 4:2 For unto us was the gospel preached, as well as unto them: but the word preached did not profit them, not being mixed with faith in them that heard it. ISA 66:2 For all those things hath mine hand made, and those things have been, saith the Lord: but to this man will I look, even to him that is poor and of a contrite spirit, and trembleth at my word.

[20] COL 3:16 Let the word of Christ dwell in you richly in all wisdom; teaching and admonishing one another in psalms and hymns and spiritual songs, singing with grace in your hearts to the Lord. EPH 5:19 Speaking to yourselves in psalms and hymns and spiritual songs, singing and making melody in your heart to the Lord. JAM 5:13 Is any among you afflicted? let him pray. Is any merry? let him sing psalms.

[21] MAT 28:19 Go ye therefore, and teach all nations, baptizing them in the name of the Father, and of the Son, and of the Holy Ghost. 1CO 11:23 For I have received of the Lord that which also I delivered unto you, That the Lord Jesus the same night in which he was betrayed took bread: 24 And when he had given thanks, he brake it, and said, Take, eat: this is my body, which is broken for you: this do in remembrance of me. 25 After the same manner also he took the cup, when he had supped, saying, This cup is the new testament in my blood: this do ye, as oft as ye drink it, in remembrance of me. 26 For as often as ye eat this bread,

fastings,[24] and thanksgivings upon special occasions,[25] which are, in their several times and seasons, to be used in an holy and religious manner.[26]

and drink this cup, ye do shew the Lord's death till he come. 27 Wherefore whosoever shall eat this bread, and drink this cup of the Lord, unworthily, shall be guilty of the body and blood of the Lord. 28 But let a man examine himself, and so let him eat of that bread, and drink of that cup. ACT 2:42 And they continued stedfastly in the apostles' doctrine and fellowship, and in breaking of bread, and in prayers.

[22] DEU 6:13 Thou shalt fear the Lord thy God, and serve him, and shalt swear by his name. NEH 10:29 They clave to their brethren, their nobles, and entered into a curse, and into an oath, to walk in God's law, which was given by Moses the servant of God, and to observe and do all the commandments of the Lord our Lord, and his judgments and his statutes.

[23] ISA 19:21 And the Lord shall be known to Egypt, and the Egyptians shall know the Lord in that day, and shall do sacrifice and oblation; yea, they shall vow a vow unto the Lord, and perform it. ECC 5:4 When thou vowest a vow unto God, defer not to pay it; for he hath no pleasure in fools: pay that which thou hast vowed. 5 Better is it that thou shouldest not vow, than that thou shouldest vow and not pay.

[24] JOE 2:12 Therefore also now, saith the Lord, turn ye even to me with all your heart, and with fasting, and with weeping, and with mourning. EST 4:16 Go, gather together all the Jews that are present in Shushan, and fast ye for me, and neither eat nor drink three days, night or day: I also and my maidens will fast likewise; and so will I go in unto the king, which is not according to the law: and if I perish, I perish. MAT 9:15 And Jesus said unto them, Can the children of the bridechamber mourn, as long as the bridegroom is with them? but the days will come, when the bridegroom shall be taken from them, and then shall they fast. 1CO 7:5 Defraud ye not one the other, except it be with consent for a time, that ye may give yourselves to fasting and prayer; and come together again, that Satan tempt you not for your incontinency.

[25] (PSA 107 throughout) EST 9:22 As the days wherein the Jews rested from their enemies, and the month which was turned unto them from sorrow to joy, and from mourning into a good day: that they should make them days of feasting and joy, and of sending portions one to another, and gifts to the poor.

[26] HEB 12:28 Wherefore we receiving a kingdom which cannot be moved, let us have grace, whereby we may serve God acceptably with reverence and godly fear.

VI. Neither prayer, nor any other part of religious worship, is now, under the Gospel, either tied unto, or made more acceptable by any place in which it is performed, or towards which it is directed:[27] but God is to be worshipped everywhere,[28] in spirit and truth;[29] as, in private families[30]

[27] JOH 4:21 Jesus saith unto her, Woman, believe me, the hour cometh, when ye shall neither in this mountain, nor yet at Jerusalem, worship the Father.

[28] MAL 1:11 For from the rising of the sun even unto the going down of the same my name shall be great among the Gentiles; and in every place incense shall be offered unto my name, and a pure offering: for my name shall be great among the heathen, saith the Lord of hosts. 1TI 2:8 I will therefore that men pray every where, lifting up holy hands, without wrath and doubting.

[29] JOH 4:23 But the hour cometh, and now is, when the true worshippers shall worship the Father in spirit and in truth: for the Father seeketh such to worship him. 24 God is a Spirit: and they that worship him must worship him in spirit and in truth.

[30] JER 10:25 Pour out thy fury upon the heathen that know thee not, and upon the families that call not on thy name: for they have eaten up Jacob, and devoured him, and consumed him, and have made his habitation desolate. DEU 6:6 And these words, which I command thee this day, shall be in thine heart: 7 And thou shalt teach them diligently unto thy children, and shalt talk of them when thou sittest in thine house, and when thou walkest by the way, and when thou liest down, and when thou risest up. JOB 1:5 And it was so, when the days of their feasting were gone about, that Job sent and sanctified them, and rose up early in the morning, and offered burnt offerings according to the number of them all: for Job said, It may be that my sons have sinned, and cursed God in their hearts. Thus did Job continually. 2SA 6:18 And as soon as David had made an end of offering burnt offerings and peace offerings, he blessed the people in the name of the Lord of hosts. 20 Then David returned to bless his household. And Michal the daughter of Saul came out to meet David, and said, How glorious was the king of Israel to-day, who uncovered himself to-day in the eyes of the handmaids of his servants, as one of the vain fellows shamelessly uncovereth himself! 1PE 3:7 Likewise, ye husbands, dwell with them according to knowledge, giving honour unto the wife, as unto the weaker vessel, and as being heirs together of the grace of life; that your prayers be not hindered. ACT 10:2 A devout man, and one that feared God with all his house, which gave much alms to the people, and prayed to God alway.

daily,[31] and in secret, each one by himself;[32] so, more solemnly in the public assemblies, which are not carelessly or wilfully to be neglected, or forsaken, when God, by His Word or providence, calls thereunto.[33]

VII. As it is the law of nature, that, in general, a due proportion of time be set apart for the worship of God; so, in His Word, by a positive, moral, and perpetual commandment binding all men in all ages, He has particularly appointed one day in seven, for a Sabbath, to be kept holy unto Him:[34] which, from the beginning of the world to the resurrection of Christ, was the last day of the week: and, from the resurrection of Christ,

[31] MAT 6:11 Give us this day our daily bread.

[32] MAT 6:6 But thou, when thou prayest, enter into thy closet, and when thou hast shut thy door, pray to thy Father which is in secret; and thy Father which seeth in secret shall reward thee openly. EPH 6:18 Praying always with all prayer and supplication in the Spirit, and watching thereunto with all perseverance and supplication for all saints.

[33] ISA 56:6 Also the sons of the stranger, that join themselves to the Lord, to serve him, and to love the name of the Lord, to be his servants, every one that keepeth the sabbath from polluting it, and taketh hold of my covenant; 7 Even them will I bring to my holy mountain, and make them joyful in my house of prayer: their burnt offerings and their sacrifices shall be accepted upon mine altar; for mine house shall be called an house of prayer for all people. HEB 10:25 Not forsaking the assembling of ourselves together, as the manner of some is; but exhorting one another: and so much the more, as ye see the day approaching. PRO 1:20 Wisdom crieth without; she uttereth her voice in the streets: 21 She crieth in the chief place of concourse, in the openings of the gates: in the city she uttereth her words, saying. 24 Because I have called, and ye refused; I have stretched out my hand, and no man regarded. 8:34 Blessed is the man that heareth me, watching daily at my gates, waiting at the posts of my doors. ACT 13:42 And when the Jews were gone out of the synagogue, the Gentiles besought that these words might be preached to them the next sabbath. LUK 4:16 And he came to Nazareth, where he had been brought up: and, as his custom was, he went into the synagogue on the sabbath day, and stood up for to read. ACT 2:42 And they continued stedfastly in the apostles' doctrine and fellowship, and in breaking of bread, and in prayers.

[34] EXO 20:8 Remember the sabbath day, to keep it holy. 10 But the seventh day is the sabbath of the Lord thy God: in it thou shalt not do any work, thou, nor thy son, nor thy daughter, thy manservant, nor thy maidservant, nor thy cattle, nor

was changed into the first day of the week,[35] which, in Scripture, is called the Lord's Day,[36] and is to be continued to the end of the world, as the Christian Sabbath.[37]

VIII. This Sabbath is then kept holy unto the Lord, when men, after a due preparing of their hearts, and ordering of their common affairs

---

thy stranger that is within thy gates: 11 For in six days the Lord made heaven and earth, the sea, and all that in them is, and rested the seventh day: wherefore the Lord blessed the sabbath day, and hallowed it. ISA 56:2 Blessed is the man that doeth this, and the son of man that layeth hold on it; that keepeth the sabbath from polluting it, and keepeth his hand from doing any evil. 4 For thus saith the Lord unto the eunuchs that keep my sabbaths, and choose the things that please me, and take hold of my covenant. 6 Also the sons of the stranger, that join themselves to the Lord, to serve him, and to love the name of the Lord, to be his servants, every one that keepeth the sabbath from polluting it, and taketh hold of my covenant; 7 Even them will I bring to my holy mountain, and make them joyful in my house of prayer: their burnt offerings and their sacrifices shall be accepted upon mine altar; for mine house shall be called an house of prayer for all people.

[35] GEN 2:2 And on the seventh day God ended his work which he had made; and he rested on the seventh day from all his work which he had made. 3 And God blessed the seventh day, and sanctified it: because that in it he had rested from all his work which God created and made. 1CO 16:1 Now concerning the collection for the saints, as I have given order to the churches of Galatia, even so do ye. 2 Upon the first day of the week let every one of you lay by him in store, as God hath prospered him, that there be no gatherings when I come. ACT 20:7 And upon the first day of the week, when the disciples came together to break bread, Paul preached unto them, ready to depart on the morrow; and continued his speech until midnight.

[36] REV 1:10 I was in the Spirit on the Lord's day, and heard behind me a great voice, as of a trumpet.

[37] EXO 20:8 Remember the sabbath day, to keep it holy. 10 But the seventh day is the sabbath of the Lord thy God: in it thou shalt not do any work, thou, nor thy son, nor thy daughter, thy manservant, nor thy maidservant, nor thy cattle, nor thy stranger that is within thy gates. MAT 5:17 Think not that I am come to destroy the law, or the prophets: I am not come to destroy, but to fulfil. 18 For verily I say unto you, Till heaven and earth pass, one jot or one tittle shall in no wise pass from the law, till all be fulfilled.

beforehand, do not only observe an holy rest, all the day, from their own works, words, and thoughts about their worldly employments and recreations,[38] but also are taken up, the whole time, in the public and

---

[38] EXO 20:8 Remember the sabbath day, to keep it holy. EXO 16:23 And he said unto them, This is that which the Lord hath said, To-morrow is the rest of the holy sabbath unto the Lord: bake that which ye will bake to-day, and seethe that ye will seethe; and that which remaineth over lay up for you to be kept until the morning. 25 And Moses said, Eat that to-day; for to-day is a sabbath unto the Lord: to-day ye shall not find it in the field. 26 Six days ye shall gather it; but on the seventh day, which is the sabbath, in it there shall be none. 29 See, for that the Lord hath given you the sabbath, therefore he giveth you on the sixth day the bread of two days; abide ye every man in his place, let no man go out of his place on the seventh day. 30 So the people rested on the seventh day. 31:15 Six days may work be done; but in the seventh is the sabbath of rest, holy to the Lord: whosoever doeth any work in the sabbath day, he shall surely be put to death. 16 Wherefore the children of Israel shall keep the sabbath, to observe the sabbath throughout their generations, for a perpetual covenant. 17 It is a sign between me and the children of Israel for ever: for in six days the Lord made heaven and earth, and on the seventh day he rested, and was refreshed. ISA 58:13 If thou turn away thy foot from the sabbath, from doing thy pleasure on my holy day; and call the sabbath a delight, the holy of the Lord, honourable; and shalt honour him, not doing thine own ways, nor finding thine own pleasure, nor speaking thine own words. NEH 13:15 In those days saw I in Judah some treading wine presses on the sabbath, and bringing in sheaves, and lading asses; as also wine, grapes, and figs, and all manner of burdens, which they brought into Jerusalem on the sabbath day: and I testified against them in the day wherein they sold victuals. 16 There dwelt men of Tyre also therein, which brought fish, and all manner of ware, and sold on the sabbath unto the children of Judah, and in Jerusalem. 17 Then I contended with the nobles of Judah, and said unto them, What evil thing is this that ye do, and profane the sabbath day? 18 Did not your fathers thus, and did not our God bring all this evil upon us, and upon this city? yet ye bring more wrath upon Israel by profaning the sabbath. 19 And it came to pass, that when the gates of Jerusalem began to be dark before the sabbath, I commanded that the gates should be shut, and charged that they should not be opened till after the sabbath: and some of my servants set I at the gates, that there should no burden be brought in on the sabbath day. 21 Then I testified against them, and said unto them, Why lodge ye about the wall? if ye do so again, I will lay hands on you. From that time forth came they no more on the sabbath. 22 And I commanded the Levites that they should cleanse themselves, and that they should come and keep the gates, to

private exercises of His worship, and in the duties of necessity and mercy.[39]

sanctify the sabbath day. Remember me, O my God, concerning this also, and spare me according to the greatness of thy mercy.

[39] ISA 58:13 If thou turn away thy foot from the sabbath, from doing thy pleasure on my holy day; and call the sabbath a delight, the holy of the Lord, honourable; and shalt honour him, not doing thine own ways, nor finding thine own pleasure, nor speaking thine own words.

Chapter XXII
Of Lawful Oaths and Vows

I. A lawful oath is part of religious worship,[1] wherein, upon just occasion, the person swearing solemnly calls God to witness what he asserts, or promises, and to judge him according to the truth or falsehood of what he swears.[2]

II. The name of God only is that by which men ought to swear, and therein it is to be used with all holy fear and reverence.[3] Therefore, to swear vainly, or rashly, by that glorious and dreadful Name; or, to swear at all by any other thing, is sinful, and to be abhorred.[4] Yet, as in matters of

---

[1] DEU 10:20 Thou shalt fear the Lord thy God; him shalt thou serve, and to him shalt thou cleave, and swear by his name.

[2] EXO 20:7 Thou shalt not take the name of the Lord thy God in vain; for the Lord will not hold him guiltless that taketh his name in vain. LEV 19:12 And ye shall not swear by my name falsely, neither shalt thou profane the name of thy God: I am the Lord. 2CO 1:23 Moreover I call God for a record upon my soul, that to spare you I came not as yet unto Corinth. 2CH 6:22 If a man sin against his neighbour, and an oath be laid upon him to make him swear, and the oath come before thine altar in this house; 23 Then hear thou from heaven, and do, and judge thy servants, by requiting the wicked, by recompensing his way upon his own head; and by justifying the righteous, by giving him according to his righteousness.

[3] DEU 6:13 Thou shalt fear the Lord thy God, and serve him, and shalt swear by his name.

[4] EXO 20:7 Thou shalt not take the name of the Lord thy God in vain; for the Lord will not hold him guiltless that taketh his name in vain. JER 5:7 How shall I pardon thee for this? thy children have forsaken me, and sworn by them that are

weight and moment, an oath is warranted by the Word of God, under the New Testament as well as under the old;[5] so a lawful oath, being imposed by lawful authority, in such matters, ought to be taken.[6]

III. Whosoever takes an oath ought duly to consider the weightiness of so solemn an act, and therein to avouch nothing but what he is fully persuaded is the truth:[7] neither may any man bind himself by oath to any thing but what is good and just, and what he believes so to be, and what he is able and resolved to perform.[8] *[Yet it is a sin to refuse an oath touching*

no gods: when I had fed them to the full, they then committed adultery, and assembled themselves by troops in the harlots' houses. MAT 5:34 But I say unto you, Swear not at all; neither by heaven; for it is God's throne. 37 But let your communication be, Yea, yea; Nay, nay: for whatsoever is more than these cometh of evil. JAM 5:12 But above all things, my brethren, swear not, neither by heaven, neither by the earth, neither by any other oath: but let your yea be yea; and your nay, nay; lest ye fall into condemnation.

[5] HEB 6:16 For men verily swear by the greater: and an oath for confirmation is to them an end of all strife. 2CO 1:23 Moreover I call God for a record upon my soul, that to spare you I came not as yet unto Corinth. ISA 65:16 That he who blesseth himself in the earth shall bless himself in the God of truth; and he that sweareth in the earth shall swear by the God of truth; because the former troubles are forgotten, and because they are hid from mine eyes.

[6] 1KI 8:31 If any man trespass against his neighbour, and an oath be laid upon him to cause him to swear, and the oath come before thine altar in this house. NEH 13:25 And I contended with them, and cursed them, and smote certain of them, and plucked off their hair, and made them swear by God, saying, Ye shall not give your daughters unto their sons, nor take their daughters unto your sons, or for yourselves. EZR 10:5 Then arose Ezra, and made the chief priests, the Levites, and all Israel, to swear that they should do according to this word. And they sware.

[7] EXO 20:7 Thou shalt not take the name of the Lord thy God in vain; for the Lord will not hold him guiltless that taketh his name in vain. JER 4:2 And thou shalt swear, The Lord liveth, in truth, in judgment, and in righteousness; and the nations shall bless themselves in him, and in him shall they glory.

[8] GEN 24:2 And Abraham said unto his eldest servant of his house, that ruled over all that he had, Put, I pray thee, thy hand under my thigh: 3 And I will make thee swear by the Lord, the God of heaven, and the God of the earth, that thou shalt not take a wife unto my son of the daughters of the Canaanites, among

any thing that is good and just, being imposed by lawful authority.] 9 IV. An oath is to be taken in the plain and common sense of the words, without equivocation, or mental reservation.[10] It cannot oblige to sin; but in any thing not sinful, being taken, it binds to performance, although to a man's own hurt.[11] Nor is it to be violated, although made to

whom I dwell. 5 And the servant said unto him, Peradventure the woman will not be willing to follow me unto this land: must I needs bring thy son again unto the land from whence thou camest? 6 And Abraham said unto him, Beware thou that thou bring not my son thither again. 8 And if the woman will not be willing to follow thee, then thou shalt be clear from this my oath: only bring not my son thither again. 9 And the servant put his hand under the thigh of Abraham his master, and sware to him concerning that matter.

[9] NUM 5:19 And the priest shall charge her by an oath, and say unto the woman, If no man have lain with thee, and if thou hast not gone aside to uncleanness with another instead of thy husband, be thou free from this bitter water that causeth the curse. 21 Then the priest shall charge the woman with an oath of cursing, and the priest shall say unto the woman, The Lord make thee a curse and an oath among thy people, when the Lord doth make thy thigh to rot, and thy belly to swell. NEH 5:12 Then said they, We will restore them, and will require nothing of them; so will we do as thou sayest. Then I called the priests, and took an oath of them, that they should do according to this promise. EXO 22:7 If a man shall deliver unto his neighbour money or stuff to keep, and it be stolen out of the man's house; if the thief be found, let him pay double. 8 If the thief be not found, then the master of the house shall be brought unto the judges, to see whether he have put his hand unto his neighbour's goods. 9 For all manner of trespass, whether it be for ox, for ass, for sheep, for raiment, or for any manner of lost thing, which another challengeth to be his, the cause of both parties shall come before the judges; and whom the judges shall condemn, he shall pay double unto his neighbour. 10 If a man deliver unto his neighbour an ass, or an ox, or a sheep, or any beast, to keep; and it die, or be hurt, or driven away, no man seeing it: 11 Then shall an oath of the Lord be between them both, that he hath not put his hand unto his neighbour's goods; and the owner of it shall accept thereof, and he shall not make it good.

[10] JER 4:2 And thou shalt swear, The Lord liveth, in truth, in judgment, and in righteousness; and the nations shall bless themselves in him, and in him shall they glory. PSA 24:4 He that hath clean hands, and a pure heart; who hath not lifted up his soul unto vanity, nor sworn deceitfully.

[11] 1SA 25:22 So and more also do God unto the enemies of David, if I leave

heretics, or infidels.¹²

V. A vow is of the like nature with a promissory oath, and ought to be made with the like religious care, and to be performed with the like faithfulness.¹³

---

of all that pertain to him by the morning light any that pisseth against the wall. 32 And David said to Abigail, Blessed be the Lord God of Israel, which sent thee this day to meet me: 33 And blessed be thy advice, and blessed be thou, which hast kept me this day from coming to shed blood, and from avenging myself with mine own hand. 34 For in very deed, as the Lord God of Israel liveth, which hath kept me back from hurting thee, except thou hadst hasted and come to meet me, surely there had not been left unto Nabal by the morning light any that pisseth against the wall. PSA 15:4 In whose eyes a vile person is contemned; but he honoureth them that fear the Lord. He that sweareth to his own hurt, and changeth not.

¹² EZE 17:16 As I live, saith the Lord God, surely in the place where the king dwelleth that made him king, whose oath he despised, and whose covenant he brake, even with him in the midst of Babylon he shall die. 18 Seeing he despised the oath by breaking the covenant, when, lo, he had given his hand, and hath done all these things, he shall not escape. 19 Therefore thus saith the Lord God; As I live, surely mine oath that he hath despised, and my covenant that he hath broken, even it will I recompense upon his own head. JOS 9:18 And the children of Israel smote them not, because the princes of the congregation had sworn unto them by the Lord God of Israel. And all the congregation murmured against the princes. 19 But all the princes said unto all the congregation, We have sworn unto them by the Lord God of Israel: now therefore we may not touch them. 2SA 21:1 Then there was a famine in the days of David three years, year after year; and David inquired of the Lord. And the Lord answered, It is for Saul, and for his bloody house, because he slew the Gibeonites.

¹³ ISA 19:21 And the Lord shall be known to Egypt, and the Egyptians shall know the Lord in that day, and shall do sacrifice and oblation; yea, they shall vow a vow unto the Lord, and perform it. ECC 5:4 When thou vowest a vow unto God, defer not to pay it; for he hath no pleasure in fools: pay that which thou hast vowed. 5 Better is it that thou shouldest not vow, than that thou shouldest vow and not pay. 6 Suffer not thy mouth to cause thy flesh to sin; neither say thou before the angel, that it was an error: wherefore should God be angry at thy voice, and destroy the work of thine hands? PSA 61:8 So will I sing praise unto thy name for ever, that I may daily perform my vows. 66:13 I will go into thy house with burnt

VI. It is not to be made to any creature, but to God alone:[14] and that it may be accepted, it is to be made voluntarily, out of faith, and conscience of duty, in way of thankfulness for mercy received, or for the obtaining of what we want, whereby we more strictly bind ourselves to necessary duties: or, to other things, so far and so long as they may fitly conduce thereunto.[15]

offerings: I will pay thee my vows, 14 Which my lips have uttered, and my mouth hath spoken, when I was in trouble.

[14] PSA 76:11 Vow, and pay unto the Lord your God: let all that be round about him bring presents unto him that ought to be feared. JER 44:25 Thus saith the Lord of hosts, the God of Israel, saying; Ye and your wives have both spoken with your mouths, and fulfilled with your hand, saying, We will surely perform our vows that we have vowed, to burn incense to the queen of heaven, and to pour out drink offerings unto her: ye will surely accomplish your vows, and surely perform your vows. 26 Therefore hear ye the word of the Lord, all Judah that dwell in the land of Egypt; Behold, I have sworn by my great name, saith the Lord, that my name shall no more be named in the mouth of any man of Judah in all the land of Egypt, saying, The Lord God liveth.

[15] DEU 23:21 When thou shalt vow a vow unto the Lord thy God, thou shalt not slack to pay it: for the Lord thy God will surely require it of thee; and it would be sin in thee. 22 But if thou shalt forbear to vow, it shall be no sin in thee. 23 That which is gone out of thy lips thou shalt keep and perform; even a freewill offering, according as thou hast vowed unto the Lord thy God, which thou hast promised with thy mouth. PSA 50:14 Offer unto God thanksgiving; and pay thy vows unto the most High. GEN 28:20 And Jacob vowed a vow, saying, If God will be with me, and will keep me in this way that I go, and will give me bread to eat, and raiment to put on, 21 So that I come again to my father's house in peace; then shall the Lord be my God: 22 And this stone, which I have set for a pillar, shall be God's house: and of all that thou shalt give me I will surely give the tenth unto thee. 1SA 1:11 And she vowed a vow, and said, O Lord of hosts, if thou wilt indeed look on the affliction of thine handmaid, and remember me, and not forget thine handmaid, but wilt give unto thine handmaid a man child, then I will give him unto the Lord all the days of his life, and there shall no razor come upon his head. PSA 66:13 I will go into thy house with burnt offerings: I will pay thee my vows, 14 Which my lips have uttered, and my mouth hath spoken, when I was in trouble. 132:2 How he sware unto the Lord, and vowed unto the mighty God of Jacob; 3 Surely I will not come into the tabernacle of my house, nor go up into my

VII. No man may vow to do any thing forbidden in the Word of God, or what would hinder any duty therein commanded, or which is not in his own power, and for the performance whereof he has no promise of ability from God.[16] In which respects, popish monastical vows of perpetual single life, professed poverty, and regular obedience, are so far from being degrees of higher perfection, that they are superstitious and sinful snares, in which no Christian may entangle himself.[17]

bed; 4 I will not give sleep to mine eyes, or slumber to mine eyelids, 5 Until I find out a place for the Lord, an habitation for the mighty God of Jacob.

[16] ACT 23:12 And when it was day, certain of the Jews banded together, and bound themselves under a curse, saying that they would neither eat nor drink till they had killed Paul. 14 And they came to the chief priests and elders, and said, We have bound ourselves under a great curse, that we will eat nothing until we have slain Paul. MAR 6:26 And the king was exceeding sorry; yet for his oath's sake, and for their sakes which sat with him, he would not reject her. NUM 30:5 But if her father disallow her in the day that he heareth; not any of her vows, or of her bonds wherewith she hath bound her soul, shall stand: and the Lord shall forgive her, because her father disallowed her. 8 But if her husband disallowed her on the day that he heard it; then he shall make her vow which she vowed, and that which she uttered with her lips, wherewith she bound her soul, of none effect: and the Lord shall forgive her. 12 But if her husband hath utterly made them void on the day he heard them; then whatsoever proceeded out of her lips concerning her vows, or concerning the bond of her soul, shall not stand: her husband hath made them void; and the Lord shall forgive her. 13 Every vow, and every binding oath to afflict the soul, her husband may establish it, or her husband may make it void.

[17] MAT 19:11 But he said unto them, All men cannot receive this saying, save they to whom it is given. 12 For there are some eunuchs, which were so born from their mother's womb: and there are some eunuchs, which were made eunuchs of men: and there be eunuchs, which have made themselves eunuchs for the kingdom of heaven's sake. He that is able to receive it, let him receive it. 1CO 7:2 Nevertheless, to avoid fornication, let every man have his own wife, and let every woman have her own husband. 9 But if they cannot contain, let them marry: for it is better to marry than to burn. EPH 4:28 Let him that stole steal no more: but rather let him labour, working with his hands the thing which is good, that he may have to give to him that needeth. 1PE 4:2 That he no longer should live the rest of his time in the flesh to the lusts of men, but to the will of God. 1CO 7:23 Ye are bought with a price; be not ye the servants of men.

Chapter XXIII
Of the Civil Magistrate

I. God, the supreme Lord and King of all the world, has ordained civil magistrates, to be, under Him, over the people, for His own glory, and the public good: and, to this end, has armed them with the power of the sword, for the defence and encouragement of them that are good, and for the punishment of evil doers.[1]

II. It is lawful for Christians to accept and execute the office of a magistrate, when called thereunto:[2] in the managing whereof, as they ought especially to maintain piety, justice, and peace, according to the

---

[1] ROM 13:1 Let every soul be subject unto the higher powers. For there is no power but of God: the powers that be are ordained of God. 2 Whosoever therefore resisteth the power, resisteth the ordinance of God: and they that resist shall receive to themselves damnation. 3 For rulers are not a terror to good works, but to the evil. Wilt thou then not be afraid of the power? do that which is good, and thou shalt have praise of the same: 4 For he is the minister of God to thee for good. But if thou do that which is evil, be afraid; for he beareth not the sword in vain: for he is the minister of God, a revenger to execute wrath upon him that doeth evil. 1PE 2:13 Submit yourselves to every ordinance of man for the Lord's sake: whether it be to the king, as supreme; 14 Or unto governors, as unto them that are sent by him for the punishment of evildoers, and for the praise of them that do well.

[2] PRO 8:15 By me kings reign, and princes decree justice. 16 By me princes rule, and nobles, even all the judges of the earth. ROM 13:1 Let every soul be subject unto the higher powers. For there is no power but of God: the powers that be are ordained of God. 2 Whosoever therefore resisteth the power, resisteth the ordinance of God: and they that resist shall receive to themselves damnation.

wholesome laws of each commonwealth;³ so, for that end, they may lawfully, now under the New Testament, wage war, upon just and necessary occasion.⁴

III. Civil magistrates may not assume to themselves the administration of the Word and sacraments; or the power of the keys of the kingdom of heaven;⁵ *[yet he has authority, and it is his duty, to take order that unity and peace be preserved in the Church, that the truth of God be kept pure and*

---

4 For he is the minister of God to thee for good. But if thou do that which is evil, be afraid; for he beareth not the sword in vain: for he is the minister of God, a revenger to execute wrath upon him that doeth evil.

³ PSA 2:10 Be wise now therefore, O ye kings: be instructed, ye judges of the earth. 12 Kiss the Son, lest he be angry, and ye perish from the way, when his wrath is kindled but a little. Blessed are all they that put their trust in him. 1TI 2:2 For kings, and for all that are in authority; that we may lead a quiet and peaceable life in all godliness and honesty. PSA 82:3 Defend the poor and fatherless: do justice to the afflicted and needy. 4 Deliver the poor and needy: rid them out of the hand of the wicked. 2SA 23:3 The God of Israel said, the Rock of Israel spake to me, He that ruleth over men must be just, ruling in the fear of God. 1PE 2:13 Submit yourselves to every ordinance of man for the Lord's sake: whether it be to the king, as supreme.

⁴ LUK 3:14 And the soldiers likewise demanded of him, saying, And what shall we do? And he said unto them, Do violence to no man, neither accuse any falsely; and be content with your wages. ROM 13:4 For he is the minister of God to thee for good. But if thou do that which is evil, be afraid; for he beareth not the sword in vain: for he is the minister of God, a revenger to execute wrath upon him that doeth evil. MAT 8:9 For I am a man under authority, having soldiers under me: and I say to this man, Go, and he goeth; and to another, Come, and he cometh; and to my servant, Do this, and he doeth it. 10 When Jesus heard it, he marvelled, and said to them that followed, Verily I say unto you, I have not found so great faith, no, not in Israel. ACT 10:1 There was a certain man in Caesarea called Cornelius, a centurion of the band called the Italian band, 2 A devout man, and one that feared God with all his house, which gave much alms to the people, and prayed to God alway. REV 17:14 These shall make war with the Lamb, and the Lamb shall overcome them: for he is Lord of lords, and King of kings: and they that are with him are called, and chosen, and faithful. 16 And the ten horns which thou sawest upon the beast, these shall hate the whore, and shall make her desolate and naked, and shall eat her flesh, and burn her with fire.

entire, that all blasphemies and heresies be suppressed, all corruptions and abuses in worship and discipline prevented or reformed, and all the ordinances of God duly settled, administrated, and observed. [6] For the better effecting whereof, he has power to call synods, to be present at them and to

[5] 2CH 26:18 And they withstood Uzziah the king, and said unto him, It appertaineth not unto thee, Uzziah, to burn incense unto the Lord, but to the priests the sons of Aaron, that are consecrated to burn incense: go out of the sanctuary; for thou hast trespassed; neither shall it be for thine honour from the Lord God. MAT 18:17 And if he shall neglect to hear them, tell it unto the church: but if he neglect to hear the church, let him be unto thee as an heathen man and a publican. MAT 16:19 And I will give unto thee the keys of the kingdom of heaven: and whatsoever thou shalt bind on earth shall be bound in heaven: and whatsoever thou shalt loose on earth shall be loosed in heaven. 1CO 12:28 And God hath set some in the church, first apostles, secondarily prophets, thirdly teachers, after that miracles, then gifts of healings, helps, governments, diversities of tongues. 29 Are all apostles? are all prophets? are all teachers? are all workers of miracles? EPH 4:11 And he gave some, apostles; and some, prophets; and some, evangelists; and some, pastors and teachers; 12 For the perfecting of the saints, for the work of the ministry, for the edifying of the body of Christ. 1CO 4:1 Let a man so account of us, as of the ministers of Christ, and stewards of the mysteries of God. 2 Moreover it is required in stewards, that a man be found faithful. ROM 10:15 And how shall they preach, except they be sent? as it is written, How beautiful are the feet of them that preach the gospel of peace, and bring glad tidings of good things! HEB 5:4 And no man taketh this honour unto himself, but he that is called of God, as was Aaron.

[6] ISA 49:23 And kings shall be thy nursing fathers, and their queens thy nursing mothers: they shall bow down to thee with their face toward the earth, and lick up the dust of thy feet; and thou shalt know that I am the Lord: for they shall not be ashamed that wait for me. PSA 122:9 Because of the house of the Lord our God I will seek thy good. EZR 7:23 Whatsoever is commanded by the God of heaven, let it be diligently done for the house of the God of heaven: for why should there be wrath against the realm of the king and his sons? 25 And thou, Ezra, after the wisdom of thy God, that is in thine hand, set magistrates and judges, which may judge all the people that are beyond the river, all such as know the laws of thy God; and teach ye them that know them not. 26 And whosoever will not do the law of thy God, and the law of the king, let judgment be executed speedily upon him, whether it be unto death, or to banishment, or to confiscation

provide that whatsoever is transacted in them be according to the mind of God⁷] or, in the least, interfere in matters of faith. Yet, as nursing fathers, it is the duty of civil magistrates to protect the Church of our common Lord, without giving the preference to any denomination of Christians above the rest, in such a manner that all ecclesiastical persons whatever shall enjoy the full, free, and unquestioned liberty of discharging every part of their sacred functions, without violence or danger. And, as Jesus Christ has appointed a regular government and discipline in his Church, no law of any commonwealth should interfere with, let, or hinder, the due exercise thereof, among the voluntary members of any denomination of Christians, according to their own profession and belief. It is the duty of civil magistrates to protect the person and good name of all their people, in such an effectual manner as that no person be suffered, either upon pretense of religion or of infidelity, to offer any indignity, violence, abuse, or injury to any other person whatsoever: and to take order, that all religious and ecclesiastical assemblies be held without molestation or disturbance.

of goods, or to imprisonment. 27 Blessed be the Lord God of our fathers, which hath put such a thing as this in the king's heart, to beautify the house of the Lord which is in Jerusalem: 28 And hath extended mercy unto me before the king, and his counsellors, and before all the king's mighty princes. And I was strengthened as the hand of the Lord my God was upon me, and I gathered together out of Israel chief men to go up with me. LEV 24:16 And he that blasphemeth the name of the Lord, he shall surely be put to death, and all the congregation shall certainly stone him: as well the stranger, as he that is born in the land, when he blasphemeth the name of the Lord, shall be put to death. DEU 13:5 And that prophet, or that dreamer of dreams, shall be put to death; because he hath spoken to turn you away from the Lord your God, which brought you out of the land of Egypt, and redeemed you out of the house of bondage, to thrust thee out of the way which the Lord thy God commanded thee to walk in. So shalt thou put the evil away from the midst of thee. 6 If thy brother, the son of thy mother, or thy son, or thy daughter, or the wife of thy bosom, or thy friend, which is as thine own soul, entice thee secretly, saying, Let us go and serve other gods, which thou hast not known, thou, nor thy fathers. 12 If thou shalt hear say in one of thy cities, which the Lord thy God hath given thee to dwell there, saying, etc. 2KI 18:4 He removed the high places, and brake the images, and cut down the groves, and brake in pieces the

Chapter XXIII / 149

IV. It is the duty of people to pray for magistrates,[8] to honor their persons,[9] to pay them tribute or other dues,[10] to obey their lawful commands, and to be subject to their authority, for conscience' sake.[11]

brasen serpent that Moses had made: for unto those days the children of Israel did burn incense to it: and he called it Nehushtan. (1CH 13:1-8; 2KI 24:1-25) 2CH 34:33 And Josiah took away all the abominations out of all the countries that pertained to the children of Israel, and made all that were present in Israel to serve, even to serve the Lord their God. And all his days they departed not from following the Lord, the God of their fathers. 2CH 15:12 And they entered into a covenant to seek the Lord God of their fathers with all their heart and with all their soul; 13 That whosoever would not seek the Lord God of Israel should be put to death, whether small or great, whether man or woman.

[7] 2CH 19:8 Moreover in Jerusalem did Jehoshaphat set of the Levites, and of the priests, and of the chief of the fathers of Israel, for the judgment of the Lord, and for controversies, when they returned to Jerusalem. 9 And he charged them, saying, Thus shall ye do in the fear of the Lord, faithfully, and with a perfect heart. 10 And what cause soever shall come to you of your brethren that dwell in their cities, between blood and blood, between law and commandment, statutes and judgments, ye shall even warn them that they trespass not against the Lord, and so wrath come upon you, and upon your brethren: this do, and ye shall not trespass. 11 And, behold, Amariah the chief priest is over you in all matters of the Lord; and Zebadiah the son of Ishmael, the ruler of the house of Judah, for all the king's matters: also the Levites shall be officers before you. Deal courageously, and the Lord shall be with the good. (2CH 29-30) MAT 2:4 And when he had gathered all the chief priests and scribes of the people together, he demanded of them where Christ should be born. 5 And they said unto him, In Bethlehem of Judaea: for thus it is written by the prophet.

[8] 1TI 2:1 I exhort therefore, that, first of all, supplications, prayers, intercessions, and giving of thanks, be made for all men; 2 For kings, and for all that are in authority; that we may lead a quiet and peaceable life in all godliness and honesty.

[9] 1PE 2:17 Honour all men. Love the brotherhood. Fear God. Honour the king.

[10] ROM 13:6 For for this cause pay ye tribute also: for they are God's ministers, attending continually upon this very thing. 7 Render therefore to all their dues: tribute to whom tribute is due; custom to whom custom; fear to whom fear; honour to whom honour.

[11] ROM 13:5 Wherefore ye must needs be subject, not only for wrath, but

Infidelity, or difference in religion, does not make void the magistrates' just and legal authority, nor free the people from their due obedience to them:[12] from which ecclesiastical persons are not exempted,[13] much less has the Pope any power and jurisdiction over them in their dominions, or over any of their people; and, least of all, to deprive them of their dominions, or lives, if he shall judge them to be heretics, or upon any other pretence whatsoever.[14]

also for conscience sake. TIT 3:1 Put them in mind to be subject to principalities and powers, to obey magistrates, to be ready to every good work.

[12] 1PE 2:13 Submit yourselves to every ordinance of man for the Lord's sake: whether it be to the king, as supreme; 14 Or unto governors, as unto them that are sent by him for the punishment of evildoers, and for the praise of them that do well. 16 As free, and not using your liberty for a cloke of maliciousness, but as the servants of God.

[13] ROM 13:1 Let every soul be subject unto the higher powers. For there is no power but of God: the powers that be are ordained of God. 1KI 2:35 And the king put Benaiah the son of Jehoiada in his room over the host: and Zadok the priest did the king put in the room of Abiathar. ACT 25:9 But Festus, willing to do the Jews a pleasure, answered Paul, and said, Wilt thou go up to Jerusalem, and there be judged of these things before me? 10 Then said Paul, I stand at Caesar's judgment seat, where I ought to be judged: to the Jews have I done no wrong, as thou very well knowest. 11 For if I be an offender, or have committed any thing worthy of death, I refuse not to die: but if there be none of these things whereof these accuse me, no man may deliver me unto them. I appeal unto Caesar. 2PE 2:1 But there were false prophets also among the people, even as there shall be false teachers among you, who privily shall bring in damnable heresies, even denying the Lord that bought them, and bring upon themselves swift destruction. 10 But chiefly them that walk after the flesh in the lust of uncleanness, and despise government. Presumptuous are they, self-willed, they are not afraid to speak evil of dignities. 11 Whereas angels, which are greater in power and might, bring not railing accusation against them before the Lord. JUD 8 Likewise also these filthy dreamers defile the flesh, despise dominion, and speak evil of dignities. 9 Yet Michael the archangel, when contending with the devil he disputed about the body of Moses, durst not bring against him a railing accusation, but said, The Lord rebuke thee. 10 But these speak evil of those things which they know not: but what they know naturally, as brute beasts, in those things they corrupt themselves. 11 Woe unto them! for they have gone in the way

of Cain, and ran greedily after the error of Balaam for reward, and perished in the gainsaying of Core.

[14] 2TH 2:4 Who opposeth and exalteth himself above all that is called God, or that is worshipped; so that he as God sitteth in the temple of God, shewing himself that he is God. REV 13:15 And he had power to give life unto the image of the beast, that the image of the beast should both speak, and cause that as many as would not worship the image of the beast should be killed. 16 And he causeth all, both small and great, rich and poor, free and bond, to receive a mark in their right hand, or in their foreheads: 17 And that no man might buy or sell, save he that had the mark, or the name of the beast, or the number of his name.

Chapter XXIV
Of Marriage and Divorce

I. Marriage is to be between one man and one woman: neither is it lawful for any man to have more than one wife, nor for any woman to have more than one husband, at the same time.[1]

II. Marriage was ordained for the mutual help of husband and wife,[2] for the increase of mankind with a legitimate issue, and of the Church with an holy seed;[3] and for preventing of uncleanness.[4]

III. It is lawful for all sorts of people to marry, who are able with judgment to give their consent.[5] Yet it is the duty of Christians to marry

---

[1] GEN 2:24 Therefore shall a man leave his father and his mother, and shall cleave unto his wife: and they shall be one flesh. MAT 19:5 And said, For this cause shall a man leave father and mother, and shall cleave to his wife: and they twain shall be one flesh? 6 Wherefore they are no more twain, but one flesh. What therefore God hath joined together, let not man put asunder. PRO 2:17 Which forsaketh the guide of her youth, and forgetteth the covenant of her God.

[2] GEN 2:18 And the Lord God said, It is not good that the man should be alone; I will make him an help meet for him.

[3] MAL 2:15 And did not he make one? Yet had he the residue of the spirit. And wherefore one? That he might seek a godly seed. Therefore take heed to your spirit, and let none deal treacherously against the wife of his youth.

[4] 1CO 7:2 Nevertheless, to avoid fornication, let every man have his own wife, and let every woman have her own husband. 9 But if they cannot contain, let them marry: for it is better to marry than to burn.

[5] HEB 13:4 Marriage is honourable in all, and the bed undefiled: but whoremongers and adulterers God will judge. 1TI 4:3 Forbidding to marry, and commanding to abstain from meats, which God hath created to be received with

only in the Lord.⁶ And therefore such as profess the true reformed religion should not marry with infidels, papists, or other idolaters: neither should such as are godly be unequally yoked, by marrying with such as are notoriously wicked in their life, or maintain damnable heresies.⁷

thanksgiving of them which believe and know the truth. 1CO 7:36 But if any man think that he behaveth himself uncomely toward his virgin, if she pass the flower of her age, and need so require, let him do what he will, he sinneth not: let them marry. 37 Nevertheless he that standeth stedfast in his heart, having no necessity, but hath power over his own will, and hath so decreed in his heart that he will keep his virgin, doeth well. 38 So then he that giveth her in marriage doeth well; but he that giveth her not in marriage doeth better. GEN 24:57 And they said, We will call the damsel, and inquire at her mouth.

⁶ 1CO 7:39 The wife is bound by the law as long as her husband liveth; but if her husband be dead, she is at liberty to be married to whom she will; only in the Lord.

⁷ GEN 34:14 And they said unto them, We cannot do this thing, to give our sister to one that is uncircumcised; for that were a reproach unto us. EXO 34:16 And thou take of their daughters unto thy sons, and their daughters go a whoring after their gods, and make thy sons go a whoring after their gods. DEU 7:3 Neither shalt thou make marriages with them; thy daughter thou shalt not give unto his son, nor his daughter shalt thou take unto thy son. 4 For they will turn away thy son from following me, that they may serve other gods: so will the anger of the Lord be kindled against you, and destroy thee suddenly. 1KI 11:4 For it came to pass, when Solomon was old, that his wives turned away his heart after other gods: and his heart was not perfect with the Lord his God, as was the heart of David his father. NEH 13:25 And I contended with them, and cursed them, and smote certain of them, and plucked off their hair, and made them swear by God, saying, Ye shall not give your daughters unto their sons, nor take their daughters unto your sons, or for yourselves. 26 Did not Solomon king of Israel sin by these things? yet among many nations was there no king like him, who was beloved of his God, and God made him king over all Israel: nevertheless even him did outlandish women cause to sin. 27 Shall we then hearken unto you to do all this great evil, to transgress against our God in marrying strange wives? MAL 2:11 Judah hath dealt treacherously, and an abomination is committed in Israel and in Jerusalem; for Judah hath profaned the holiness of the Lord which he loved, and hath married the daughter of a strange god. 12 The Lord will cut off the man that doeth this, the master and the scholar, out of the tabernacles of Jacob, and him that offereth an offering unto the Lord of hosts. 2CO 6:14 Be ye not unequally

IV. Marriage ought not to be within the degrees of consanguinity or affinity forbidden by the Word.[8] Nor can such incestuous marriages ever be made lawful by any law of man or consent of parties, so as those persons may live together as man and wife.[9] *[The man may not marry any of his wife's kindred, nearer in blood then he may of his own: nor the woman of her husband's kindred, nearer in blood than of her own.[10]]*
V. Adultery or fornication committed after a contract, being detected before marriage, gives just occasion to the innocent party to dissolve that contract.[11] In the case of adultery after marriage, it is lawful

yoked together with unbelievers: for what fellowship hath righteousness with unrighteousness? and what communion hath light with darkness?

[8] (LEV 18) 1CO 5:1 It is reported commonly that there is fornication among you, and such fornication as is not so much as named among the Gentiles, that one should have his father's wife. AMO 2:7 That pant after the dust of the earth on the head of the poor, and turn aside the way of the meek: and a man and his father will go in unto the same maid, to profane my holy name.

[9] MAR 6:18 For John had said unto Herod, It is not lawful for thee to have thy brother's wife. LEV 18:24 Defile not ye yourselves in any of these things: for in all these the nations are defiled which I cast out before you: 25 And the land is defiled: therefore I do visit the iniquity thereof upon it, and the land itself vomiteth out her inhabitants. 26 Ye shall therefore keep my statutes and my judgments, and shall not commit any of these abominations; neither any of your own nation, nor any stranger that sojourneth among you: 27 (For all these abominations have the men of the land done, which were before you, and the land is defiled;) 28 That the land spue not you out also, when ye defile it, as it spued out the nations that were before you.

[10] LEV 20:19 And thou shalt not uncover the nakedness of thy mother's sister, nor of thy father's sister: for he uncovereth his near kin: they shall bear their iniquity. 20 And if a man shall lie with his uncle's wife, he hath uncovered his uncle's nakedness: they shall bear their sin; they shall die childless. 21 And if a man shall take his brother's wife, it is an unclean thing: he hath uncovered his brother's nakedness; they shall be childless.

[11] MAT 1:18 Now the birth of Jesus Christ was on this wise: When as his mother Mary was espoused to Joseph, before they came together, she was found with child of the Holy Ghost. 19 Then Joseph her husband, being a just man, and not willing to make her a publick example, was minded to put her away privily.

for the innocent party to sue out a divorce and, after the divorce,[12] to marry another, as if the offending party were dead.[13]

VI. Although the corruption of man be such as is apt to study arguments unduly to put asunder those whom God has joined together in marriage: yet, nothing but adultery, or such wilful desertion as can no way be remedied by the Church, or civil magistrate, is cause sufficient of dissolving the bond of marriage:[14] wherein, a public and orderly course of proceeding is to be observed; and the persons concerned in it not left to their own wills, and discretion, in their own case.[15]

---

20 But while he thought on these things, behold, the angel of the Lord appeared unto him in a dream, saying, Joseph, thou son of David, fear not to take unto thee Mary thy wife: for that which is conceived in her is of the Holy Ghost.

[12] MAT 5:31 It hath been said, Whosoever shall put away his wife, let him give her a writing of divorcement: 32 But I say unto you, That whosoever shall put away his wife, saving for the cause of fornication, causeth her to commit adultery: and whosoever shall marry her that is divorced committeth adultery.

[13] MAT 19:9 And I say unto you, Whosoever shall put away his wife, except it be for fornication, and shall marry another, committeth adultery: and whoso marrieth her which is put away doth commit adultery. ROM 7:2 For the woman which hath an husband is bound by the law to her husband so long as he liveth; but if the husband be dead, she is loosed from the law of her husband. 3 So then if, while her husband liveth, she be married to another man, she shall be called an adulteress: but if her husband be dead, she is free from that law; so that she is no adulteress, though she be married to another man.

[14] MAT 19:8 He saith unto them, Moses because of the hardness of your hearts suffered you to put away your wives: but from the beginning it was not so. 9 And I say unto you, Whosoever shall put away his wife, except it be for fornication, and shall marry another, committeth adultery: and whoso marrieth her which is put away doth commit adultery. 1CO 7:15 But if the unbelieving depart, let him depart. A brother or a sister is not under bondage in such cases: but God hath called us to peace. MAT 19:6 Wherefore they are no more twain, but one flesh. What therefore God hath joined together, let not man put asunder.

[15] DEU 24:1 When a man hath taken a wife, and married her, and it come to pass that she find no favour in his eyes, because he hath found some uncleanness in her: then let him write her a bill of divorcement, and give it in her hand, and send her out of his house. 2 And when she is departed out of his house, she may go

and be another man's wife. 3 And if the latter husband hate her, and write her a bill of divorcement, and giveth it in her hand, and sendeth her out of his house; or if the latter husband die, which took her to be his wife; 4 Her former husband, which sent her away, may not take her again to be his wife, after that she is defiled; for that is abomination before the Lord: and thou shalt not cause the land to sin, which the Lord thy God giveth thee for an inheritance.

Chapter XXV
Of the Church

I. The catholic or universal Church, which is invisible, consists of the whole number of the elect, that have been, are, or shall be gathered into one, under Christ the Head thereof; and is the spouse, the body, the fulness of Him that fills all in all.[1]

II. The visible Church, which is also catholic or universal under the Gospel (not confined to one nation, as before under the law), consists of all those throughout the world that profess the true religion;[2] and of their

---

[1] EPH 1:10 That in the dispensation of the fulness of times he might gather together in one all things in Christ, both which are in heaven, and which are on earth; even in him. 22 And hath put all things under his feet, and gave him to be the head over all things to the church, 23 Which is his body, the fulness of him that filleth all in all. 5:23 For the husband is the head of the wife, even as Christ is the head of the church: and he is the saviour of the body. 27 That he might present it to himself a glorious church, not having spot, or wrinkle, or any such thing; but that it should be holy and without blemish. 32 This is a great mystery: but I speak concerning Christ and the church. COL 1:18 And he is the head of the body, the church: who is the beginning, the firstborn from the dead; that in all things he might have the preeminence.

[2] 1CO 1:2 Unto the church of God which is at Corinth, to them that are sanctified in Christ Jesus, called to be saints, with all that in every place call upon the name of Jesus Christ our Lord, both theirs and ours. 1CO 12:12 For as the body is one, and hath many members, and all the members of that one body, being many, are one body: so also is Christ. 13 For by one Spirit are we all baptized into one body, whether we be Jews or Gentiles, whether we be bond or free; and have been all made to drink into one Spirit. PSA 2:8 Ask of me, and I shall give thee the

children:³ and is the kingdom of the Lord Jesus Christ,⁴ the house and family of God,⁵ out of which there is no ordinary possibility of salvation.⁶

heathen for thine inheritance, and the uttermost parts of the earth for thy possession. REV 7:9 After this I beheld, and, lo, a great multitude, which no man could number, of all nations, and kindreds, and people, and tongues, stood before the throne, and before the Lamb, clothed with white robes, and palms in their hands. ROM 15:9 And that the Gentiles might glorify God for his mercy; as it is written, For this cause I will confess to thee among the Gentiles, and sing unto thy name. 10 And again he saith, Rejoice, ye Gentiles, with his people. 11 And again, Praise the Lord, all ye Gentiles; and laud him, all ye people. 12 And again, Esaias saith, There shall be a root of Jesse, and he that shall rise to reign over the Gentiles; in him shall the Gentiles trust.

³ 1CO 7:14 For the unbelieving husband is sanctified by the wife, and the unbelieving wife is sanctified by the husband: else were your children unclean; but now are they holy. ACT 2:39 For the promise is unto you, and to your children, and to all that are afar off, even as many as the Lord our God shall call. EZE 16:20 Moreover thou hast taken thy sons and thy daughters, whom thou hast borne unto me, and these hast thou sacrificed unto them to be devoured. Is this of thy whoredoms a small matter, 21 That thou hast slain my children, and delivered them to cause them to pass through the fire for them? ROM 11:16 For if the firstfruit be holy, the lump is also holy: and if the root be holy, so are the branches. GEN 3:15 And I will put enmity between thee and the woman, and between thy seed and her seed; it shall bruise thy head, and thou shalt bruise his heel. 17:7 And I will establish my covenant between me and thee and thy seed after thee in their generations for an everlasting covenant, to be a God unto thee, and to thy seed after thee.

⁴ MAT 13:47 Again, the kingdom of heaven is like unto a net, that was cast into the sea, and gathered of every kind. ISA 9:7 Of the increase of his government and peace there shall be no end, upon the throne of David, and upon his kingdom, to order it, and to establish it with judgment and with justice from henceforth even for ever. The zeal of the Lord of hosts will perform this.

⁵ EPH 2:19 Now therefore ye are no more strangers and foreigners, but fellow citizens with the saints, and of the household of God. 3:15 Of whom the whole family in heaven and earth is named.

⁶ ACT 2:47 Praising God, and having favour with all the people. And the Lord added to the church daily such as should be saved.

III. Unto this catholic visible Church Christ has given the ministry, oracles, and ordinances of God, for the gathering and perfecting of the saints, in this life, to the end of the world: and does, by His own presence and Spirit, according to His promise, make them effectual thereunto.[7]

IV. This catholic Church has been sometimes more, sometimes less visible.[8] And particular Churches, which are members thereof, are more or less pure, according as the doctrine of the Gospel is taught and embraced, ordinances administered, and public worship performed more or less purely in them.[9]

[7] 1CO 12:28 And God hath set some in the church, first apostles, secondarily prophets, thirdly teachers, after that miracles, then gifts of healings, helps, governments, diversities of tongues. EPH 4:11 And he gave some, apostles; and some, prophets; and some, evangelists; and some, pastors and teachers; 12 For the perfecting of the saints, for the work of the ministry, for the edifying of the body of Christ: 13 Till we all come in the unity of the faith, and of the knowledge of the Son of God, unto a perfect man, unto the measure of the stature of the fulness of Christ. MAT 28:19 Go ye therefore, and teach all nations, baptizing them in the name of the Father, and of the Son, and of the Holy Ghost: 20 Teaching them to observe all things whatsoever I have commanded you: and, lo, I am with you alway, even unto the end of the world. Amen. ISA 59:21 As for me, this is my covenant with them, saith the Lord; My spirit that is upon thee, and my words which I have put in thy mouth, shall not depart out of thy mouth, nor out of the mouth of thy seed, nor out of the mouth of thy seed's seed, saith the Lord, from henceforth and for ever.

[8] ROM 11:3 Lord, they have killed thy prophets, and digged down thine altars; and I am left alone, and they seek my life. 4 But what saith the answer of God unto him? I have reserved to myself seven thousand men, who have not bowed the knee to the image of Baal. REV 12:6 And the woman fled into the wilderness, where she hath a place prepared of God, that they should feed her there a thousand two hundred and threescore days. 14 And to the woman were given two wings of a great eagle, that she might fly into the wilderness, into her place, where she is nourished for a time, and times, and half a time, from the face of the serpent.

[9] (REV 2-3 throughout) 1CO 5:6 Your glorying is not good. Know ye not that a little leaven leaveneth the whole lump? 7 Purge out therefore the old leaven, that ye may be a new lump, as ye are unleavened. For even Christ our passover is sacrificed for us.

V. The purest Churches under heaven are subject both to mixture and error;[10] and some have so degenerated, as to become no Churches of Christ, but synagogues of Satan.[11] Nevertheless, there shall be always a Church on earth to worship God according to His will.[12]

VI. There is no other head of the Church but the Lord Jesus Christ.[13] Nor can the Pope of Rome, in any sense, be head thereof. *[but is that Antichrist, that man of sin, and son of perdition, that exalts himself, in the Church, against Christ and all that is called God.[14]]*

[10] 1CO 13:12 For now we see through a glass, darkly; but then face to face: now I know in part; but then shall I know even as also I am known. MAT 13:24-30, 47 Again, the kingdom of heaven is like unto a net, that was cast into the sea, and gathered of every kind.

[11] REV 18:2 And he cried mightily with a strong voice, saying, Babylon the great is fallen, is fallen, and is become the habitation of devils, and the hold of every foul spirit, and a cage of every unclean and hateful bird. ROM 11:18 Boast not against the branches. But if thou boast, thou bearest not the root, but the root thee. 19 Thou wilt say then, The branches were broken off, that I might be graffed in. 20 Well; because of unbelief they were broken off, and thou standest by faith. Be not highminded, but fear: 21 For if God spared not the natural branches, take heed lest he also spare not thee. 22 Behold therefore the goodness and severity of God: on them which fell, severity; but toward thee, goodness, if thou continue in his goodness: otherwise thou also shalt be cut off.

[12] MAT 16:18 And I say also unto thee, That thou art Peter, and upon this rock I will build my church; and the gates of hell shall not prevail against it. PSA 72:17 His name shall endure for ever: his name shall be continued as long as the sun: and men shall be blessed in him: all nations shall call him blessed. 102:28 The children of thy servants shall continue, and their seed shall be established before thee. MAT 28:19 Go ye therefore, and teach all nations, baptizing them in the name of the Father, and of the Son, and of the Holy Ghost: 20 Teaching them to observe all things whatsoever I have commanded you: and, lo, I am with you alway, even unto the end of the world. Amen.

[13] COL 1:18 And he is the head of the body, the church: who is the beginning, the firstborn from the dead; that in all things he might have the preeminence. EPH 1:22 And hath put all things under his feet, and gave him to be the head over all things to the church.

[14] MAT 23:8 But be not ye called Rabbi: for one is your Master, even Christ; and all ye are brethren. 9 And call no man your father upon the earth: for one is

your Father, which is in heaven. 10 Neither be ye called masters: for one is your Master, even Christ. 2TH 2:3 Let no man deceive you by any means: for that day shall not come, except there come a falling away first, and that man of sin be revealed, the son of perdition; 4 Who opposeth and exalteth himself above all that is called God, or that is worshipped; so that he as God sitteth in the temple of God, shewing himself that he is God. 8 And then shall that Wicked be revealed, whom the Lord shall consume with the spirit of his mouth, and shall destroy with the brightness of his coming: 9 Even him, whose coming is after the working of Satan with all power and signs and lying wonders. REV 13:6 And he opened his mouth in blasphemy against God, to blaspheme his name, and his tabernacle, and them that dwell in heaven.

Chapter XXVI
Of the Communion of Saints

I. All saints, that are united to Jesus Christ their Head, by His Spirit, and by faith, have fellowship with Him in His grace, sufferings, death, resurrection, and glory:[1] and, being united to one another in love, they have communion in each other's gifts and graces,[2] and are obliged to the

---

[1] 1JO 1:3 That which we have seen and heard declare we unto you, that ye also may have fellowship with us: and truly our fellowship is with the Father, and with his Son Jesus Christ. EPH 3:16 That he would grant you, according to the riches of his glory, to be strengthened with might by his Spirit in the inner man; 17 That Christ may dwell in your hearts by faith; that ye, being rooted and grounded in love, 18 May be able to comprehend with all saints what is the breadth, and length, and depth, and height; 19 And to know the love of Christ, which passeth knowledge, that ye might be filled with all the fulness of God. JOH 1:16 And of his fulness have all we received, and grace for grace. EPH 2:5 Even when we were dead in sins, hath quickened us together with Christ, (by grace ye are saved;) 6 And hath raised us up together, and made us sit together in heavenly places in Christ Jesus. PHI 3:10 That I may know him, and the power of his resurrection, and the fellowship of his sufferings, being made conformable unto his death. ROM 6:5 For if we have been planted together in the likeness of his death, we shall be also in the likeness of his resurrection: 6 Knowing this, that our old man is crucified with him, that the body of sin might be destroyed, that henceforth we should not serve sin. 2TI 2:12 If we suffer, we shall also reign with him: if we deny him, he also will deny us.

[2] EPH 4:15 But speaking the truth in love, may grow up into him in all things, which is the head, even Christ: 16 From whom the whole body fitly joined together and compacted by that which every joint supplieth, according to the effectual working in the measure of every part, maketh increase of the body unto

performance of such duties, public and private, as do conduce to their mutual good, both in the inward and outward man.³

II. Saints by profession are bound to maintain an holy fellowship and communion in the worship of God, and in performing such other spiritual services as tend to their mutual edification;⁴ as also in relieving each other in outward things, according to their several abilities and

the edifying of itself in love. 1CO 12:7 But the manifestation of the Spirit is given to every man to profit withal. 1CO 3:21 Therefore let no man glory in men. For all things are yours; 22 Whether Paul, or Apollos, or Cephas, or the world, or life, or death, or things present, or things to come; all are yours; 23 And ye are Christ's; and Christ is God's. COL 2:19 And not holding the Head, from which all the body by joints and bands having nourishment ministered, and knit together, increaseth with the increase of God.

³ 1TH 5:11 Wherefore comfort yourselves together, and edify one another, even as also ye do. 14 Now we exhort you, brethren, warn them that are unruly, comfort the feebleminded, support the weak, be patient toward all men. ROM 1:11 For I long to see you, that I may impart unto you some spiritual gift, to the end ye may be established; 12 That is, that I may be comforted together with you by the mutual faith both of you and me. 14 I am debtor both to the Greeks, and to the Barbarians; both to the wise, and to the unwise. 1JO 3:16 Hereby perceive we the love of God, because he laid down his life for us: and we ought to lay down our lives for the brethren. 17 But whoso hath this world's good, and seeth his brother have need, and shutteth up his bowels of compassion from him, how dwelleth the love of God in him? 18 My little children, let us not love in word, neither in tongue; but in deed and in truth. GAL 6:10 As we have therefore opportunity, let us do good unto all men, especially unto them who are of the household of faith.

⁴ HEB 10:24 And let us consider one another to provoke unto love and to good works: 25 Not forsaking the assembling of ourselves together, as the manner of some is; but exhorting one another: and so much the more, as ye see the day approaching. ACT 2:42 And they continued stedfastly in the apostles' doctrine and fellowship, and in breaking of bread, and in prayers. 46 And they, continuing daily with one accord in the temple, and breaking bread from house to house, did eat their meat with gladness and singleness of heart. ISA 2:3 And many people shall go and say, Come ye, and let us go up to the mountain of the Lord, to the house of the God of Jacob; and he will teach us of his ways, and we will walk in his paths: for out of Zion shall go forth the law, and the word of the Lord from

necessities. Which communion, as God offers opportunity, is to be extended unto all those who, in every place, call upon the name of the Lord Jesus.[5]

III. This communion which the saints have with Christ, does not make them in any wise partakers of the substance of His Godhead; or to be equal with Christ in any respect: either of which to affirm is impious and blasphemous.[6] Nor does their communion one with another, as saints, take away, or infringe the title or propriety which each man has in his goods and possessions.[7]

Jerusalem. 1CO 11:20 When ye come together therefore into one place, this is not to eat the Lord's supper.

[5] ACT 2:44 And all that believed were together, and had all things common; 45 And sold their possessions and goods, and parted them to all men, as every man had need. 1JO 3:17 But whoso hath this world's good, and seeth his brother have need, and shutteth up his bowels of compassion from him, how dwelleth the love of God in him? (2CO 8-9) ACT 11:29 Then the disciples, every man according to his ability, determined to send relief unto the brethren which dwelt in Judaea: 30 Which also they did, and sent it to the elders by the hands of Barnabas and Saul.

[6] COL 1:18 And he is the head of the body, the church: who is the beginning, the firstborn from the dead; that in all things he might have the preeminence. 19 For it pleased the Father that in him should all fulness dwell. 1CO 8:6 But to us there is but one God, the Father, of whom are all things, and we in him; and one Lord Jesus Christ, by whom are all things, and we by him. ISA 42:8 I am the Lord: that is my name: and my glory will I not give to another, neither my praise to graven images. 1TI 6:15 Which in his times he shall shew, who is the blessed and only Potentate, the King of kings, and Lord of lords; 16 Who only hath immortality, dwelling in the light which no man can approach unto; whom no man hath seen, nor can see: to whom be honour and power everlasting. Amen. PSA 45:7 Thou lovest righteousness, and hatest wickedness: therefore God, thy God, hath anointed thee with the oil of gladness above thy fellows. HEB 1:8 But unto the Son he saith, Thy throne, O God, is for ever and ever: a sceptre of righteousness is the sceptre of thy kingdom. 9 Thou hast loved righteousness, and hated iniquity; therefore God, even thy God, hath anointed thee with the oil of gladness above thy fellows.

[7] EXO 20:15 Thou shalt not steal. EPH 4:28 Let him that stole steal no more:

but rather let him labour, working with his hands the thing which is good, that he may have to give to him that needeth. ACT 5:4 While it remained, was it not thine own? and after it was sold, was it not in thine own power? why hast thou conceived this thing in thine heart? thou hast not lied unto men, but unto God.

Chapter XXVII
Of the Sacraments

I. Sacraments are holy signs and seals of the covenant of grace,[1] immediately instituted by God,[2] to represent Christ and His benefits; and to confirm our interest in Him:[3] as also, to put a visible difference

---

[1] ROM 4:11 And he received the sign of circumcision, a seal of the righteousness of the faith which he had yet being uncircumcised: that he might be the father of all them that believe, though they be not circumcised; that righteousness might be imputed unto them also. GEN 17:7 And I will establish my covenant between me and thee and thy seed after thee in their generations for an everlasting covenant, to be a God unto thee, and to thy seed after thee. 10 This is my covenant, which ye shall keep, between me and you and thy seed after thee; Every man child among you shall be circumcised.
[2] MAT 28:19 Go ye therefore, and teach all nations, baptizing them in the name of the Father, and of the Son, and of the Holy Ghost. 1CO 11:23 For I have received of the Lord that which also I delivered unto you, That the Lord Jesus the same night in which he was betrayed took bread.
[3] 1CO 10:16 The cup of blessing which we bless, is it not the communion of the blood of Christ? The bread which we break, is it not the communion of the body of Christ? 11:25 After the same manner also he took the cup, when he had supped, saying, This cup is the new testament in my blood: this do ye, as oft as ye drink it, in remembrance of me. 26 For as often as ye eat this bread, and drink this cup, ye do shew the Lord's death till he come. GAL 3:27 For as many of you as have been baptized into Christ have put on Christ. 3:17 And this I say, that the covenant, that was confirmed before of God in Christ, the law, which was four hundred and thirty years after, cannot disannul, that it should make the promise of none effect.

between those that belong unto the Church and the rest of the world;[4] and solemnly to engage them to the service of God in Christ, according to His Word.[5]

II. There is, in every sacrament, a spiritual relation, or sacramental union, between the sign and the thing signified: whence it comes to pass, that the names and effects of the one are attributed to the other.[6]

III. The grace which is exhibited in or by the sacraments rightly used, is not conferred by any power in them; neither does the efficacy of a sacrament depend upon the piety or intention of him that does administer it:[7] but upon the work of the Spirit,[8] and the word of institution, which

---

[4] ROM 15:8 Now I say that Jesus Christ was a minister of the circumcision for the truth of God, to confirm the promises made unto the fathers. EXO 12:48 And when a stranger shall sojourn with thee, and will keep the passover to the Lord, let all his males be circumcised, and then let him come near and keep it; and he shall be as one that is born in the land: for no uncircumcised person shall eat thereof. GEN 34:14 And they said unto them, We cannot do this thing, to give our sister to one that is uncircumcised; for that were a reproach unto us.

[5] ROM 6:3 Know ye not, that so many of us as were baptized into Jesus Christ were baptized into his death? 4 Therefore we are buried with him by baptism into death: that like as Christ was raised up from the dead by the glory of the Father, even so we also should walk in newness of life. 1CO 10:16 The cup of blessing which we bless, is it not the communion of the blood of Christ? The bread which we break, is it not the communion of the body of Christ? 21 Ye cannot drink the cup of the Lord, and the cup of devils: ye cannot be partakers of the Lord's table, and of the table of devils.

[6] GEN 17:10 This is my covenant, which ye shall keep, between me and you and thy seed after thee; Every man child among you shall be circumcised. MAT 26:27 And he took the cup, and gave thanks, and gave it to them, saying, Drink ye all of it; 28 For this is my blood of the new testament, which is shed for many for the remission of sins. TIT 3:5 Not by works of righteousness which we have done, but according to his mercy he saved us, by the washing of regeneration, and renewing of the Holy Ghost.

[7] ROM 2:28 For he is not a Jew, which is one outwardly; neither is that circumcision, which is outward in the flesh: 29 But he is a Jew, which is one inwardly; and circumcision is that of the heart, in the spirit, and not in the letter; whose praise is not of men, but of God. 1PE 3:21 The like figure whereunto even

contains, together with a precept authorizing the use thereof, a promise of benefit to worthy receivers.[9]

IV. There are only two sacraments ordained by Christ our Lord in the Gospel; that is to say, Baptism, and the Supper of the Lord: neither of which may be dispensed by any, but by a minister of the Word lawfully ordained.[10]

V. The sacraments of the Old Testament in regard to the spiritual things thereby signified and exhibited, were, for substance, the same with those of the new.[11]

baptism doth also now save us (not the putting away of the filth of the flesh, but the answer of a good conscience toward God,) by the resurrection of Jesus Christ.

[8] MAT 3:11 I indeed baptize you with water unto repentance: but he that cometh after me is mightier than I, whose shoes I am not worthy to bear: he shall baptize you with the Holy Ghost, and with fire. 1CO 12:13 For by one Spirit are we all baptized into one body, whether we be Jews or Gentiles, whether we be bond or free; and have been all made to drink into one Spirit.

[9] MAT 26:27 And he took the cup, and gave thanks, and gave it to them, saying, Drink ye all of it; 28 For this is my blood of the new testament, which is shed for many for the remission of sins. 28:19 Go ye therefore, and teach all nations, baptizing them in the name of the Father, and of the Son, and of the Holy Ghost: 20 Teaching them to observe all things whatsoever I have commanded you: and, lo, I am with you alway, even unto the end of the world. Amen.

[10] MAT 28:19 Go ye therefore, and teach all nations, baptizing them in the name of the Father, and of the Son, and of the Holy Ghost. 1CO 11:20 When ye come together therefore into one place, this is not to eat the Lord's supper. 23 For I have received of the Lord that which also I delivered unto you, That the Lord Jesus the same night in which he was betrayed took bread. 1CO 4:1 Let a man so account of us, as of the ministers of Christ, and stewards of the mysteries of God. HEB 5:4 And no man taketh this honour unto himself, but he that is called of God, as was Aaron.

[11] 1CO 10:1 Moreover, brethren, I would not that ye should be ignorant, how that all our fathers were under the cloud, and all passed through the sea; 2 And were all baptized unto Moses in the cloud and in the sea; 3 And did all eat the same spiritual meat; 4 And did all drink the same spiritual drink: for they drank of that spiritual Rock that followed them: and that Rock was Christ.

Chapter XXVIII
Of Baptism

I. Baptism is a sacrament of the New Testament, ordained by Jesus Christ,[1] not only for the solemn admission of the party baptized into the visible Church;[2] but also to be unto him a sign and seal of the covenant of grace,[3] of his ingrafting into Christ,[4] of regeneration,[5] of remission of sins,[6] and of his giving up unto God, through Jesus Christ, to walk in the

---

[1] MAT 28:19 Go ye therefore, and teach all nations, baptizing them in the name of the Father, and of the Son, and of the Holy Ghost.

[2] 1CO 12:13 For by one Spirit are we all baptized into one body, whether we be Jews or Gentiles, whether we be bond or free; and have been all made to drink into one Spirit.

[3] ROM 4:11 And he received the sign of circumcision, a seal of the righteousness of the faith which he had yet being uncircumcised: that he might be the father of all them that believe, though they be not circumcised; that righteousness might be imputed unto them also. COL 2:11 In whom also ye are circumcised with the circumcision made without hands, in putting off the body of the sins of the flesh by the circumcision of Christ: 12 Buried with him in baptism, wherein also ye are risen with him through the faith of the operation of God, who hath raised him from the dead.

[4] GAL 3:27 For as many of you as have been baptized into Christ have put on Christ. ROM 6:5 For if we have been planted together in the likeness of his death, we shall be also in the likeness of his resurrection.

[5] TIT 3:5 Not by works of righteousness which we have done, but according to his mercy he saved us, by the washing of regeneration, and renewing of the Holy Ghost.

[6] MAR 1:4 John did baptize in the wilderness, and preach the baptism of repentance for the remission of sins.

newness of life.[7] Which sacrament is, by Christ's own appointment, to be continued in His Church until the end of the world.[8]

II. The outward element to be used in this sacrament is water, wherewith the party is to be baptized, in the name of the Father, and of the Son, and of the Holy Ghost, by a minister of the Gospel, lawfully called thereunto.[9]

III. Dipping of the person into the water is not necessary; but Baptism is rightly administered by pouring, or sprinkling water upon the person.[10]

[7] ROM 6:3 Know ye not, that so many of us as were baptized into Jesus Christ were baptized into his death? 4 Therefore we are buried with him by baptism into death: that like as Christ was raised up from the dead by the glory of the Father, even so we also should walk in newness of life.

[8] MAT 28:19 Go ye therefore, and teach all nations, baptizing them in the name of the Father, and of the Son, and of the Holy Ghost.

[9] MAT 3:11 I indeed baptize you with water unto repentance: but he that cometh after me is mightier than I, whose shoes I am not worthy to bear: he shall baptize you with the Holy Ghost, and with fire. JOH 1:33 And I knew him not: but he that sent me to baptize with water, the same said unto me, Upon whom thou shalt see the Spirit descending, and remaining on him, the same is he which baptizeth with the Holy Ghost. MAT 28:19 Go ye therefore, and teach all nations, baptizing them in the name of the Father, and of the Son, and of the Holy Ghost: 20 Teaching them to observe all things whatsoever I have commanded you: and, lo, I am with you alway, even unto the end of the world. Amen.

[10] HEB 9:10 Which stood only in meats and drinks, and divers washings, and carnal ordinances, imposed on them until the time of reformation. 19 For when Moses had spoken every precept to all the people according to the law, he took the blood of calves and of goats, with water, and scarlet wool, and hyssop, and sprinkled both the book, and all the people, 20 Saying, This is the blood of the testament which God hath enjoined unto you. 21 Moreover he sprinkled with blood both the tabernacle, and all the vessels of the ministry. 22 And almost all things are by the law purged with blood; and without shedding of blood is no remission. ACT 2:41 Then they that gladly received his word were baptized: and the same day there were added unto them about three thousand souls. 16:33 And he took them the same hour of the night, and washed their stripes; and was baptized, he and all his, straightway. MAR 7:4 And when they come from the market, except they wash, they eat not. And many other things there be, which

IV. Not only those that do actually profess faith in and obedience unto Christ,[11] but also the infants of one, or both, believing parents, are to be baptized.[12]

they have received to hold, as the washing of cups, and pots, brasen vessels, and of tables.
   [11] MAR 16:15 And he said unto them, Go ye into all the world, and preach the gospel to every creature. 16 He that believeth and is baptized shall be saved; but he that believeth not shall be damned. ACT 8:37 And Philip said, If thou believest with all thine heart, thou mayest. And he answered and said, I believe that Jesus Christ is the Son of God. 38 And he commanded the chariot to stand still: and they went down both into the water, both Philip and the eunuch; and he baptized him.
   [12] GEN 17:7 And I will establish my covenant between me and thee and thy seed after thee in their generations for an everlasting covenant, to be a God unto thee, and to thy seed after thee. 9 And God said unto Abraham, Thou shalt keep my covenant therefore, thou, and thy seed after thee in their generations. GAL 3:9 So then they which be of faith are blessed with faithful Abraham. 14 That the blessing of Abraham might come on the Gentiles through Jesus Christ; that we might receive the promise of the Spirit through faith. COL 2:11 In whom also ye are circumcised with the circumcision made without hands, in putting off the body of the sins of the flesh by the circumcision of Christ: 12 Buried with him in baptism, wherein also ye are risen with him through the faith of the operation of God, who hath raised him from the dead. ACT 2:38 Then Peter said unto them, Repent, and be baptized every one of you in the name of Jesus Christ for the remission of sins, and ye shall receive the gift of the Holy Ghost. 39 For the promise is unto you, and to your children, and to all that are afar off, even as many as the Lord our God shall call. ROM 4:11 And he received the sign of circumcision, a seal of the righteousness of the faith which he had yet being uncircumcised: that he might be the father of all them that believe, though they be not circumcised; that righteousness might be imputed unto them also: 12 And the father of circumcision to them who are not of the circumcision only, but who also walk in the steps of that faith of our father Abraham, which he had being yet uncircumcised. 1CO 7:14 For the unbelieving husband is sanctified by the wife, and the unbelieving wife is sanctified by the husband: else were your children unclean; but now are they holy. MAT 28:19 Go ye therefore, and teach all nations, baptizing them in the name of the Father, and of the Son, and of the Holy Ghost. MAR 10:13 And they brought young children to him, that he should

V. Although it is a great sin to contemn or neglect this ordinance,[13] yet grace and salvation are not so inseparably annexed unto it, as that no person can be regenerated, or saved, without it:[14] or, that all that are baptized are undoubtedly regenerated.[15]

touch them: and his disciples rebuked those that brought them. 14 But when Jesus saw it, he was much displeased, and said unto them, Suffer the little children to come unto me, and forbid them not: for of such is the kingdom of God. 15 Verily I say unto you, Whosoever shall not receive the kingdom of God as a little child, he shall not enter therein. 16 And he took them up in his arms, put his hands upon them, and blessed them. LUK 18:15 And they brought unto him also infants, that he would touch them: but when his disciples saw it, they rebuked them.

[13] LUK 7:30 But the Pharisees and lawyers rejected the counsel of God against themselves, being not baptized of him. EXO 4:24 And it came to pass by the way in the inn, that the Lord met him, and sought to kill him. 25 Then Zipporah took a sharp stone, and cut off the foreskin of her son, and cast it at his feet, and said, Surely a bloody husband art thou to me. 26 So he let him go: then she said, A bloody husband thou art, because of the circumcision.

[14] ROM 4:11 And he received the sign of circumcision, a seal of the righteousness of the faith which he had yet being uncircumcised: that he might be the father of all them that believe, though they be not circumcised; that righteousness might be imputed unto them also. ACT 10:2 A devout man, and one that feared God with all his house, which gave much alms to the people, and prayed to God alway. 4 And when he looked on him, he was afraid, and said, What is it, Lord? And he said unto him, Thy prayers and thine alms are come up for a memorial before God. 22 And they said, Cornelius the centurion, a just man, and one that feareth God, and of good report among all the nation of the Jews, was warned from God by an holy angel to send for thee into his house, and to hear words of thee. 31 And said, Cornelius, thy prayer is heard, and thine alms are had in remembrance in the sight of God. 45 And they of the circumcision which believed were astonished, as many as came with Peter, because that on the Gentiles also was poured out the gift of the Holy Ghost. 47 Can any man forbid water, that these should not be baptized, which have received the Holy Ghost as well as we?

[15] ACT 8:13 Then Simon himself believed also: and when he was baptized, he continued with Philip, and wondered, beholding the miracles and signs which were done. 23 For I perceive that thou art in the gall of bitterness, and in the bond of iniquity.

VI. The efficacy of Baptism is not tied to that moment of time wherein it is administered;[16] yet, notwithstanding, by the right use of this ordinance, the grace promised is not only offered, but really exhibited, and conferred, by the Holy Ghost, to such (whether of age or infants) as that grace belongs unto, according to the counsel of God's own will, in His appointed time.[17]

VII. The sacrament of Baptism is but once to be administered unto any person.[18]

[16] JOH 3:5 Jesus answered, Verily, verily, I say unto thee, Except a man be born of water and of the Spirit, he cannot enter into the kingdom of God. 8 The wind bloweth where it listeth, and thou hearest the sound thereof, but canst not tell whence it cometh, and whither it goeth: so is every one that is born of the Spirit.

[17] GAL 3:27 For as many of you as have been baptized into Christ have put on Christ. TIT 3:5 Not by works of righteousness which we have done, but according to his mercy he saved us, by the washing of regeneration, and renewing of the Holy Ghost. EPH 5:25 Husbands, love your wives, even as Christ also loved the church, and gave himself for it; 26 That he might sanctify and cleanse it with the washing of water by the word. ACT 2:38 Then Peter said unto them, Repent, and be baptized every one of you in the name of Jesus Christ for the remission of sins, and ye shall receive the gift of the Holy Ghost. 41 Then they that gladly received his word were baptized: and the same day there were added unto them about three thousand souls.

[18] TIT 3:5 Not by works of righteousness which we have done, but according to his mercy he saved us, by the washing of regeneration, and renewing of the Holy Ghost.

Chapter XXIX
Of the Lord's Supper

I. Our Lord Jesus, in the night wherein He was betrayed, instituted the sacrament of His body and blood, called the Lord's Supper, to be observed in His Church, unto the end of the world, for the perpetual remembrance of the sacrifice of Himself in His death; the sealing all benefits thereof unto true believers, their spiritual nourishment and growth in Him, their further engagement in and to all duties which they owe unto Him; and, to be a bond and pledge of their communion with Him, and with each other, as members of His mystical body.[1]

II. In this sacrament, Christ is not offered up to His Father; nor any real sacrifice made at all, for remission of sins of the quick or dead;[2] but

---

[1] 1CO 11:23 For I have received of the Lord that which also I delivered unto you, That the Lord Jesus the same night in which he was betrayed took bread: 24 And when he had given thanks, he brake it, and said, Take, eat: this is my body, which is broken for you: this do in remembrance of me. 25 After the same manner also he took the cup, when he had supped, saying, This cup is the new testament in my blood: this do ye, as oft as ye drink it, in remembrance of me. 26 For as often as ye eat this bread, and drink this cup, ye do shew the Lord's death till he come. 1CO 10:16 The cup of blessing which we bless, is it not the communion of the blood of Christ? The bread which we break, is it not the communion of the body of Christ? 17 For we being many are one bread, and one body: for we are all partakers of that one bread. 21 Ye cannot drink the cup of the Lord, and the cup of devils: ye cannot be partakers of the Lord's table, and of the table of devils. 12:13 For by one Spirit are we all baptized into one body, whether we be Jews or Gentiles, whether we be bond or free; and have been all made to drink into one Spirit.

[2] HEB 9:22 And almost all things are by the law purged with blood; and

only a commemoration of that one offering up of Himself, by Himself, upon the cross, once for all: and a spiritual oblation of all possible praise unto God, for the same:[3] so that the popish sacrifice of the mass (as they call it) is most abominably injurious to Christ's one, only sacrifice, the alone propitiation for all the sins of His elect.[4]

without shedding of blood is no remission. 25 Nor yet that he should offer himself often, as the high priest entereth into the holy place every year with blood of others; 26 For then must he often have suffered since the foundation of the world: but now once in the end of the world hath he appeared to put away sin by the sacrifice of himself. 28 So Christ was once offered to bear the sins of many; and unto them that look for him shall he appear the second time without sin unto salvation.

[3] 1CO 11:24 And when he had given thanks, he brake it, and said, Take, eat: this is my body, which is broken for you: this do in remembrance of me. 25 After the same manner also he took the cup, when he had supped, saying, This cup is the new testament in my blood: this do ye, as oft as ye drink it, in remembrance of me. 26 For as often as ye eat this bread, and drink this cup, ye do shew the Lord's death till he come. MAT 26:26 And as they were eating, Jesus took bread, and blessed it, and brake it, and gave it to the disciples, and said, Take, eat; this is my body. 27 And he took the cup, and gave thanks, and gave it to them, saying, Drink ye all of it.

[4] HEB 7:23 And they truly were many priests, because they were not suffered to continue by reason of death: 24 But this man, because he continueth ever, hath an unchangeable priesthood. 27 Who needeth not daily, as those high priests, to offer up sacrifice, first for his own sins, and then for the people's: for this he did once, when he offered up himself. 10:11 And every priest standeth daily ministering and offering oftentimes the same sacrifices, which can never take away sins: 12 But this man, after he had offered one sacrifice for sins for ever, sat down on the right hand of God. 14 For by one offering he hath perfected for ever them that are sanctified. 18 Now where remission of these is, there is no more offering for sin.

[5] MAT 26:26 And as they were eating, Jesus took bread, and blessed it, and brake it, and gave it to the disciples, and said, Take, eat; this is my body. 27 And he took the cup, and gave thanks, and gave it to them, saying, Drink ye all of it; 28 For this is my blood of the new testament, which is shed for many for the remission of sins. MAR 14:22 And as they did eat, Jesus took bread, and blessed, and brake it, and gave to them, and said, Take, eat: this is my body. 23 And he took the cup, and when he had given thanks, he gave it to them: and they all drank of it.

III. The Lord Jesus has, in this ordinance, appointed His ministers to declare His word of institution to the people, to pray, and bless the elements of bread and wine, and thereby to set them apart from a common to an holy use; and to take and break the bread, to take the cup, and (they communicating also themselves) to give both to the communicants;[5] but to none who are not then present in the congregation.[6]

IV. Private masses, or receiving this sacrament by a priest, or any other alone;[7] as likewise, the denial of the cup to the people,[8] worshipping the elements, the lifting them up, or carrying them about, for adoration,

24 And he said unto them, This is my blood of the new testament, which is shed for many. LUK 22:19 And he took bread, and gave thanks, and brake it, and gave unto them, saying, This is my body which is given for you: this do in remembrance of me. 20 Likewise also the cup after supper, saying, This cup is the new testament in my blood, which is shed for you. 1CO 11:23 For I have received of the Lord that which also I delivered unto you, That the Lord Jesus the same night in which he was betrayed took bread: 24 And when he had given thanks, he brake it, and said, Take, eat: this is my body, which is broken for you: this do in remembrance of me. 25 After the same manner also he took the cup, when he had supped, saying, This cup is the new testament in my blood: this do ye, as oft as ye drink it, in remembrance of me. 26 For as often as ye eat this bread, and drink this cup, ye do shew the Lord's death till he come.

[6] ACT 20:7 And upon the first day of the week, when the disciples came together to break bread, Paul preached unto them, ready to depart on the morrow; and continued his speech until midnight. 1CO 11:20 When ye come together therefore into one place, this is not to eat the Lord's supper.

[7] 1CO 10:6 Now these things were our examples, to the intent we should not lust after evil things, as they also lusted.

[8] MAR 14:23 And he took the cup, and when he had given thanks, he gave it to them: and they all drank of it. 1CO 11:25 After the same manner also he took the cup, when he had supped, saying, This cup is the new testament in my blood: this do ye, as oft as ye drink it, in remembrance of me. 26 For as often as ye eat this bread, and drink this cup, ye do shew the Lord's death till he come. 27 Wherefore whosoever shall eat this bread, and drink this cup of the Lord, unworthily, shall be guilty of the body and blood of the Lord. 28 But let a man examine himself, and so let him eat of that bread, and drink of that cup. 29 For he that eateth and drinketh unworthily, eateth and drinketh damnation to himself, not discerning the Lord's body.

and the reserving them for any pretended religious use; are all contrary to the nature of this sacrament, and to the institution of Christ.[9]

V. The outward elements in this sacrament, duly set apart to the uses ordained by Christ, have such relation to Him crucified, as that, truly, yet sacramentally only, they are sometimes called by the name of the things they represent, to wit, the body and blood of Christ;[10] albeit, in substance and nature, they still remain truly and only bread and wine, as they were before.[11]

VI. That doctrine which maintains a change of the substance of bread and wine, into the substance of Christ's body and blood (commonly called transubstantiation) by consecration of a priest, or by any other way, is repugnant, not to Scripture alone, but even to common sense, and reason; overthrows the nature of the sacrament, and has been, and is, the cause of manifold superstitions; yes, of gross idolatries.[12]

---

[9] MAT 15:9 But in vain they do worship me, teaching for doctrines the commandments of men.

[10] MAT 26:26 And as they were eating, Jesus took bread, and blessed it, and brake it, and gave it to the disciples, and said, Take, eat; this is my body. 27 And he took the cup, and gave thanks, and gave it to them, saying, Drink ye all of it; 28 For this is my blood of the new testament, which is shed for many for the remission of sins.

[11] 1CO 11:26 For as often as ye eat this bread, and drink this cup, ye do shew the Lord's death till he come. 27 Wherefore whosoever shall eat this bread, and drink this cup of the Lord, unworthily, shall be guilty of the body and blood of the Lord. 28 But let a man examine himself, and so let him eat of that bread, and drink of that cup. MAT 26:29 But I say unto you, I will not drink henceforth of this fruit of the vine, until that day when I drink it new with you in my Father's kingdom.

[12] ACT 3:21 Whom the heaven must receive until the times of restitution of all things, which God hath spoken by the mouth of all his holy prophets since the world began. 1CO 11:24 And when he had given thanks, he brake it, and said, Take, eat: this is my body, which is broken for you: this do in remembrance of me. 25 After the same manner also he took the cup, when he had supped, saying, This cup is the new testament in my blood: this do ye, as oft as ye drink it, in remembrance of me. 26 For as often as ye eat this bread, and drink this cup, ye do shew the Lord's death till he come. LUK 24:6 He is not here, but is risen:

VII. Worthy receivers, outwardly partaking of the visible elements, in this sacrament,[13] do then also, inwardly by faith, really and indeed, yet not carnally and corporally but spiritually, receive and feed upon, Christ crucified, and all benefits of His death: the body and blood of Christ being then, not corporally or carnally, in, with, or under the bread and wine; yet, as really, but spiritually, present to the faith of believers in that ordinance, as the elements themselves are to their outward senses.[14]

VIII. Although ignorant and wicked men receive the outward elements in this sacrament; yet, they receive not the thing signified thereby; but, by their unworthy coming thereunto, are guilty of the body and blood of the Lord, to their own damnation. Wherefore, all ignorant and ungodly persons, as they are unfit to enjoy communion with Him, so are they unworthy of the Lord's table; and cannot, without great sin against Christ, while they remain such, partake of these holy mysteries,[15] or be admitted thereunto.[16]

---

remember how he spake unto you when he was yet in Galilee. 39 Behold my hands and my feet, that it is I myself: handle me, and see; for a spirit hath not flesh and bones, as ye see me have.

[13] 1CO 11:28 But let a man examine himself, and so let him eat of that bread, and drink of that cup.

[14] 1CO 10:16 The cup of blessing which we bless, is it not the communion of the blood of Christ? The bread which we break, is it not the communion of the body of Christ?

[15] 1CO 11:27 Wherefore whosoever shall eat this bread, and drink this cup of the Lord, unworthily, shall be guilty of the body and blood of the Lord. 28 But let a man examine himself, and so let him eat of that bread, and drink of that cup. 29 For he that eateth and drinketh unworthily, eateth and drinketh damnation to himself, not discerning the Lord's body. 2CO 6:14 Be ye not unequally yoked together with unbelievers: for what fellowship hath righteousness with unrighteousness? and what communion hath light with darkness? 15 And what concord hath Christ with Belial? or what part hath he that believeth with an infidel? 16 And what agreement hath the temple of God with idols? for ye are the temple of the living God; as God hath said, I will dwell in them, and walk in them; and I will be their God, and they shall be my people.

[16] 1CO 5:6 Your glorying is not good. Know ye not that a little leaven

leaveneth the whole lump? 7 Purge out therefore the old leaven, that ye may be a new lump, as ye are unleavened. For even Christ our passover is sacrificed for us. 13 But them that are without God judgeth. Therefore put away from among yourselves that wicked person. 2TH 3:6 Now we command you, brethren, in the name of our Lord Jesus Christ, that ye withdraw yourselves from every brother that walketh disorderly, and not after the tradition which he received of us. 14 And if any man obey not our word by this epistle, note that man, and have no company with him, that he may be ashamed. 15 Yet count him not as an enemy, but admonish him as a brother. MAT 7:6 Give not that which is holy unto the dogs, neither cast ye your pearls before swine, lest they trample them under their feet, and turn again and rend you.

Chapter XXX
Of Church Censures

I. The Lord Jesus, as king and head of His Church, has therein appointed a government, in the hand of Church officers, distinct from the civil magistrate.[1]

---

[1] ISA 9:6 For unto us a child is born, unto us a son is given: and the government shall be upon his shoulder: and his name shall be called Wonderful, Counsellor, The mighty God, The everlasting Father, The Prince of Peace. 7 Of the increase of his government and peace there shall be no end, upon the throne of David, and upon his kingdom, to order it, and to establish it with judgment and with justice from henceforth even for ever. The zeal of the Lord of hosts will perform this. 1TI 5:17 Let the elders that rule well be counted worthy of double honour, especially they who labour in the word and doctrine. 1TH 5:12 And we beseech you, brethren, to know them which labour among you, and are over you in the Lord, and admonish you. ACT 20:17 And from Miletus he sent to Ephesus, and called the elders of the church. 18 And when they were come to him, he said unto them, Ye know, from the first day that I came into Asia, after what manner I have been with you at all seasons. HEB 13:7 Remember them which have the rule over you, who have spoken unto you the word of God: whose faith follow, considering the end of their conversation. 17 Obey them that have the rule over you, and submit yourselves: for they watch for your souls, as they that must give account, that they may do it with joy, and not with grief: for that is unprofitable for you. 24 Salute all them that have the rule over you, and all the saints. They of Italy salute you. 1CO 12:28 And God hath set some in the church, first apostles, secondarily prophets, thirdly teachers, after that miracles, then gifts of healings, helps, governments, diversities of tongues. MAT 28:18 And Jesus came and spake unto them, saying, All power is given unto me in heaven and in earth. 19 Go ye therefore, and teach all nations, baptizing them in the name of the Father, and

II. To these officers the keys of the kingdom of heaven are committed; by virtue whereof, they have power, respectively, to retain, and remit sins; to shut that kingdom against the impenitent, both by the Word, and censures; and to open it unto penitent sinners, by the ministry of the Gospel; and by absolution from censures, as occasion shall require.[2]

III. Church censures are necessary, for the reclaiming and gaining of offending brethren, for deterring of others from the like offenses, for purging out of that leaven which might infect the whole lump, for vindicating the honor of Christ, and the holy profession of the Gospel, and for preventing the wrath of God, which might justly fall upon the Church, if they should suffer His covenant, and the seals thereof, to be profaned by notorious and obstinate offenders.[3]

---

of the Son, and of the Holy Ghost: 20 Teaching them to observe all things whatsoever I have commanded you: and, lo, I am with you alway, even unto the end of the world. Amen.

[2] MAT 16:19 And I will give unto thee the keys of the kingdom of heaven: and whatsoever thou shalt bind on earth shall be bound in heaven: and whatsoever thou shalt loose on earth shall be loosed in heaven. 18:17 And if he shall neglect to hear them, tell it unto the church: but if he neglect to hear the church, let him be unto thee as an heathen man and a publican. 18 Verily I say unto you, Whatsoever ye shall bind on earth shall be bound in heaven: and whatsoever ye shall loose on earth shall be loosed in heaven. JOH 20:21 Then said Jesus to them again, Peace be unto you: as my Father hath sent me, even so send I you. 22 And when he had said this, he breathed on them, and saith unto them, Receive ye the Holy Ghost: 23 Whose soever sins ye remit, they are remitted unto them; and whose soever sins ye retain, they are retained. 2CO 2:6 Sufficient to such a man is this punishment, which was inflicted of many. 7 So that contrariwise ye ought rather to forgive him, and comfort him, lest perhaps such a one should be swallowed up with overmuch sorrow. 8 Wherefore I beseech you that ye would confirm your love toward him.

[3] (1CO 5 throughout) 1TI 5:20 Them that sin rebuke before all, that others also may fear. MAT 7:6 Give not that which is holy unto the dogs, neither cast ye your pearls before swine, lest they trample them under their feet, and turn again and rend you. 1TI 1:20 Of whom is Hymenaeus and Alexander; whom I have delivered unto Satan, that they may learn not to blaspheme. 1CO 11:27 Wherefore

IV. For the better attaining of these ends, the officers of the Church are to proceed by admonition; suspension from the sacrament of the Lord's Supper for a season; and by excommunication from the Church; according to the nature of the crime, and demerit of the person.[4]

whosoever shall eat this bread, and drink this cup of the Lord, unworthily, shall be guilty of the body and blood of the Lord. 28 But let a man examine himself, and so let him eat of that bread, and drink of that cup. 29 For he that eateth and drinketh unworthily, eateth and drinketh damnation to himself, not discerning the Lord's body. 30 For this cause many are weak and sickly among you, and many sleep. 31 For if we would judge ourselves, we should not be judged. 32 But when we are judged, we are chastened of the Lord, that we should not be condemned with the world. 33 Wherefore, my brethren, when ye come together to eat, tarry one for another. 34 And if any man hunger, let him eat at home; that ye come not together unto condemnation. And the rest will I set in order when I come. JUD 23 And others save with fear, pulling them out of the fire; hating even the garment spotted by the flesh.

[4] 1TH 5:12 And we beseech you, brethren, to know them which labour among you, and are over you in the Lord, and admonish you. 2TH 3:6 Now we command you, brethren, in the name of our Lord Jesus Christ, that ye withdraw yourselves from every brother that walketh disorderly, and not after the tradition which he received of us. 14 And if any man obey not our word by this epistle, note that man, and have no company with him, that he may be ashamed. 15 Yet count him not as an enemy, but admonish him as a brother. 1CO 5:4 In the name of our Lord Jesus Christ, when ye are gathered together, and my spirit, with the power of our Lord Jesus Christ, 5 To deliver such an one unto Satan for the destruction of the flesh, that the spirit may be saved in the day of the Lord Jesus. 13 But them that are without God judgeth. Therefore put away from among yourselves that wicked person. MAT 18:17 And if he shall neglect to hear them, tell it unto the church: but if he neglect to hear the church, let him be unto thee as an heathen man and a publican. TIT 3:10 A man that is an heretick after the first and second admonition reject.

Chapter XXXI
Of Synods and Councils

I. For the better government, and further edification of the Church, there ought to be such assemblies as are commonly called synods or councils:[1] and it belongs to the overseers and other rulers of the particular Churches, by virtue of their office, and the power which Christ has given them for edification and not for destruction, to appoint such assemblies; and to convene together in them, as often as they shall judge it expedient for the good of the Church.

[II. As magistrates may lawfully call a synod of ministers, and other fit persons, to consult and advise with, about matters of religion;[2] so, if magistrates be open enemies to the Church, the ministers of Christ, of

---

[1] ACT 15:2 When therefore Paul and Barnabas had no small dissension and disputation with them, they determined that Paul and Barnabas, and certain other of them, should go up to Jerusalem unto the apostles and elders about this question. 4 And when they were come to Jerusalem, they were received of the church, and of the apostles and elders, and they declared all things that God had done with them. 6 And the apostles and elders came together for to consider of this matter.

[2] ISA 49:23 And kings shall be thy nursing fathers, and their queens thy nursing mothers: they shall bow down to thee with their face toward the earth, and lick up the dust of thy feet; and thou shalt know that I am the Lord: for they shall not be ashamed that wait for me. 1TI 2:1 I exhort therefore, that, first of all, supplications, prayers, intercessions, and giving of thanks, be made for all men; 2 For kings, and for all that are in authority; that we may lead a quiet and peaceable life in all godliness and honesty. 2CH 19:8 Moreover in Jerusalem did Jehoshaphat set of the Levites, and of the priests, and of the chief of the fathers of Israel, for the judgment of the Lord, and for controversies, when they returned to

themselves, by virtue of their office, or they, with other fit persons upon delegation from their Churches, may meet together in such assemblies.³]
II. It belongs to synods and councils, ministerially to determine controversies of faith, and cases of conscience; to set down rules and directions for the better ordering of the public worship of God, and government of his Church; to receive complaints in cases of maladministration, and authoritatively to determine the same; which decrees and determinations, if consonant to the Word of God, are to be received with reverence and submission; not only for their agreement with the Word, but also for the power whereby they are made, as being an ordinance of

Jerusalem. 9 And he charged them, saying, Thus shall ye do in the fear of the Lord, faithfully, and with a perfect heart. 10 And what cause soever shall come to you of your brethren that dwell in their cities, between blood and blood, between law and commandment, statutes and judgments, ye shall even warn them that they trespass not against the Lord, and so wrath come upon you, and upon your brethren: this do, and ye shall not trespass. 11 And, behold, Amariah the chief priest is over you in all matters of the Lord; and Zebadiah the son of Ishmael, the ruler of the house of Judah, for all the king's matters: also the Levites shall be officers before you. Deal courageously, and the Lord shall be with the good. (2CH 29-30 throughout) MAT 2:4 And when he had gathered all the chief priests and scribes of the people together, he demanded of them where Christ should be born. 5 And they said unto him, In Bethlehem of Judaea: for thus it is written by the prophet. PRO 11:14 Where no counsel is, the people fall: but in the multitude of counsellors there is safety.

³ ACT 15:2 When therefore Paul and Barnabas had no small dissension and disputation with them, they determined that Paul and Barnabas, and certain other of them, should go up to Jerusalem unto the apostles and elders about this question. 4 And when they were come to Jerusalem, they were received of the church, and of the apostles and elders, and they declared all things that God had done with them. 22 Then pleased it the apostles and elders, with the whole church, to send chosen men of their own company to Antioch with Paul and Barnabas; namely, Judas surnamed Barsabas, and Silas, chief men among the brethren: 23 And they wrote letters by them after this manner; The apostles and elders and brethren send greeting unto the brethren which are of the Gentiles in Antioch and Syria and Cilicia. 25 It seemed good unto us, being assembled with one accord, to send chosen men unto you with our beloved Barnabas and Paul.

God appointed thereunto in His Word.[4]

III. All synods or councils, since the apostles' times, whether general or particular, may err; and many have erred. Therefore they are not to be made the rule of faith, or practice; but to be used as a help in both.[5]

IV. Synods and councils are to handle, or conclude nothing, but that which is ecclesiastical: and are not to intermeddle with civil affairs which concern the commonwealth, unless by way of humble petition in cases

---

[4] ACT 15:15 And to this agree the words of the prophets; as it is written. 19 Wherefore my sentence is, that we trouble not them, which from among the Gentiles are turned to God. 24 Forasmuch as we have heard, that certain which went out from us have troubled you with words, subverting your souls, saying, Ye must be circumcised, and keep the law: to whom we gave no such commandment. 27 We have sent therefore Judas and Silas, who shall also tell you the same things by mouth. 28 For it seemed good to the Holy Ghost, and to us, to lay upon you no greater burden than these necessary things; 29 That ye abstain from meats offered to idols, and from blood, and from things strangled, and from fornication: from which if ye keep yourselves, ye shall do well. Fare ye well. 30 So when they were dismissed, they came to Antioch: and when they had gathered the multitude together, they delivered the epistle: 31 Which when they had read, they rejoiced for the consolation. 16:4 And as they went through the cities, they delivered them the decrees for to keep, that were ordained of the apostles and elders which were at Jerusalem. MAT 18:17 And if he shall neglect to hear them, tell it unto the church: but if he neglect to hear the church, let him be unto thee as an heathen man and a publican. 18 Verily I say unto you, Whatsoever ye shall bind on earth shall be bound in heaven: and whatsoever ye shall loose on earth shall be loosed in heaven. 19 Again I say unto you, That if two of you shall agree on earth as touching any thing that they shall ask, it shall be done for them of my Father which is in heaven. 20 For where two or three are gathered together in my name, there am I in the midst of them.

[5] EPH 2:20 And are built upon the foundation of the apostles and prophets, Jesus Christ himself being the chief corner stone. ACT 17:11 These were more noble than those in Thessalonica, in that they received the word with all readiness of mind, and searched the scriptures daily, whether those things were so. 1CO 2:5 That your faith should not stand in the wisdom of men, but in the power of God. 2CO 1:24 Not for that we have dominion over your faith, but are helpers of your joy: for by faith ye stand.

extraordinary; or, by way of advice, for satisfaction of conscience, if they be thereunto required by the civil magistrate.[6]

[6] LUK 12:13 And one of the company said unto him, Master, speak to my brother, that he divide the inheritance with me. 14 And he said unto him, Man, who made me a judge or a divider over you? JOH 18:36 Jesus answered, My kingdom is not of this world: if my kingdom were of this world, then would my servants fight, that I should not be delivered to the Jews: but now is my kingdom not from hence.

Chapter XXXII

Of the State of Men after Death, and of the Resurrection of the Dead

I. The bodies of men, after death, return to dust, and see corruption:[1] but their souls, which neither die nor sleep, having an immortal subsistence, immediately return to God who gave them:[2] the souls of the righteous, being then made perfect in holiness, are received into the highest heavens, where they behold the face of God, in light and glory, waiting for the full redemption of their bodies.[3] And the souls of the wicked are cast into hell, where they remain in torments and utter

---

[1] GEN 3:19 In the sweat of thy face shalt thou eat bread, till thou return unto the ground; for out of it wast thou taken: for dust thou art, and unto dust shalt thou return. ACT 13:36 For David, after he had served his own generation by the will of God, fell on sleep, and was laid unto his fathers, and saw corruption.

[2] LUK 23:43 And Jesus said unto him, Verily I say unto thee, To-day shalt thou be with me in paradise. ECC 12:7 Then shall the dust return to the earth as it was: and the spirit shall return unto God who gave it.

[3] HEB 12:23 To the general assembly and church of the firstborn, which are written in heaven, and to God the Judge of all, and to the spirits of just men made perfect. 2CO 5:1 For we know that if our earthly house of this tabernacle were dissolved, we have a building of God, an house not made with hands, eternal in the heavens. 6 Therefore we are always confident, knowing that, whilst we are at home in the body, we are absent from the Lord. 8 We are confident, I say, and willing rather to be absent from the body, and to be present with the Lord. PHI 1:23 For I am in a strait betwixt two, having a desire to depart, and to be with Christ; which is far better. ACT 3:21 Whom the heaven must receive until the times of restitution of all things, which God hath spoken by the mouth of all his holy prophets since the world began. EPH 4:10 He that descended is the same also that ascended up far above all heavens, that he might fill all things.

darkness, reserved to the judgment of the great day.⁴ Beside these two places, for souls separated from their bodies, the Scripture acknowledges none.

II. At the last day, such as are found alive shall not die, but be changed:⁵ and all the dead shall be raised up, with the selfsame bodies, and none other (although with different qualities), which shall be united again to their souls forever.⁶

III. The bodies of the unjust shall, by the power of Christ, be raised to dishonor: the bodies of the just, by His Spirit, unto honor; and be made conformable to His own glorious body.⁷

⁴ LUK 16:23 And in hell he lift up his eyes, being in torments, and seeth Abraham afar off, and Lazarus in his bosom. 24 And he cried and said, Father Abraham, have mercy on me, and send Lazarus, that he may dip the tip of his finger in water, and cool my tongue; for I am tormented in this flame. ACT 1:25 That he may take part of this ministry and apostleship, from which Judas by transgression fell, that he might go to his own place. JUD 6 And the angels which kept not their first estate, but left their own habitation, he hath reserved in everlasting chains under darkness unto the judgment of the great day. 7 Even as Sodom and Gomorrah, and the cities about them in like manner, giving themselves over to fornication, and going after strange flesh, are set forth for an example, suffering the vengeance of eternal fire. 1PE 3:19 By which also he went and preached unto the spirits in prison.

⁵ 1TH 4:17 Then we which are alive and remain shall be caught up together with them in the clouds, to meet the Lord in the air: and so shall we ever be with the Lord. 1CO 15:51 Behold, I shew you a mystery; We shall not all sleep, but we shall all be changed, 52 In a moment, in the twinkling of an eye, at the last trump: for the trumpet shall sound, and the dead shall be raised incorruptible, and we shall be changed.

⁶ JOB 19:26 And though after my skin worms destroy this body, yet in my flesh shall I see God: 27 Whom I shall see for myself, and mine eyes shall behold, and not another; though my reins be consumed within me. 1CO 15:42 So also is the resurrection of the dead. It is sown in corruption; it is raised in incorruption: 43 It is sown in dishonour; it is raised in glory: it is sown in weakness; it is raised in power: 44 It is sown a natural body; it is raised a spiritual body. There is a natural body, and there is a spiritual body.

⁷ ACT 24:15 And have hope toward God, which they themselves also allow,

that there shall be a resurrection of the dead, both of the just and unjust. JOH 5:28 Marvel not at this: for the hour is coming, in the which all that are in the graves shall hear his voice, 29 And shall come forth; they that have done good, unto the resurrection of life; and they that have done evil, unto the resurrection of damnation. 1CO 15:43 It is sown in dishonour; it is raised in glory: it is sown in weakness; it is raised in power. PHI 3:21 Who shall change our vile body, that it may be fashioned like unto his glorious body, according to the working whereby he is able even to subdue all things unto himself.

Chapter XXXIII
Of the Last Judgment

I. God has appointed a day, wherein He will judge the world, in righteousness, by Jesus Christ,[1] to whom all power and judgment is given of the Father.[2] In which day, not only the apostate angels shall be judged,[3] but likewise all persons that have lived upon earth shall appear before the tribunal of Christ, to give an account of their thoughts, words, and deeds; and to receive according to what they have done in the body, whether good or evil.[4]

---

[1] ACT 17:31 Because he hath appointed a day, in the which he will judge the world in righteousness by that man whom he hath ordained; whereof he hath given assurance unto all men, in that he hath raised him from the dead.

[2] JOH 5:27 And hath given him authority to execute judgment also, because he is the Son of man.

[3] 1CO 6:3 Know ye not that we shall judge angels? how much more things that pertain to this life? JUD 6 And the angels which kept not their first estate, but left their own habitation, he hath reserved in everlasting chains under darkness unto the judgment of the great day. 2PE 2:4 For if God spared not the angels that sinned, but cast them down to hell, and delivered them into chains of darkness, to be reserved unto judgment.

[4] 2CO 5:10 For we must all appear before the judgment seat of Christ; that every one may receive the things done in his body, according to that he hath done, whether it be good or bad. ECC 12:14 For God shall bring every work into judgment, with every secret thing, whether it be good, or whether it be evil. ROM 2:16 In the day when God shall judge the secrets of men by Jesus Christ according to my gospel. 14:10 But why dost thou judge thy brother? or why dost thou set at nought thy brother? for we shall all stand before the judgment seat of Christ. 12 So then every one of us shall give account of himself to God.

II. The end of God's appointing this day is for the manifestation of the glory of His mercy, in the eternal salvation of the elect; and of His justice, in the damnation of the reprobate, who are wicked and disobedient. For then shall the righteous go into everlasting life, and receive that fulness of joy and refreshing, which shall come from the presence of the Lord; but the wicked who know not God, and obey not the gospel of Jesus Christ, shall be cast into eternal torments, and be punished with everlasting destruction from the presence of the Lord, and from the glory of His power.[5]

MAT 12:36 But I say unto you, That every idle word that men shall speak, they shall give account thereof in the day of judgment. 37 For by thy words thou shalt be justified, and by thy words thou shalt be condemned.

[5] MAT 25:31 When the Son of man shall come in his glory, and all the holy angels with him, then shall he sit upon the throne of his glory: 32 And before him shall be gathered all nations: and he shall separate them one from another, as a shepherd divideth his sheep from the goats: 33 And he shall set the sheep on his right hand, but the goats on the left. 34 Then shall the King say unto them on his right hand, Come, ye blessed of my Father, inherit the kingdom prepared for you from the foundation of the world: 35 For I was an hungred, and ye gave me meat: I was thirsty, and ye gave me drink: I was a stranger, and ye took me in: 36 Naked, and ye clothed me: I was sick, and ye visited me: I was in prison, and ye came unto me. 37 Then shall the righteous answer him, saying, Lord, when saw we thee an hungred, and fed thee? or thirsty, and gave thee drink? 38 When saw we thee a stranger, and took thee in? or naked, and clothed thee? 39 Or when saw we thee sick, or in prison, and came unto thee? 40 And the King shall answer and say unto them, Verily I say unto you, Inasmuch as ye have done it unto one of the least of these my brethren, ye have done it unto me. 41 Then shall he say also unto them on the left hand, Depart from me, ye cursed, into everlasting fire, prepared for the devil and his angels: 42 For I was an hungred, and ye gave me no meat: I was thirsty, and ye gave me no drink: 43 I was a stranger, and ye took me not in: naked, and ye clothed me not: sick, and in prison, and ye visited me not. 44 Then shall they also answer him, saying, Lord, when saw we thee an hungred, or athirst, or a stranger, or naked, or sick, or in prison, and did not minister unto thee? 45 Then shall he answer them, saying, Verily I say unto you, Inasmuch as ye did it not to one of the least of these, ye did it not to me. 46 And these shall go away into everlasting punishment: but the righteous into life eternal. ROM 2:5 But after thy hardness and impenitent heart treasurest up unto thyself wrath against the day of

III. As Christ would have us to be certainly persuaded that there shall be a day of judgment, both to deter all men from sin; and for the greater consolation of the godly in their adversity:[6] so will He have that day unknown to men, that they may shake off all carnal security, and be

wrath and revelation of the righteous judgment of God; 6 Who will render to every man according to his deeds. ROM 9:22 What if God, willing to shew his wrath, and to make his power known, endured with much longsuffering the vessels of wrath fitted to destruction: 23 And that he might make known the riches of his glory on the vessels of mercy, which he had afore prepared unto glory. MAT 5:21 His lord said unto him, Well done, thou good and faithful servant: thou hast been faithful over a few things, I will make thee ruler over many things: enter thou into the joy of thy lord. ACT 3:19 Repent ye therefore, and be converted, that your sins may be blotted out, when the times of refreshing shall come from the presence of the Lord. 2TH 1:7 And to you who are troubled rest with us, when the Lord Jesus shall be revealed from heaven with his mighty angels, 8 In flaming fire taking vengeance on them that know not God, and that obey not the gospel of our Lord Jesus Christ: 9 Who shall be punished with everlasting destruction from the presence of the Lord, and from the glory of his power; 10 When he shall come to be glorified in his saints, and to be admired in all them that believe (because our testimony among you was believed) in that day.

[6] 2PE 3:11 Seeing then that all these things shall be dissolved, what manner of persons ought ye to be in all holy conversation and godliness. 14 Wherefore, beloved, seeing that ye look for such things, be diligent that ye may be found of him in peace, without spot, and blameless. 2CO 5:10 For we must all appear before the judgment seat of Christ; that every one may receive the things done in his body, according to that he hath done, whether it be good or bad. 11 Knowing therefore the terror of the Lord, we persuade men; but we are made manifest unto God; and I trust also are made manifest in your consciences. 2TH 1:5 Which is a manifest token of the righteous judgment of God, that ye may be counted worthy of the kingdom of God, for which ye also suffer: 6 Seeing it is a righteous thing with God to recompense tribulation to them that trouble you; 7 And to you who are troubled rest with us, when the Lord Jesus shall be revealed from heaven with his mighty angels. LUK 21:7 And they asked him, saying, Master, but when shall these things be? and what sign will there be when these things shall come to pass? 28 And when these things begin to come to pass, then look up, and lift up your heads; for your redemption draweth nigh. ROM 8:23 And not only they, but ourselves also, which have the firstfruits of the Spirit, even we ourselves groan

always watchful, because they know not at what hour the Lord will come; and may be ever prepared to say, Come Lord Jesus, come quickly, Amen.[7]

within ourselves, waiting for the adoption, to wit, the redemption of our body. 24 For we are saved by hope: but hope that is seen is not hope: for what a man seeth, why doth he yet hope for? 25 But if we hope for that we see not, then do we with patience wait for it.

[7] MAT 24:36 But of that day and hour knoweth no man, no, not the angels of heaven, but my Father only. 42 Watch therefore: for ye know not what hour your Lord doth come. 43 But know this, that if the goodman of the house had known in what watch the thief would come, he would have watched, and would not have suffered his house to be broken up. 44 Therefore be ye also ready: for in such an hour as ye think not the Son of man cometh. MAR 13:35 Watch ye therefore: for ye know not when the master of the house cometh, at even, or at midnight, or at the cockcrowing, or in the morning: 36 Lest coming suddenly he find you sleeping. 37 And what I say unto you I say unto all, Watch. LUK 12:35 Let your loins be girded about, and your lights burning; 36 And ye yourselves like unto men that wait for their lord, when he will return from the wedding; that when he cometh and knocketh, they may open unto him immediately. REV 22:20 He which testifieth these things saith, Surely I come quickly. Amen. Even so, come, Lord Jesus.

Index to the Westminster Confession of Faith and the Larger Catechism

The parentheses contain the chapter number-paragraph number as found in the Confession or the question number if referring to the Larger Catechism (LC).

Ability
   Adam was endued with the power and ability to keep the covenant of works (19-1), *(see also Man—and his original state)*

Abortion
   (cf. exposition of the Sixth Commandment LC 134-136)

Actual Sin
   is a transgression of the righteous law of God (6-6) proceeds from our original corruption (6-4), *(cf. LC 194)*

Adam
   and his posterity in the covenant of works (7-2), (LC 22, 92), *(cf. LC 193)*
   endued with the power and ability to keep the covenant of works (19-1), *(see also Man—and his original state)*
   given a law by God, a covenant of works (19-1), *(cf. LC 92)*
   those elect who were fallen in Adam are effectually called (3-6)

Administration
   of the covenant of grace (7-5), (LC 33-35)
   of the sacraments
      civil magistrates may not assume to themselves the administration of the Word and sacraments (23-3)

one key in determining the purity of a particular church (25-4)
part of the ordinary worship of God (21-5)

Admiration of God
for the doctrine of predestination (3-8)

Admonition
Church officers are to make use of admonition, suspension from the Lord's table and excommunication in order to protect the Church (30-4)

Adoption
(12), (LC 74)
all those who are justified are adopted as the children of God (12)
elect in Christ are adopted as the sons of God (3-6), (LC 39)
Spirit of adoption witnesses with our spirits (18-2)

Adultery
(24-5), *(cf. exposition of the Seventh Commandment LC 137-139)*

All-Knowing
God is all-knowing (2-2)

Angels
and God's providence (5-4), (LC 19)
creation of angels (LC 16)
in God's eternal decree (3-3), (LC 12, 13)
judgment of angels (33-1), (LC 88-90)
their service to God a pattern for man (LC 192)
will accompany Christ when He returns in judgment (LC 56)

Anger
(cf. exposition of the Sixth Commandment LC 134-136)

Annihilationism
doctrine of Annihilationism disputed (32), (33)

Anointing
(see Jesus Christ—and the Holy Spirit)

Antichrist
Pope of Rome is that antichrist (25-6 original version)

Antinomianism
(see Law of God)

Index / 203

Apocrypha
> (1-3)

Apostles
> Christ conversed with the apostles after His resurrection (LC 53)
> Since the apostles' time, all synods and councils may err (31-3)

Approver
> God is not the approver of sin (5-4)

Ascension of Christ
> (8-4), (LC 51-54)

Assemblies
> civil magistrate is to see that all religious and ecclesiastical assemblies may be held without molestation or disturbance (23-3)
> public assemblies for worship are not to be neglected (21-6)
> there ought to be assemblies commonly called synods and councils for the better government and edification of the Church (31-1)

Assurance
> (18), (LC 80, 81)
> of believers
>> believer's assurance is strengthened by good works (16-2)
>> fruits of assurance (18-3)
>> infallible assurance does not belong to the essence of faith (18-3)
>> infallible assurance of faith is founded upon the divine truth of the promises of salvation (18-2)
>> is conveyed by the Spirit without extraordinary revelation (18-3)
>> only those who truly believe in the Lord Jesus can be certainly assured that they are in the state of grace (18-1)
>> true believers may have their assurance shaken, but are never utterly destitute of that seed of God (18-4)
> of truth
>> assurance of the infallible truth of the Word of God (1-5)
> unregenerate men
>> unregenerate men may deceive themselves with false hopes and carnal presumptions of being in the favor of God (18-1)

Atheism
> first petition of the Lord's Prayer calls on God to remove atheism (LC 190)
> forbidden by the First Commandment (LC 105)

Atonement
> *(see also Jesus Christ—and the atonement)*
> design of the atonement (3-6), (8-1), *(cf. LC 38)*
> work of the atonement (6-5), (8-4), (8-5), (11-1, 3, 4), (29-2), (LC 44, 49)

Attributes of God
> (2-1, 2), (LC 7, 112) *(see also God)*

Author
> God is not the author of sin (5-4)

Authority
> civil magistrate has the authority to preserve unity and peace in the Church, etc. (23-3 original version)
> in the Church of God (1-3)
> of the civil magistrate is not negated by infidelity or difference in religion (23-4)
> of the Holy Scriptures (1-4, 5)

Baptism
> (28), (LC 165-167, 176, 177)
> administration of baptism
>> baptism is to be administered but once unto any person (28-7)
>> baptism is to be administered by a minister of the Gospel lawfully called thereunto (28-2)
>> baptism is to be administered in the name of the Father, and of the Son and of the Holy Ghost (28-2)
> a sacrament of the New Testament (28-1), (LC 35)
> and grace
>> grace and salvation are not inseparably annexed to this ordinance (28-5)
> and regeneration
>> all who are baptized are not necessarily regenerated (28-5)

definition of baptism (LC 165)
efficacy of baptism (28-6)
element of baptism
    outward element to be used is water (28-2)
improving our baptism (LC 167)
meaning of baptism (28-1)
mode of baptism (28-3)
neglect of baptism
    it a great sin to neglect this ordinance (28-5)
obligation of those baptized (LC 167)
of infants *(see subjects of baptism)*
ordained by Christ (28-1)
    one of the two sacraments ordained by Christ in the Gospel (27-4)
subjects of baptism
    baptism is to be administered to infants of believing parents (28-4), (LC 166)
    those who profess faith in and obedience unto Christ are to be baptized (28-4), (LC 166)
to be continued in Christ's Church until the end of the world (28-1)

Baptismal Regeneration
(see Baptism—and regeneration)

Believe
believing and assurance
    only those who truly believe in the Lord Jesus may be certainly assured that they are in the state of grace (18-1)
believing parents
    infants of believing parents are to be baptized (28-4)
Spirit of Christ persuades the elect to believe and obey (8-8)

Believers
(see also Elect, Saints)
and Christ
    believers are members of Christ's mystical body (29-1)
    Christ has delivered believers from this present evil world, bondage to Satan and dominion of sin (20-1)
    Christ has purchased liberty for believers (20-1)

and God
    believers have free access to God (20-1)
and sin
    corruption remains in believers (17-3)
and the law of God
    moral law of God is of great use to true believers (19-6)
    true believers are freed from the curse of the law (19-6)
and the magistracy
    it is lawful for Christians to accept and execute the office of magistrate (23-2)
and the sacraments
    believer's communion with Christ in the Lord's Supper (29-1)
    benefits of Christ's sacrifice are sealed to true believers in the sacrament of the Lord's Supper (29-1)
    body and blood of Christ are spiritually present to the faith of believers in the sacrament of the Lord's Supper (29-7)
and the Scriptures (LC 4)
and the Spirit
    believers have fuller communications of the free Spirit of God under the New Testament (20-1)
and war
    believers may wage war upon just and necessary occasion (23-2)
assurance of believers (LC 80, 81)
    true believers may have their assurance shaken, but are never utterly destitute of that seed of God (18-4)
    true believers may wait long for assurance (18-3)
liberty of believers
    under the New Testament, Christians have enlarged liberty (20-1)
marriage of believers
    it is the duty of Christians to marry only in the Lord (24-3)
perseverance of believers (LC 79-81)

Blood of Christ
    only the blood of Christ can expiate sin (LC 152)
    (see also Atonement, Jesus Christ—and the atonement)
Boasting
    (cf. exposition of the Ninth Commandment LC 143-145)
Body
    after death, the bodies of men return to dust but their souls return to God (32-1)
    all shall give an account of their thoughts, words and deeds done in the body (33-1)
    Christ suffered in His body and arose from the dead with it (8-4)
    dead shall be raised at the last day with the self-same bodies which shall again be united to their souls (32-2)
    of the just and the unjust shall be raised by the power of Christ (32-3)
    righteous wait in heaven for the redemption of their bodies (32-1)
Body and Blood
    Christ instituted the sacrament of His body and blood (29-1)
    doctrine of transubstantiation maintains that the elements of bread and wine change into the substance of Christ's body and blood (29-6)
    elements of bread and wine represent the body and blood of Christ in the sacrament of the Lord's Supper (29-5)
    of Christ are spiritually present to the faith of believers in the sacrament of the Lord's Supper (29-7)
    those who receive the Lord's Supper in an unworthy manner are guilty of the body and blood of Christ (29-8)
Bondage
    sinner is freed from his natural bondage at conversion (9-4)
Books
    of the New Testament (1-2)
    of the Old Testament (1-2)
Bread
    and wine remain bread and wine in the sacrament of the Lord's Supper (29-5)
    and wine represent the body and blood of Christ (29-5)

Bribery
forbidden by the Eighth Commandment (LC 140-142)
Business Ethics
(cf. exposition of the Eighth Commandment LC 140-142 and Ninth Commandment 143-145)

Call
(Calling, see Effectual Calling)
Canon of the Scripture
(1-3)
Catholic Church
(see Church)
Censures
(see Church—censures of the Church)
Ceremonial Law
all ceremonial laws have been abrogated under the New Testament (19-3)
God gave Israel ceremonial laws in addition to the ten commandments (19-3)
Jewish Church was subjected to the yoke of the ceremonial law (20-1)
Chastisement of God
(5-5), *(cf. LC 195)*
Chastity
in body, mind, etc. required by the Seventh Commandment (LC 137-139)
Children
of God *(see also Believers, Elect, Saints)*
all those who are justified are adopted as the children of God (12)
are exposed to manifold temptations (5-5)
are sealed to the day of redemption (12)
are sometimes left to the corruption of their own hearts (5-5)
Spirit of adoption witnesses with our spirits that we are the

children of God (18-2)
of professing parents
are members of the visible Church and should be baptized (25-2)
Chosen
those of mankind that are predestinated unto life were chosen in Christ (3-5)
Christ
(see Jesus Christ)
Christian
(see Believers, Elect, Saints)
Christian Liberty
(20)
destroyed when it is used as a pretense for sin (20-3)
enlarged under the New Testament (20-1)
those who, upon the pretense of Christian liberty resist any lawful power are resisting the ordinance of God (20-4)
Christian Sabbath
(21-7) *(see also Lord's Day, Sabbath)*
Christology
(see Jesus Christ)
Church
(25)
and civil magistrates
civil magistrates are nursing fathers to the Church (23-3)
civil magistrate has the authority to preserve unity and peace in the Church, etc. (23-3 original version)
civil magistrates may lawfully call a synod of ministers of the Church (23-3 and 31-2 original version)
ministers of the Church have the authority to call for a synod or council themselves if the civil magistrate is an open enemy of the Church (31-2 original version)
and God's providence
Church is taken care of in a special manner by God's providence (5-7)
and Jesus Christ

Christ executes the offices of prophet, priest and king of the Church (LC 42-45)

Christ has appointed a government in the Church distinct from the civil magistrate (30-1)

Christ has appointed a regular government and discipline in His Church (23-3)

Christ has established external peace and order in the Church (20-4)

Christ has given the ministry, oracles and ordinances of God to the visible Church (25-3)

Christ is the Head and Savior of the Church (8-1), (25-1, 6), (LC 52-54, 60)

Christ's honor is vindicated through the use of Church censures (30-3)

Christ's promise of the Spirit is being fulfilled in the visible Church (25-3)

visible Church is the kingdom of Christ (25-2)

and marriage

Church may attempt to remedy a case of wilful desertion in a marriage (24-6)

marriage was ordained to provide the Church with an holy seed (24-2)

and salvation

ordinarily there is no salvation outside of the visible Church (25-2)

and Scripture

Church has been given the Scripture to establish and comfort her against the malice of Satan and the world (1-1)

censures of the Church (30), (LC 45)

are necessary for the reclaiming and gaining of offending brethren, etc. (30-3)

Church officers have the power to shut the kingdom of heaven against the impenitent, both by the Word and censures, and to open it unto penitent sinners by the ministry of the Gospel (30-2)

Index / 211

may prevent the wrath of God from falling upon the Church (30-3)
those who publish or maintain false opinions may be proceeded against by the censures of the Church (20-4)

government of the Church
Christ has appointed a government in the Church distinct from the civil magistrate (30-1)
Jesus Christ has appointed a regular government and discipline in His Church (23-3), *(cf. LC 45)*

Head of the Church
there is no other Head of the Church but the Lord Jesus Christ (25-6)

invisible Church
catholic or universal Church is invisible and consists of the whole number of the elect (25-1), (LC 64)
communion of the members of the invisible Church with Christ (LC 65, 69, 82, 83, 86)

members of the Church (LC 61, 62)
baptism admits the party into the visible Church (28-1)
catholic or universal Church is invisible and consists of the whole number of the elect (25-1)
sacraments put a visible difference between those in the Church and the rest of the world (27-1)
visible Church consists of those throughout the world that profess the true religion; and their children (25-2)

ministers of the Church
have the authority to call for a synod or council themselves if the civil magistrate is an open enemy of the Church (31-2 original version)

officers of the Church
are to make use of admonition, suspension from the Lord's table and excommunication in order to protect the Church (30-4)
have the duty to appoint synods and councils as often as is necessary for the good of the Church (31-1)
have the power to shut the kingdom of heaven against the

     impenitent, both by the Word and censures, and to open it
     unto penitent sinners by the ministry of the Gospel
     (30-2)
  hold the keys of the kingdom of heaven (30-2)
  second petition of the Lord's Prayer calls on God to furnish the
     Church with officers, purge her from corruption, etc. (LC
     191)
perseverance of the Church
  there will always be a Church on earth to worship God
     (25-5)
purity of the Church
  purest Churches under heaven are subject both to mixture and
     error (25-5)
  purity of the visible Church is determined by the degree to
     which the doctrine of the Gospel is taught and embraced,
     etc. (25-4)
  second petition of the Lord's Prayer calls on God to furnish the
     Church with officers, purge her from corruption, etc. (LC
     191)
sacraments of the Church *(see also Sacraments)*
  allowing the profaning of the covenant and its seals can result in
     the wrath of God falling upon the Church (30-3)
  baptism admits the party into the visible Church (28-1)
  sacrament of the Lord's Supper was instituted by Christ to be
     observed in His Church until the end of the world (29-1)
  sacraments put a visible difference between those in the Church
     and the rest of the world (27-1)
synods and councils of the Church
  decrees and determinations of synods and councils are to be
     received with reverence and submission if consonant to the
     Word of God (31-2)
  have the responsibility to set down rules and directions for the
     better ordering of the worship and government of the
     Church (31-2)
  may be petitioned by the civil magistrate for advice (31-4)
  serve for the better government and edification of the Church
     (31-1)

visible Church (25-2), (LC 61, 63)
> consists of those throughout the world that profess the true religion; and their children (25-2), (LC 62)
> has been given the ministry, oracles and ordinances of God for the gathering and perfecting of the saints (25-3)
> has been sometimes more, sometimes less visible and pure (25-4)
> is no longer confined to one nation as under the law (25-2)
> is the kingdom of the Lord Jesus Christ (25-2)

worship of the Church
> acceptable way of worshipping God is instituted by Himself and is limited by His revealed will (21-1)
> by profession, saints are bound to maintain an holy fellowship and communion in the worship of God (26-2)
> God is to be worshipped everywhere in spirit and truth (21-6)
> God may not be worshipped under any visible representation (21-1)
> lawful oath is part of religious worship (22-1)
> law of nature teaches that a proportion of time is to be set aside for the worship of God (21-7)
> parts of the ordinary religious worship of God (21-5)
> prayer with thanksgiving is one special part of religious worship (21-3)
> public assemblies for worship are not to be neglected (21-6)
> public worship is one key in determining the purity of a particular Church (25-4)
> religious worship (21-1)
> religious worship is to be given to God alone and not to angels, saints or any other creature (21-2)
> since the Fall, God cannot be worshipped without a Mediator (21-2)
> synods and councils have the responsibility to set down rules and directions for the better ordering of the public worship of God (31-2)
> there will always be a Church on earth to worship God (25-5)

those who publish or maintain false opinions about worship may be proceeded against by the censures of the Church and the power of the civil magistrate (20-4)

under the Gospel, worship is not tied to or made more acceptable by any place in which it is performed (21-6)

worship is due to God from all creatures (2-2)

Civil Magistrate
(23)
and Christians
it is lawful for Christians to accept and execute the office of magistrate (23-2)

it is the duty of people to pray for magistrates, to honor them, etc. (23-4)

and marriage
civil magistrate may attempt to remedy a case of wilful desertion in a marriage (24-6)

and the Church
Christ has appointed a government in the Church distinct from the civil magistrate (30-1)

civil magistrate has the authority to preserve unity and peace in the Church, etc. (23-3 original version)

civil magistrate is a nursing father to the Church (23-3), *(cf. second petition of the Lord's Prayer LC 191)*

civil magistrate should give no preference to any denomination of Christians above the rest (23-3)

may lawfully call a synod of ministers (23-3 and 31-2 original version)

may not assume to themselves the power of the keys of the kingdom (23-3)

may petition the Church for advice (31-4)

ministers of the Church have the authority to call for a synod or council themselves if the civil magistrate is an open enemy of the Church (31-2 original version)

those who destroy the external peace and order Christ has established in the Church may be proceeded against by the power of the civil magistrate (20-4 original version)

Index / 215

authority of the civil magistrate
    authority of the civil magistrate is not negated by infidelity or difference in religion (23-4)
    civil magistrate has the authority to preserve unity and peace in the Church, etc. (23-3 original version)
    civil magistrate may lawfully call a synod of ministers (23-3 and 31-2 original version)
    civil magistrate may not assume to themselves the power of the keys of the kingdom of heaven (23-3)
    civil magistrate may petition the Church (31-4)
    civil magistrate must not interfere in matters of faith (23-3)
    those who destroy the external peace and order Christ has established in the Church may be proceeded against by the power of the civil magistrate (20-4 original version)
duties of the civil magistrate
    civil magistrate must not interfere in matters of faith (23-3)
    it is the duty of the civil magistrate to protect the person and good name of all people (23-3)
ordained by God (23-1)
purpose of civil magistrates (23-1)

Civil Power
(see also Civil Magistrate)
    synods and councils are not to intermeddle with civil affairs which concern the commonwealth unless petitioned (31-4)
    those who, upon the pretense of Christian liberty, resist a lawful civil power are resisting the ordinance of God (20-4)

Clothing
    modesty in clothing required by the Seventh Commandment (LC 137-139)

Commands of God
(see also Holy Scripture, Law, Word of God)
    man was commanded not to eat of the tree at creation (4-2)
    obedience is yielded to God's commands in the Word by faith (14-2)

Commandments
(see also Holy Scripture, Law, Word of God)
God delivered the law upon Mount Sinai in ten commandments (19-2)
God has given a perpetual Sabbath commandment binding all men in all ages (21-7)
Ten Commandments *(see Ten Commandments)*
Commission, The Great
(LC 53)
Common Grace
(10-4), *(cf. LC 60, 61)*
Communicants
receive the sacrament of the Lord's Supper (29-3)
Communion
man was in communion with God at creation (4-2), *(cf. LC 27)*
of saints does not infringe the title or propriety which each man has in his goods and possessions (26-3)
of the saints (26-1)
of the saints and the worship of God (26-2)
of the saints with Christ (26-3), (LC 63, 65, 69, 82, 83, 86, 90)
Communion
(as in Lord's Supper), (see also Lord's Supper, Sacraments—of the Lord's Supper)
all ignorant and ungodly persons are unfit to enjoy communion with Christ (29-8)
of believers with Christ and each other in the Lord's Supper (29-1)
Condescension of God
(7-1)
Conditions
of the covenant of grace (7-3)
of the covenant of works (7-2)
Confession of Sin
every man is bound to make private confession of his sins before God (15-6)

he that sins ought to be willing to make a private or public confession (15-6)
Conscience
God alone is Lord of the conscience (20-2)
liberty of conscience (20-1)
is destroyed by requiring an implicit faith and absolute and blind obedience (20-2)
Conscionable Hearing
(LC 160)
Consecration
baptism is a sign and seal of consecration before God (28-1)
Consolation
certainty of a day of judgment deters men from sin and gives consolation to the godly (33-3)
produced by the doctrine of predestination (3-8)
Consubstantiation
doctrine of consubstantiation disputed (29-7)
Controversies
of religion (1-10)
synods and councils have the responsibility to determine controversies of faith (31-2)
Corrupt
(see also Sin)
corrupted nature of our first parents is conveyed to their posterity (6-3) *(see also Imputation, Original Sin)*
corrupted nature remains in the regenerated (6-5), (13-2), *(see also Man—his present state)*
Corruption
body of Christ did not see corruption (LC 52)
moral law restrains our corruptions (19-6) *(see also Law of God)*
Councils
(31)
all synods and councils, since the apostles' time, are subject to error (31-3)
and synods serve for the better government and edification of the Church (31-1)

are an ordinance of God (31-2)
are to handle or conclude nothing but that which is ecclesiastical and are not to intermeddle with civil affairs unless petitioned (31-4)
Church officers have the duty to appoint synods and councils as often as is necessary for the good of the Church (31-1)
decrees and determinations of synods and councils are to be received with reverence and submission if consonant to the Word of God (31-2)
responsibilities of synods and councils (31-2)

Counsel of God
God's secret counsel (3-5)
is wise and holy (3-1)
unsearchable counsel of God's will in passing by the non-elect (3-7)
whole counsel of God (1-6)

Covenant
(7)
of grace (7-3, 4), (LC 30, 31, 57)
    administered with more simplicity under the Gospel (7-6), (LC 35)
    allowing the profaning of the covenant and its seals can result in the wrath of God falling upon the Church (30-3)
    and the perseverance of the saints (17-2)
    baptism is a sign and seal of the covenant of grace (28-1)
    conditions of the covenant of grace (7-3)
    differently administered (7-5, 6), (LC 33, 34)
    Jesus Christ is the Mediator of the covenant of grace (LC 36)
    Jesus Christ the Testator of the covenant of grace (7-4)
    sacraments are signs and seals of the covenant of grace (27-1)
of life (LC 20)
of works (7-1, 2), (LC 30)
    conditions of the covenant of works (7-2)
    God gave Adam a law, a covenant of works (19-1)

Covenant Theology
   (see Covenant)
Covetousness
   forbidden by the Eighth Commandment (LC 140-142), Tenth Commandment (LC 146-148)
Creation
   (4), (LC 15)
   and the execution of God's decrees (LC 14)
   of angels (LC 16)
   of man (LC 17, 20, 21)
Creator
   (7-1)
Creature
   all creatures are made by God (4-2)
   all creatures are reached by the providence of God (5-7)
   distance between God and the creature is great (7-1)
Curse of the Law
   Christ has purchased freedom from the curse of the moral law for believers (20-1)
Damnation
   Christ has delivered believers from everlasting damnation (20-1)
   God's justice shall be glorified in the damnation of the reprobate on the day of judgment (33-2)
   of the law of God (6-6)
   those who receive the sacrament of the Lord's Supper in an unworthy manner do so to their own damnation (29-8)
Darkness
   (see Hell)
Day
   Lord's Day (21-7)
   of judgment (LC 82), *(see also Judgment)*
      certainty of a day of judgment deters men from sin and gives consolation to the godly (33-3)
      goal of the judgment day is the manifestation of the glory of God's mercy and justice (33-2)

God has appointed a day wherein He will judge the world by Jesus Christ (33-1)
last day (32-2)
righteous shall go into everlasting life on the day of judgment (33-2)
unknown to men (33-3)
wicked are cast into hell at death where they remain reserved for judgment on the great day (32-1)
of redemption
adopted children of God are sealed to the day of redemption (12), (18-2)
Sabbath Day (21-1)
God has appointed one day in seven for a Sabbath (21-7)

Dead
all the dead shall be raised at the last day (32-2)
natural man is dead in sin (9-3) *(see also Man–and his present state)*
our first parents became dead in sin as a result of the Fall (6-2)
prayer is not to be made for the dead (21-4)
resurrection from the dead (32)

Death
of angels
some men and angels are predestinated unto everlasting death (3-3)
of Christ (8-4), *(see also Jesus Christ–and the atonement)*
all saints that are united to Christ share in His death (26-1)
of man
after death, the bodies of men return to dust but their souls return to God (32-1)
after death, the souls of the righteous are received into the highest heavens (32-1)
all men are appointed unto death (LC 84)
Christ has delivered believers from the sting of death (20-1)
sinner is made subject to death by transgressions of God's law (6-6)
some men and angels are predestinated unto everlasting death (3-3)

state of men after death (32)
threatened upon the breach of the covenant of works (19-1), (LC 20)
prayer is not to be made for those who have sinned the sin unto death (21-4)

Debt of Former Sins
is not satisfied by good works (16-5)

Decalogue
(see Ten Commandments)

Decree of God
(3), (LC 12-14)
and election
God decreed from all eternity to justify the elect (11-4)
God's decree of election guarantees the perseverance of the saints (17-2)
and providence (5-2)
and second causes (3-1)
before the foundation of the world (3-5)
concerning men and angels (3-3), (LC 13)
execution of God's decree (LC 14)
not based on foreseen future events (3-2)
Scripture makes known God's decrees (LC 6)

Denomination
civil magistrate should give no preference to any denomination of Christians above the rest (23-3)

Depravity, Total
(6-2, 4), (9-3), (LC 28), *(cf. exposition of the Lord's Prayer LC 190-194)*
(see also Man–and his present state, Sin–and man)

Desertion
wilful desertion as grounds for divorce (24-6), *(cf. exposition of the Seventh Commandment LC 137-139)*

Destruction
wicked shall be punished with everlasting destruction (33- 2)

Devil
(see Satan)

Diet
    (cf. exposition of the Sixth Commandment LC 134-136)
Diligence
    produced by the doctrine of predestination (3-8)
Discontentment
    forbidden by the Tenth Commandment (LC 146-148)
Dishonor
    of the non-elect (3-7)
Discipline
    civil magistrates have the authority to prevent or reform all abuses in worship and discipline (23-3 original version)
    Jesus Christ has appointed a regular government and discipline in His Church (23-3)
Divorce
    (24), *(cf. exposition of the Seventh Commandment LC 137-139)*
    on the grounds of adultery (24-5)
    on the grounds of wilful desertion (24-6)
    rights of the innocent party in the matter of adultery (24-5)
Doctrine
    degree to which the doctrine of the Gospel is taught and embraced partially determines the purity of a particular Church (25-4)
    efficacy of doctrine (1-5)
Dominion
    of God
        God has sovereign dominion over all things (2-2)
    of man
        man originally had dominion over the creatures (4- 2), (LC 17, 20)
    of sin
        all mankind is under the dominion of sin and Satan (LC 191)
        Christ has delivered believers from the dominion of sin (20-1)
Duty
    of inferiors/superiors to one another *(cf. exposition of the Fifth Commandment LC 123-132)*
    of man toward God (19-2), (LC 91, 98)
    of man toward his fellowman (19-2), (LC 98)

Ecclesiastical
ecclesiastical persons are not exempt from obedience to the civil magistrate (23-4)
synods and councils are to handle or conclude nothing but that which is ecclesiastical (31-4)
those who, upon the pretense of Christian liberty resist a lawful ecclesiastical power are resisting the ordinance of God (20-4)

Effectual Calling
(10), (LC 58, 59, 66-68)
elect are effectually called unto faith according to God's will (3-6)
is of God's free and special grace alone (10-2)
it is the duty of everyone to make his calling and election sure (18-3)
non-elect may be called by the ministry of the Word (10-4)
those effectually called and regenerated are also sanctified (13-1)
those effectually called are justified, pardoned, accounted righteous (11-1)
those effectually called shall persevere to the end (17-1)

Eighth Commandment
(LC 140-142)

Elect
(see also Believers, Saints)
and adoption
> as adopted children of God the elect are sealed to the day of redemption (12)

and Christ
> Christ governs the hearts of the elect by His Word and Spirit (8-8), *(cf. LC 45)*
> Christ intercedes for the elect (LC 54, 55)
> Christ satisfied the Father's justice on behalf of the elect (11-3)
> Christ's sacrifice is the propitiation for all the sins of the elect (29-2), (LC 38), *(cf. LC 44)*

elect are redeemed by Christ (3-6), (LC 52)
elect enjoy union with Christ (LC 65, 66)
elect have Christ's obedience and satisfaction imputed to them (11-1)
elect receive and rest in Christ by faith (11-1)
elect receive the benefits of Christ's mediation (LC 57-59, 153, 154)

and effectual calling (LC 58, 59, 66-68)
>   elect are called by the Spirit of Christ (3-6)
>   elect are effectually called, justified, pardoned, accounted righteous (11-1)
>   elect are effectually called out of a state of sin and death to grace and salvation (10-1)
>   elect are effectually called, regenerated and sanctified (13-1)
>   elect are enabled to believe to the saving of their souls by the grace of faith (14-1)
>   elect are made willing to come to Christ by God's grace (10-1)
>   elect are persuaded by Christ's Spirit to believe and obey (8-8)
>   elect are to be redeemed, called, justified, sanctified and glorified (8-1)
>   even those elect who are incapable of being outwardly called are saved (10-3)
>   only the elect are effectually called, justified, adopted, sanctified and saved (3-6)
>   wills of the elect are renewed when they are effectually called (10-1)

and God
>   elect are appointed by God unto glory (3-6)
>   God continues to forgive the sins of the justified (11-5)
>   God decreed from all eternity to justify the elect (11-4)

and sin
>   Christ satisfied the Father's justice on behalf of the elect (11-3)
>   Christ's sacrifice is the propitiation for all the sins of the elect (29-2)
>   elect can come under God's Fatherly displeasure by sinning (11-5)
>   God continues to forgive the sins of the justified (11-5)

and the benefits of redemption (8-6)

and the Church
>   catholic or universal Church is invisible and consists of the whole number of the elect (25-1), (LC 64)

and the covenants of God (LC 30, 31, 32, 34)

and the day of judgment

God's mercy shall be glorified in the eternal salvation of the elect on the day of judgment (33-2)
and the law (7-5)
and the Word of God
    mysteries of salvation are revealed in and by the Word to the elect (8-8)
elect infants
    are regenerated and saved (10-3)
enemies of the elect
    all the enemies of the elect are overcome by Christ's almighty power and wisdom (8-8), (LC 38, 45, 52-54)
perseverance of the elect (LC 79-81)
    elect are kept by the power of Christ (3-6)
    elect can never fall away from the state of justification (11-5), *(cf. 18-4)*

Election
(LC 12, 13)
decree of election guarantees the perseverance of the saints (17-2)
eternal election (3-8)
it is the duty of everyone to make his calling and election sure (18-3)
of angels and men (LC 13)

Elements
in the sacrament of baptism (28-2)
in the sacrament of the Lord's Supper (29-3, 5), (LC 169)
outward elements of the Lord's Supper may be received by ignorant and wicked men (29-8)
those who partake of the visible elements of the Lord's Supper do spiritually receive and feed upon Christ crucified (29-7)

Enemy
all enemies of the elect are overcome by Christ (8-8), (LC 38, 45, 52-54)

Enlighten
minds of the elect are spiritually and savingly enlightened (10-1)

Envy
(cf. exposition of the Eighth Commandment LC 140-142, Ninth Commandment LC 143-145, Tenth Commandment LC 146-148)

Eschatology
    (32), (33), (LC 51-53, 56), *(see also Return of Christ, Second Coming of Christ)*

Eternal
    election (3-8)
    God is eternal (2-1)
    God's eternal power was manifested in the act of creation (4-1)
    God's mercy shall be glorified in the eternal salvation of the elect on the day of judgment (33-2)
    wicked shall be cast into eternal torments (33-2)
    will of God in predestination (3-6)

Eternity
    for the righteous and the wicked (33-2)
    God decreed from all eternity to justify the elect (11-4)

Eucharist
    (see Lord's Supper, Sacraments-of the Lord's Supper)

Euthanasia
    (cf. exposition of the Sixth Commandment LC 134-136)

Evidence
    good works are the fruits and evidences of a true and lively faith (16-2), *(cf. LC 32)*

Evil
    converted sinner continues to do that which is evil (9-4)
    tree of the knowledge of good and evil (4-2)

Exaltation of Jesus Christ
    (8-4), (LC 42, 51-56)

Excommunication
    Church officers are to make use of admonition, suspension from the Lord's table and excommunication in order to protect the Church (30-4)

Existence of God
    (1-1), (21-1), (LC 2)

Expiate
    only the blood of Christ can expiate sin (LC 152)

Extortion
    (cf. exposition of the Eighth Commandment LC 140-142)

Faith
- (14)
- and assurance
    - assurance of faith is conveyed by the Spirit without extraordinary revelation (18-3)
    - infallible assurance does not belong to the essence of faith (18-3)
- and Christ
    - Christ is the author and finisher of our faith (14-3)
    - faith receives and rests on Christ and His righteousness (11-2)
    - grace of faith is a work of Christ's Spirit (14-1)
- and grace
    - grace of faith enables the elect to believe to the saving of their souls (14-1), *(cf. LC 32)*
- and justification (LC 72, 73)
    - faith is the instrument of justification (11-2)
- and predestination
    - foreseen faith was not the basis of predestination (3-5)
- and the conscience (20-2)
- and the elect
    - covenant of grace was administered under the Old Testament in such a way that was sufficient to build up the elect in faith in the promised Messiah (LC 34)
    - elect are kept by Christ's power through faith (3-6)
    - elect in Christ are called to faith (3-6)
- and the sacraments
    - body and blood of Christ are spiritually present to the faith of believers in the sacrament of the Lord's Supper (29-7)
    - faith is increased and strengthened by the ministry of the Word and the administration of the sacraments (14-1)
- and the Spirit
    - grace of faith is a work of Christ's Spirit (14-1)
- and the Word of God
    - by faith, a Christian believes the Word to be true (14-2)
    - faith is increased and strengthened by the ministry of the Word and the administration of the sacraments (14-1)
    - faith is ordinarily wrought by the ministry of the Word (14-1)

controversies of faith
    synods and councils have the responsibility to determine controversies of faith (31-2)
is a gift of God (11-1)
matters of faith
    civil magistrates must not interfere in matters of faith (23-3)
    those who publish or maintain false opinions about faith may be proceeded against by the censures of the Church and the power of the civil magistrate (20-4 original version)
saving faith (14-1), (LC 72, 73)
    may differ in degrees (14-3)
    principal acts of saving faith (14-2)
works by love (11-2)

Fall from Grace
    those who are justified can never fall away from that state (11-5), *(cf. LC 79-81)*

Fall of Man
    (6), (LC 21-23)
    and the covenant of works (7-3)
    by his Fall man lost all ability to do spiritual good (9-3)
    God's providence and the first Fall (5-4)
    law given to Adam continued to be a perfect rule of righteousness after the Fall (19-2), *(cf. LC 94-97)*
    results of the Fall (6-2)
    since the Fall, God cannot be worshipped without a Mediator (21-2)

False Testimony
    (cf. exposition of the Ninth Commandment LC 143-145)

Family
    visible Church is the house and family of God (25-2)
    Word of God should be read by families (LC 156)
    worship is to take place in private families (21-6)

Fasting
    part of religious worship (21-5)

Father
    God the Father (2-3)
    God the Father's justice was fully satisfied by Jesus Christ (8-5)

Fear of God
    (1-8)
Fellowship of the Saints
    and the worship of God (26-2)
    with Christ (26-1)
Fencing the Lord's Table
    (see Lord's Supper-fencing of the Lord's Table)
Fifth Commandment
    (LC 123-133)
First Cause
    (5-2)
First Commandment
    (LC 103-106)
Flesh
    wages war against the Spirit (13-2)
Foreknowledge of God
    and providence (5-1, 2)
    and the execution of His decrees (LC 14)
Foreordain (Ordain)
    God ordained some to dishonor and wrath for their sin (3-7)
    God ordained whatsoever comes to pass (3-1), (LC 12)
    God's foreordination of all means in predestination (3-6)
    number of men and angels foreordained to life/death is certain and definite (3-4)
    some men and angels are foreordained to everlasting life/death (3-3)
    those ordained unto eternal life are promised the Holy Spirit (7-3)
Foresignify
    Christ was foresignified by types and ordinances (7-5)
Forgery
    forbidden by the Ninth Commandment (LC 143-145)
Forgiveness
    baptism is a sign and seal of the remission of sins (28-1)
    Church officers have the power to retain and remit sins (30-2)
    corruption of man's nature, which remains in the regenerate, is pardoned through Christ (6-5)

God pardons the sins of those whom He effectually calls (11-1, 5)
Fornication
(cf. exposition of the Seventh Commandment LC 137-139)
committed after a contract of marriage has been made but detected before the marriage (24-5)
Fountain of all Being
God is the fountain of all being (2-2)
Fourth Commandment
(LC 115-121)
Freedom
Christ has purchased freedom for believers (20-1)
in his state of innocency man had freedom and power to do good (9-2), *(see also Man–and his original state)*
Free Will
(9)
Fruit
forbidden fruit (6-1), (LC 21)
good works are the fruits and evidences of a true and lively faith (16-2)
of assurance (18-3)
Gifts
of the Spirit
God's former ways of revealing His will have ceased (1-1, 6)
of wicked and ungodly men are sometimes withdrawn by God (5-6)
Glory
of Christ
all saints that are united to Christ share in His glory (26-1)
of God
manifested in the act of creation (4-1)
man's chief end is to glorify God (LC 1)
purpose of reprobation (3-7)
Scripture gives glory to God (1-5), (LC 4)
sought in the Lord's Prayer (LC 191, 196)
of the elect
God has appointed the elect unto glory (3-6)
state of glory
and the will of man (9-5)

Gluttony
    forbidden by the Sixth and Seventh Commandments (LC 134-136, 137-139)

God
    (2), (LC 5, 7-11)
    and adoption
        God adopts all those who are justified as His children (12)
        God pities, protects, provides for and chastens His adopted children (12)
    and death
        after death, the bodies of men return to dust but their souls return to God (32-1)
    and man (LC 1)
    and marriage
        in marriage, God joins two together (24-6)
    and means
        God's use of means in providence (5-3)
    and oaths
        God's name and the swearing of oaths (22-2)
        God's Word warrants oaths (22-2)
    and prayer
        God requires prayer of all men (21-3)
        prayer is one special part of the worship of God (21-3)
    and sin
        every sin is a transgression of God's righteous law (6-6)
        God is not the author of sin (3-1), (5-4)
        God's permission of the sin of our first parents (6-1)
    and sinners
        God's conversion of a sinner (9-4)
        God's exact justice and rich grace are glorified in the justification of sinners (11-3)
        God's grace enables the converted sinner to do good (9-4)
    and the Church
        Church censures may prevent the wrath of God from falling upon the Church (30-3)
        God's providence takes care of the Church in a special manner (5-7)

there will always be a Church on earth to worship God (25-5)
visible Church is the house and family of God (25-2)
and the creation (LC 15)
of man
distance between God and the creature is great (7-1), *(see also 16-5)*
God created man in His own image (4-2), (LC 17)
God endued the will of man with natural liberty (9-1)
God made man and all other creatures (4-2)
God's authority as Creator and the giving of the law (19-5)
God's law was written on man's heart at creation (4-2)
God was in communion with man at creation (4-2)
great disproportion exists between God and man (16-5), *(see also 7-1)*
of the world
God created the world out of nothing (4-1)
God's eternal power, glory, goodness, wisdom and power are manifested in the act of creation (4-1)
God the Father, Son, and Holy Ghost in the act of creation (4-1)
and the elect
believers have free access to God (20-1)
Christ has purchased freedom from the wrath of God for believers (20-1)
duty of the elect toward God is found in the first four commandments (19-2)
God appointed the elect unto glory (3-6)
God effectually calls the elect by His Word and Spirit (10-1)
God may withdraw the light of His countenance from true believers (18-4)
God's decree of election guarantees the perseverance of the saints (17-2)
and the sacraments
baptism is a sign and seal of consecration before God (28-1)
God instituted the sacraments (27-1)

and the wicked
> God blinds and hardens wicked and ungodly men and withholds His grace from them (5-6)
> wicked who do not know God and obey not the Gospel shall be cast into eternal torments (33-2)

and the world
> God created the world out of nothing (4-1)
> God has appointed a day wherein He will judge the world by Jesus Christ (33-1)
> God's decree before the foundation of the world (3-5)

and vows
> vows are to be made to God alone (22-6)

as Creator (7-1)
> as Creator God upholds, directs, disposes and governs all things (5-1)
> God made man and all other creatures (4-2)
> God's authority as Creator and the giving of the law (19-5)
> God the Father, Son, and Holy Ghost in the act of creation (4-1)

attributes of God (2-1), (2-2), (LC 7)

authority of God
> God's authority as Creator and the giving of the law (19-5)

chastisement of God (5-5)

commandments of God *(see also Commands, Commandments)*
> angels were created to execute the commandments of God (LC 16)
> man transgressed the commandment of God in eating the forbidden fruit (LC 21)

covenants of God (7)

decree of God (3), (LC 6, 12-14)
> God decreed from all eternity to justify the elect (11-4)
> God's decree and providence (5-2)
> God's decree before the foundation of the world (3-5)
> God's decree of election guarantees the perseverance of the saints (17-2)

existence of God (LC 2)
> light of nature shows that there is a God (1-1), (21-1)

foreknowledge of God
    God exercises providence according to His infallible foreknowledge (5-1), (LC 14)
    God's foreknowledge in providence (5-2)
forgiveness of God
    God continues to forgive the sins of the justified (11-5)
glory of God (LC 1, 4)
    God exercises providence to the praise of His glory (5-1)
    God is glorified in the good works of His people (16-2)
    God's exact justice and rich grace are glorified in the justification of sinners (11-3), *(cf. 11-3)*
    God's glory is manifested in creation (4-1)
    God's mercy and justice shall be glorified on the day of judgment (33-2)
    sought in the Lord's Prayer (LC 190, 196)
God alone is Lord of the conscience (20-2)
God is the first Cause (5-2)
God is to be feared, loved, praised, called upon, trusted in and served (21-1)
God's condescension to man (7-1)
goodness of God
    God's goodness is manifested in the act of creation (4-1)
    God's goodness, wisdom and power are manifested by the light of nature and the works of creation and providence (1-1), (5-4)
grace of God
    and the second covenant (LC 32)
    effectual calling is of God's free and special grace alone (10-2)
    elect are made willing to come to Christ by God's grace (10-1)
    God's exact justice and rich grace are glorified in the justification of sinners (11-3), *(cf. LC 13)*
    God's free grace and love in predestination (3-5)
    God's grace enables the converted sinner to do good (9-4)
    God's grace is withheld from wicked and ungodly men (5-6)
    praise of God's glorious grace, the purpose of predestination (3-5)

repentance is an act of God's free grace in Christ (15-3)
image of God (LC 17)
judgment of God *(see also Judgment)*
    God has appointed a day wherein He will judge the world by Jesus Christ (33-1)
justice of God
    God's exact justice and rich grace are glorified in the justification of sinners (11-3)
    God's justice in reprobation (3-7), (LC 13)
    God's justice praised in His exercise of providence (5-1)
    God's mercy and justice shall be glorified on the day of judgment (33-2)
    God the Father's justice was fully satisfied by Jesus Christ (8-5), (LC 38)
knowledge of God
    God knows whatsoever may or can come to pass (3-2)
    Scriptures make known what God is, etc. (LC 6)
law of God (19)
    every sin is a transgression of God's righteous law (6-6)
    God delivered the law upon Mount Sinai in ten commandments (19-2)
    God gave Israel ceremonial laws in addition to the ten commandments (19-3)
    God gave Israel judicial laws in addition to the ten commandments (19-4)
    God's authority as Creator and the giving of the law (19-5)
    God's law and repentance (15-2)
    God's law was written on man's heart at creation (4-2), (LC 17)
    God's will is revealed in the moral law (19-6, 7)
    man's duty toward God is found in the first four commandments (19-2)
    moral law (LC 92, 93)
        exposition of the moral law (Ten Commandments) (LC 98-148)
        uses of the moral law (LC 94-97)

God's law and repentance (15-2)
God's law was written on man's heart at creation (4-2), (LC 17)
God's will is revealed in the moral law (19-6, 7)
man's duty toward God is found in the first four commandments (19-2)
moral law (LC 92, 93)
    exposition of the moral law (Ten Commandments) (LC 98-148)
    uses of the moral law (LC 94-97)
lordship
    God has lordship and sovereignty over all (21-1)
love of God
    and the perseverance of the saints (LC 79)
    God's free grace and love in predestination (3-5), (LC 13)
name of God *(cf. exposition of the Third Commandment LC 111-114)*
    God's name and the swearing of oaths (22-2)
nature of God *(see also Attributes of God)*
    definition/description of God (2-1) (LC 7)
power of God
    acknowledged in the Lord's Prayer (LC 196)
    by the word of His power, God made the world of nothing (LC 15)
    God's eternal power is manifested in the act of creation (4-1)
    God's goodness, wisdom and power are manifested by the light of nature and the works of creation and providence (1-1), (5-4)
praise of God
    God's praise in reprobation (3-7)
    God's praise, reverence and admiration because of predestination (3-8)
predestination of God
    a high mystery (3-8)
    doctrine of predestination is to be handled with special prudence and care (3-8)
    God's free grace and love in predestination (3-5)

God's praise, reverence and admiration because of predestination (3-8)
    of angels and men (3-3), (3-4)
    not based on foreseen faith, good works or perseverance (3-5)
    praise of God's glorious grace, the purpose of predestination (3-5)
    those of mankind predestinated unto life (3-5)
providence of God (5), (LC 18-20)
    and the first Fall (5-4)
    and the nature of second causes (5-2)
    and the sins of angels and men (5-4)
    God exercises providence according to His infallible foreknowledge (5-1)
    God exercises providence to the praise of His glory (5-1)
    God's decree and providence (5-2)
    God's goodness, wisdom and power are manifested by the light of nature and the works of creation and providence (1-1)
    God's power, wisdom and goodness are manifested in providence (5-4)
    God's providence is most wise and holy (5-1)
    God's providence reaches all creatures (5-7)
    God's providence takes care of the Church in a special manner (5-7)
    God's use of means in providence (5-3)
    God's will and the exercise of providence (5-1)
purpose of God
    God's eternal and immutable purpose (3-5)
    God's eternal purpose in choosing Christ to be the Mediator (8-1)
purpose of God's will in predestination (3-6)
reprobation of God
    God passed by the non-elect and ordained them to dishonor and wrath (3-7)
    God's justice, praise and sovereign power in reprobation (3-7)
revelation of God
    God's former ways of revealing God's will have now ceased (1-1)

      natural revelation (1-1)
      necessary for salvation (1-1)
  reverence of God
      God's praise, reverence and admiration because of predestination (3-8)
  Son of God
      God's Son the second person of the trinity (8-2)
      God the Son in the Godhead (2-3)
  sovereignty of God
      acknowledged in the Lord's Prayer (LC 196)
      God has lordship and sovereignty over all (21-1)
      God's sovereign power in reprobation (3-7), (LC 13)
  Spirit of God (LC 2), *(see also Holy Spirit)*
      God effectually calls the elect by His Word and Spirit (10-1)
      God the Holy Ghost in the Godhead (2-3)
  will of God
      God's decrees are the holy acts of the counsel of His will (LC 12), *(cf. LC 13, 14)*
      God's will and the exercise of providence (5-1)
      God's will is revealed in His Word (3-8)
      God's will is revealed in the moral law (19-6), (19-7)
      sought in the Lord's Prayer (LC 192)
  wisdom of God
      God's goodness, wisdom and power are manifested by the light of nature and the works of creation and providence (1-1), (5-4)
      God's wisdom is manifested in the act of creation (4-1)
  Word of God *(see Word of God)*
  works of God (LC 2)
  worship of God (1-6, 8), *(cf. exposition of the First Commandment LC 103-106 and the Second Commandment 107-110)*
      acceptable way of worshipping God is instituted by Himself (21-1)
      by profession, saints are bound to maintain an holy fellowship and communion in the worship of God (26-2)
      God is to be worshipped everywhere in spirit and truth (21-6)

God may not be worshipped under any visible representation (21-1)
is to take place in private families (21-6)
lawful oath is part of religious worship (22-1)
law of nature teaches that a proportion of time is to be set aside for the worship of God (21-7)
parts of the ordinary worship of God (21-5)
prayer is one special part of the worship of God (21-3)
public assemblies for worship are not to be neglected (21-6)
public worship is one key in determining the purity of a particular Church (25-4)
religious worship (21-1)
religious worship is to be given to God alone and not to angels, saints or any other creature (21-2)
since the Fall, God cannot be worshipped without a Mediator (21-2)
synods and councils have the responsibility to set down rules and directions for the better ordering of the public worship of God (31-2)
there will always be a Church on earth to worship God (25-5)
those who publish or maintain false opinions about worship may be proceeded against by the censures of the Church and the power of the civil magistrate (20-4)
under the Gospel, worship is not tied to or made more acceptable by any place in which it is performed (21-6)
worship is due to God from all creatures (2-2)

wrath of God
against sinners (6-6)
against the non-elect (3-7)
allowing the profaning of the covenant and its seals can result in the wrath of God falling upon the Church (30-3)
Christ has purchased freedom from the wrath of God for believers (20-1)
Church censures may prevent the wrath of God from falling upon the Church (30-3)

Godhead
    (LC 9)
    communion of the saints with Christ does not make them partakers of His Godhead (26-3)
    properties of the persons in the Godhead (LC 10)
    Scriptures make known the Godhead (LC 6)
    unity and persons of the Godhead (2-3)

Good
    Church officers have the duty to appoint synods and councils as often as is necessary for the good of the Church (31-1)
    God is good (2-1), (21-1)
    tree of the knowledge of good and evil (4-2)

Goodness of God
    God's goodness is manifested in the act of creation (4-1)
    God's goodness is praised in His exercise of providence (5-1)
    God's goodness, wisdom and power are manifested by the light of nature and the works of creation and providence (1-1), (5-4)

Good Works
    (16)
    ability to do good works is wholly from the Spirit of Christ (16-3)
    are not the basis of predestination (3-5)
    are only such as God has commanded in His Word (16-1)
    are the fruits and evidences of a true and lively faith (16-2), *(cf. LC 73)*
    by good works believers manifest their thankfulness, strengthen their assurance, edify their brethren, etc. (16-2)
    do not merit pardon of sin (16-5)
    do not satisfy the debt of former sins (16-5)
    of believers are accepted in Christ (16-6)
    of unregenerate men (16-7)

Gospel
    and the Church
        Church officers have the power to shut the kingdom of heaven against the impenitent, both by the Word and censures, and to open it unto penitent sinners by the ministry of the Gospel (30-2)

degree to which the doctrine of the Gospel is taught and embraced partially determines the purity of a particular Church (25-4)
holy profession of the Gospel is vindicated through the use of Church censures (30-3)
visible Church is no longer confined to one nation under the Gospel (25-2)
and the covenant of grace
administration of the covenant of grace under the gospel (7-6)
and the sacraments
baptism is to be by a minister of the Gospel lawfully called thereunto (28-2)
Jesus Christ ordained only two sacraments in the Gospel (27-4)
and the wicked
wicked who do not know God and obey not the Gospel shall be cast into eternal torments (33-2), *(cf. LC 45)*
and the worship of God
under the Gospel, worship is not tied to or made more acceptable by any place in which it is performed (21-6)
ministry of the Gospel
Church officers have the power to shut the kingdom of heaven against the impenitent, both by the Word and censures, and to open it unto penitent sinners by the ministry of the Gospel (30-2)
propagation of the Gospel prayed for in the Lord's Prayer (LC 191)

Gossiping
forbidden by the Ninth Commandment (LC 143-145)

Govern
Christ governs the hearts of the elect by His Word and Spirit (8-8)

Government
civil government *(see Civil Government)*
of the Church
Jesus Christ has appointed a government in the Church distinct from the civil magistrate (30-1)
Jesus Christ has appointed a regular government and discipline in His Church (23-3), (LC 45)

synods and councils have the responsibility to set down rules and directions for the better ordering of the government of the Church (31-2)
synods and councils serve for the better government and edification of the Church (31-1)
there are some circumstances concerning the government of the Church which are ordered by the light of nature, etc. (1-6)

Grace
    and adoption (LC 74)
    and assurance
        assurance of grace and salvation (18-1)
    and justification (LC 70-73)
    and predestination
        God's free grace in predestination (3-5)
    and repentance (LC 76)
        repentance is an act of God's free grace in Christ (15-3)
    and sanctification (LC 75)
    and the elect
        elect are effectually called to grace and salvation (10-1)
        elect are made willing to come to Christ by God's grace (10-1)
    and the Gospel
        uses of the law for true believers is not contrary to the grace of the Gospel (19-7)
    and the sacraments (27-3)
        baptism is a sign and seal of the covenant of grace (28-1)
        grace is not inseparably annexed to the ordinance of baptism (28-5)
        sacraments are signs and seals of the covenant of grace (27-1), *(cf. LC 35)*
    and the Spirit
        grace of faith is a work of Christ's Spirit (14-1)
        grace which is promised in baptism is offered, exhibited and conferred by the Holy Ghost (28-6)
    covenant of grace (7-3), (7-4)
        baptism is a sign and seal of the covenant of grace (28-1)
        covenant of grace and the perseverance of the saints (17-2)

covenant of grace is administered with more simplicity (7-6)
covenant of grace is differently administered (7-5)
Jesus Christ, the Testator of the covenant of grace (7-4)
of Christ
    all saints that are united to Christ share in His grace (26-1)
    bestowed upon the elect (LC 45)
    grace of faith is a work of Christ's Spirit (14-1)
of God
    and adoption (LC 74)
    and justification (LC 70-73)
    and predestination
        God's free grace in predestination (3-5)
    and repentance (LC 76)
        repentance is an act of God's free grace in Christ (15-3)
    and sanctification (LC 75)
    effectual calling is of God's free and special grace alone (10-2)
    elect are made willing to come to Christ by God's grace (10-1)
    God's grace frees the sinner and enables him to do good (9-4)
    God's grace is withheld from wicked and ungodly men (5-6)
    God's grace praised in the election of some angels and men (LC 13)
state of grace
    converted sinner is translated into the state of grace (9-4)
    those effectually called cannot fall away from the state of grace (17-1), (LC 79)

Grave
Christ has delivered believers from the victory of the grave (20-1)
Greek
New Testament in Greek (1-8)
Grieving the Spirit
(LC 105)
Holy Spirit is grieved by sinning believers (17-3), (18-4)
Guilt
brought upon the sinner by every transgression of God's law (6-6)
of our first parents' sin imputed to their posterity (6-3)
unworthy recipients of the Lord's supper are guilty of His body and blood (29-8)

Hand
  Jesus Christ now sits at the right hand of God (8-4), (LC 51)
Hatred
  forbidden by the Sixth Commandment (LC 134-136)
Head
  Jesus Christ is the Head and Savior of the Church (8-1), (25-1, 6)
  serpent's head should be bruised by the seed of the woman (8-6)
Hearing
  conscionable hearing of the Word is part of the ordinary worship of God (21-5)
Heart
  law of God was written on man's heart at creation (4-2)
  new heart and a new spirit are created in those effectually called and regenerated (13-1)
  of stone taken away when the elect are effectually called (10-1)
Heathen
  fate of the heathen (LC 60)
Heaven
  (33-2), (LC 90)
  civil magistrates may not assume to themselves the power of the keys of the kingdom of heaven (23-3)
Hebrew
  Old Testament in Hebrew (1-8)
Heir
  adopted children of God are heirs of everlasting salvation (12)
  Jesus Christ, the Heir of all things (8-1)
Hell
  Christ's descent into hell (LC 50)
  place of torment and utter darkness (32-1), *(cf. LC 29, 83)*
  wicked are cast into hell where they remain reserved for judgment on the great day (32-1), *(cf. LC 86, 89)*
Heresy
  civil magistrates have the authority to suppress all blasphemies and heresies (23-3 original version)
Holiness
  man was endued with true holiness at creation (4-2)

sanctification is imperfect in this life (13-2)
true holiness is the goal of sanctification (13-1)
Holy
God is most holy (2-1)
Holy Ghost
(see Holy Spirit)
Holy Scripture
(1) *(see also Scripture, Word of God)*
Holy Spirit
and adoption (LC 74)
and assurance
assurance of faith is conveyed by the Holy Spirit (18-3)
assurance of faith is founded upon the testimony of the Spirit (18-2)
and Christ
Jesus Christ, as a prophet, reveals the will of God to the Church by His Spirit (LC 43)
Jesus Christ was conceived by the power of the Holy Ghost (8-2), (LC 37)
prayer is to be made in the name of the Son by the help of His Spirit (21-3)
Spirit anointed Jesus Christ above measure (8-3), (LC 42)
Spirit of Christ in the calling of the elect (3-6)
Spirit of Christ is active in the gathering and perfecting of the saints (25-3)
Spirit of Christ persuades the elect to believe and obey (8-8)
and creation (4-1)
and justification (LC 72, 73)
and prayer
prayer is to be made in the name of the Son by the help of His Spirit (21-3)
and regeneration
Spirit quickens and renews passive man (10-2)
Spirit regenerates and saves elect infants who die in infancy (10-3)
and repentance (LC 76)

and sanctification (LC 75)
    Spirit is responsible for good works in believers (16-3, 5)
    Spirit subdues and enables the will of man to do the will of God revealed in the law (19-7)
and the application of redemption (LC 58, 59)
and the elect
    elect are effectually called by God's Word and Spirit (10-1)
    in due time the Spirit applies Christ to the elect (11-4)
    Spirit is promised to all who are ordained unto eternal life (7-3), (LC 32), *(cf. LC 38)*
    Spirit of Christ in the calling of the elect (3-6)
    Spirit of Christ persuades the elect to believe and obey (8-8)
    Spirit regenerates and saves elect infants who die in infancy (10-3)
and the law (7-5)
and the perseverance of the saints (17-2)
and the revelation of God (LC 2)
and the sacraments
    efficacy of a sacrament depends upon the work of the Spirit and the word of institution (27-3)
    Spirit offers, exhibits and confers grace in baptism to such as that grace belongs (28-6)
equal with the Father (LC 11)
grieving the Spirit (17-3), (18-4)
illumination of the Spirit (1-6)
promise of the Spirit (7-3)
witness of the Spirit (18-2), (LC 4)

Homosexuality
    forbidden by the Seventh Commandment (LC 137-139)

Humiliation of Christ
    (8-4), (LC 42, 46-50)

Humility
    produced by the doctrine of predestination (3-8)

Hypostatic Union
    (see Jesus Christ-natures of Christ)

Idolatry
> first petition of the Lord's Prayer calls on God to remove idolatry (LC 190)
> forbidden by the First Commandment (LC 103-106)

Illumination of the Spirit
> (1-6)

Image of God in Man
> (LC 17), *(see also Man-and his original state)*

Images
> creation of images forbidden by the Second Commandment (LC 107-110)

Imagination
> God may not be worshipped according to the imaginations and devices of men (21-1)

Immortal
> man was created with an immortal soul (4-2)

Immutable
> God is immutable (2-1)

Imputation
> Christ's obedience and satisfaction are imputed to those who are effectually called (11-1), (LC 70, 71, 77)
> guilt of our first parents' sin is imputed to their posterity (6-3), (LC 22, 25, 26)
> of the sin of the elect to Christ *(see Jesus Christ-and the elect)*

Incarnation
> (8-2), (LC 36, 37)

Incest
> forbidden by the Seventh Commandment (LC 137-139)

Infants
> elect infants who die in infancy are regenerated and saved (10-3)
> of believing parents are to be baptized (28-4), (LC 166)

Infinite
> God is infinite in His being and perfection (2-1)

Inflation
> *(cf. exposition of the Eighth Commandment LC 140-142)*

Inherit
    adopted children of God inherit promises as heirs of everlasting salvation (12)
Inheritance
    everlasting inheritance and the covenant of grace (7-4)
    everlasting inheritance purchased by Jesus Christ for the elect (8-5)
    Holy Spirit is the earnest of our inheritance (18-2)
Innocency
    in man's state of innocency he had freedom and power to do good (9-2), *(see also Man-and his original state)*
    man fell from his state of innocency (LC 21)
Innocent
    protection of the innocent required by the Sixth Commandment (LC 134-136)
Inspiration
    books of the Apocrypha were not of divine inspiration (1-3)
    of the Scripture (1-2)
Inspired
    Old and New Testaments were immediately inspired by God (1-8)
Institution
    word of institution and the efficacy of the sacraments (27-3)
Intercession
    and the necessity of the Mediator being both God and man (LC 38, 39)
    Jesus Christ is now making intercession (8-4, 8), (LC 54, 55, 79)
Interpretation
    infallible rule of interpretation (1-9)
Invisible Church
    benefits enjoyed by the members of the invisible Church (LC 65, 69)
    catholic or universal Church is invisible and consists of the whole number of the elect (25-1), (LC 64)
Irresistible Grace
    (see Effectual Calling, God-grace of God)
Israel
    Christ was prefigured in Israel's ceremonial laws (19-3)
    God gave Israel ceremonial laws in addition to the ten commandments (19-3)

God gave Israel judicial laws in addition to the ten commandments (19-4)

Jesus Christ
(8)
and our faith
Christ is the author and finisher of our faith (14-3)
grace of faith is a work of Christ's Spirit (14-1)
and prayer
prayer is to be made in the name of the Son (21-3)
and the atonement
Christ died for the sins of the elect and rose for their justification (11-4), (LC 52)
Christ effectually applies and communicates redemption to the elect (8-8)
Christ's sacrifice is the propitiation for all the sins of His elect (29-2)
design of the atonement (3-6), (8-1)
through Christ our original corruption is pardoned and mortified (6-5)
work of the atonement (6-5), (8-4, 5), (11-1, 3, 4), (29-2)
and the Church
Christ has appointed a government in the Church distinct from the civil magistrate (30-1)
Christ has appointed a regular government and discipline in His Church (23-3)
Christ has established external peace and order in the Church (20-4)
Christ has given the ministry, oracles and ordinances of God to the visible Church (25-3)
Christ is the Head and Savior of the Church (8-1), (25-1, 6), (LC 52, 54, 60)
Christ's honor is vindicated through the use of Church censures (30-3)
Christ's promise of the Spirit is being fulfilled in the visible Church (25-3)
visible Church is the kingdom of Christ (25-2)

and the covenant of grace
    Christ is the substance of the covenant of grace (7-6), (LC 35)
    Christ is the Testator of the covenant of grace (7-4)
and the elect (believers, saints)
    all saints that are united to Christ have fellowship with Him in His graces, sufferings, death, resurrection and glory (26-1)
    believers are created in Christ unto good works (16-2)
    Christ died for the sins of the elect and rose for their justification (11-4)
    Christ effectually applies and communicates redemption to the elect (8-8)
    Christ has delivered believers from this present evil world, bondage to Satan and dominion of sin, etc. (20-1)
    Christ has purchased liberty for believers (20-1)
    Christ is applied to the elect in due time by the Holy Spirit (11-4)
    Christ makes intercession for the elect (8-4), (8-8)
    Christ's intercession and the perseverance of the saints (17-2)
    Christ's obedience and satisfaction are imputed to those who are effectually called (11-1)
    Christ's sacrifice is the propitiation for all the sins of His elect (29-2)
    Christ's Spirit is active in the gathering and perfecting of the saints (25-3)
    Christ's Spirit is wholly responsible for the good works of believers (16-3)
    Christ's Spirit persuades the elect to believe and obey (8-8)
    Christ was given by the Father for those who are effectually called (11-3)
    elect are chosen to eternal life in Christ (LC 13)
    elect are redeemed by Christ (3-6)
    good works of believers are accepted in Christ (16-6)
    saints have communion with Christ (26-3)
    those of mankind that are predestinated unto life in Christ (3-5)
    through Him our original corruption is pardoned and mortified (6-5)

and the Holy Spirit
    Christ's promise of the Spirit is being fulfilled in the visible Church (25-3)
    Christ's sanctifying Spirit supplies strength (13-3)
    Christ was anointed with the Holy Spirit above measure (8-3)
    Christ was conceived by the power of the Holy Ghost (8-2)
    grace of faith is a work of Christ's Spirit (14-1)
    Spirit of Christ subdues and enables the will of man to do the will of God revealed in the law (19-7)
and the imputation of His obedience and satisfaction (11-1), (LC 70, 71, 77)
and the law
    attention to the moral law makes clearer our need of Christ (19-6)
    Christ in the Gospel does not in any way dissolve the moral law (19-5)
    Christ was made under the law and did perfectly fulfil it (8-4)
    Christ was prefigured in Israel's ceremonial laws (19-3)
    Spirit of Christ subdues and enables the will of man to do the will of God revealed in the law (19-7)
and the Old Testament
    Christ was foresignified in types and ordinances (7-5), (LC 34)
    Christ was prefigured in Israel's ceremonial laws (19-3)
    Christ was revealed in promises, types and sacrifices (8-6)
and the sacraments
    baptism is a sign and seal of ingrafting into Christ (28-1)
    Christ has appointed baptism to be continued in His Church until the end of the world (28-1)
    Christ instituted the sacrament of the Lord's Supper (29-1)
    Christ is not re-sacrificed in the sacrament of the Lord's Supper (29-2)
    Christ ordained only two sacraments in the Gospel (27-4)
    ignorant and ungodly persons commit great sin against Christ when they partake of the Lord's Supper (29-8)
    Lord's Supper is a perpetual remembrance of the sacrifice of Christ (29-1)

   relation between the elements in the sacrament of the Lord's Supper and Christ (29-5)
   sacraments represent Christ and His benefits (27-1)
   those who partake of the Lord's Supper do spiritually receive and feed upon Christ crucified (29-7)
  and types
   Christ was foresignified in types and ordinances (7-5)
   Christ was prefigured in Israel's ceremonial laws (19-3)
   Christ was revealed in promises, types and sacrifices (8-6)
  ascension of Christ (LC 51-54)
  as Mediator (LC 38-40)
   Christ was chosen, ordained and furnished by God to execute the office of a Mediator (8-1)
   Christ willingly undertook the office of Mediator (8-4)
   freely provided and offered to sinners (LC 32)
   of the covenant of grace (36)
   since the Fall, God cannot be worshipped without a Mediator (21-2)
  as Messiah (7-5)
  as the second Adam (LC 31)
  burial of Christ (8-4)
  Christ is the Heir of all things (8-1)
  Christ was signified to be the seed of the woman (8-6)
  communion with Christ
   all ignorant and ungodly persons are unfit to enjoy communion with Him (29-8)
   saints have communion with Christ (26-3)
  crucifixion of Christ (8-4)
  death of Christ (8-4)
  equal with the Father (LC 11)
  exaltation of Christ (8-4), (LC 51-56)
  God's mercy in Christ is apprehended in repentance (15-2)
  humiliation of Christ (8-4), (LC 47-50)
  incarnation of Christ (8-3), (LC 36, 37)
  intercession of Christ
   Christ makes intercession for the elect (8-4, 8), (LC 54, 55, 79)

Christ's intercession and the perseverance of the saints (17-2)
judgment of Christ
    all power and judgment has been given to Christ by the Father (33-1)
    Christ is the Judge of the world (8-1, 4), (33-1)
    Christ would have the day of judgment unknown to men (33-3)
mediation of Christ
    by His mediation, Christ has procured redemption (LC 57-59)
names of Christ (LC 41, 42)
natures of Christ
    all fullness dwells in Christ (8-3)
    Christ acts according to both natures in the work of mediation (8-7)
    Christ has all the treasures of wisdom and knowledge (8-3)
    Christ is holy, harmless, undefiled, and full of grace and truth (8-3)
    Christ is the same yesterday, today and forever (8-6)
    Christ is very and eternal God, of one substance and equal with the Father (8-2)
    Christ's pre-existence (8-2)
    Christ took upon Himself man's nature (8-2), *(cf. LC 52)*
    in Christ, the human and divine natures are united (8-3)
    in Christ, two whole, perfect, and distinct natures are inseparably joined (8-2)
obedience of Christ
    Christ rendered perfect obedience (8-5)
    Christ's obedience and satisfaction are imputed to those who are effectually called (11-1)
offices of Christ (8-1), (LC 43-45)
power of Christ
    by Christ's power, all enemies of the elect are overcome (8-8)
    by Christ's power, the bodies of the just and the unjust shall be raised (32-3), (LC 87)
    over all things in heaven and earth (LC 54)
promise of Christ

Christ's promise of the Spirit is being fulfilled in the visible
Church (25-3)
resurrection of Christ (LC 51-53)
Christ arose from the dead on the third day and ascended into
heaven (8-4)
Christ died for the sins of the elect and rose for their justification
(11-4), (LC 52)
virtue of Christ's death and resurrection is the ground of
sanctification (13-1)
satisfaction of Christ
Christ fully satisfied the justice of His Father (8-5)
Christ's obedience and satisfaction are imputed to those who
are effectually called (11-1)
states of Christ (8-4), (LC 42, 46-50)
suffering of Christ (8-4)
union with Christ
all saints that are united to Christ have fellowship with Him in
His graces, sufferings, death, resurrection and glory (26-1)
work of Christ *(see also Atonement, Intercession)*
Christ died for the sins of the elect and rose for their justification
(11-4)
Christ was signified to be the Lamb slain from the beginning of
the world (8-6)

Judas
(LC 49)

Judge
God has appointed a day wherein He will judge the world by Jesus
Christ (33-1)
Jesus Christ is the Judge of the world (8-1), (LC 51, 56)

Judgment
all power and judgment has been given to Jesus Christ by the Father
(33-1)
certainty of a day of judgment deters men from sin and gives
consolation to the godly (33-3)
day of judgment is unknown to men (33-3)
God's mercy and justice shall be glorified on the day of judgment
(33-2)

of the last judgment (33), (LC 86, 88, 89, 90)
temporal judgments are brought upon sinning believers (17-3)
wicked are cast into hell where they remain reserved for judgment on the great day (32-1)

Judicial Laws
God gave Israel judicial laws in addition to the ten commandments (19-4)

Just
bodies of the just and the unjust shall be raised by the power of Christ (32-3)
God is just (2-1)

Justice
God's justice in reprobation (3-7)
God's justice praised in His exercise of providence (5-1)
God's justice shall be glorified on the day of judgment (33-2)
Jesus Christ fully satisfied the justice of His Father (8-5), (LC 38)

Justification
(11)
definition of justification (LC 70)
difference between justification and sanctification (LC 77)
elect can never fall away from the state of justification (11-5)
of believers under the Old Testament (11-6)
of sinners glorifies God's exact justice and rich grace (11-3)
only of free grace (11-3), (LC 71)

Justify (Justified)
all those justified are adopted as the children of God (12)
elect in Christ are justified (3-6)
God decreed from all eternity to justify the elect (11-4)
justifying faith (LC 72, 73)
those effectually called are justified, pardoned, accounted righteous (11-1)

Kidnapping
forbidden by the Eighth Commandment (LC 140-142)

King
Jesus Christ is a King (8-1)

Kingdom
    of Christ
        in the second petition of the Lord's Prayer, we ask Christ to exercise the kingdom of His power in all the world (LC 191)
    of God
        Christ conversed with the apostles concerning the kingdom of God after His resurrection (LC 53)
    of heaven
        Church officers have the power to shut/open the kingdom of heaven (30-2)
        civil magistrates may not assume to themselves the power of the keys of the kingdom of heaven (23-3)
        keys of the kingdom of heaven have been committed to Church officers (30-2)
    of sin and Satan
        in the second petition of the Lord's Prayer, we pray that the kingdom of sin and Satan may be destroyed (LC 191)
    of the Lord Jesus Christ
        visible Church is the kingdom of the Lord Jesus Christ (25-2)

Knowledge
    all the treasures of wisdom and knowledge are in Jesus Christ (8-3)
    man was endued with knowledge at creation (4-2)
    of God (1-1), *(cf. 21-1)*, (LC 6)
    tree of the knowledge of good and evil (4-2)

Lamb of God
    (8-6)

Last Day
    Christ shall come again at the last day (LC 56)
    elect are assured of their resurrection on the last day (LC 52)

Last Judgment
    (33)
    certainty of a day of judgment deters men from sin and gives consolation to the godly (33-3)
    day of judgment is unknown to men (33-3)

God's mercy and justice shall be glorified on the day of judgment (33-2)
wicked are cast into hell where they remain reserved for judgment on the great day (32-1)
Law of God
(19)
and believers
Christ has purchased freedom from the curse of the moral law for believers (20-1), *(cf. 19-6)*
law's usefulness to true believers is not contrary to the grace of the Gospel (19-7)
true believers are freed from the curse of the law (19- 6), *(cf. 20-1)*
and Christ
Christ has purchased freedom from the curse of the moral law for believers (20-1)
Christ was made under the law and did perfectly fulfil it (8-4), (LC 48)
and repentance (15-2)
and sin
every sin is a transgression of the righteous law of God (6-6), (LC 24)
and the covenant of grace
administration of the covenant of grace under the law (7-5)
and unregenerate men (LC 96)
as a covenant of works (19-1)
ceremonial law (19-3)
all ceremonial laws have been abrogated under the New Testament (19-3)
Jewish Church was subjected to the yoke of the ceremonial law (20-1)
curse of the law (6-6)
exposition of the Ten Commandments (LC 98-148)
judicial law
God gave Israel judicial laws in addition to the ten commandments which expired together with Israel (19-4)

moral law (LC 92-148)
> Christ has purchased freedom from the curse of the moral law for believers (20-1)
> moral law forever binds all (19-5)
> moral law is a rule of life informing us of the will of God (19-6)
> moral law is of great use to true believers (19-6)

under the law, the Church was confined to one nation (25-2)
was written on man's heart at creation (4-2), (LC 17)
which was given to Adam continued to be a perfect rule of righteousness after the Fall (19-2)

Lawful
civil magistrates may lawfully call a synod of ministers (31-2 original version)
it is lawful for Christians to accept and execute the office of magistrate (23-2)
lawful commands of the civil magistrate are to be obeyed (23-4)
marriages
> incestuous marriages are not lawful (24-4)
> it is lawful for all sorts of people to marry (24-3)
> it is not lawful for any man to have more than one wife at a time (24-1)
> it is not lawful for any woman to have more than one husband at a time (24-1)

oaths
> it is a sin to refuse an oath which is imposed by lawful authority (22-3 original version)

prayer is to be made for all things lawful (21-4)

Law of Nature
teaches that a proportion of time is to set aside for the worship of God (21-7)

Laziness
fobidden by the Eighth Commandment (LC 140-142)

Lending
(cf. exposition of the Eighth Commandment (LC 140-142)

Lesbianism
    forbidden by the Seventh Commandment (LC 137-139)

Liberty
    all ecclesiastical persons should enjoy unquestioned liberty in the discharge of their duties (23-3)
    Christian liberty (20)
        destroyed when it is used as a pretense for sin (20-3)
        enlarged under the New Testament (20-1)
        those who, upon the pretense of Christian liberty resist any lawful power are resisting the ordinance of God (20-4)
    man was left to the liberty of his will at creation (4-2)
    of conscience (20-1)
    of conscience is destroyed by requiring an implicit faith and an absolute and blind obedience (20-2)
    will of man was endued with natural liberty (9-1)

Life
    offered to sinners in the covenant of grace (7-3)
    righteous shall go into everlasting life (33-2)
    some men and angels predestined unto everlasting life (3-3)
    was promised upon the fulfillment of the covenant of works (19-1)

Light of Nature
    living according to the light of nature cannot save (10-4), (LC 60)
    manifests the goodness, wisdom and power of God so that men are left unexcusable (1-1)
    shows that there is a God (21-1), (LC 2)

Limited Atonement
    (LC 38, 44), *(see also Atonement, Jesus Christ—and the Atonement)*
    only the elect in Christ are redeemed (3-6)

Lord
    (see Jesus Christ)
    God alone is Lord of the conscience (20-2)

Lord's Day
    (21-7), *(cf. exposition of the Fourth Commandment LC 115-122), (see also Sabbath)*

Lordship
God has lordship and sovereignty over all (21-1)
Lord's Prayer
(LC 186-196)
conclusion (LC 196)
parts of the Lord's Prayer (LC 188)
preface (LC 189)
six petitions (LC 190-195)
use of the Lord's Prayer (LC 187)
Lord's Supper
(29), (LC 168-177)
administration of the Lord's Supper (LC 174)
agreement with the sacrament of baptism (LC 176), *(cf. LC 177)*
and one who doubts of his being in Christ (LC 172)
and the Church
> Church officers are to make use of admonition, suspension from the Lord's table and excommunication in order to protect the Church (30-4)
> procedure to be used for the observance of the Lord's Supper (29-3)
> sacrament of the Lord's Supper should be given only to those present in the congregation (29-3)

difference from the sacrament of baptism (LC 177), *(cf. LC 176)*
elements of the Lord's Supper
> bread and wine represent Christ's body and blood (29-5), (LC 169)
> elements in the sacrament of the Lord's Supper and their relation to Christ (29-5)
> ignorant and wicked men may receive the outward elements, but do not receive the thing signified (29-8)

fencing of the Lord's table
> all ignorant and ungodly persons are not to be admitted to the Lord's table (29-8), (LC 173)
> Church officers are to make use of admonition, suspension from the Lord's table and excommunication in order to protect the Church (30-4)

instituted by Jesus Christ (29-1), (LC 164)
meaning of the Lord's Supper (29-1, 2), (LC 168)
    doctrine of transubstantiation is repugnant (29-6)
    sacrament of the Lord's Supper does not involve any real sacrifice (29-2)
    sacrament of the Lord's Supper is a commemoration of Christ's one offering up of Himself (29-2)
obligation of those who have received the sacrament of the Lord's Supper (LC 175)
practices that are contrary to the nature of this sacrament (29-4)
preparation for the sacrament of the Lord's Supper (LC 171)
those who partake of the Lord's Supper do spiritually receive and feed upon Christ crucified (29-7)
worthy communication in the sacrament of the Lord's Supper (LC 170)

Love
believers have a child-like love toward God (20-1)
faith works by love (11-2)
in love believers are to receive the one who repents of his sins (15-6)
of God
    and the perseverance of believers (LC 79)
    in election (3-5), (LC 13, 30)

Luck
(cf. exposition of the First Commandment LC 103-106)

Lying
forbidden by the Ninth Commandment (LC 143-145)

Man
(see also Men)
and God (LC 1, 2, 5)
and his Fall (6-1), (LC 21-23)
    man lost all ability to do spiritual good when he fell into sin (9-3)
    man's Fall and the covenant of works (7-3)
and his original state (LC 17, 20, 21)

man had dominion over the creatures at creation (4-2)
man had freedom and power to do good (9-2)
man had power to fulfill law of God at creation (4-2)
man was commanded not to eat of the tree at creation (4-2)
man was created by God in His image with a reasonable soul (4-2)
man was endued with knowledge, righteousness and true holiness at creation (4-2)
man was in communion with God at creation (4-2)
man was left to the liberty of his will at creation (4-2), (9-1)
man was subject to the transgression of God's law at creation (4-2)
and his present state (LC 25, 28), *(cf. the petitions of the Lord's Prayer LC 190-195)*
man is in a state of sin and death by nature (10-1), (LC 26, 27)
man is passive until quickened and renewed by the Holy Spirit (10-2)
man's corruption may lead him to consider unbiblical arguments in the matter of divorce (24-6)
natural man is averse from good and dead in sin (9-3)
no man is able to perfectly keep the commandments of God (LC 149)
and his will (9-5), (LC 21)
and marriage
incestuous marriages are not lawful (24-4; *cf. 24-4 original version)*
it is not lawful for any man to have more than one wife at a time (24-1)
marriage is to be between one man and one woman (24-1)
marriage was ordained for the increase of mankind (24-2)
and sin
every man has a duty to repent of particular sins (15-5)
every man is bound to make private confession of his sins before God (15-6)
and the law of God *(see also Law of God)*

curse of the law (6-6)
duty which God requires of man is obedience (LC 91)
every sin is a transgression of the righteous law of God (6-6)
God has given a perpetual Sabbath commandment binding all men in all ages (21-7)
man's duty toward God is found in the first four commandments (19-2)
man's duty toward his fellow man is found in the last six commandments (19-2)
moral law forever binds all men (19-5)
moral law is a rule of life informing man of the will of God (19-6)
was written on man's heart at creation (4-2)
which was given to Adam continued to be a perfect rule of righteousness after the Fall (19-2)
and the providence of God (LC 20), *(see also Providence)*

Mankind
(see also Man, Men)
all mankind are not left to perish in the estate of sin and misery (LC 30)
Fall brought mankind into an estate of sin and misery (LC 23)
moral law is the rule of obedience binding upon all mankind (LC 92, 93)
our first parents were the root of all mankind (6-3), *(cf. LC 22)*
uses of the moral law for mankind (LC 94-97)

Man of Sin
Pope of Rome is that man of sin (25-6 original version)

Marks of the Church
(cf. 25-4)

Marriage
(24), *(cf. exposition of the Seventh Commandment LC 137-139)*
adultery after marriage (24-5)
contract of marriage may be dissolved if adultery or fornication is detected prior to the marriage (24-5)
incestuous marriages are not lawful (24-4; *cf. 24-4 original version)*

is the joining by God of a man and a woman (24-6)
　　　is to be between one man and one woman (24-1)
　　　it is lawful for all sorts of people to marry (24-3)
　　　it is the duty of Christians to marry only in the Lord (24-3)
　　　ordained by God for man's help (LC 20)
　　　purposes of marriage (24-2)
Mass
　　　popish sacrifice of the mass is most abominably injurious to Christ's one, only sacrifice (29-2)
　　　private masses are contrary to the nature of the sacrament of the Lord's Supper (29-4)
Materialism
　　　forbidden by the Eighth Commandment (LC 140-142)
Means
　　　God's use of means in providence (5-3)
Mediation
　　　Jesus Christ's work of mediation (8-7), (LC 57-59, 153, 154)
Mediator
　　　Christ is the Mediator between God and man (8-1), *(cf. LC 32, 36, 38-42)*
　　　since the Fall, God cannot be worshipped without a Mediator (21-2)
Men
　　(see also Man)
　　and death
　　　　after death, the bodies of men return to dust but their souls return to God (32-1)
　　　　all persons who have ever lived upon the earth shall appear before the tribunal of Christ (33-1)
　　　　state of men after death (32)
　　and prayer
　　　　God requires prayer of all men (21-3)
　　and salvation
　　　　man cannot be saved without professing the Christian religion (10-4)
　　and the day of judgment (LC 87-90)

certainty of a day of judgment deters men from sin and gives
consolation to the godly (33-3)
day of judgment is unknown to men (33-3)
and the law of God
moral law is the declaration of God's will to mankind (LC 93)
unregenerate men and the law of God (LC 96)
uses of the moral law for men (LC 94-97)
and the Sabbath (see also Sabbath)
God has given a perpetual Sabbath commandment binding all men in all ages (21-7)
in God's eternal decree (3-3), (LC 12, 13)
sins of men and God's providence (5-4)
wicked and unregenerate men
ignorant and wicked men may receive the outward elements in the Lord's Supper, but they do not receive the thing signified (29-8)
unregenerate men may deceive themselves with false hopes and carnal presumptions of being in the favor of God (18-1)
wicked and ungodly men are blinded and hardened by God, given over to their own lusts and sometimes have their gifts withdrawn (5-6)
works of unregenerate men (16-7)

Mercy of God
is praised in His exercise of providence (5-1)
shall be glorified on the day of judgment (33-2)
withheld from the non-elect (3-7)

Messiah
promised to the elect under the law (7-5), (LC 34)

Miracles (5-3)

Miseries
sinner is made subject to spiritual, temporal and eternal miseries (6-6)

Mode of baptism
(28-3)

Moral Law
    all are forever bound by the moral law (19-5), (LC 93)
    definition of the moral law (LC 93)
    exposition of the Ten Commandments (LC 98-148)
    uses of the moral law (LC 94-97)
Mortification
    (see Sanctification)
Murder
    forbidden by the Sixth Commandment (LC 134-136)
Mystery
    holy mysteries in the sacrament of the Lord's Supper (29-8)
    of predestination (3-8)
    of salvation is revealed in and by the Word (8-8)

Name of God
    (cf. exposition of the Third Commandment LC 111-114)
Nature
    of God
        revealed in His law (LC 95)
    of the elements of the Lord's Supper
        elements remain the same in nature in the sacrament of the Lord's Supper (29-5)
    law of nature
        teaches that a proportion of time is to set aside for the worship of God (21-7)
    light of nature
        living according to the light of nature cannot save (10-4)
        shows that there is a God (21-1)
Natures of Christ
    (see Jesus Christ—natures of Christ)
Nature of Man
    (see Man—and his original state, and his present state)
New Testament
    all ceremonial laws have been abrogated under the New Testament (19-3)
    baptism is a sacrament of the New Testament (28-1)

books of the New Testament (1-2)
designates the period under the gospel (7-6)
liberty of Christians is enlarged under the New Testament (20-1)
Scriptures of the New Testament are the Word of God (LC 3)

Ninth Commandment
(LC 143-145)

Non-Elect
(see also Reprobate)
may be called by the ministry of the Word without being saved and may experience some common operations of the Spirit (10-4)

Number
of men and angels foreordained to life/death is certain and definite (3-4)

Oath
binds in anything not sinful (22-4)
God's name is that by which men ought to swear (22-2)
it is a sin to refuse an oath which is lawfully imposed (22-3 original version)
lawful oath is part of religious worship (21-5), (22-1)
lawful oaths and vows (22-1)
not to be violated even if it is made to heretics or infidels (22-4)
to be taken in the plain and common sense of the words (22-4)
vain or rash oaths (22-2)
warranted by the Word of God (22-2)
whosoever takes an oath should duly consider so solemn an act (22-3)

Obedience
Adam's posterity were bound to perpetual obedience in the covenant of works (19-1)
due to God from all creatures (2-2)
elect are enabled to obey by the Holy Spirit (LC 32)
Jesus Christ rendered perfect obedience (8-5), *(see also Satisfaction)*
perfect and personal obedience is required in the covenant of works (7-2)

to the revealed Word of God and the doctrine of predestination (3-8)
yielded to the commands of God in the Word by faith (14-2)
Obey
people have a duty to obey the civil magistrate (23-4)
Spirit of Christ persuades the elect to believe and obey (8-8)
Office
of Mediator and Surety was executed by Jesus Christ (8-3)
of Mediator was willingly undertaken by Jesus Christ (8-4)
Officers
(see Church Officers)
Offices of Christ
(8-1), (LC 42-45)
Old Testament
books of the Old Testament (1-2)
designating the period under the law (7-5)
justification of believers under the Old Testament (11-6)
sacraments of the Old Testament were, for substance, the same with those of the New (27-5)
Scriptures of the Old Testament are the Word of God (LC 3)
Omnipotence of God
(2-1, 2), (LC 7, 196), *(see also God—power of God, God—sovereignty of God)*
Omnipresence of God
(2-1), (LC 7)
Omniscience of God
(2-2), (LC 7)
Ordain
(as in Appoint)
baptism was ordained by Jesus Christ (28-1)
only two sacraments have been ordained by Christ in the Gospel (27-4)
sacraments can only be dispensed by a minister of the Word lawfully ordained (27-4)
Ordain
(as in Foreordain, see Foreordain)

Ordinance
   Christ was signified by ordinances under the law (7-5)
Ordo Salutis
   (8-1), (10), (11), (12), (13), (14), (15), (LC 67, 68, 70-76)
Original Righteousness
   of our first parents (6-2)
Original Sin
   (see also Imputation)
   basis from which proceeds all actual transgressions (6-4), *(cf. LC 193, 194)*
   definition of original sin (6-3), (LC 25), *(cf. LC 22, 26)*
   is a transgression of the righteous law of God (6-6)

Pantheism
   doctrine of pantheism disputed (2-2), (5-1)
Parents
   duty to parents *(cf. exposition of the Fifth Commandment LC 123-133)*
   our first parents (6-1)
   our first parents became dead in sin as a result of the Fall (6-2)
   our first parents were the root of all mankind (6-3)
   sin of our first parents (6-1)
Passover
   covenant of grace was administered under the Old Testament by the passover (LC 34)
Perfection
   not obtainable in this life (13-2)
   should be sought (13-3)
Perjury
   forbidden by the Ninth Commandment (LC 143-145)
Perspicuity of Scripture (1-9)
Perseverance (17)
   of the Church (25-5)
   of the saints (17-1)
      and the intercession of Jesus Christ (17-2)
         depends upon the immutability of the decree of election (17-2)

270 / Guide to the Westminster Standards

    foreseen perseverance was not the basis of predestination (3-5)
Persuade
    elect are persuaded by Christ's Spirit to believe and obey (8-8)
Pilate
    Christ was condemned by Pilate (LC 49)
Polygamy
    forbidden by the Seventh Commandment (LC 137-139)
    unlawful (24-1)
Pope
    antichrist, that man of sin, son of perdition (25-6 original version)
    has no power or jurisdiction over the civil magistrate (23-4)
    in no sense is the Pope of Rome the head of the Church (25-6)
    popish monastical vows are superstitious and sinful snares (22-7)
    popish sacrifice of the mass is most abominably injurious to Christ's one, only sacrifice (29-2)
Pornography
    forbidden by the Seventh Commandment (LC 137-139)
Posterity
    Adam's posterity were bound to perpetual obedience in the covenant of works (19-1)
    of our first parents affected by their Fall (6-3), (LC 26)
Power(s)
    Adam was endued with the power and ability to keep the covenant of works (19-1)
    ecclesiastical power
        power of the keys of kingdom of heaven (30-2)
        those who, upon the pretense of Christian liberty resist a lawful ecclesiastical power, are resisting the ordinance of God (20-4)
    man had power to fulfil the law of God at creation (4-2)
    of Christ
        all power and judgment has been given to Jesus Christ by the Father (33-1)
        by the power of Christ, the bodies of the just and the unjust shall be raised (32-3)

overcomes all enemies of the elect (8-8)
of death
    Jesus Christ remained under the power of death for three days (8-4)
of God
    ascribed to Him alone in the Lord's Prayer (LC 196)
    God's eternal power was manifested in the act of creation (4-1)
    God's power is manifested in providence (5-4)
    God's power is praised in His exercise of providence (5-1)
    God's power is revealed by the light of nature and in the works of creation and providence (1-1)
of synods and councils (31)
of the civil magistrate (23)
    civil magistrates may not assume to themselves the power of the keys of the kingdom of heaven (23-3)
    power of the sword has been given to civil magistrates (23-1)
powers which God has ordained are for upholding and preserving (20-4)

Powerful
God is infinitely powerful (2-1)

Praise of God
for the doctrine of predestination (3-8)
God's exercise of providence to the praise of His glory (5-1)
praise of His grace the purpose of predestination (3-5)
praise of His justice the purpose of reprobation (3-7)

Prayer
(LC 178-185)
an outward means whereby Christ communicates to His Church the benefits of His mediation (LC 154)
attitude in prayer (LC 185, 189)
definition of prayer (LC 178)
faith is increased and strengthened by prayer (14-1)
Lord's Prayer (LC 186-196)
    meaning of the Lord's Prayer
        conclusion (LC 196)

preface (LC 189)
six petitions (LC 190-195)
    parts of the Lord's Prayer (LC 188)
    use of the Lord's Prayer (LC 187)
one special part of religious worship (21-3)
required by God of all men (21-3)
subjects of prayer (LC 183, 184)
to be made for all things lawful and for all sorts of men living or that shall live hereafter (21-4)
to be made in the name of the Son, by the help of His Spirit (21-3), (LC 178, 180-182)
to be made unto God only (LC 179)
to be made with understanding, reverence, humility, fervency, faith, love and perseverance (21-3)

Preaching of the Word
covenant of grace is administered in the preaching of the Word (LC 35)
manner of preaching (LC 159)
obligation of those who hear the Word preached (LC 160)
only by those sufficiently gifted, duly approved and called (LC 158)
part of the ordinary worship of God (21-5)

Predestination
(3)
a high mystery (3-8)
doctrine of predestination is to be handled with special prudence and care (3-8)
not based on foreseen faith, good works or perseverance (3-5)
of angels and men (3-3, 4)
those of mankind predestinated unto life (3-5)

Pre-existence of Christ
(8-2)

Preservation
of all things by God (5-1)
of life required by the Sixth Commandment (LC 134-136)

Priest
    Jesus Christ is a Priest (8-1)
Profess
    professing the Christian religion is necessary for salvation (10-4)
Promise(s)
    and believers
        adopted children of God inherit promises as heirs of everlasting salvation (12)
        infallible assurance of faith is founded upon the divine truth of the promises of salvation (18-2)
        Jesus Christ was revealed in promises (8-6)
    and faith
        infallible assurance of faith is founded upon the divine truth of the promises of salvation (18-2)
        promises in the Word are embraced by faith (14-2)
    and the Church
        Christ's promise of the Spirit is being fulfilled in the visible Church (25-3)
    and the Spirit
        Holy Spirit is promised to all who are ordained unto eternal life (7-3)
    of Christ
        Christ's promise of the Spirit is being fulfilled in the visible Church (25-3)
    of God
        adopted children of God inherit promises as heirs of everlasting salvation (12)
        life was promised upon the fulfillment of the covenant of works (19-1)
    of salvation
        adopted children of God inherit promises as heirs of everlasting salvation (12)
        benefits of redemption are communicated in promises (8-6)
        Holy Spirit is promised to all who are ordained unto eternal life (7-3)

infallible assurance of faith is founded upon the divine truth of the promises of salvation (18-2)

Jesus Christ was revealed in promises (8-6)

of the covenants
    adopted children of God inherit promises as heirs of everlasting salvation (12)
    benefits of redemption are communicated in promises (8-6)
    Holy Spirit is promised to all who are ordained unto eternal life (7-3)
    Jesus Christ was revealed in promises (8-6), *(cf. LC 34)*
    life was promised upon the fulfillment of the covenant of works (19-1)

Promise of the Spirit
(7-3), (LC 32)

Prophet
Jesus Christ is a Prophet (8-1)

Properties
peculiar to each person of the Trinity (2-3), (LC 10)

Propitiation
sacrifice of Christ is the propitiation for all the sins of His elect (29-2)

Providence
(5), (LC 14, 18-20), *(cf. exposition of the Lord's Prayer LC 191-193, 195)*
and the first fall (5-4)
and the nature of second causes (5-2)
and the sins of angels and men (5-4), *(cf. LC 19, 20)*
God executes His decrees in the works of providence (LC 14)
God's providence is most wise and holy (5-1)
God's providence reaches all creatures (5-7)
God's providence takes care of the Church in a special manner (5-7)
God's use of means in providence (5-3)

Provision
daily provision is prayed for in fourth petition of the Lord's Prayer (LC 193)

Psalms
    singing of psalms is part of the ordinary worship of God (21-5)
Punish
    wicked shall be punished with everlasting destruction (33-2)
Punishment
    Fall made all men liable to all punishments in this world and that which is to come (LC 27), *(cf. LC 28, 29)*
Purgatory
    prayers for the dead are not to be offered (21-4)
    doctrine of purgatory disputed (32-1)
Purpose
    God's eternal and immutable purpose (3-5)
    of God's will in predestination (3-6)
Rape
    forbidden by the Seventh Commandment (LC 137-139)
Reading of Scripture
    part of religious worship (21-5), (LC 156, 157)
Reasonable
    man was created with a reasonable soul (4-2)
Reconciliation
    purchased by Jesus Christ by obedience and sacrifice (8-5), *(cf. LC 40, 44)*
Recreation
    moderation in recreation is required by the Sixth Commandment (LC 134-136)
Redeemed
    only the elect in Christ are redeemed (3-6)
Redemption
    (see also Atonement, Jesus Christ-and the atonement)
    adopted children of God are sealed to the day of redemption (12), (18-2)
    application of Christ's redemption (LC 58, 59)
    benefits of redemption are communicated to the elect in all ages (8-6)
    Christ's work of redemption (8-4, 5, 6)
    effectually applied and communicated to the elect by Christ (8-8)

procured by Christ by His mediation (LC 57)
souls of the righteous wait in heaven for the redemption of their bodies (32-1)

Regenerate
(see also Believers)
moral law is of use to the regenerate (19-6), (LC 97)
those regenerated retain a corrupt nature (6-5)

Regeneration
baptism is a sign and seal of regeneration (28-1)
can occur without baptism (28-5)
Spirit quickens and renews passive man (10-2)
Spirit regenerates and saves elect infants who die in infancy (10-3)

Regulative Principle
(see also Worship–of God)
(21-1), *(cf. exposition of the Second Commandment LC 107-110)*

Religion
controversies of religion are to be judged by the Holy Spirit speaking in the Scripture (1-10)
professing the Christian religion is necessary for salvation (10-4)

Religious Worship
(21-1, 2) *(see also Worship–of God)*

Repent
no sin is so great that it can damn those who truly repent (15-4)

Repentance
(15), (LC 76)
an act of God's free grace (15-3)
an evangelical grace (15-1)
definition of repentance (15-2)
man has a duty to repent of particular sins (15-5)
necessary to all sinners (15-3)
not a satisfaction for sin (15-3)
to be preached by every minister of the Gospel (15-1)

Reprobate
(see also Non-Elect)
God's justice shall be glorified in the damnation of the reprobate on the day of judgment (33-2)

Reprobation
    (3-7), (LC 13, 68)
Reputation
    guarding of our own and our neighbor's reputation is required by the Ninth Commandment (LC 143-145)
Restoration
    (15-6)
Resurrection
    of believers
        all saints that are united to Christ share in His resurrection (26-1), (LC 82)
    of the dead (LC 86-90)
        state of men after death and the resurrection from the dead (32)
    of the Lord Jesus Christ (8-4), (LC 51, 52)
Return of Christ
    (see also Second Coming)
    (32-3), (33)
    Jesus Christ shall return to judge men and angels (8- 4)
Revelation
    assurance of faith can be obtained without extraordinary revelation (18-3)
    God's former ways of revealing His will have now ceased (1-1)
    natural revelation (1-1) *(see also Light of Nature)*
    necessary for salvation (1-1)
Reverence
    of God for the doctrine of predestination (3-8)
Righteous
    after death, the souls of the righteous are received into the highest heavens (32-1)
    shall go into everlasting life on the day of judgment (33-2), (LC 90)
    those effectually called are justified, pardoned, accounted righteous (11-1)
Righteousness
    law given to Adam continued to be a perfect rule of righteousness after the Fall (19-2)
    man was endued with righteousness at creation (4-2)
    our first parents fell from their original righteousness (6-2)

Robbery
   forbidden by the Eighth Commandment (LC 140-142)
Rule
   law given to Adam continued to be a perfect rule of righteousness after the Fall (19-2)
   moral law is a rule of life informing us of the will of God (19-6)
   of faith and life (1-2), (LC 3)
   of obedience revealed to Adam was the moral law (LC 92)
   of the Word (1-6)

Sabbath
   (21), *(cf. exposition of the Fourth Commandment LC 115-121)*
   and worship (21-8)
   Christian Sabbath (21-7)
   God has given a perpetual Sabbath commandment binding all men in all ages (21-7)
   instituted by God while man was in his original state (LC 20)
   is to be kept holy unto the Lord (21-7, 8), (LC 117-121)
   requirements of the Fourth Commandment (LC 116)
   seventh day in the Old Testament, first day in the New Testament (21-7)

Sacraments
   (27), (LC 161-177)
   administration of the sacraments
      can only be dispensed by a minister of the Word lawfully ordained (27-4)
      civil magistrates may not assume to themselves the administration of the Word and sacraments (23-3)
      covenant of grace is administered through sacraments (7-6), (LC 35)
      faith is increased and strengthened by the administration of the sacraments (14-1)
      Lord's Supper to be given only to those present in the congregation (29-3)
      only two sacraments were ordained by Christ our Lord in the Gospel (27-4)

part of the ordinary worship of God (21-5)
procedure to be used in the observance of the Lord's Supper (29-3)
agreement of the two sacraments with each other (LC 176), *(cf. LC 177)*
and Christ
- elements in the sacrament of the Lord's Supper and their relation to Christ (29-5)
- elements of bread and wine represent Christ's body and blood in the sacrament of the Lord's Supper (29-5)
- only two sacraments were ordained by Christ our Lord in the Gospel (27-4)
- sacrament of the Lord's Supper is a commemoration of Christ's once offering up of Himself (29-2)
- sacrament of the Lord's Supper was instituted by Jesus Christ (29-1)
- sacraments are an outward means whereby Christ communicates the benefits of His mediation (LC 154)
- sacraments represent Christ and His benefits (27-1)
- those who partake of the sacrament of the Lord's Supper spiritually receive and feed upon Christ crucified (29-7)

and faith
- faith is increased and strengthened by the administration of the sacraments (14-1)

and grace (27-3)
- grace and salvation are not inseparably annexed to the sacrament of baptism (28-5)

and the Church
- Church officers are to make use of admonition, suspension from the Lord's table and excommunication in order to protect the Church (30-4)
- Lord's Supper is to be given only to those present in the congregation (29-3)

and the civil magistrate
- civil magistrates may not assume to themselves the administration of the Word and sacraments (23-3)

and the covenant of grace
  covenant of grace is administered through sacraments (7-6)
and the Spirit
  efficacy of the sacraments depends upon the work of the Spirit and the word of institution (27-3)
and the wrath of God
  allowing the profaning of the covenant and its seals can result in the wrath of God falling upon the Church (30-3)
and worship
  administration of the sacraments is part of the ordinary worship of God (21-5)
are effectual means of salvation (LC 161)
definition of a sacrament (27-1), (LC 162)
  every sacrament contains a spiritual relation between the sign and the thing signified (27-2)
differences between the two sacraments (LC 177), *(cf. LC 176)*
efficacy of the sacraments
  depends upon the work of the Spirit and the word of institution (27-3)
  efficacy of the sacrament of baptism (28-6)
elements of the sacraments
  bread and wine represent Christ's body and blood (29-5)
  elements in the sacrament of the Lord's Supper and their relation to Christ (29-5)
  ignorant and wicked men may receive the outward elements, but do not receive the thing signified (29-8)
  outward element to be used in baptism is water (28-2)
fencing the Lord's table
  all ignorant and ungodly persons are not to be admitted to the Lord's table (29-8)
  allowing the profaning of the covenant and its seals can result in the wrath of God falling upon the Church (30-3)
  Church officers are to make use of admonition, suspension from the Lord's table and excommunication in order to protect the Church (30-4)
instituted by Christ (LC 164)

instituted by God (27-1)
meaning of the sacraments
  sacraments put a visible difference between those in the Church and the rest of the world (27-1)
  sacraments represent Christ and His benefits (27-1)
of baptism (LC 165-167, 176, 177), *(see also Baptism)*
  agreement with the sacrament of the Lord's Supper (LC 176), *(cf. LC 177)*
  a sacrament of the New Testament (28-1)
  can only be dispensed by a minister of the Word lawfully ordained (27-4)
  definition of baptism (LC 165)
  efficacy of the sacrament of baptism (28-6)
  grace and salvation are not inseparably annexed to the sacrament of baptism (28-5)
  neglect of baptism
    it is a great sin to neglect the sacrament of baptism (28-5)
  obligation of those baptized (LC 167)
  outward element to be used in baptism is water (28-2)
  subjects of baptism
    those who profess faith in and obedience unto Christ are to be baptized (28-4), (LC 166)
    to be administered to infants of believing parents (28-4), (LC 166)
  to be administered but once unto any person (28-7)
  to be continued in Christ's Church until the end of the world (28-1)
of the Lord's Supper (LC 168-177), *(see also Lord's Supper)*
  administration of the sacrament (29-3), (LC 174)
    can only be dispensed by a minister of the Word lawfully ordained (27-4)
    to be given only to those present in the congregation (29-3)
  agreement with the sacrament of baptism (LC 176), *(cf. LC 177)*
  and one who doubts of his being in Christ (LC 172)
  consubstantiation
    doctrine of consubstantiation disputed (29-7)

definition of the Lord's Supper (LC 168)
difference from the sacrament of baptism (LC 177), *(cf. LC 176)*
does not involve any real sacrifice (29-2)
elements in the sacrament of the Lord's Supper
    represent Christ's body and blood (29-5), (LC 169, 170)
    their relation to Christ (29-5)
fencing of the table
    all ignorant and ungodly persons are not to be admitted to the Lord's table (29-8), (LC 173)
    Church officers are to make use of admonition, suspension from the Lord's table and excommunication in order to protect the Church (30-4)
ignorant and wicked men may receive the outward elements of the Lord's Supper, but they do not receive the thing signified (29-8)
instituted by Jesus Christ (29-1)
meaning of the sacrament of the Lord's Supper (LC 168)
    commemoration of Christ's one offering up of Himself (29-2)
    those who partake of the sacrament of the Lord's Supper spiritually receive and feed upon Christ crucified (29-7)
obligation of those who have received the Lord's Supper (LC 175)
practices that are contrary to the nature of the sacrament of the Lord's Supper (29-4)
preparation for the Lord's Supper (LC 171)

Old Testament sacraments
    substance of the sacraments of the Old Testament were the same with those of the New (27-5)

only two sacraments were ordained by Christ our Lord in the Gospel (27-4), (LC 164)

parts of a sacrament (LC 163)

substance of the sacraments
    substance of the sacraments of the Old Testament were the same with those of the New (27-5)

Transubstantiation
    doctrine of transubstantiation is repugnant (29-6)

Sacrifice
    benefits of redemption were communicated in sacrifices (8-6)
    Jesus Christ was revealed in sacrifices (8-6)
    Lord's Supper is a perpetual remembrance of Christ's sacrifice (29-1)
    sacrament of the Lord's Supper does not involve any real sacrifice (29-2)

Saints
    (see also Believers, Elect)
    (26)
    and their duty toward one another (26-1), (26-2)
    and their union with Christ
        all saints that are united to Christ have fellowship with Him in His graces, sufferings, death, resurrection and glory (26-1)
        saints have communion with Christ (26-3)
    and the visible Church
        saints are to be gathered and perfected by the visible Church (25-3)
    and worship
        by profession they are bound to maintain an holy fellowship and communion in the worship of God (26-2)
        worship is not to be given to saints (21-2)
    communion of the saints
        communion of saints does not infringe the title or propriety which each man has in his goods and possessions (26-3)
        communion of the saints with one another (26-1)
        saints have communion with Christ (26-3)
    grieving the Holy Spirit
        saints can grieve the Holy Spirit by sinning (17-3)
    perseverance of the saints (17-1)
        their perseverance and the intercession of Jesus Christ (17-2)
        their perseverance is guaranteed by the decree of election (17-2)
    worship is not to be given to saints (21-2)

Salvation
    and assurance

assurance of grace and salvation (18-1)
infallible assurance of faith is founded upon the divine truth of the promises of salvation (18-2)
true believers may have their assurance shaken, but are never utterly destitute of that seed of God (18-4)

and the covenant of grace
salvation is offered to sinners in the covenant of grace (7-3), (LC 30, 32)

and the mercy of God
God's mercy shall be glorified in the eternal salvation of the elect on the day of judgment (33-2)

and the sacraments
salvation is held forth in the preaching of the Word and the administration of the sacraments (LC 35)
salvation is not inseparably annexed to the ordinance of baptism (28-5)

and the visible Church
all who live in the visible Church are not saved (LC 61)
Christ is revealing the whole will of God concerning salvation to the Church as a prophet (LC 43)
salvation is ordinarily possible only through the visible Church (25-2)

and the Word of God
Holy Spirit makes the Word an effectual means of enlightening, convincing and humbling sinners, etc. (LC 155)
mysteries of salvation are revealed in and by the Word (8-8), (LC 2)
Scripture comforts and builds up believers unto salvation (LC 4)

and unregenerate men
unregenerate men may deceive themselves with false hopes and carnal presumptions of being in the favor of God (18-1)

fallen man has lost all ability to convert himself (9-3)
light of nature and the works of creation and providence are not sufficient for salvation (1-1), *(cf. LC 2, 60)*
of the elect *(see also Believers, Elect)*
adopted children of God are heirs of everlasting salvation (12)

elect are effectually called to grace and salvation (10-1)
elect are kept by Christ's power, through faith, unto salvation (3-6), *(cf. LC 38)*
elect under the Old Testament had full remission of sin and eternal salvation by faith in the promised Messiah (LC 34)
God's mercy shall be glorified in the eternal salvation of the elect on the day of judgment (33-2)
promises of salvation
    infallible assurance of faith is founded upon the divine truth of the promises of salvation (18-2)

Sanctification
(see also Holy Spirit–and sanctification)
(13)
and justification (LC 77)
Christ's sanctifying Spirit supplies strength (13-3)
definition of sanctification (LC 75)
grounded in Christ's death and resurrection (13-1)
involves the destruction of sin's dominion through the indwelling of Christ's Word and Spirit (13-1), (LC 195)
is imperfect in this life (13-2), (LC 78)
through Christ our original corruption is pardoned and mortified (6-5)
true holiness is the goal of sanctification (13-1)

Sanctify (Sanctified)
elect in Christ are sanctified (3-6)
sanctifying Spirit of Christ supplies strength (13-3)
those effectually called and sanctified shall persevere to the end (17-1)

Satan
by nature, we are wholly inclined to do the will of the devil (LC 192)
Christ has delivered believers from the bondage of Satan (20-1), (LC 52)
God may not be worshipped according to Satan's suggestions (21-1)
malice of Satan (1-1)
power of Satan over wicked and ungodly men (5-6), *(cf. LC 27)*
Satan's temptation of our first parents (6-1), (LC 21)

second petition of the Lord's Prayer calls for the destruction of Satan's kingdom (LC 191)

some Churches have so degenerated as to become synagogues of Satan (25-5)

through Satan's temptations saints may fall into grievous sins (17-3), (LC 195)

wicked will be cast into hell with the devil and his angels (LC 89)

Satisfaction

Christ's obedience and satisfaction are imputed to those who are effectually called (11-1), (LC 70, 71), *(cf. LC 194)*

of the Father's justice was made on behalf of the elect by Christ (11-3), (LC 38, 48, 52)

repentance is not a satisfaction for sin (15-3)

Saving Faith

(see also Faith)

(14)

its principal acts (14-2)

Savior

(see Jesus Christ)

Scripture

(see also Holy Scripture, Word of God)

(LC 2-6)

acknowledges only two places for souls separated from their bodies, heaven or hell (32-1)

makes God known (LC 6)

reading of the Scriptures is part of the ordinary worship of God (21-5)

supreme judge in controversies (1-10)

teaches what man is to believe concerning God (LC 5)

Second Causes

and providence (5-2)

in God's decree (3-1)

Second Coming of Christ

(32-3), (33)

at the end of the world (LC 53, 56)

in the second petition of the Lord's Prayer, we ask Christ to hasten the time of His second coming (LC 191)

to judge angels, men, the world (8-4), (LC 51)

Second Commandment
    (LC 107-110)
Seed
    Jesus Christ was signified to be the seed of the woman (8-6)
Self-Existent
    God is self-existent and independent (2-2)
Serpent
    serpent's head should be bruised by the seed of the woman (8-6)
Service
    due to God from all creatures (2-2)
Seventh Commandment
    (LC 137-139)
Sin(s)
    actual sin
        is a transgression of the righteous law of God (6-6), (LC 24)
        proceeds from our original corruption (6-4)
    all sins are not equally heinous (LC 150, 151)
    and believers
        believers can fall into grievous sins (17-3)
        Christ has delivered believers from the dominion of sin (20-1)
        Christ has purchased freedom from the guilt of sin for believers (20-1)
        elect under the Old Testament had full remission of sin (LC 34)
        sacrifice of Christ is the propitiation for all the sins of His elect (29-2)
        those effectually called have their sins pardoned (11-1)
    and Christ
        Christ executed the office of priest in His once offering Himself a sacrifice for the sins of His people (LC 44)
        Christ was conceived and born without sin (LC 37)
        Mediator was called Jesus because He saves His people from their sins (LC 41)
        only the blood of Christ can expiate sin (LC 152)
    and God
        God is not the author of sin (3-1)
        God's providence and the sins of angels and men (5-4)

sin of our first parents was permitted by God (6-1)
and good works
    debt of former sins is not satisfied by good works (16-5)
and man (9-3), *(cf. LC 22, 23, 25, 28-30 and the exposition of the Lord's Prayer LC 190-195), (see also Man–and his present state)*
and repentance
    man has a duty to repent of particular sins (15-5)
    no sin is so great that it can damn those who truly repent (15-4)
and the Church
    Church officers, who hold the keys of the kingdom of heaven, have the power to retain and remit sins, etc. (30-2)
and the moral law of God
    attention to the moral law of God produces a hatred of sin (19-6)
    every sin is a transgression of the righteous law of God (6-6)
and the reprobate (LC 13)
and the sacraments
    baptism is a sign and seal of remission of sins (28-1)
    great sin is committed against Christ when ignorant or ungodly persons partake of the Lord's Supper (29-8)
    it is a great sin to neglect the ordinance of baptism (28-5)
and the taking of oaths
    it is a sin to refuse an oath which is lawfully imposed (22-3 original version)
confession of sin
    every man is bound to make private confession of his sins before God (15-6)
debt of sin
    debt of former sins is not satisfied by good works (16-5)
definition of sin
    every sin is a transgression of the righteous law of God (6-6)
dominion of sin
    Christ has delivered believers from the dominion of sin (20-1)
    dominion of sin is destroyed in sanctification (13-1)
guilt of sin
    Christ has purchased freedom from the guilt of sin for believers (20-1)

judgment of sin
> certainty of a day of judgment deters men from sin and gives consolation to the godly (33-3)
> every sin, no matter how small, deserves damnation (15-4), (LC 152)

of angels
> God's providence and the sins of angels and men (5-4)

of our first parents permitted by God (6-1)

original sin *(see Original Sin)*

prayer is not to be made for those who have sinned the sin unto death (21-4)

propitiation of sin
> sacrifice of Christ is the propitiation for all the sins of His elect (29-2)

result of sin
> death results from sin (LC 84, 85)
> every sin, no matter how small, deserves damnation (15-4), (LC 152)

those effectually called have their sins pardoned (11-1)

transmission of the sin of our first parents *(see Original Sin)*

Sinful
lawful oaths bind in anything not sinful (22-4)
works of unregenerate men are sinful (16-7)

Singing
singing of psalms is part of the ordinary worship of God (21-5)

Sinner
converted by God and translated into the state of grace (9-4)
converted sinner can will and do that which is spiritually good (9-4)
converted sinner continues to do that which is evil (9-4)
God's exact justice and rich grace are glorified in the sinner's justification (11-3)
guilty for every transgression of God's law (6-6)
made subject to death and miseries by transgressions of God's law (6-6)
Mediator is freely provided and offered to sinners in the covenant of grace (LC 32)
offered life and salvation in the covenant of grace (7-3)

repentance is necessary for all sinners (15-3)
Scriptures are able to convert sinners (LC 4)
Sixth Commandment
(LC 134-136)
Slain
Jesus Christ was signified to be the Lamb slain (8-6)
Slander
forbidden by the Ninth Commandment (LC 143-145)
Sodomy
forbidden by the Seventh Commandment (LC 137-139)
Son of God
(see also Jesus Christ)
became man (LC 37)
Christ was declared to be the Son of God by His resurrection (LC 52)
in the act of creation (4-1)
Mediator of the covenant of grace is the eternal Son of God (LC 36)
prayer is to be made in the name of the Son (21-3)
second person of the Trinity (8-2)
Son of Perdition
Pope of Rome is the son of perdition (25-6 original version)
Soteriology
(see Redemption, Salvation)
Soul(s)
after death, the bodies of men return to dust but their souls return to God (32-1)
Christ took to Himself a true body and a reasonable soul (LC 37)
dead shall be raised at the last day with the self-same bodies which shall again be united to their souls (32-2)
has an immortal substance (32-1)
man was created with a reasonable and immortal soul (4-2), (LC 17)
of the righteous are received into the highest heavens, souls of the wicked are cast into hell (32-1)
Scripture acknowledges only two places for souls separated from their bodies, heaven or hell (32-1)
Soul Sleep
doctrine of soul sleep disputed (32-1)

Sovereignty of God
    (see also God)
    God has lordship and sovereignty over all (21-1), (LC 196)
    God's sovereign power in reprobation (3-7), (LC 13)
Spirit
    (see Holy Spirit)
State
    of adoption
        given to all those justified (12)
    of glory
        and the will of man (9-5)
    of grace (9-4)
        true believers cannot fall away from the state of grace (LC 79)
    of innocency
        in man's state of innocency he had freedom and power to do good (9-2)
    of sin
        elect are effectually called out of a state of sin and death (10-1)
        man's state of sin (9-3)
States of Christ
    (8-4), (LC 42, 46-50)
Stealing
    forbidden by the Eighth Commandment (LC 140-142)
Stewardship
    required by the Eighth Commandment (LC 140-142)
Subjects of Baptism
    (see Baptism, Sacraments-of baptism)
Substance
    Christ is the substance of the covenant of grace (7-6), (LC 35)
    Christ was conceived by the power of the Holy Ghost in the womb of the Virgin Mary of her substance (LC 37)
    doctrine of transubstantiation, which maintains a change of the substance of the bread and wine in the sacrament of the Lord's Supper, is repugnant to Scripture, common sense and reason (29-6)
    elements remain the same in substance in the sacrament of the Lord's Supper (29-5)

sacraments of the Old Testament were, for substance, the same with those of the New (27-5)
souls have an immortal substance (32-1)
Suffering
all saints that are united to Christ share in His sufferings (26-1)
of Christ as Mediator (LC 38, 39)
Suicide
forbidden by the Sixth Commandment (LC 134-136)
Supererogation
works of supererogation are impossible (16-5)
Supper
(see also Lord's Supper)
Lord's Supper (29)
of the Lord, one of the two sacraments ordained by Christ in the Gospel (27-4)
Surety
Jesus Christ executed the office of Mediator and Surety (8-3), (LC 71)
Suspension
Church officers are to make use of admonition, suspension from the Lord's table and excommunication in order to protect the Church (30-4)
Synods
(31)
all synods and councils, since the Apostles' time, are subject to error (31-3)
and councils serve for the better government and edification of the Church (31-1)
are to handle or conclude nothing but that which is ecclesiastical and are not to intermeddle with civil affairs unless petitioned (31-4)
Church officers have the duty to appoint synods and councils as often as is necessary for the good of the Church (31-1)
civil magistrates may lawfully call a synod of ministers (23-3 and 31-2 original version)
decrees and determinations of synods and councils are to be received with reverence and submission if consonant to the Word of God (31-2)

ordinance of God (31-2)
responsibilities of synods and councils (31-2)
Temptation
Christ conflicted with the temptations of Satan (LC 48)
Christ supports His people in their temptations (LC 45)
God's children are exposed to manifold temptations (5-5)
our first parents, through the temptation of Satan, transgressed the commandment of God (LC 21)
saints may fall into sin through the temptations of Satan and the world (17-3), (LC 195)
Ten Commandments
(LC 98-148)
Tenth Commandment
(LC 146-148)
Testimony
of the Church regarding Holy Scripture (1-5)
of the Spirit of adoption (18-2)
Thanksgiving
part of religious worship (21-5)
Theft
forbidden by the Eighth Commandment (LC 140-142)
Theonomy
(see Law of God)
Third Commandment
(LC 111-114)
Throne
all those justified are adopted and have access to the throne of grace (12)
Tongue
prayer, if vocal, is to be made in a known tongue (21-3)
Torment
souls of the wicked are being kept in torments and utter darkness (32-1)
wicked shall be cast into eternal torments (33-2)
Transgression(s)
all actual transgressions proceed from our original corruption (6-4)

every transgression of God's law brings guilt upon the sinner (6-6)
sin is any transgression of the law of God (LC 24)
Transubstantiation
a repugnant doctrine (29-6)
Tree
of life (LC 20)
of the knowledge of good and evil (4-2), (LC 20)
Trinity
(2-3), (LC 9, 10)
Truth
civil magistrates have the authority to keep the truth of God pure and entire (23-3 original version)
Holy Scripture is designed to propagate truth (1-1)
infallible truth of Scripture (1-5)
Type(s)
benefits of redemption were communicated in types (8-6)
Christ was signified by types under the law (7-5), (LC 34)
in the ceremonial law (19-3)
Jesus Christ was revealed in types (8-6)

Unconditional Election
(see Effectual Calling, Elect, Election)
Union
of saints with Christ and one another (26-1)
Unity
of the Godhead (2-3)
of the person of Jesus Christ (8-7)

Virgin Mary
Christ was conceived by the power of the Holy Ghost in the womb of the Virgin Mary (LC 37)
Visible
sacraments put a visible difference between those in the Church and the rest of the world (27-1)
those who partake of the visible elements in the Lord's Supper do spiritually receive and feed upon Christ crucified (29-7)

Visible Church
(25-2)
all who live in the visible Church are not saved (LC 61)
baptism admits the party into the visible Church (28-1)
has been sometimes more, sometimes less visible and particular Churches are more or less pure according as the doctrine of the Gospel is taught and embraced, etc. (25-4)
membership of the visible Church (LC 62)
special privileges of the visible Church (LC 63)

Vow
lawful oaths and vows (22-1)
no vow may be made to do anything forbidden in the Word of God (22-7)
of the like nature with a promissory oath (22-5)
part of religious worship (21-5)
popish monastical vows are superstitious and sinful snares (22-7)
to be made to God alone (22-6)
to be made voluntarily (22-6)

War
may be waged by Christians upon just and necessary occasion (23-2), *(cf. exposition of the Sixth Commandment LC 134-136)*
there is a continual and irreconcilable war between the flesh and Spirit (13-2)

Water
outward element to be used in the sacrament of baptism is water (28-2)

Wicked
after death, the souls of the wicked are cast into hell where they await judgment (32-1)
God blinds and hardens wicked and ungodly men (5-6)
God's grace is withheld from wicked and ungodly men (5-6)
wicked who do not know God and obey not the Gospel shall be cast into eternal torments (33-2), (LC 87, 89)

Will
free will (9-1)

of creatures in God's decree (3-1)
of God (1-1)
    and His decree (LC 12, 14)
        will of creatures in God's decree (3-1)
        will of God in reference to His eternal decree (3-1), (LC 13)
    and His Word
        will of God is revealed in His Word (3-8)
    and predestination (3-5)
    and providence (5-1)
    and revelation
        God's former ways of revealing His will have now ceased (1-1)
    and the moral law
        uses of the moral law to men (LC 95-97)
        will of God is revealed in the moral law (19-6, 7), (LC 93)

    and worship
        acceptable way of worshipping God is instituted by Him and limited by His revealed will (21-1)
    eternal and most free purpose of God's will (3-6)
    is revealed by Christ to the Church (LC 43)
of man at creation
    man had freedom and power to do good (9-2)
    man had power to fulfill law of God at creation (4-2)
    man was left to the liberty of his will at creation (4-2), (LC 21)
    man was subject to the transgression of God's law at creation (4-2)
    will of man was endued with natural liberty (9-1)
of regenerate man
    converted sinner can will and do that which is spiritually good (9-4)
    will of man is enabled to do good alone in the state of glory (9-5)
    will of the elect is renewed when they are effectually called (10-1)

of unregenerate man
>will of man is enabled to do good alone in the state of glory (9-5)

Wine
bread and wine remain bread and wine in the sacrament of the Lord's Supper (29-5)
bread and wine represent the body and blood of Christ (29-5)
bread and wine, the elements in the sacrament of the Lord's Supper (29-3)

Wisdom
all the treasures of wisdom and knowledge are in Jesus Christ (8-3)
God's wisdom was manifested in the act of creation (4-1)
God's wisdom praised in His exercise of providence (5-1)
of Christ overcomes all enemies of the elect (8-8)
of God revealed by the light of nature and the works of creation and providence (1-1)
of God is manifested in providence (5-4)

Wise
God is most wise (2-1)

Witness of the Spirit
(18-2), (LC 4, 80, 81)

Woman
incestuous marriages are not lawful (24-4; *cf. 24-4 original version*)
it is not lawful for any woman to have more than one husband at a time (24-1)
marriage is to be between one man and one woman (24-1)

Word(s)
all shall give an account of their words and deeds before the tribunal of Christ (33-1)
of institution and the efficacy of the sacraments (27-3)

Word of God
(LC 2-6), *(see also Scripture, Holy Scripture)*
and faith
>by faith, a Christian believes the Word to be true (14-2)
>grace of faith is ordinary wrought by the ministry of the Word (14-1)

and good works
>   God has commanded good works in His Word (16-1)
and grace
>   grace of faith is ordinary wrought by the ministry of the Word (14-1)
and marriage
>   marriage ought not to be within the degrees of consanguinity or affinity forbidden by the Word (24-4)
and oaths
>   oaths are warranted by the Word of God (22-2)
and preaching *(see also Preaching of the Word)*
>   covenant of grace is administered through the preaching of the Word (7-6)
and salvation
>   Holy Spirit makes the Word an effectual means of enlightening, convincing and humbling sinners, etc. (LC 155)
>   mysteries of salvation are revealed in and by the Word (8-8), (LC 2)
and the Church
>   Church officers have the power to shut the kingdom of heaven against the impenitent, both by the Word and censures, and to open it unto penitent sinners by the ministry of the Gospel (30-2)
>   decrees and determinations of synods and councils are to be received with reverence and submission if consonant to the Word of God (31-2)
and the civil magistrate
>   civil magistrates may not assume to themselves the administration of the Word and sacraments (23-3)
and the covenant of grace
>   covenant of grace is administered through the preaching of the Word (7-6), (LC 35)
and the elect
>   Christ governs the hearts of the elect by His Word and Spirit (8-8)

elect are effectually called by God's Word and Spirit (10-1)
and the pronouncements of synods and councils
    decrees and determinations of synods and councils are to be received with reverence and submission if consonant to the Word of God (31-2)
and the Sabbath
    in His Word, God has given a perpetual Sabbath commandment binding all men in all ages (21-7)
and the sacraments
    sacraments can only be dispensed by a minister of the Word lawfully ordained (27-4)
and vows
    no man may vow to do anything forbidden in the Word of God (22-7)
and worship
    acceptable way of worshipping God is prescribed in His Word (21-1)
    conscionable hearing of the Word is part of the ordinary worship of God (21-5)
an outward means whereby Christ communicates the benefits of His mediation (LC 154)
concerning predestination
    will of God concerning predestination is revealed in His Word (3-8)
hearing of the Word (LC 160)
reading of the Word
    part of religious worship (21-5), (LC 156, 157)
translation of the Word (LC 156)
written Word of God (1-2)

Work(s)
God gave Adam a law, a covenant of works (19-1)
good works *(see Good Works)*
of Christ in mediation (8-7)
of creation and providence (1-1)
of God declare that there is a God (LC 2)
of unbelievers are sinful (16-7)

World
    Christ has appointed baptism to be continued in His Church until the end of the world (28-1)
    created out of nothing by God (4-1)
    God has appointed a day wherein He will judge the world by Jesus Christ (33-1)
    Jesus Christ shall return to judge at the end of the world (8-4)
    sacraments put a visible difference between those in the Church and the rest of the world (27-1)
    Scripture was given to establish and comfort the Church against the malice of the world (1-1)
    through the temptations of the world, saints may fall into grievous sins (17-3)

Worship
    and the ceremonial laws (19-3)
    and the conscience (20-2)
    and the Sabbath (21-8)
    of God (1-6), (1-8), *(cf. exposition of the First Commandment LC 103-106 and the Second Commandment LC 107-110)*
        acceptable way of worshipping God is instituted by Himself and is limited by His revealed will (21-1)
        by profession, saints are bound to maintain an holy fellowship and communion in the worship of God (26-2)
        civil magistrates have the authority to prevent or reform all abuses in worship (23-3 original version)
        God is to be worshipped everywhere in spirit and truth (21-6)
        God may not be worshipped under any visible representation (21-1)
        is to take place in private families (21-6)
        lawful oath is part of religious worship (22-1)
        law of nature teaches that a proportion of time is to be set aside for the worship of God (21-7)
        parts of the ordinary religious worship of God (21-5)
        prayer with thanksgiving is one special part of religious worship (21-3)

public assemblies for worship are not to be neglected (21-6)
public worship is one key in determining the purity of a particular Church (25-4)
religious worship (21-1)
religious worship is to be given to God alone and not to angels, saints or any other creature (21-2)
since the Fall, God cannot be worshipped without a Mediator (21-2)
synods and councils have the responsibility to set down rules and directions for the better ordering of the public worship of God (31-2)
there will always be a Church on earth to worship God (25-5)
those who publish or maintain false opinions about worship may be proceeded against by the censures of the Church and the power of the civil magistrate (20-4)
under the Gospel, worship is not tied to or made more acceptable by any place in which it is performed (21-6)
worship is due to God from all creatures (2-2)

public worship
public assemblies for worship are not to be neglected (21-6)
public worship is one key in determining the purity of a particular Church (25-4)
synods and councils have the responsibility to set down rules and directions for the better ordering of the public worship of God (31-2)
those who publish or maintain false opinions about worship may be proceeded against by the censures of the Church and the power of the civil magistrate (20-4)

Wrath of God
against sinners (6-6), (LC 27)
against the non-elect (3-7)
allowing the profaning of the covenant and its seals can result in the wrath of God falling upon the Church (30-3)
Christ endured the weight of God's wrath (LC 49)
Christ has purchased freedom from the wrath of God for believers (20-1), *(cf. LC 38, 77)*

Church censures may prevent the wrath of God from falling upon the Church (30-3)
deserved for every sin (LC 152)
for abuse of His name (LC 114)
for false worship (LC 110)
repentance and faith are required to escape the wrath of God (LC 153)

Westminster Larger Catechism

Question 1: What is the chief and highest end of man?
Answer: Man's chief and highest end is to glorify God, and fully to enjoy Him forever.

Question 2: How does it appear that there is a God?
Answer: The very light of nature in man, and the works of God, declare plainly that there is a God; but His Word and Spirit only do sufficiently and effectually reveal Him unto men for their salvation.

Question 3: What is the Word of God?
Answer: The holy Scriptures of the Old and New Testaments are the Word of God, the only rule of faith and obedience.

Question 4: How does it appear that the Scriptures are the Word of God?
Answer: The Scriptures manifest themselves to be the Word of God, by their majesty and purity; by the consent of all the parts, and the scope of the whole, which is to give all glory to God; by their light and power to convince and convert sinners, to comfort and build up believers unto salvation: but the Spirit of God bearing witness by and with the Scriptures in the heart of man, is alone able fully to persuade it that they are the very Word of God.

Question 5: What do the Scriptures principally teach?
Answer: The Scriptures principally teach, what man is to believe concerning God, and what duty God requires of man.

Question 6: What do the Scriptures make known of God?
Answer: The Scriptures make known what God is, the persons in the Godhead, His decrees, and the execution of His decrees.

Question 7: What is God?
Answer: God is a Spirit, in and of Himself infinite in being, glory, blessedness, and perfection; all-sufficient, eternal, unchangeable, incomprehensible, everywhere present, almighty, knowing all things, most wise, most holy, most just, most merciful and gracious, long-suffering, and abundant in goodness and truth.

Question 8: Are there more Gods than one?
Answer: There is but one only, the living and true God.

Question 9: How many persons are there in the Godhead?
Answer: There be three persons in the Godhead, the Father, the Son, and the Holy Ghost; and these three are one true, eternal God, the same in substance, equal in power and glory; although distinguished by Their personal properties.

Question 10: What are the personal properties of the three persons in the Godhead?
Answer: It is proper to the Father to beget the Son, and to the Son to be begotten of the Father, and to the Holy Ghost to proceed from the Father and the Son from all eternity.

Question 11: How does it appear that the Son and the Holy Ghost are God equal with the Father?
Answer: The Scriptures manifest that the Son and the Holy Ghost are God equal with the Father, ascribing unto Them such

names, attributes, works, and worship, as are proper to God only.

Question 12: What are the decrees of God?
Answer: God's decrees are the wise, free, and holy acts of the counsel of His will, whereby, from all eternity, He has, for His own glory, unchangeably foreordained whatsoever comes to pass in time, especially concerning angels and men.

Question 13: What has God especially decreed concerning angels and men?
Answer: God, by an eternal and immutable decree, out of His mere love, for the praise of His glorious grace, to be manifested in due time, has elected some angels to glory; and in Christ has chosen some men to eternal life, and the means thereof: and also, according to His sovereign power, and the unsearchable counsel of His own will (whereby He extends or withholds favor as He pleases), has passed by and foreordained the rest to dishonor and wrath, to be for their sin inflicted, to the praise of the glory of His justice.

Question 14: How does God execute His decrees?
Answer: God executes His decrees in the works of creation and providence, according to His infallible foreknowledge, and the free and immutable counsel of His own will.

Question 15: What is the work of creation?
Answer: The work of creation is that wherein God did in the beginning, by the word of His power, make of nothing the world, and all things therein, for Himself, within the space of six days, and all very good.

Question 16: How did God create angels?
Answer: God created all the angels spirits, immortal, holy, excell-

ing in knowledge, mighty in power, to execute His commandments, and to praise His name, yet subject to change.

Question 17: How did God create man?
Answer: After God had made all other creatures, He created man male and female; formed the body of the man of the dust of the ground, and the woman of the rib of the man, endued them with living, reasonable, and immortal souls; made them after His own image, in knowledge, righteousness, and holiness; having the law of God written in their hearts, and power to fulfil it, and dominion over the creatures; yet subject to fall.

Question 18: What are God's works of providence?
Answer: God's works of providence are His most holy, wise, and powerful preserving and governing all His creatures; ordering them, and all their actions, to His own glory.

Question 19: What is God's providence towards the angels?
Answer: God by his providence permitted some of the angels, wilfully and irrecoverably, to fall into sin and damnation, limiting and ordering that, and all their sins, to His own glory; and established the rest in holiness and happiness; employing them all, at His pleasure, in the administrations of His power, mercy, and justice.

Question 20: What was the providence of God toward man in the estate in which he was created?
Answer: The providence of God toward man in the estate in which he was created, was the placing him in paradise, appointing him to dress it, giving him liberty to eat of the fruit of the earth; putting the creatures under his dominion, and ordaining marriage for his help; affording him communion with Himself; instituting the sabbath; entering into a covenant of life with him, upon condition of personal,

perfect, and perpetual obedience, of which the tree of life was a pledge; and forbidding to eat of the tree of the knowledge of good and evil, upon the pain of death.

Question 21: Did man continue in that estate wherein God at first created him?

Answer: Our first parents being left to the freedom of their own will, through the temptation of Satan, transgressed the commandment of God in eating the forbidden fruit; and thereby fell from the estate of innocency wherein they were created.

Question 22: Did all mankind fall in that first transgression?

Answer: The covenant being made with Adam as a public person, not for himself only, but for his posterity, all mankind descending from him by ordinary generation, sinned in him, and fell with him in that first transgression.

Question 23: Into what estate did the fall bring mankind?

Answer: The fall brought mankind into an estate of sin and misery.

Question 24: What is sin?

Answer: Sin is any want of conformity unto, or transgression of, any law of God, given as a rule to the reasonable creature.

Question 25: Wherein consists the sinfulness of that estate whereinto man fell?

Answer: The sinfulness of that estate whereinto man fell, consists in the guilt of Adam's first sin, the want of that righteousness wherein he was created, and the corruption of his nature, whereby he is utterly indisposed, disabled, and made opposite unto all that is spiritually good, and wholly inclined to all evil, and that continually; which is commonly called original sin, and from which do proceed all actual transgressions.

Question 26: How is original sin conveyed from our first parents unto their posterity?
Answer: Original sin is conveyed from our first parents unto their posterity by natural generation, so as all that proceed from them in that way are conceived and born in sin.

Question 27: What misery did the fall bring upon mankind?
Answer: The fall brought upon mankind the loss of communion with God, His displeasure and curse; so as we are by nature children of wrath, bond slaves to Satan, and justly liable to all punishments in this world, and that which is to come.

Question 28: What are the punishments of sin in this world?
Answer: The punishments of sin in this world are either inward, as blindness of mind, a reprobate sense, strong delusions, hardness of heart, horror of conscience, and vile affections; or outward, as the curse of God upon the creatures for our sakes, and all other evils that befall us in our bodies, names, estates, relations, and employments; together with death itself.

Question 29: What are the punishments of sin in the world to come?
Answer: The punishments of sin in the world to come, are everlasting separation from the comfortable presence of God, and most grievous torments in soul and body, without intermission, in hell fire forever.

Question 30: Does God leave all mankind to perish in the estate of sin and misery?
Answer: God does not leave all men to perish in the estate of sin and misery, into which they fell by the breach of the first covenant, commonly called the covenant of works; but of His mere love and mercy delivers His elect out of it, and brings them into an estate of salvation by the second covenant, commonly called the covenant of grace.

Question 31: With whom was the covenant of grace made?
Answer: The covenant of grace was made with Christ as the second Adam, and in Him with all the elect as his seed.

Question 32: How is the grace of God manifested in the second covenant?
Answer: The grace of God is manifested in the second covenant, in that He freely provides and offers to sinners a Mediator, and life and salvation by Him; and requiring faith as the condition to interest them in Him, promises and gives His Holy Spirit to all His elect, to work in them that faith, with all other saving graces; and to enable them unto all holy obedience, as the evidence of the truth of their faith and thankfulness to God, and as the way which He has appointed them to salvation.

Question 33: Was the covenant of grace always administered after one and the same manner?
Answer: The covenant of grace was not always administered after the same manner, but the administrations of it under the Old Testament were different from those under the New.

Question 34: How was the covenant of grace administered under the Old Testament?
Answer: The covenant of grace was administered under the Old Testament, by promises, prophecies, sacrifices, circumcision, the passover, and other types and ordinances, which did all foresignify Christ then to come, and were for that time sufficient to build up the elect in faith in the promised Messiah, by whom they then had full remission of sin, and eternal salvation.

Question 35: How is the covenant of grace administered under the New Testament?
Answer: Under the New Testament, when Christ the substance was

exhibited, the same covenant of grace was and still is to be administered in the preaching of the Word, and the administration of the sacraments of Baptism and the Lord's Supper; in which grace and salvation are held forth in more fulness, evidence, and efficacy, to all nations.

Question 36: Who is the Mediator of the covenant of grace?
Answer: The only Mediator of the covenant of grace is the Lord Jesus Christ, who, being the eternal Son of God, of one substance and equal with the Father, in the fulness of time became man, and so was and continues to be God and man, in two entire distinct natures, and one person, forever.

Question 37: How did Christ, being the Son of God, become man?
Answer: Christ the Son of God became man, by taking to Himself a true body, and a reasonable soul, being conceived by the power of the Holy Ghost in the womb of the virgin Mary, of her substance, and born of her, yet without sin.

Question 38: Why was it requisite that the Mediator should be God?
Answer: It was requisite that the Mediator should be God, that He might sustain and keep the human nature from sinking under the infinite wrath of God, and the power of death; give worth and efficacy to His sufferings, obedience, and intercession; and to satisfy God's justice, procure His favor, purchase a peculiar people, give His Spirit to them, conquer all their enemies, and bring them to everlasting salvation.

Question 39: Why was it requisite that the Mediator should be man?
Answer: It was requisite that the Mediator should be man, that He might advance our nature, perform obedience to the law, suffer and make intercession for us in our nature, have a fellow feeling of our infirmities; that we might receive the adoption of sons, and have comfort and access with boldness unto the throne of grace.

Question 40: Why was it requisite that the Mediator should be God and man in one person?

Answer: It was requisite that the Mediator, who was to reconcile God and man, should Himself be both God and man, and this in one person, that the proper works of each nature might be accepted of God for us, and relied on by us, as the works of the whole person.

Question 41: Why was our Mediator called Jesus?

Answer: Our Mediator was called Jesus, because He saves His people from their sins.

Question 42: Why was our Mediator called Christ?

Answer: Our Mediator was called Christ, because He was anointed with the Holy Ghost above measure; and so set apart, and fully furnished with all authority and ability, to execute the offices of prophet, priest, and king of His church, in the estate both of His humiliation and exaltation.

Question 43: How does Christ execute the office of a prophet?

Answer: Christ executes the office of a prophet, in His revealing to the church, in all ages, by His Spirit and Word, in divers ways of administration, the whole will of God, in all things concerning their edification and salvation.

Question 44: How does Christ execute the office of a priest?

Answer: Christ executes the office of a priest, in His once offering Himself a sacrifice without spot to God, to be a reconciliation for the sins of His people; and in making continual intercession for them.

Question 45: How does Christ execute the office of a king?

Answer: Christ executes the office of a king, in calling out of the world a people to Himself, and giving them officers, laws, and censures, by which He visibly governs them; in bestowing saving grace upon His elect, rewarding their obedience, and correcting them for their sins, preserving and supporting them under all their temptations and sufferings, restraining and overcoming all their enemies, and powerfully ordering all things for His own glory, and their good; and also in taking vengeance on the rest, who know not God, and obey not the gospel.

Question 46: What was the estate of Christ's humiliation?
Answer: The estate of Christ's humiliation was that low condition, wherein He for our sakes, emptying Himself of His glory, took upon him the form of a servant, in His conception and birth, life, death, and after His death, until His resurrection.

Question 47: How did Christ humble Himself in His conception and birth?
Answer: Christ humbled Himself in His conception and birth, in that, being from all eternity the Son of God, in the bosom of the Father, He was pleased in the fulness of time to become the son of man, made of a woman of low estate, and to be born of her; with divers circumstances of more than ordinary abasement.

Question 48: How did Christ humble Himself in His life?
Answer: Christ humbled Himself in His life, by subjecting Himself to the law, which He perfectly fulfilled; and by conflicting with the indignities of the world, temptations of Satan, and infirmities in His flesh, whether common to the nature of man, or particularly accompanying that His low condition.

Question 49: How did Christ humble Himself in His death?
Answer: Christ humbled Himself in His death, in that having been betrayed by Judas, forsaken by His disciples, scorned and rejected by the world, condemned by Pilate, and tormented by His persecutors; having also conflicted with the terrors of death, and the powers of darkness, felt and

borne the weight of God's wrath, He laid down His life an offering for sin, enduring the painful, shameful, and cursed death of the cross.

Question 50: Wherein consisted Christ's humiliation after His death?
Answer: Christ's humiliation after His death consisted in His being buried, and continuing in the state of the dead, and under the power of death till the third day; which has been otherwise expressed in these words, He descended into hell.

Question 51: What was the estate of Christ's exaltation?
Answer: The estate of Christ's exaltation comprehends His resurrection, ascension, sitting at the right hand of the Father, and His coming again to judge the world.

Question 52: How was Christ exalted in His resurrection?
Answer: Christ was exalted in His resurrection, in that, not having seen corruption in death (of which it was not possible for Him to be held), and having the very same body in which He suffered, with the essential properties thereof (but without mortality, and other common infirmities belonging to this life), really united to His soul, He rose again from the dead the third day by His own power; whereby He declared Himself to be the Son of God, to have satisfied divine justice, to have vanquished death, and him that had the power of it, and to be Lord of quick and dead: all which He did as a public person, the head of His church, for their justification, quickening in grace, support against enemies, and to assure them of their resurrection from the dead at the last day.

Question 53: How was Christ exalted in His ascension?
Answer: Christ was exalted in His ascension, in that having after His resurrection often appeared unto and conversed with His apostles, speaking to them of the things pertaining to

the kingdom of God, and giving them commission to preach the gospel to all nations, forty days after His resurrection, He, in our nature, and as our head, triumphing over enemies, visibly went up into the highest heavens, there to receive gifts for men, to raise up our affections thither, and to prepare a place for us, where Himself is, and shall continue till His second coming at the end of the world.

Question 54: How is Christ exalted in His sitting at the right hand of God?

Answer: Christ is exalted in His sitting at the right hand of God, in that as God-man He is advanced to the highest favor with God the Father, with all fulness of joy, glory, and power over all things in heaven and earth; and does gather and defend His church, and subdue their enemies; furnishes His ministers and people with gifts and graces, and makes intercession for them.

Question 55: How does Christ make intercession?

Answer: Christ makes intercession, by His appearing in our nature continually before the Father in heaven, in the merit of His obedience and sacrifice on earth, declaring His will to have it applied to all believers; answering all accusations against them, and procuring for them quiet of conscience, notwithstanding daily failings, access with boldness to the throne of grace, and acceptance of their persons and services.

Question 56: How is Christ to be exalted in His coming again to judge the world?

Answer: Christ is to be exalted in His coming again to judge the world, in that He, who was unjustly judged and condemned by wicked men, shall come again at the last day in great power, and in the full manifestation of His own glory, and of His Father's, with all His holy angels, with a shout, with the voice of the archangel, and with the trumpet of God, to judge the world in righteousness.

Question 57: What benefits has Christ procured by His mediation?
Answer: Christ, by His mediation, has procured redemption, with all other benefits of the covenant of grace.

Question 58: How do we come to be made partakers of the benefits which Christ has procured?
Answer: We are made partakers of the benefits which Christ has procured, by the application of them unto us, which is the work especially of God the Holy Ghost.

Question 59: Who are made partakers of redemption through Christ?
Answer: Redemption is certainly applied, and effectually communicated, to all those for whom Christ has purchased it; who are in time by the Holy Ghost enabled to believe in Christ according to the gospel.

Question 60: Can they who have never heard the gospel, and so know not Jesus Christ, nor believe in Him, be saved by their living according to the light of nature?
Answer: They who, having never heard the gospel, know not Jesus Christ, and believe not in Him, cannot be saved, be they never so diligent to frame their lives according to the light of nature, or the laws of that religion which they profess; neither is there salvation in any other, but in Christ alone, who is the Savior only of His body the church.

Question 61: Are all they saved who hear the gospel, and live in the church?
Answer: All that hear the gospel, and live in the visible church, are not saved; but they only who are true members of the church invisible.

Question 62: What is the visible church?

Answer: The visible church is a society made up of all such as in all ages and places of the world do profess the true religion, and of their children.

Question 63: What are the special privileges of the visible church?
Answer: The visible church has the privilege of being under God's special care and government; of being protected and preserved in all ages, not withstanding the opposition of all enemies; and of enjoying the communion of saints, the ordinary means of salvation, and offers of grace by Christ to all the members of it in the ministry of the gospel, testifying, that whosoever believes in Him shall be saved, and excluding none that will come unto Him.

Question 64: What is the invisible church?
Answer: The invisible church is the whole number of the elect, that have been, are, or shall be gathered into one under Christ the head.

Question 65: What special benefits do the members of the invisible church enjoy by Christ?
Answer: The members of the invisible church by Christ enjoy union and communion with Him in grace and glory.

Question 66: What is that union which the elect have with Christ?
Answer: The union which the elect have with Christ is the work of God's grace, whereby they are spiritually and mystically, yet really and inseparably, joined to Christ as their head and husband; which is done in their effectual calling.

Question 67: What is effectual calling?
Answer: Effectual calling is the work of God's almighty power and grace, whereby (out of His free and special love to His elect, and from nothing in them moving Him thereunto) He does, in His accepted time, invite and draw them to Jesus Christ, by His Word and Spirit; savingly enlighten-

ing their minds, renewing and powerfully determining their wills, so as they (although in themselves dead in sin) are hereby made willing and able freely to answer His call, and to accept and embrace the grace offered and conveyed therein.

Question 68: Are the elect only effectually called?
Answer: All the elect, and they only, are effectually called; although others may be, and often are, outwardly called by the ministry of the Word, and have some common operations of the Spirit; who, for their wilful neglect and contempt of the grace offered to them, being justly left in their unbelief, do never truly come to Jesus Christ.

Question 69: What is the communion in grace which the members of the invisible church have with Christ?
Answer: The communion in grace which the members of the invisible church have with Christ, is their partaking of the virtue of His mediation, in their justification, adoption, sanctification, and whatever else, in this life, manifests their union with Him.

Question 70: What is justification?
Answer: Justification is an act of God's free grace unto sinners, in which He pardons all their sins, accepts and accounts their persons righteous in His sight; not for any thing wrought in them, or done by them, but only for the perfect obedience and full satisfaction of Christ, by God imputed to them, and received by faith alone.

Question 71: How is justification an act of God's free grace?
Answer: Although Christ, by His obedience and death, did make a proper, real, and full satisfaction to God's justice in the behalf of them that are justified; yet inasmuch as God accepts the satisfaction from a surety, which He might have demanded of them, and did provide this surety, His

own only Son, imputing His righteousness to them, and requiring nothing of them for their justification but faith, which also is His gift, their justification is to them of free grace.

Question 72: What is justifying faith?
Answer: Justifying faith is a saving grace, wrought in the heart of a sinner by the Spirit and Word of God, whereby he, being convinced of his sin and misery, and of the disability in himself and all other creatures to recover him out of his lost condition, not only assents to the truth of the promise of the gospel, but receives and rests upon Christ and His righteousness, therein held forth, for pardon of sin, and for the accepting and accounting of his person righteous in the sight of God for salvation.

Question 73: How does faith justify a sinner in the sight of God?
Answer: Faith justifies a sinner in the sight of God, not because of those other graces which do always accompany it, or of good works that are the fruits of it, nor as if the grace of faith, or any act thereof, were imputed to him for his justification; but only as it is an instrument by which he receives and applies Christ and His righteousness.

Question 74: What is adoption?
Answer: Adoption is an act of the free grace of God, in and for His only Son Jesus Christ, whereby all those that are justified are received into the number of His children, have His name put upon them, the Spirit of His Son given to them, are under His fatherly care and dispensations, admitted to all the liberties and privileges of the sons of God, made heirs of all the promises, and fellow heirs with Christ in glory.

Question 75: What is sanctification?
Answer: Sanctification is a work of God's grace, whereby they

whom God has, before the foundation of the world, chosen to be holy, are in time, through the powerful operation of His Spirit applying the death and resurrection of Christ unto them, renewed in their whole man after the image of God; having the seeds of repentance unto life, and all other saving graces, put into their hearts, and those graces so stirred up, increased, and strengthened, as that they more and more die unto sin, and rise unto newness of life.

Question 76: What is repentance unto life?
Answer: Repentance unto life is a saving grace, wrought in the heart of a sinner by the Spirit and Word of God, whereby, out of the sight and sense, not only of the danger, but also of the filthiness and odiousness of his sins, and upon the apprehension of God's mercy in Christ to such as are penitent, he so grieves for and hates his sins, as that he turns from them all to God, purposing and endeavoring constantly to walk with Him in all the ways of new obedience.

Question 77: Wherein do justification and sanctification differ?
Answer: Although sanctification be inseparably joined with justification, yet they differ, in that God in justification imputes the righteousness of Christ; in sanctification His Spirit infuses grace, and enables to the exercise thereof; in the former, sin is pardoned; in the other, it is subdued: the one does equally free all believers from the revenging wrath of God, and that perfectly in this life, that they never fall into condemnation; the other is neither equal in all, nor in this life perfect in any, but growing up to perfection.

Question 78: Whence arises the imperfection of sanctification in believers?
Answer: The imperfection of sanctification in believers arises from the remnants of sin abiding in every part of them, and the

perpetual lustings of the flesh against the spirit; whereby they are often foiled with temptations, and fall into many sins, are hindered in all their spiritual services, and their best works are imperfect and defiled in the sight of God.

Question 79: May not true believers, by reason of their imperfections, and the many temptations and sins they are overtaken with, fall away from the state of grace?

Answer: True believers, by reason of the unchangeable love of God, and His decree and covenant to give them perseverance, their inseparable union with Christ, His continual intercession for them, and the Spirit and seed of God abiding in them, can neither totally nor finally fall away from the state of grace, but are kept by the power of God through faith unto salvation.

Question 80: Can true believers be infallibly assured that they are in the estate of grace, and that they shall persevere therein unto salvation?

Answer: Such as truly believe in Christ, and endeavor to walk in all good conscience before Him, may, without extraordinary revelation, by faith grounded upon the truth of God's promises, and by the Spirit enabling them to discern in themselves those graces to which the promises of life are made, and bearing witness with their spirits that they are the children of God, be infallibly assured that they are in the estate of grace, and shall persevere therein unto salvation.

Question 81: Are all true believers at all times assured of their present being in the estate of grace, and that they shall be saved?

Answer: Assurance of grace and salvation not being of the essence of faith, true believers may wait long before they obtain it; and, after the enjoyment thereof, may have it weakened and intermitted, through manifold distempers, sins, temptations, and desertions; yet are they never left without such a presence and support of the Spirit of God as keeps them from sinking into utter despair.

Question 82: What is the communion in glory which the members of the invisible church have with Christ?
Answer: The communion in glory which the members of the invisible church have with Christ, is in this life, immediately after death, and at last perfected at the resurrection and day of judgment.

Question 83: What is the communion in glory with Christ which the members of the invisible church enjoy in this life?
Answer: The members of the invisible church have communicated to them in this life the firstfruits of glory with Christ, as they are members of Him their head, and so in Him are interested in that glory which He is fully possessed of; and, as an earnest thereof, enjoy the sense of God's love, peace of conscience, joy in the Holy Ghost, and hope of glory; as, on the contrary, sense of God's revenging wrath, horror of conscience, and a fearful expectation of judgment, are to the wicked the beginning of their torments which they shall endure after death.

Question 84: Shall all men die?
Answer: Death being threatened as the wages of sin, it is appointed unto all men once to die; for that all have sinned.

Question 85: Death, being the wages of sin, why are not the righteous delivered from death, seeing all their sins are forgiven in Christ?
Answer: The righteous shall be delivered from death itself at the last day, and even in death are delivered from the sting and curse of it; so that, although they die, yet it is out of God's love, to free them perfectly from sin and misery, and to make them capable of further communion with Christ in glory, which they then enter upon.

Question 86: What is the communion in glory with Christ, which the members of the invisible church enjoy immediately after death?
Answer: The communion in glory with Christ, which the members of the invisible church enjoy immediately after death, is, in that their souls are then made perfect in holiness, and received into the highest heavens, where they behold the face of God in light and glory, waiting for the full redemption of their bodies, which even in death continue united to Christ, and rest in their graves as in their beds, till at the last day they be again united to their souls. Whereas the souls of the wicked are at their death cast into hell, where they remain in torments and utter darkness, and their bodies kept in their graves, as in their prisons, till the resurrection and judgment of the great day.

Question 87: What are we to believe concerning the resurrection?
Answer: We are to believe, that at the last day there shall be a general resurrection of the dead, both of the just and unjust: when they that are then found alive shall in a moment be changed; and the selfsame bodies of the dead which were laid in the grave, being then again united to their souls forever, shall be raised up by the power of Christ. The bodies of the just, by the Spirit of Christ, and by virtue of His resurrection as their head, shall be raised in power, spiritual, incorruptible, and made like to His glorious body; and the bodies of the wicked shall be raised up in dishonor by Him, as an offended judge.

Question 88: What shall immediately follow after the resurrection?
Answer: Immediately after the resurrection shall follow the general and final judgment of angels and men; the day and hour whereof no man knows, that all may watch and pray, and be ever ready for the coming of the Lord.

Question 89: What shall be done to the wicked at the day of judgment?
Answer: At the day of judgment, the wicked shall be set on Christ's left hand, and, upon clear evidence, and full conviction of their own consciences, shall have the fearful but just sentence of condemnation pronounced against them; and thereupon shall be cast out from the favorable presence of God, and the glorious fellowship with Christ, His saints, and all His holy angels, into hell, to be punished with unspeakable torments, both of body and soul, with the devil and his angels forever.

Question 90: What shall be done to the righteous at the day of judgment?
Answer: At the day of judgment, the righteous, being caught up to Christ in the clouds, shall be set on His right hand, and there openly acknowledged and acquitted, shall join with Him in the judging of reprobate angels and men, and shall be received into heaven, where they shall be fully and forever freed from all sin and misery; filled with inconceivable joys, made perfectly holy and happy both in body and soul, in the company of innumerable saints and holy angels, but especially in the immediate vision and fruition of God the Father, of our Lord Jesus Christ, and of the Holy Spirit, to all eternity. And this is the perfect and full communion, which the members of the invisible church shall enjoy with Christ in glory, at the resurrection and day of judgment.

Question 91: What is the duty which God requires of man?
Answer: The duty which God requires of man, is obedience to His revealed will.

Question 92: What did God at first reveal unto man as the rule of his obedience?
Answer: The rule of obedience revealed to Adam in the estate of

innocence, and to all mankind in him, besides a special command not to eat of the fruit of the tree of the knowledge of good and evil, was the moral law.

Question 93: What is the moral law?
Answer: The moral law is the declaration of the will of God to mankind, directing and binding everyone to personal, perfect, and perpetual conformity and obedience thereunto, in the frame and disposition of the whole man, soul and body, and in performance of all those duties of holiness and righteousness which he owes to God and man: promising life upon the fulfilling, and threatening death upon the breach of it.

Question 94: Is there any use of the moral law to man since the fall?
Answer: Although no man, since the fall, can attain to righteousness and life by the moral law; yet there is great use thereof, as well common to all men, as peculiar either to the unregenerate, or the regenerate.

Question 95: Of what use is the moral law to all men?
Answer: The moral law is of use to all men, to inform them of the holy nature and will of God, and of their duty, binding them to walk accordingly; to convince them of their disability to keep it, and of the sinful pollution of their nature, hearts, and lives; to humble them in the sense of their sin and misery, and thereby help them to a clearer sight of the need they have of Christ, and of the perfection of His obedience.

Question 96: What particular use is there of the moral law to unregenerate men?
Answer: The moral law is of use to unregenerate men, to awaken their consciences to flee from wrath to come, and to drive them to Christ; or, upon their continuance in the estate and way of sin, to leave them inexcusable, and under the curse thereof.

Question 97: What special use is there of the moral law to the regenerate?
Answer: Although they that are regenerate, and believe in Christ, be delivered from the moral law as a covenant of works, so as thereby they are neither justified nor condemned; yet, besides the general uses thereof common to them with all men, it is of special use, to show them how much they are bound to Christ for His fulfilling it, and enduring the curse thereof in their stead, and for their good; and thereby to provoke them to more thankfulness, and to express the same in their greater care to conform themselves thereunto as the rule of their obedience.

Question 98: Where is the moral law summarily comprehended?
Answer: The moral law is summarily comprehended in the ten commandments, which were delivered by the voice of God upon Mount Sinai, and written by Him in two tables of stone; and are recorded in the twentieth chapter of Exodus. The four first commandments containing our duty to God, and the other six our duty to man.

Question 99: What rules are to be observed for the right understanding of the ten commandments?
Answer: For the right understanding of the ten commandments, these rules are to be observed: That the law is perfect, and binds everyone to full conformity in the whole man unto the righteousness thereof, and unto entire obedience forever; so as to require the utmost perfection of every duty, and to forbid the least degree of every sin. That it is spiritual, and so reaches the understanding, will, affections, and all other powers of the soul; as well as words, works, and gestures. That one and the same thing, in divers respects, is required or forbidden in several commandments. That as, where a duty is commanded, the contrary sin is forbidden; and, where a sin is forbidden, the contrary duty is commanded: so, where a promise is annexed, the contrary threatening is included; and, where

a threatening is annexed, the contrary promise is included. That what God forbids, is at no time to be done; what He commands, is always our duty; and yet every particular duty is not to be done at all times. That under one sin or duty, all of the same kind are forbidden or commanded; together with all the causes, means, occasions, and appearances thereof, and provocations thereunto. That what is forbidden or commanded to ourselves, we are bound, according to our places, to endeavor that it may be avoided or performed by others, according to the duty of their places. That in what is commanded to others, we are bound, according to our places and callings, to be helpful to them; and to take heed of partaking with others in what is forbidden them.

Question 100: What special things are we to consider in the ten commandments?
Answer: We are to consider, in the ten commandments, the preface, the substance of the commandments themselves, and several reasons annexed to some of them, the more to enforce them.

Question 101: What is the preface to the ten commandments?
Answer: The preface to the ten commandments is contained in these words, *I am the Lord thy God, which have brought thee out of the land of Egypt, out of the house of bondage.* Wherein God manifests His sovereignty, as being JEHOVAH, the eternal, immutable, and almighty God; having His being in and of Himself, and giving being to all His words and works: and that He is a God in covenant, as with Israel of old, so with all His people; who, as He brought them out of their bondage in Egypt, so He delivers us from our spiritual thraldom; and that therefore we are bound to take Him for our God alone, and to keep all His commandments.

Question 102: What is the sum of the four commandments which contain our duty to God?
Answer: The sum of the four commandments containing our duty to God is, to love the Lord our God with all our heart, and with all our soul, and with all our strength, and with all our mind.

Question 103: Which is the first commandment?
Answer: The first commandment is, *Thou shall have no other gods before Me.*

Question 104: What are the duties required in the first commandment?
Answer: The duties required in the first commandment are, the knowing and acknowledging of God to be the only true God, and our God; and to worship and glorify Him accordingly, by thinking, meditating, remembering, highly esteeming, honoring, adoring, choosing, loving, desiring, fearing of Him; believing Him; trusting, hoping, delighting, rejoicing in Him; being zealous for Him; calling upon Him, giving all praise and thanks, and yielding all obedience and submission to Him with the whole man; being careful in all things to please Him, and sorrowful when in anything He is offended; and walking humbly with Him.

Question 105: What are the sins forbidden in the first commandment?
Answer: The sins forbidden in the first commandment are, atheism, in denying or not having a God; idolatry, in having or worshiping more gods than one, or any with or instead of the true God; the not having and avouching Him for God, and our God; the omission or neglect of anything due to Him, required in this commandment; ignorance, forgetfulness, misapprehensions, false opinions, unworthy and wicked thoughts of Him; bold and curious searching into His secrets; all profaneness,

hatred of God; self-love, self-seeking, and all other inordinate and immoderate setting of our mind, will, or affections upon other things, and taking them off from Him in whole or in part; vain credulity, unbelief, heresy, misbelief, distrust, despair, incorrigibleness, and insensibleness under judgments, hardness of heart, pride, presumption, carnal security, tempting of God; using unlawful means, and trusting in lawful means; carnal delights and joys; corrupt, blind, and indiscreet zeal; lukewarmness, and deadness in the things of God; estranging ourselves, and apostatizing from God; praying, or giving any religious worship, to saints, angels, or any other creatures; all compacts and consulting with the devil, and hearkening to his suggestions; making men the lords of our faith and conscience; slighting and despising God and His commands; resisting and grieving of His Spirit, discontent and impatience at His dispensations, charging Him foolishly for the evils He inflicts on us; and ascribing the praise of any good we either are, have, or can do, to fortune, idols, ourselves, or any other creature.

Question 106: What are we specially taught by these words *before Me* in the first commandment?
Answer: These words *before Me*, or *before My face*, in the first commandment, teach us, that God, who sees all things, takes special notice of, and is much displeased with, the sin of having any other God: that so it may be an argument to dissuade from it, and to aggravate it as a most impudent provocation: as also to persuade us to do as in His sight, whatever we do in His service.

Question 107: Which is the second commandment?
Answer: The second commandment is, *Thou shalt not make unto thee any graven image, or any likeness of anything that is in heaven above, or that is in the earth beneath, or that is in the water under the earth: Thou shalt not bow down thyself*

to them, nor serve them: for I the Lord thy God am a jealous God, visiting the iniquity of the fathers upon the children unto the third and fourth generation of them that hate Me; and showing mercy unto thousands of them that love Me, and keep My commandments.

Question 108: What are the duties required in the second commandment?
Answer: The duties required in the second commandment are, the receiving, observing, and keeping pure and entire, all such religious worship and ordinances as God has instituted in His Word; particularly prayer and thanksgiving in the name of Christ; the reading, preaching, and hearing of the Word; the administration and receiving of the sacraments; church government and discipline; the ministry and maintenance thereof; religious fasting; swearing by the name of God, and vowing unto Him: as also the disapproving, detesting, opposing, all false worship; and, according to each one's place and calling, removing it, and all monuments of idolatry.

Question 109: What are the sins forbidden in the second commandment?
Answer: The sins forbidden in the second commandment are, all devising, counseling, commanding, using, and anywise approving, any religious worship not instituted by God Himself; tolerating a false religion; the making any representation of God, of all or of any of the three persons, either inwardly in our mind, or outwardly in any kind of image or likeness of any creature whatsoever; all worshiping of it, or God in it or by it; the making of any representation of feigned deities, and all worship of them, or service belonging to them; all superstitious devices, corrupting the worship of God, adding to it, or taking from it, whether invented and taken up of ourselves, or received by tradition from others, though under the title of antiquity, custom, devotion, good intent,

or any other pretense whatsoever; simony; sacrilege; all neglect, contempt, hindering, and opposing the worship and ordinances which God has appointed.

Question 110: What are the reasons annexed to the second commandment, the more to enforce it?

Answer: The reasons annexed to the second commandment, the more to enforce it, contained in these words, *For I the Lord thy God am a jealous God, visiting the iniquity of the fathers upon the children unto the third and fourth generation of them that hate Me; and showing mercy unto thousands of them that love Me, and keep My commandments;* are, besides God's sovereignty over us, and propriety in us, His fervent zeal for His own worship, and His revengeful indignation against all false worship, as being a spiritual whoredom; accounting the breakers of this commandment such as hate Him, and threatening to punish them unto divers generations; and esteeming the observers of it such as love Him and keep His commandments, and promising mercy to them unto many generations.

Question 111: Which is the third commandment?

Answer: The third commandment is, *Thou shalt not take the name of the Lord thy God in vain: for the Lord will not hold him guiltless that takes His name in vain.*

Question 112: What is required in the third commandment?

Answer: The third commandment requires, That the name of God, His titles, attributes, ordinances, the Word, sacraments, prayer, oaths, vows, lots, His works, and whatsoever else there is whereby He makes Himself known, be holily and reverently used in thought, meditation, word, and writing; by an holy profession, and answerable conversation, to the glory of God, and the good of ourselves, and others.

Question 113: What are the sins forbidden in the third commandment?
Answer: The sins forbidden in the third commandment are, the not using of God's name as is required; and the abuse of it in an ignorant, vain, irreverent, profane, superstitious, or wicked mentioning, or otherwise using His titles, attributes, ordinances, or works, by blasphemy, perjury; all sinful cursings, oaths, vows, and lots; violating of our oaths and vows, if lawful; and fulfilling them, if of things unlawful; murmuring and quarreling at, curious prying into, and misapplying of God's decrees and providences; misinterpreting, misapplying, or any way perverting the Word, or any part of it, to profane jests, curious or unprofitable questions, vain janglings, or the maintaining of false doctrines; abusing it, the creatures, or anything contained under the name of God, to charms, or sinful lusts and practices; the maligning, scorning, reviling, or anywise opposing of God's truth, grace, and ways; making profession of religion in hypocrisy, or for sinister ends; being ashamed of it, or a shame to it, by unconformable, unwise, unfruitful, and offensive walking, or backsliding from it.

Question 114: What reasons are annexed to the third commandment?
Answer: The reasons annexed to the third commandment, in these words, *The Lord thy God,* and, *For the Lord will not hold him guiltless that takes His name in vain,* are, because He is the Lord and our God, therefore His name is not to be profaned, or any way abused by us; especially because He will be so far from acquitting and sparing the transgressors of this commandment, as that He will not suffer them to escape His righteous judgment, albeit many such escape the censures and punishments of men.

Question 115: Which is the fourth commandment?
Answer: The fourth commandment is, *Remember the sabbath day, to keep it holy. Six days shalt thou labor, and do all thy*

work: but the seventh day is the sabbath of the Lord thy God: in it thou shalt not do any work, thou, nor thy son, nor thy daughter, thy manservant, nor thy maidservant, nor thy cattle, nor thy stranger that is within thy gates: For in six days the Lord made heaven and earth, the sea, and all that in them is, and rested the seventh day: wherefore the Lord blessed the sabbath day, and hallowed it.

Question 116: What is required in the fourth commandment?
Answer: The fourth commandment requires of all men the sanctifying or keeping holy to God such set times as He has appointed in His Word, expressly one whole day in seven; which was the seventh from the beginning of the world to the resurrection of Christ, and the first day of the week ever since, and so to continue to the end of the world; which is the Christian sabbath, and in the New Testament called the Lord's day.

Question 117: How is the sabbath or the Lord's day to be sanctified?
Answer: The sabbath or Lord's day is to be sanctified by an holy resting all the day, not only from such works as are at all times sinful, but even from such worldly employments and recreations as are on other days lawful; and making it our delight to spend the whole time (except so much of it as is to betaken up in works of necessity and mercy) in the public and private exercises of God's worship: and, to that end, we are to prepare our hearts, and with such foresight, diligence, and moderation, to dispose and seasonably dispatch our worldly business, that we may be the more free and fit for the duties of that day.

Question 118: Why is the charge of keeping the sabbath more specially directed to governors of families, and other superiors?
Answer: The charge of keeping the sabbath is more specially directed to governors of families, and other superiors, because they are bound not only to keep it themselves,

but to see that it be observed by all those that are under their charge; and because they are prone ofttimes to hinder them by employments of their own.

Question 119: What are the sins forbidden in the fourth commandment?
Answer: The sins forbidden in the fourth commandment are, all omissions of the duties required, all careless, negligent, and unprofitable performing of them, and being weary of them; all profaning the day by idleness, and doing that which is in itself sinful; and by all needless works, words, and thoughts, about our worldly employments and recreations.

Question 120: What are the reasons annexed to the fourth commandment, the more to enforce it?
Answer: The reasons annexed to the fourth commandment, the more to enforce it, are taken from the equity of it, God allowing us six days of seven for our own affairs, and reserving but one for Himself, in these words, *Six days shalt thou labor, and do all thy work:* from God's challenging a special propriety in that day, *The seventh day is the sabbath of the Lord thy God:* from the example of God, who *in six days made heaven and earth, the sea, and all that in them is, and rested the seventh day:* and from that blessing which God put upon that day, not only in sanctifying it to be a day for His service, but in ordaining it to be a means of blessing to us in our sanctifying it; *Wherefore the Lord blessed the sabbath day, and hallowed it.*

Question 121: Why is the word *Remember* set in the beginning of the fourth commandment?
Answer: The word *Remember* is set in the beginning of the fourth commandment, partly, because of the great benefit of remembering it, we being thereby helped in our preparation to keep it, and, in keeping it, better to keep all the rest

of the commandments, and to continue a thankful remembrance of the two great benefits of creation and redemption, which contain a short abridgment of religion; and partly, because we are very ready to forget it, for that there is less light of nature for it, and yet it restrains our natural liberty in things at other times lawful; that it comes but once in seven days, and many worldly businesses come between, and too often take off our minds from thinking of it, either to prepare for it, or to sanctify it; and that Satan with his instruments much labor to blot out the glory, and even the memory of it, to bring in all irreligion and impiety.

Question 122: What is the sum of the six commandments which contain our duty to man?
Answer: The sum of the six commandments which contain our duty to man is, to love our neighbor as ourselves, and to do to others what we would have them to do to us.

Question 123: Which is the fifth commandment?
Answer: The fifth commandment is, *Honor thy father and thy mother; that thy days may be long upon the land which the Lord thy God gives thee.*

Question 124: Who are meant by father and mother in the fifth commandment?
Answer: By father and mother, in the fifth commandment, are meant, not only natural parents, but all superiors in age and gifts; and especially such as, by God's ordinance, are over us in place of authority, whether in family, church, or commonwealth.

Question 125: Why are superiors styled father and mother?
Answer: Superiors are styled father and mother, both to teach them in all duties toward their inferiors, like natural parents, to express love and tenderness to them, accord-

ing to their several relations; and to work inferiors to a greater willingness and cheerfulness in performing their duties to their superiors, as to their parents.

Question 126: What is the general scope of the fifth commandment?
Answer: The general scope of the fifth commandment is, the performance of those duties which we mutually owe in our several relations, as inferiors, superiors, or equals.

Question 127: What is the honor that inferiors owe to their superiors?
Answer: The honor which inferiors owe to their superiors is, all due reverence in heart, word, and behavior; prayer and thanksgiving for them; imitation of their virtues and graces; willing obedience to their lawful commands and counsels; due submission to their corrections; fidelity to, defense and maintenance of their persons and authority, according to their several ranks, and the nature of their places; bearing with their infirmities, and covering them in love, that so they may be an honor to them and to their government.

Question 128: What are the sins of inferiors against their superiors?
Answer: The sins of inferiors against their superiors are, all neglect of the duties required toward them; envying at, contempt of, and rebellion against, their persons and places, in their lawful counsels, commands, and corrections; cursing, mocking, and all such refractory and scandalous carriage, as proves a shame and dishonor to them and their government.

Question 129: What is required of superiors towards their inferiors?
Answer: It is required of superiors, according to that power they receive from God, and that relation wherein they stand, to love, pray for, and bless their inferiors; to instruct, counsel, and admonish them; countenancing, commending, and rewarding such as do well; and discountenan-

cing, reproving, and chastising such as do ill; protecting, and providing for them all things necessary for soul and body: and by grave, wise, holy, and exemplary carriage, to procure glory to God, honor to themselves, and so to preserve that authority which God has put upon them.

Question 130: What are the sins of superiors?
Answer: The sins of superiors are, besides the neglect of the duties required of them, an inordinate seeking of themselves, their own glory, ease, profit, or pleasure; commanding things unlawful, or not in the power of inferiors to perform; counseling, encouraging, or favoring them in that which is evil; dissuading, discouraging, or discountenancing them in that which is good; correcting them unduly; careless exposing, or leaving them to wrong, temptation, and danger; provoking them to wrath; or any way dishonoring themselves, or lessening their authority, by an unjust, indiscreet, rigorous, or remiss behavior.

Question 131: What are the duties of equals?
Answer: The duties of equals are, to regard the dignity and worth of each other, in giving honor to go one before another; and to rejoice in each other's gifts and advancement, as their own.

Question 132: What are the sins of equals?
Answer: The sins of equals are, besides the neglect of the duties required, the undervaluing of the worth, envying the gifts, grieving at the advancement of prosperity one of another; and usurping preeminence one over another.

Question 133: What is the reason annexed to the fifth commandment, the more to enforce it?
Answer: The reason annexed to the fifth commandment, in these words, *That thy days may be long upon the land which the Lord thy God gives thee,* is an express promise of long life

and prosperity, as far as it shall serve for God's glory and their own good, to all such as keep this commandment.

Question 134: Which is the sixth commandment?
Answer: The sixth commandment is, *Thou shalt not kill.*

Question 135: What are the duties required in the sixth commandment?
Answer: The duties required in the sixth commandment are, all careful studies, and lawful endeavors, to preserve the life of ourselves and others by resisting all thoughts and purposes, subduing all passions, and avoiding all occasions, temptations, and practices, which tend to the unjust taking away the life of any; by just defense thereof against violence, patient bearing of the hand of God, quietness of mind, cheerfulness of spirit; a sober use of meat, drink, physic, sleep, labor, and recreations; by charitable thoughts, love, compassion, meekness, gentleness, kindness; peaceable, mild and courteous speeches and behavior; forbearance, readiness to be reconciled, patient bearing and forgiving of injuries, and requiting good for evil; comforting and succoring the distressed, and protecting and defending the innocent.

Question 136: What are the sins forbidden in the sixth commandment?
Answer: The sins forbidden in the sixth commandment are, all taking away the life of ourselves, or of others, except in case of public justice, lawful war, or necessary defense; the neglecting or withdrawing the lawful and necessary means of preservation of life; sinful anger, hatred, envy, desire of revenge; all excessive passions, distracting cares; immoderate use of meat, drink, labor, and recreations; provoking words, oppression, quarreling, striking, wounding, and whatsoever else tends to the destruction of the life of any.

Question 137: Which is the seventh commandment?

Answer: The seventh commandment is, *Thou shalt not commit adultery.*

Question 138: What are the duties required in the seventh commandment?
Answer: The duties required in the seventh commandment are, chastity in body, mind, affections, words, and behavior; and the preservation of it in ourselves and others; watchfulness over the eyes and all the senses; temperance, keeping of chaste company, modesty in apparel; marriage by those that have not the gift of continency, conjugal love, and cohabitation; diligent labor in our callings; shunning all occasions of uncleanness, and resisting temptations thereunto.

Question 139: What are the sins forbidden in the seventh commandment?
Answer: The sins forbidden in the seventh commandment, besides the neglect of the duties required, are, adultery, fornication, rape, incest, sodomy, and all unnatural lusts; all unclean imaginations, thoughts, purposes, and affections; all corrupt or filthy communications, or listening thereunto; wanton looks, impudent or light behavior, immodest apparel; prohibiting of lawful, and dispensing with unlawful marriages; allowing, tolerating, keeping of stews, and resorting to them; entangling vows of single life, undue delay of marriage; having more wives or husbands than one at the same time; unjust divorce, or desertion; idleness, gluttony, drunkenness, unchaste company; lascivious songs, books, pictures, dancings, stage plays; and all other provocations to, or acts of uncleanness, either in ourselves or others.

Question 140: Which is the eighth commandment?
Answer: The eighth commandment is, *Thou shalt not steal.*

Question 141: What are the duties required in the eighth commandment?

Answer: The duties required in the eighth commandment are, truth, faithfulness, and justice in contracts and commerce between man and man; rendering to everyone his due; restitution of goods unlawfully detained from the right owners thereof; giving and lending freely, according to our abilities, and the necessities of others; moderation of our judgments, wills, and affections concerning worldly goods; a provident care and study to get, keep, use, and dispose these things which are necessary and convenient for the sustentation of our nature, and suitable to our condition; a lawful calling, and diligence in it; frugality; avoiding unnecessary lawsuits and suretyship, or other like engagements; and an endeavor, by all just and lawful means, to procure, preserve, and further the wealth and outward estate of others, as well as our own.

Question 142: What are the sins forbidden in the eighth commandment?

Answer: The sins forbidden in the eighth commandment, besides the neglect of the duties required, are, theft, robbery, manstealing, and receiving anything that is stolen; fraudulent dealing, false weights and measures, removing land marks, injustice and unfaithfulness in contracts between man and man, or in matters of trust; oppression, extortion, usury, bribery, vexatious lawsuits, unjust enclosures and depopulations; engrossing commodities to enhance the price; unlawful callings, and all other unjust or sinful ways of taking or withholding from our neighbor what belongs to him, or of enriching ourselves; covetousness; inordinate prizing and affecting worldly goods; distrustful and distracting cares and studies in getting, keeping, and using them; envying at the prosperity of others; as likewise idleness, prodigality, wasteful gaming; and all other ways whereby we do unduly prejudice our own outward estate, and defrauding ourselves of the due use and comfort of that estate which God has given us.

Question 143: Which is the ninth commandment?
Answer: The ninth commandment is, *Thou shalt not bear false witness against thy neighbor.*

Question 144: What are the duties required in the ninth commandment?
Answer: The duties required in the ninth commandment are, the preserving and promoting of truth between man and man, and the good name of our neighbor, as well as our own; appearing and standing for the truth; and from the heart, sincerely, freely, clearly, and fully, speaking the truth, and only the truth, in matters of judgment and justice, and in all other things whatsoever; a charitable esteem of our neighbors; loving, desiring, and rejoicing in their good name; sorrowing for, and covering of their infirmities; freely acknowledging of their gifts and graces, defending their innocency; a ready receiving of a good report, and unwillingness to admit of an evil report, concerning them; discouraging talebearers, flatterers, and slanderers; love and care of our own good name, and defending it when need requires; keeping of lawful promises; studying and practicing of whatsoever things are true, honest, lovely, and of good report.

Question 145: What are the sins forbidden in the ninth commandment?
Answer: The sins forbidden in the ninth commandment are, all prejudicing the truth, and the good name of our neighbors, as well as our own, especially in public judicature; giving false evidence, suborning false witnesses, wittingly appearing and pleading for an evil cause, outfacing and overbearing the truth; passing unjust sentence, calling evil good, and good evil; rewarding the wicked

according to the work of the righteous, and the righteous according to the work of the wicked; forgery, concealing the truth, undue silence in a just cause, and holding our peace when iniquity calls for either a reproof from ourselves, or complaint to others; speaking the truth unseasonably, or maliciously to a wrong end, or perverting it to a wrong meaning, or in doubtful and equivocal expressions, to the prejudice of truth or justice; speaking untruth, lying, slandering, backbiting, detracting, tale bearing, whispering, scoffing, reviling, rash, harsh, and partial censuring; misconstructing intentions, words, and actions; flattering, vainglorious boasting, thinking or speaking too highly or too meanly of ourselves or others; denying the gifts and graces of God; aggravating smaller faults; hiding, excusing, or extenuating of sins, when called to a free confession;unnecessary discovering of infirmities; raising false rumors, receiving and countenancing evil reports, and stopping our ears against just defense; evil suspicion; envying or grieving at the deserved credit of any, endeavoring or desiring to impair it, rejoicing in their disgrace and infamy; scornful contempt, fond admiration; breach of lawful promises; neglecting such things as are of good report, and practicing, or not avoiding ourselves, or not hindering what we can in others, such things as procure an ill name.

Question 146: Which is the tenth commandment?
Answer: The tenth commandment is, *Thou shalt not covet thy neighbor's house, thou shalt not covet thy neighbor's wife, nor his manservant, nor his maidservant, nor his ox, nor his ass, nor any thing that is thy neighbor's.*

Question 147: What are the duties required in the tenth commandment?
Answer: The duties required in the tenth commandment are, such a full contentment with our own condition, and such a charitable frame of the whole soul toward our neighbor,

as that all our inward motions and affections touching him, tend unto, and further all that good which is his.

Question 148: What are the sins forbidden in the tenth commandment?
Answer: The sins forbidden in the tenth commandment are, discontentment with our own estate; envying and grieving at the good of our neighbor, together with all inordinate motions and affections to anything that is his.

Question 149: Is any man able perfectly to keep the commandments of God?
Answer: No man is able, either of himself, or by any grace received in this life, perfectly to keep the commandments of God; but does daily break them in thought, word, and deed.

Question 150: Are all transgressions of the law of God equally heinous in themselves, and in the sight of God?
Answer: All transgressions of the law of God are not equally heinous; but some sins in themselves, and by reason of several aggravations, are more heinous in the sight of God than others.

Question 151: What are those aggravations that make some sins more heinous than others?
Answer: Sins receive their aggravations, From the persons offending: if they be of riper age, greater experience or grace, eminent for profession, gifts, place, office, guides to others, and whose example is likely to be followed by others. From the parties offended: if immediately against God, his attributes, and worship; against Christ, and His grace; the Holy Spirit, His witness, and workings; against superiors, men of eminency, and such as we stand especially related and engaged unto; against any of the saints, particularly weak brethren, the souls of them, or any other, and the common good of all or many. From the

nature and quality of the offense: if it be against the express letter of the law, break many commandments, contain in it many sins: if not only conceived in the heart, but breaks forth in words and actions, scandalize others, and admit of no reparation: if against means, mercies, judgments, light of nature, conviction of conscience, public or private admonition, censures of the church, civil punishments; and our prayers, purposes, promises, vows, covenants, and engagements to God or men: if done deliberately, wilfully, presumptuously, impudently, boastingly, maliciously, frequently, obstinately, with delight, continuance, or relapsing after repentance. From circumstances of time and place: if on the Lord's day, or other times of divine worship; or immediately before or after these, or other helps to prevent or remedy such miscarriages: if in public, or in the presence of others, who are thereby likely to be provoked or defiled.

Question 152: What does every sin deserve at the hands of God?
Answer: Every sin, even the least, being against the sovereignty, goodness, and holiness of God, and against His righteous law, deserves His wrath and curse, both in this life, and that which is to come; and cannot be expiated but by the blood of Christ.

Question 153: What does God require of us, that we may escape His wrath and curse due to us by reason of the transgression of the law?
Answer: That we may escape the wrath and curse of God due to us by reason of the transgression of the law, He requires of us repentance toward God, and faith toward our Lord Jesus Christ, and the diligent use of the outward means whereby Christ communicates to us the benefits of His mediation.

Question 154: What are the outward means whereby Christ communi-

Answer: cates to us the benefits of His mediation? The outward and ordinary means whereby Christ communicates to His church the benefits of His mediation, are all His ordinances; especially the Word, sacraments, and prayer; all which are made effectual to the elect for their salvation.

Question 155: How is the Word made effectual to salvation?
Answer: The Spirit of God makes the reading, but especially the preaching of the Word, an effectual means of enlightening, convincing, and humbling sinners; of driving them out of themselves, and drawing them unto Christ; of conforming them to His image, and subduing them to His will; of strengthening them against temptations and corruptions; of building them up in grace, and establishing their hearts in holiness and comfort through faith unto salvation.

Question 156: Is the Word of God to be read by all?
Answer: Although all are not to be permitted to read the Word publicly to the congregation, yet all sorts of people are bound to read it apart by themselves, and with their families: to which end, the holy Scriptures are to be translated out of the original into vulgar languages.

Question 157: How is the Word of God to be read?
Answer: The holy Scriptures are to be read with an high and reverent esteem of them; with a firm persuasion that they are the very Word of God, and that He only can enable us to understand them; with desire to know, believe, and obey the will of God revealed in them; with diligence, and attention to the matter and scope of them; with meditation, application, self-denial, and prayer.

Question 158: By whom is the Word of God to be preached?
Answer: The Word of God is to be preached only by such as are

sufficiently gifted, and also duly approved and called to that office.

Question 159: How is the Word of God to be preached by those that are called thereunto?
Answer: They that are called to labor in the ministry of the Word, are to preach sound doctrine, diligently, in season and out of season; plainly, not in the enticing words of man's wisdom, but in demonstration of the Spirit, and of power; faithfully, making known the whole counsel of God; wisely, applying themselves to the necessities and capacities of the hearers; zealously, with fervent love to God and the souls of His people; sincerely, aiming at His glory, and their conversion, edification, and salvation.

Question 160: What is required of those that hear the Word preached?
Answer: It is required of those that hear the Word preached, that they attend upon it with diligence, preparation, and prayer; examine what they hear by the Scriptures; receive the truth with faith, love, meekness, and readiness of mind, as the Word of God; meditate, and confer of it; hide it in their hearts, and bring forth the fruit of it in their lives.

Question 161: How do the sacraments become effectual means of salvation?
Answer: The sacraments become effectual means of salvation, not by any power in themselves, or any virtue derived from the piety or intention of him by whom they are administered, but only by the working of the Holy Ghost, and the blessing of Christ, by whom they are instituted.

Question 162: What is a sacrament?
Answer: A sacrament is a holy ordinance instituted by Christ in His church, to signify, seal, and exhibit unto those that are within the covenant of grace, the benefits of His

mediation; to strengthen and increase their faith, and all other graces; to oblige them to obedience; to testify and cherish their love and communion one with another; and to distinguish them from those that are without.

Question 163: What are the parts of a sacrament?
Answer: The parts of a sacrament are two; the one an outward and sensible sign, used according to Christ's own appointment; the other an inward and spiritual grace thereby signified.

Question 164: How many sacraments has Christ instituted in His church under the New Testament?
Answer: Under the New Testament Christ has instituted in His church only two sacraments, Baptism and the Lord's Supper.

Question 165: What is Baptism?
Answer: Baptism is a sacrament of the New Testament, wherein Christ has ordained the washing with water in the name of the Father, and of the Son, and of the Holy Ghost, to be a sign and seal of ingrafting into Himself, of remission of sins by His blood, and regeneration by His Spirit; of adoption, and resurrection unto everlasting life; and whereby the parties baptized are solemnly admitted into the visible church, and enter into an open and professed engagement to be wholly and only the Lord's.

Question 166: Unto whom is Baptism to be administered?
Answer: Baptism is not to be administered to any that are out of the visible church, and so strangers from the covenant of promise, till they profess their faith in Christ, and obedience to Him, but infants descending from parents, either both, or but one of them, professing faith in Christ, and obedience to Him, are in that respect within the covenant, and to be baptized.

Question 167: How is our Baptism to be improved by us?
Answer: The needful but much neglected duty of improving our Baptism, is to be performed by us all our life long, especially in the time of temptation, and when we are present at the administration of it to others; by serious and thankful consideration of the nature of it, and of the ends for which Christ instituted it, the privileges and benefits conferred and sealed thereby, and our solemn vow made therein; by being humbled for our sinful defilement, our falling short of, and walking contrary to, the grace of baptism, and our engagements; by growing up to assurance of pardon of sin, and of all other blessings sealed to us in that sacrament; by drawing strength from the death and resurrection of Christ, into whom we are baptized, for the mortifying of sin, and quickening of grace; and by endeavoring to live by faith, to have our conversation in holiness and righteousness, as those that have therein given up their names to Christ; and to walk in brotherly love, as being baptized by the same Spirit into one body.

Question 168: What is the Lord's Supper?
Answer: The Lord's Supper is a sacrament of the New Testament, wherein, by giving and receiving bread and wine according to the appointment of Jesus Christ, His death is showed forth; and they that worthily communicate feed upon His body and blood, to their spiritual nourishment and growth in grace; have their union and communion with Him confirmed; testify and renew their thankfulness, and engagement to God, and their mutual love and fellowship each with other, as members of the same mystical body.

Question 169: How has Christ appointed bread and wine to be given and received in the sacrament of the Lord's Supper?
Answer: Christ has appointed the ministers of His Word, in the

administration of this sacrament of the Lord's Supper, to set apart the bread and wine from common use, by the word of institution, thanksgiving, and prayer; to take and break the bread, and to give both the bread and the wine to the communicants: who are, by the same appointment, to take and eat the bread, and to drink the wine, in thankful remembrance that the body of Christ was broken and given, and His blood shed, for them.

Question 170: How do they that worthily communicate in the Lord's Supper feed upon the body and blood of Christ therein?

Answer: As the body and blood of Christ are not corporally or carnally present in, with, or under the bread and wine in the Lord's Supper, and yet are spiritually present to the faith of the receiver, no less truly and really than the elements themselves are to their outward senses; so they that worthily communicate in the sacrament of the Lord's Supper, do therein feed upon the body and blood of Christ, not after a corporal and carnal, but in a spiritual manner; yet truly and really, while by faith they receive and apply unto themselves Christ crucified, and all the benefits of His death.

Question 171: How are they that receive the sacrament of the Lord's Supper to prepare themselves before they come unto it?

Answer: They that receive the sacrament of the Lord's Supper are, before they come, to prepare themselves thereunto, by examining themselves of their being in Christ, of their sins and wants; of the truth and measure of their knowledge, faith, repentance; love to God and the brethren, charity to all men, forgiving those that have done them wrong; of their desires after Christ, and of their new obedience; and by renewing the exercise of these graces, by serious meditation, and fervent prayer.

Question 172: May one who doubts of his being in Christ, or of his due

Answer: preparation, come to the Lord's Supper? One who doubts of his being in Christ, or of his due preparation to the sacrament of the Lord's Supper, may have true interest in Christ, though he be not yet assured thereof; and in God's account has it, if he be duly affected with the apprehension of the want of it, and unfeignedly desires to be found in Christ, and to depart from iniquity: in which case (because promises are made, and this sacrament is appointed, for the relief even of weak and doubting Christians) he is to bewail his unbelief, and labor to have his doubts resolved; and, so doing, he may and ought to come to the Lord's Supper, that he may be further strengthened.

Question 173: May any who profess the faith, and desire to come to the Lord's Supper, be kept from it?
Answer: Such as are found to be ignorant or scandalous, notwithstanding their profession of the faith, and desire to come to the Lord's Supper, may and ought to be kept from that sacrament, by the power which Christ has left in His church, until they receive instruction, and manifest their reformation.

Question 174: What is required of them that receive the sacrament of the Lord's Supper in the time of the administration of it?
Answer: It is required of them that receive the sacrament of the Lord's Supper, that, during the time of the administration of it, with all holy reverence and attention they wait upon God in that ordinance, diligently observe the sacramental elements and actions, heedfully discern the Lord's body, and affectionately meditate on His death and sufferings, and thereby stir up themselves to a vigorous exercise of their graces; in judging themselves, and sorrowing for sin; in earnest hungering and thirsting after Christ, feeding on Him by faith, receiving of His fulness, trusting in His merits, rejoicing in His love, giving thanks

for His grace; in renewing of their covenant with God, and love to all the saints.

Question 175: What is the duty of Christians, after they have received the sacrament of the Lord's Supper?

Answer: The duty of Christians, after they have received the sacrament of the Lord's Supper, is seriously to consider how they have behaved themselves therein, and with what success; if they find quickening and comfort, to bless God for it, beg the continuance of it, watch against relapses, fulfil their vows, and encourage themselves to a frequent attendance on that ordinance: but if they find no present benefit, more exactly to review their preparation to, and carriage at, the sacrament; in both which, if they can approve themselves to God and their own consciences, they are to wait for the fruit of it in due time: but, if they see they have failed in either, they are to be humbled, and to attend upon it afterwards with more care and diligence.

Question 176: Wherein do the sacraments of Baptism and the Lord's Supper agree?

Answer: The sacraments of Baptism and the Lord's Supper agree, in that the author of both is God; the spiritual part of both is Christ and His benefits; both are seals of the same covenant, are to be dispensed by ministers of the gospel, and by none other; and to be continued in the church of Christ until His second coming.

Question 177: Wherein do the sacraments of Baptism and the Lord's Supper differ?

Answer: The sacraments of Baptism and the Lord's Supper differ, in that Baptism is to be administered but once, with water, to be a sign and seal of our regeneration and ingrafting into Christ, and that even to infants; whereas the Lord's Supper is to be administered often, in the elements of bread and wine, to represent and exhibit Christ as spiritual nourishment to the soul, and to confirm our continuance and growth in Him, and that only to such as are of years and ability to examine themselves.

Question 178: What is prayer?
Answer: Prayer is an offering up of our desires unto God, in the name of Christ, by the help of His Spirit; with confession of our sins, and thankful acknowledgment of His mercies.

Question 179: Are we to pray unto God only?
Answer: God only being able to search the hearts, hear the requests, pardon the sins, and fulfil the desires of all; and only to be believed in, and worshiped with religious worship; prayer, which is a special part thereof, is to be made by all to Him alone, and to none other.

Question 180: What is it to pray in the name of Christ?
Answer: To pray in the name of Christ is, in obedience to His command, and in confidence on His promises, to ask mercy for His sake; not by bare mentioning of His name, but by drawing our encouragement to pray, and our boldness, strength, and hope of acceptance in prayer, from Christ and His mediation.

Question 181: Why are we to pray in the name of Christ?
Answer: The sinfulness of man, and his distance from God by reason thereof, being so great, as that we can have no access into His presence without a mediator; and there being none in heaven or earth appointed to, or fit for, that glorious work but Christ alone, we are to pray in no other name but His only.

Question 182: How does the Spirit help us to pray?
Answer: We not knowing what to pray for as we ought, the Spirit

helps our infirmities, by enabling us to understand both for whom, and what, and how prayer is to be made; and by working and quickening in our hearts (although not in all persons, nor at all times, in the same measure) those apprehensions, affections, and graces which are requisite for the right performance of that duty.

Question 183: For whom are we to pray?
Answer: We are to pray for the whole church of Christ upon earth; for magistrates, and ministers; for ourselves, our brethren, yea, our enemies; and for all sorts of men living, or that shall live hereafter; but not for the dead, nor for those that are known to have sinned the sin unto death.

Question 184: For what things are we to pray?
Answer: We are to pray for all things tending to the glory of God, the welfare of the church, our own or others' good; but not for anything that is unlawful.

Question 185: How are we to pray?
Answer: We are to pray with an awful apprehension of the majesty of God, and deep sense of our own unworthiness, necessities, and sins; with penitent, thankful, and enlarged hearts; with understanding, faith, sincerity, fervency, love, and perseverance, waiting upon Him, with humble submission to His will.

Question 186: What rule has God given for our direction in the duty of prayer?
Answer: The whole Word of God is of use to direct us in the duty of prayer; but the special rule of direction is that form of prayer which our Savior Christ taught His disciples, commonly called the Lord's Prayer.

Question 187: How is the Lord's Prayer to be used?
Answer: The Lord's Prayer is not only for direction, as a pattern,

according to which we are to make other prayers; but may also be used as a prayer, so that it be done with understanding, faith, reverence, and other graces necessary to the right performance of the duty of prayer.

Question 188: Of how many parts does the Lord's Prayer consist?
Answer: The Lord's Prayer consists of three parts; a preface, petitions, and a conclusion.

Question 189: What does the preface of the Lord's Prayer teach us?
Answer: The preface of the Lord's Prayer (contained in these words, *Our Father which art in heaven*), teaches us, when we pray, to draw near to God with confidence of His fatherly goodness, and our interest therein; with reverence, and all other childlike dispositions, heavenly affections, and due apprehensions of His sovereign power, majesty, and gracious condescension: as also, to pray with and for others.

Question 190: What do we pray for in the first petition?
Answer: In the first petition (which is, *Hallowed be thy name*), acknowledging the utter inability and indisposition that is in ourselves and all men to honor God aright, we pray, that God would by His grace enable and incline us and others to know, to acknowledge, and highly to esteem Him, His titles, attributes, ordinances, Word, works, and whatsoever He is pleased to make Himself known by; and to glorify Him in thought, word, and deed: that He would prevent and remove atheism, ignorance, idolatry, profaneness, and whatsoever is dishonorable to Him; and, by His overruling providence, direct and dispose of all things to His own glory.

Question 191: What do we pray for in the second petition?
Answer: In the second petition (which is, *Thy kingdom come*), acknowledging ourselves and all mankind to be by

nature under the dominion of sin and Satan, we pray, that the kingdom of sin and Satan may be destroyed, the gospel propagated throughout the world, the Jews called, the fulness of the Gentiles brought in; the church furnished with all gospel officers and ordinances, purged from corruption, countenanced and maintained by the civil magistrate: that the ordinances of Christ may be purely dispensed, and made effectual to the converting of those that are yet in their sins, and the confirming, comforting, and building up of those that are already converted: that Christ would rule in our hearts here, and hasten the time of His second coming, and our reigning with Him forever: and that He would be pleased so to exercise the kingdom of His power in all the world, as may best conduce to these ends.

Question 192: What do we pray for in the third petition?
Answer: In the third petition (which is, *Thy will be done in earth, as it is in heaven*), acknowledging, that by nature we and all men are not only utterly unable and unwilling to know and do the will of God, but prone to rebel against His Word, to repine and murmur against His providence, and wholly inclined to do the will of the flesh, and of the devil: we pray, that God would by His Spirit take away from ourselves and others all blindness, weakness, indisposedness, and perverseness of heart; and by His grace make us able and willing to know, do, and submit to His will in all things, with the like humility, cheerfulness, faithfulness, diligence, zeal, sincerity, and constancy, as the angels do in heaven.

Question 193: What do we pray for in the fourth petition?
Answer: In the fourth petition (which is, *Give us this day our daily bread*), acknowledging, that in Adam, and by our own sin, we have forfeited our right to all the outward blessings of this life, and deserve to be wholly deprived of

them by God, and to have them cursed to us in the use of them; and that neither they of themselves are able to sustain us, nor we to merit, or by our own industry to procure them; but prone to desire, get, and use them unlawfully: we pray for ourselves and others, that both they and we, waiting upon the providence of God from day to day in the use of lawful means, may, of His free gift, and as to His fatherly wisdom shall seem best, enjoy a competent portion of them; and have the same continued and blessed unto us in our holy and comfortable use of them, and contentment in them; and be kept from all things that are contrary to our temporal support and comfort.

Question 194: What do we pray for in the fifth petition?
Answer: In the fifth petition (which is, *Forgive us our debts, as we forgive our debtors*), acknowledging, that we and all others are guilty both of original and actual sin, and thereby become debtors to the justice of God; and that neither we, nor any other creature, can make the least satisfaction for that debt: we pray for ourselves and others, that God of His free grace would, through the obedience and satisfaction of Christ, apprehended and applied by faith, acquit us both from the guilt and punishment of sin, accept us in his Beloved; continue His favor and grace to us, pardon our daily failings, and fill us with peace and joy, in giving us daily more and more assurance of forgiveness; which we are the rather emboldened to ask, and encouraged to expect, when we have this testimony in ourselves, that we from the heart forgive others their offenses.

Question 195: What do we pray for in the sixth petition?
Answer: In the sixth petition (which is, *And lead us not into temptation, but deliver us from evil*), acknowledging, that the most wise, righteous, and gracious God, for divers

holy and just ends, may so order things, that we may be assaulted, foiled, and for a time led captive by temptations; that Satan, the world, and the flesh, are ready powerfully to draw us aside, and ensnare us; and that we, even after the pardon of our sins, by reason of our corruption, weakness, and want of watchfulness, are not only subject to be tempted, and forward to expose ourselves unto temptations, but also of ourselves unable and unwilling to resist them, to recover out of them, and to improve them; and worthy to be left under the power of them: we pray, that God would so overrule the world and all in it, subdue the flesh, and restrain Satan, order all things, bestow and bless all means of grace, and quicken us to watchfulness in the use of them, that we and all His people may by His providence be kept from being tempted to sin; or, if tempted, that by His Spirit we may be powerfully supported and enabled to stand in the hour of temptation: or when fallen, raised again and recovered out of it, and have a sanctified use and improvement thereof: that our sanctification and salvation may be perfected, Satan trodden under our feet, and we fully freed from sin, temptation, and all evil, forever.

Question 196: What does the conclusion of the Lord's Prayer teach us?
Answer: The conclusion of the Lord's Prayer (which is, *For thine is the kingdom, and the power, and the glory, forever. Amen.*), teaches us to enforce our petitions with arguments, which are to be taken, not from any worthiness in ourselves, or in any other creature, but from God; and with our prayers to join praises, ascribing to God alone eternal sovereignty, omnipotency, and glorious excellency; in regard whereof, as He is able and willing to help us, so we by faith are emboldened to plead with Him that He would, and quietly to rely upon Him, that He will fulfil our requests. And, to testify this our desire and assurance, we say, Amen.

The Crisis of Our Time

Historians have christened the thirteenth century the Age of Faith and termed the eighteenth century the Age of Reason. The twentieth century has been called many things: the Atomic Age, the Age of Inflation, the Age of the Tyrant, the Age of Aquarius. But it deserves one name more than the others: the Age of Irrationalism. Contemporary secular intellectuals are anti-intellectual. Contemporary philosophers are anti-philosophy. Contemporary theologians are anti-theology.

In past centuries secular philosophers have generally believed that knowledge is possible to man. Consequently they expended a great deal of thought and effort trying to justify knowledge. In the twentieth century, however, the optimism of the secular philosophers has all but disappeared. They despair of knowledge.

Like their secular counterparts, the great theologians and doctors of the church taught that knowledge is possible to man. Yet the theologians of the twentieth century have repudiated that belief. They also despair of knowledge. This radical skepticism has filtered down from the philosophers and theologians and penetrated our entire culture, from television to music to literature. *The Christian in the twentieth century is confronted with an overwhelming cultural consensus—sometimes stated explicitly, but most often implicitly: Man does not and cannot know anything truly.*

What does this have to do with Christianity? Simply this: If man can know nothing truly, man can truly know nothing. We cannot know that the Bible is the Word of God, that Christ died for sin, or that Christ is alive today at the right hand of the Father. Unless knowledge is possible, Christianity is nonsensical, for it claims to be knowledge. What is at stake in the twentieth century is not simply a single doctrine, such as the Virgin Birth, or the existence of hell, as important as those doctrines may be, but the whole of Christianity itself. If knowledge is not possible to man, it is worse than silly to argue points of doctrine—it is insane.

The irrationalism of the present age is so thorough-going and pervasive that even the Remnant—the segment of the professing church that remains faithful—has accepted much of it, frequently without even being aware of what it was accepting. In some circles this irrationalism has become synonymous with piety and humility, and those who oppose it are denounced as rationalists—as though to be logical were a sin. Our contemporary anti-theologians make a contradiction and call it a Mystery. The faithful ask for truth and are given Paradox. If any balk at swallowing the absurdities of the anti-theologians, they are frequently marked as heretics or schismatics who seek to act independently of God.

There is no greater threat facing the true Church of Christ at this moment than the irrationalism that now controls our entire culture. Communism, guilty of tens of millions of murders, including those of millions of Christians, is to be feared, but not nearly so much as the idea that we do not and cannot know the truth. Hedonism, the popular philosophy of America, is not to be feared so much as the belief that logic —that "mere human logic," to use the religious irrationalists' own phrase—is futile. The attacks on truth, on revelation, on the intellect, and on logic are renewed daily. But note well: The misologists—the haters of logic—use logic to demonstrate the futility of using logic. The anti-intellectuals construct intricate intellectual arguments to prove the insufficiency of the intellect. The anti-theologians use the revealed Word of God to show that there can be no revealed Word of God—or that if there could, it would remain impenetrable darkness and Mystery to our finite minds.

Nonsense Has Come

Is it any wonder that the world is grasping at straws—the straws of experientialism, mysticism and drugs? After all, if people are told that the Bible contains insoluble mysteries, then is not a flight into mysticism to be expected? On what grounds can it be condemned? Certainly not on logical grounds or Biblical grounds, if logic is futile and the Bible unintelligible. Moreover, if it cannot be condemned on logical or Biblical grounds, it cannot be condemned at all. If people are going to have a religion of the mysterious, they will not adopt Christianity: They will have a genuine mystery religion. "Those who call for Nonsense," C.S. Lewis once wrote, "will find that it comes." And that is precisely what has happened. The popularity of Eastern mysticism, of drugs, and of religious experience is the logical consequence of the irrationalism of the twentieth century. There can and will be no Christian revival—and no reconstruction of society—unless and until the irrationalism of the age is totally repudiated by Christians.

The Church Defenseless

Yet how shall they do it? The spokesmen for Christianity have been fatally infected with irrationalism. The seminaries, which annually train thousands of men to teach millions of Christians, are the finishing schools of irrationalism, completing the job begun by the government schools and colleges. Some of the pulpits of the most conservative churches (we are not speaking of the apostate churches) are occupied by graduates of the anti-theological schools. These products of modern anti-theological education, when asked to give a reason for the hope that is in them, can generally respond with only the intellectual analogue of a shrug—a mumble about Mystery. They have not grasped—and therefore cannot teach those for whom they are responsible—the first truth: "And ye shall know the truth." Many, in fact, explicitly deny it, saying that, at best, we possess only "pointers" to the truth, or something "similar" to the truth, a mere analogy. Is the impotence of the Christian Church a puzzle? Is the fascination with pentecostalism and faith healing among members of conservative churches an enigma? Not when one understands the sort of studied nonsense that is purveyed in the name of God in the seminaries.

The Trinity Foundation

The creators of The Trinity Foundation firmly believe that theology is too important to be left to the licensed theologians — the graduates of the schools of theology. They have created The Trinity Foundation for the express purpose of teaching the faithful all that the Scriptures contain—not warmed over, baptized, secular philosophies. Each member of the board of directors of The Trinity Foundation has signed this oath: "I believe that the Bible alone and the Bible in its entirety is the Word of God and, therefore, inerrant in the autographs. I believe that the system of truth presented in the Bible is best summarized in the Westminster Confession of Faith. So help me God."

The ministry of The Trinity Foundation is the presentation of the system of truth taught in Scripture as clearly and as completely as possible. We do not regard obscurity as a virtue, nor confusion as a sign of spirituality. Confusion, like all error, is sin, and teaching that confusion is all that Christians can hope for is doubly sin.

The presentation of the truth of Scripture necessarily involves the rejection of error. The Foundation has exposed and will continue to expose the irrationalism of the twentieth century, whether its current spokesman be an existentialist philosopher or a professed Reformed theologian. We oppose anti-intellectualism, whether it be espoused by a neo-orthodox theologian or a fundamentalist evangelist. We reject misology, whether it be on the lips of a neo-evangelical or those of a Roman Catholic charismatic. To each error we bring the brilliant light of Scripture, proving all things, and holding fast to that which is true.

The Primacy of Theory

The ministry of The Trinity Foundation is not a "practical" ministry. If you are a pastor, we will not enlighten you on how to organize an ecumenical prayer meeting in your community or how to double church attendance in a year. If you are a homemaker, you will have to read elsewhere to find out how to become a total woman. If you are a businessman, we will not tell you how to develop a social conscience. The professing church is drowning in such "practical" advice.

The Trinity Foundation is unapologetically theoretical in its outlook, believing that theory without practice is dead, and that practice without theory is blind. The trouble with the professing church is not primarily in its practice, but in its theory. Christians do not know, and many do not even care to know, the doctrines of Scripture. Doctrine is intellectual, and Christians are generally anti-intellectual. Doctrine is ivory tower philosophy, and they scorn ivory towers. The ivory tower, however, is the control tower of a civilization. It is a fundamental, theoretical mistake of the practical men to think that they can be merely practical, for practice is always the practice of some theory. The relationship between theory and practice is the relationship between cause and effect. If a person believes correct theory, his practice will tend to be correct. The practice of contemporary Christians is immoral because it is the practice of false theories. It is a major theoretical mistake of the practical men to think that they can ignore the ivory towers of the philosophers and theologians as irrelevant to their lives. Every action that the "practical" men take is governed by the thinking that has occurred in some ivory tower—whether that tower be the British Museum, the Academy, a home in Basel, Switzerland, or a tent in Israel.

In Understanding Be Men

It is the first duty of the Christian to understand correct theory—correct doctrine—and thereby implement correct practice. This order—first theory, then practice—is both logical and Biblical. It is, for example, exhibited in Paul's epistle to the Romans, in which he spends the first eleven chapters expounding theory and the last five discussing practice. The contemporary teachers of Christians have not only reversed the order, they have inverted the Pauline emphasis on theory and practice. The virtually complete failure of the teachers of the professing church to instruct the faithful in correct doctrine is the cause of the misconduct and cultural impotence of Christians. The Church's lack of power is the result of its lack of truth. The *Gospel* is the power of God, not religious experience or personal relationship. The Church has no power because it has abandoned the Gospel, the good news, for a religion of experientialism. Twentieth century American Christians are children carried about by every wind of doctrine, not knowing what they believe, or even if they believe anything for certain.

The chief purpose of The Trinity Foundation is to counteract the irrationalism of the age and to expose the errors of the teachers of the church. Our emphasis—on the Bible as the sole source of truth, on the primacy of the intellect, on the supreme importance of correct doctrine, and on the necessity for systematic and logical thinking—is almost unique in Christendom. To the extent that the church survives—and she will survive and flourish—it will be because of her increasing acceptance of these basic ideas and their logical implications.

We believe that the Trinity Foundation is filling a vacuum in Christendom. We are saying that Christianity is intellectually defensible —that, in fact, it is the only intellectually defensible system of thought. We are saying that God has made the wisdom of this world—whether that wisdom be called science, religion, philosophy, or common sense— foolishness. We are appealing to all Christians who have not conceded defeat in the intellectual battle with the world to join us in our efforts to raise a standard to which all men of sound mind can repair.

The love of truth, of God's Word, has all but disappeared in our time. We are committed to and pray for a great instauration. But though we may not see this reformation of Christendom in our lifetimes, we believe it is our duty to present the whole counsel of God because Christ has commanded it. The results of our teaching are in God's hands, not ours. Whatever those results, His Word is never taught in vain, but always accomplishes the result that He intended it to accomplish. Professor Gordon H. Clark has stated our view well:

> There have been times in the history of God's people, for example, in the days of Jeremiah, when refreshing grace and widespread revival were not to be expected: the time was one of chastisement. If this twentieth century is of a similar nature, individual Christians here and there can find comfort and strength in a study of God's Word. But if God has decreed happier days for us and if we may expect a world-shaking and genuine spiritual awakening, then it is the author's belief that a zeal for souls, however necessary, is not the sufficient condition. Have there not been devout saints in every age, numerous enough to carry on a revival? Twelve such persons are plenty. What distinguishes the arid ages from the period of the Reformation, when nations were moved as they had not been since Paul preached in Ephesus, Corinth, and Rome, is the latter's fullness of

knowledge of God's Word. To echo an early Reformation thought, when the ploughman and the garage attendant know the Bible as well as the theologian does, and know it better than some contemporary theologians, then the desired awakening shall have already occurred.

In addition to publishing books, of which *Guide to the Westminster Confession and Catechism* is the 30th, the Foundation publishes a bimonthly newsletter, *The Trinity Review*. Subscriptions to *The Review* are free; please write to the address below to become a subscriber. If you would like further information or would like to join us in our work, please let us know.

The Trinity Foundation is a non-profit foundation tax-exempt under section 501 (c)(3) of the Internal Revenue Code of 1954. You can help us disseminate the Word of God through your tax-deductible contributions to the Foundation.

And we know that the Son of God is come, and hath given us an understanding, that we may know him that is true, and we are in him that is true, in his Son Jesus Christ. This is the true God, and eternal life.

John W. Robbins
President

Intellectual Ammunition

The Trinity Foundation is committed to the reconstruction of philosophy and theology along Biblical lines. We regard God's command to bring all our thoughts into conformity with Christ very seriously, and the books listed below are designed to accomplish that goal. They are written with two subordinate purposes: (1) to demolish all secular claims to knowledge; and (2) to build a system of truth based upon the Bible alone.

Works of Philosophy

Behaviorism and Christianity, Gordon H. Clark $5.95
  Behaviorism is a critique of both secular and religious behaviorists. It includes chapters on John Watson, Edgar S. Singer Jr., Gilbert Ryle, B.F. Skinner, and Donald MacKay. Clark's refutation of behaviorism and his argument for a Christian doctrine of man are unanswerable.

A Christian Philosophy of Education, Gordon H. Clark $8.95
  The first edition of this book was published in 1946. It sparked the contemporary interest in Christian schools. Dr. Clark has thoroughly revised and updated it, and it is needed now more than ever. Its chapters include: The Need for a World-View, The Christian World-View, The Alternative to Christian Theism, Neutrality, Ethics, The Christian Philoso-

phy of Education, Academic Matters, Kindergarten to University. Three appendices are included as well: *The Relationship of Public Education to Christianity, A Protestant World-View,* and *Art and the Gospel.*

A Christian View of Men and Things, Gordon H. Clark $9.95
No other book achieves what A Christian View *does: the presentation of Christianity as it applies to history, politics, ethics, science, religion, and epistemology. Clark's command of both worldly philosophy and Scripture is evident on every page, and the result is a breathtaking and invigorating challenge to the wisdom of this world.*

Clark Speaks From The Grave, Gordon H. Clark $3.95
Dr. Clark chides some of his critics for their failure to defend Christianity competently. Clark Speaks *is a stimulating and illuminating discussion of the errors of contemporary apologists.*

Education, Christianity, and the State $7.95
J. Gresham Machen
Machen was one of the foremost educators, theologians, and defenders of Christianity in the twentieth century. The author of numerous scholarly books, Machen saw clearly that if Christianity is to survive and flourish, a system of Christian grade schools must be established. This collection of essays captures his thought on education over nearly three decades.

Gordon H. Clark: Personal Recollections, $6.95
John W. Robbins, editor
Friends of Dr. Clark have written their recollections of the man. Contributors include family members, colleagues, students, and friends such as Harold Lindsell, Carl Henry, Ronald Nash, Dwight Zeller, and Mary Crumpacker. The book includes an extensive bibliography of Clark's work.

John Dewey, Gordon H. Clark $2.00
America has not produced many philosophers, but John Dewey has been extremely influential. Clark examines his philosophy of Instrumentalism.

Logic, Gordon H. Clark $8.95
  Written as a textbook for Christian schools, Logic *is another unique book from Clark's pen. His presentation of the laws of thought, which must be followed if Scripture is to be understood correctly, and which are found in Scripture itself, is both clear and thorough.* Logic *is an indispensable book for the thinking Christian.*

The Philosophy of Science and Belief in God $5.95
Gordon H. Clark
  In opposing the contemporary idolatry of science, Clark analyzes three major aspects of science: the problem of motion, Newtonian science, and modern theories of physics. His conclusion is that science, while it may be useful, is always false; and he demonstrates its falsity in numerous ways. Since science is always false, it can offer no objection to the Bible and Christianity.

Religion, Reason and Revelation, Gordon H. Clark $7.95
  One of Clark's apologetical masterpieces, Religion, Reason and Revelation *has been praised for the clarity of its thought and language. It includes chapters on Is Christianity a Religion? Faith and Reason, Inspiration and Language, Revelation and Morality, and God and Evil. It is must reading for all serious Christians.*

Thales to Dewey: A History of Philosophy,   paper $11.95
Gordon H. Clark   hardback $16.95
  This volume is the best one volume history of philosophy in English.

Three Types of Religious Philosophy, Gordon H. Clark $6.95
  In this book on apologetics, Clark examines empiricism, rationalism, dogmatism, and contemporary irrationalism, which does not rise to the level of philosophy. He offers a solution to the question, "How can Christianity be defended before the world?"

Works of Theology

The Atonement, Gordon H. Clark $8.95
This is a major addition to Clark's multi-volume systematic theology. In The Atonement, Clark discusses the Covenants, the Virgin Birth and Incarnation, federal headship and representation, the relationship between God's sovereignty and justice, and much more. He analyzes traditional views of the Atonement and criticizes them in the light of Scripture alone.

The Biblical Doctrine of Man, Gordon H. Clark $5.95
Is man soul and body or soul, spirit, and body? What is the image of God? Is Adam's sin imputed to his children? Is evolution true? Are men totally depraved? What is the heart? These are some of the questions discussed and answered from Scripture in this book.

Cornelius Van Til: The Man and The Myth $2.45
John W. Robbins
The actual teachings of this eminent Philadelphia theologian have been obscured by the myths that surround him. This book penetrates those myths and criticizes Van Til's surprisingly unorthodox views of God and the Bible.

Faith and Saving Faith, Gordon H. Clark $6.95
The views of the Roman Catholic church, John Calvin, Thomas Manton, John Owen, Charles Hodge, and B.B. Warfield are discussed in this book. Is the object of faith a person or a proposition? Is faith more than belief? Is belief more than thinking with assent, as Augustine said? In a world chaotic with differing views of faith, Clark clearly explains the Biblical view of faith and saving faith.

God's Hammer: The Bible and Its Critics, Gordon H. Clark $6.95
The starting point of Christianity, the doctrine on which all other doctrines depend, is "The Bible alone is the Word of God written, and therefore inerrant in the autographs." Over the centuries the opponents of Christianity, with Satanic shrewdness, have concentrated their attacks on

the truthfulness and completeness of the Bible. In the twentieth century the attack is not so much in the fields of history and archaeology as in philosophy. Clark's brilliant defense of the complete truthfulness of the Bible is captured in this collection of eleven major essays.

Guide to the Westminster Confession and Catechism, $13.95
James E. Bordwine
  This large book contains the full text of both the Westminster Confession (both original and American versions) and the Larger Catechism. In addition, it offers a chapter-by-chapter summary of the Confession and a unique index to both the Confession and the Catechism.

The Incarnation, Gordon H. Clark $8.95
  Who was Christ? The attack on the Incarnation in the nineteenth and twentieth centuries has been vigorous, but the orthodox response has been lame. Clark reconstructs the doctrine of the Incarnation building upon and improving upon the Chalcedonian definition.

In Defense of Theology, Gordon H. Clark $12.95
  There are four groups to whom Clark addresses this book: the average Christians who are uninterested in theology, the atheists and agnostics, the religious experientialists, and the serious Christians. The vindication of the knowledge of God against the objections of three of these groups is the first step in theology.

The Johannine Logos, Gordon H. Clark $5.95
  Clark analyzes the relationship between Christ, who is the truth, and the Bible. He explains why John used the same word to refer to both Christ and his teaching. Chapters deal with the Prologue to John's Gospel, Logos and Rheemata, Truth, and Saving Faith.

Logical Criticisms of Textual Criticism, Gordon H. Clark $3.25
  In this critique of the science of textual criticism, Dr. Clark exposes the fallacious argumentation of the modern textual critics and defends the view that the early Christians knew better than the modern critics which manuscripts of the New Testament were more accurate.

Pat Robertson: A Warning to America, John W. Robbins $6.95
The Protestant Reformation was based on the Biblical principle that the Bible is the only revelation from God, yet a growing religious movement, led by Pat Robertson, asserts that God speaks to them directly. This book addresses the serious issue of religious fanaticism in America by examining the theological views of Pat Robertson.

Predestination, Gordon H. Clark $7.95
Clark thoroughly discusses one of the most controversial and pervasive doctrines of the Bible: that God is, quite literally, Almighty. Free will, the origin of evil, God's omniscience, creation, and the new birth are all presented within a Scriptural framework. The objections of those who do not believe in the Almighty God are considered and refuted. This edition also contains the text of the booklet, Predestination in the Old Testament.

Scripture Twisting in the Seminaries. Part 1: Feminism $5.95
John W. Robbins
An analysis of the views of three graduates of Westminster Seminary on the role of women in the church.

Today's Evangelism: Counterfeit or Genuine? $6.95
Gordon H. Clark
Clark compares the methods and messages of today's evangelists with Scripture, and finds that Christianity is on the wane because the Gospel has been distorted or lost. This is an extremely useful and enlightening book.

The Trinity, Gordon H. Clark $8.95
Apart from the doctrine of Scripture, no teaching of the Bible is more important than the doctrine of God. Clark's defense of the orthodox doctrine of the Trinity is a principal portion of a major new work of Systematic Theology now in progress. There are chapters on the deity of Christ, Augustine, the incomprehensibility of God, Bavinck and Van Til, and the Holy Spirit, among others.

What Do Presbyterians Believe? Gordon H. Clark $7.95
   This classic introduction to Christian doctrine has been republished. It is the best commentary on the Westminster Confession of Faith that has ever been written.

Commentaries on the New Testament

Colossians, Gordon H. Clark $6.95
Ephesians, Gordon H. Clark $8.95
First and Second Thessalonians, Gordon H. Clark $5.95
First Corinthians, Gordon H. Clark $10.95
The Pastoral Epistles (I and II Timothy and Titus) $9.95
   Gordon H. Clark

   All of Clark's commentaries are expository, not technical, and are written for the Christian layman. His purpose is to explain the text clearly and accurately so that the Word of God will be thoroughly known by every Christian. Revivals of Christianity come only through the spread of God's truth. The sound exposition of the Bible, through preaching and through commentaries on Scripture, is the only method of spreading that truth.

The Trinity Library

   We will send you one copy of each of the 33 books listed above for the low price of $150. The regular price of these books is $240. You may also order the books you want individually on the order blank on the next page. Because some of the books are in short supply, we must reserve the right to substitute others of equal or greater value in The Trinity Library.

   Thank you for your attention. We hope to hear from you soon. This special offer expires June 30, 1993.

Order Form

Name _____

Address _____

_____

Please: ☐ add my name to the mailing list for *The Trinity Review*. I understand that there is no charge for the *Review*.

☐ accept my tax deductible contribution of $ _____ for the work of the Foundation.

☐ send me _____ copies of *Guide to the Confession and Catechism*. I enclose as payment $ _____ .

☐ send me the Trinity Library of 33 books. I enclose $150 as full payment for it.

☐ send me the following books. I enclose full payment in the amount of $ _____ for them.

_____
_____
_____
_____
_____
_____

Mail to: The Trinity Foundation
Post Office Box 700
Jefferson, MD 21755

Please add $1.00 for postage on orders less than $10. Thank you.
For quantity discounts, please write to the Foundation.